THE MINOR PROPHETS

AN
EXPOSITIONAL
COMMENTARY

Volume 2
Micah-Malachi

Books by Dr. Boice . . .

Witness and Revelation in the Gospel of John
Philippians: An Expositional Commentary
The Sermon on the Mount
How to Live the Christian Life (originally, *How to Really Live It Up*)
Ordinary Men Called by God (originally, *How God Can Use Nobodies*)
The Last and Future World
The Gospel of John: An Expositional Commentary (5 volumes in one)
"Galatians" in the *Expositor's Bible Commentary*
Can You Run Away From God?
Our Sovereign God, editor
Our Savior God: Studies on Man, Christ and the Atonement, editor
Foundations of the Christian Faith (4 volumes in one)
The Foundation of Biblical Authority, editor
The Epistles of John
Does Inerrancy Matter?
Making God's Word Plain, editor
Genesis: An Expositional Commentary (3 volumes)
The Parables of Jesus
The Christ of Christmas
The Christ of the Open Tomb
Standing on the Rock
The Minor Prophets: An Expositional Commentary (2 volumes)
Christ's Call to Discipleship
Daniel: An Expositional Commentary (available in 1989)
Ephesians: An Expositional Commentary (available in 1989)

Volume 2   Micah-Malachi

THE MINOR PROPHETS

AN EXPOSITIONAL COMMENTARY

JAMES MONTGOMERY BOICE

Ministry Resources Library

Zondervan Publishing House • Grand Rapids, MI

THE MINOR PROPHETS
VOLUME 2: MICAH–MALACHI
Copyright © 1986 by
The Zondervan Corporation
Grand Rapids, Michigan

MINISTRY RESOURCES LIBRARY
is an imprint of
Zondervan Publishing House
1415 Lake Drive S.E.
Grand Rapids, Michigan 49506

Library of Congress Cataloging in Publication Data

Boice, James Montgomery, 1938–
    The Minor Prophets.

    Includes bibliographical references and indexes.
    Contents: v. 1. Hosea–Jonah.   —   v. 2. Micah–Malachi.
    1. Bible. O.T. Minor Prophets—Commentaries.
I. Bible. O.T. Minor Prophets. English 1983.

BS1560.B57   1985   224'.9077   83–5794

ISBN   0–310–21580–3   (v. 2)

ISBN 0-310-21581-1 (v. 2)

Edited by Joseph Comanda

Printed in the United States of America

91   92   93   94 / CH / 12   11   10   9   8   7   6

To
The Lord God Almighty,
who changes not

Contents

MALACHI

Preface

I always enjoy writing a preface to a volume of my studies of Scripture, for a preface is written last and is therefore a reward for having brought the volume itself to completion. My pleasure is doubled in this instance, for it signals not only the end of this volume but the completion of the two-volume set on the Minor Prophets. The first volume, covering Hosea through Jonah, was released in 1983.

Few portions of Scripture have been so challenging to me as the Minor Prophets. It is not that they are hard to interpret, though some of them are (Zechariah is possibly the most difficult section of all the Word of God). Rather it is because they speak so directly and powerfully to present sins. It is just not possible to read them carefully without having one's life challenged and without determining to go out and live differently. One must study them slowly, digesting what one reads and obeying it before moving on. I discovered that when I first preached from them, and I found that I had to spread out my preaching on the Minor Prophets over more than ten years.

First, they highlight God's sovereignty. Indeed, they do more than merely highlight it; they breathe it throughout. Nothing is more central to the thinking of these twelve writers than the fact that God is the sovereign Lord of history and that nothing happens, either to Israel or to the gentile nations, that is not the result of His direct determination. The locust plague of Joel was His doing. The destruction of Nineveh was from Him, just as its earlier repentance under the preaching of Jonah was God-given. When Israel was invaded by Assyria and Judah by

Babylon, it was the Lord who did it. Whatever problems the prophets may have with the specific nature of God's actions—Habakkuk is one who had great problems—they never doubt for a second that the almighty God is in charge of history.

The second great attribute of God seen in the Minor Prophets is holiness. An awareness of holiness was the driving force behind their sharp denunciations of sin. It made no difference where the sin was found, whether in foreign lands (Edom, as in Obadiah; Assyria, as in Nahum) or among God's people—it was still an offense to God and called for judgment. Nowhere in the Bible are there stiffer denunciations of sin and heartier calls for a deep and pervasive repentance. Apart from repentance, judgment falls.

Third, the prophets speak of God's love. The conjunction of love and justice is sometimes so stark that critical, liberal scholars resort to excluding sections of the books that deal with God's love. They miss a great truth when they do this, for love is not incompatible with justice. On the contrary, it is because of God's great love for His people (even His love for Nineveh) that He sends prophets with the message of judgment and, indeed, eventually sends the judgment itself. God knows that sin is an outrage against Himself, humanity, and even the one pursuing it. He knows that sin is destructive. So He judges sin—in the case of His own people in order to turn them back from sin to Himself.

We need these emphases today. We need them as individuals, for we sin and run away from God just as Israel did. We need them as a nation also, for

God will not deal with America or Britain or any other contemporary nation differently in regard to its sin than He dealt with the nations of antiquity. We need to learn—deeply and in a way that changes us—that "righteousness exalts a nation, but sin is a disgrace to any people" (Prov. 14:34).

As I write this preface I have completed more than sixteen years of ministry at Tenth Presbyterian Church in Philadelphia and have produced, at last count, thirty volumes of Bible study material. Needless to say, I could not have produced this large quantity of writing if the congregation of the church had not supported me in this effort and provided the kind of secretarial help and additional pastoral assistance that made it possible. Two pastors in particular have been supportive: the Reverend Glenn N. McDowell, who bears the brunt of the administrative responsibility, and the Reverend Linward A. Crow, who works with church leadership and does much of the pastoral visitation.

My secretary, Miss Caecilie M. Foelster, has assisted me in the production of all but the earliest of my books. She types the manuscript, checks points of reference, and assists in the production of the index.

JAMES MONTGOMERY BOICE
Philadelphia, Pennsylvania

MICAH

1

A Prophet Who Was Remembered

(Micah 1:1–16)

The word of the LORD that came to Micah of Moresheth during the reigns of Jotham, Ahaz and Hezekiah, kings of Judah—the vision he saw concerning Samaria and Jerusalem.

> *Hear, O peoples, all of you,*
> *listen, O earth and all who are in it,*
> *that the Sovereign LORD may witness against you,*
> *the Lord from his holy temple.*
> *Look! The LORD is coming from his dwelling place;*
> *he comes down and treads the high places of the earth.*
> *The mountains melt beneath him*
> *and the valleys split apart,*
> *like wax before the fire,*
> *like water rushing down a slope.*
> *All this is because of Jacob's transgression,*
> *because of the sins of the house of Israel.*
> *What is Jacob's transgression?*
> *Is it not Samaria?*
> *What is Judah's high place?*
> *Is it not Jerusalem?*

In the summer of 1981, I again visited the lake country of England after many years, and I walked along the shore of Windermere where William Wordsworth wrote some of his most memorable poetry. It was a brilliant day, the kind that makes you thrill to be alive. But I have been there when the clouds hung low on the mountains and the damp gray seemed to seep into my bones. It must have been on such a day that Wordsworth, walking along the lake with his sister Dorothy, suddenly came upon the field of daffodils that he described in one of his best-known poems.

I wandered lonely as a cloud
That floats on high o'er vales and
    hills,
When all at once I saw a crowd,
A host, of golden daffodils,
Beside the lake, beneath the trees,
Fluttering and dancing in the
    breeze.

As the poem goes on Wordsworth describes how that scene brightened his spirits and served as a rejuvenating force years afterward.

Something similar happens in coming to the prophet Micah. The minor prophets largely convey a message of

God's judgment. This has been true of all those considered thus far: Hosea, Joel, Amos, Obadiah, and Jonah. With the sole exception of Jonah, moreover, their messages of judgment went unheeded. The prophets appeared. Their warnings were rejected. Judgment came.

This is a depressing picture. But suddenly we come to Micah, and the daffodils flourish. This is not because Micah is any less concerned with judgment. He begins by describing the destruction of Samaria, the capital of the northern kingdom of Israel, and Jerusalem, the capital of Judah, and he carries on in that vein. No, the encouraging part is not that some other message has replaced judgment. It is rather that in Micah's case the message of judgment was heeded, repentance followed, and the disaster was postponed for a century. Hosea and Amos were ignored. Jeremiah was imprisoned. But here was one prophet who was listened to and whose preaching therefore changed history. In coming to Micah we should be encouraged to learn that one man did make a difference.

A Turbulent Century

Micah was also remembered.

The preaching of Micah about the impending judgment of God bore fruit during the reign of King Hezekiah, whose story is told in 2 Kings 18–20. During Hezekiah's reign, Shalmaneser of Assyria attacked the northern capital of Samaria and overthrew it. Then he deported the people of that kingdom. Eight years later Sennacherib, Shalmaneser's successor, attacked the southern kingdom of Judah, and Hezekiah was forced to pay tribute. On one occasion the Assyrian field commander appeared before the walls and demanded that Jerusalem surrender. Shortly after that Sennacherib sent a letter to Hezekiah saying, "Do not let the God you depend on deceive you when he says,

'Jerusalem will not be handed over to the king of Assyria.' Surely you have heard what the kings of Assyria have done to all the countries, destroying them completely. And will you be delivered? Did the gods of the nations that were destroyed by my forefathers deliver them?" (2 Kings 19:10–12). Hezekiah spread this letter before the Lord and received an answer through Isaiah: the city would not be destroyed and Sennacherib would himself fall.

Of Hezekiah it is said, "He did what was right in the eyes of the Lord, just as his father David had done. He removed the high places, smashed the sacred stones and cut down the Asherah poles. He broke into pieces the bronze snake Moses had made, for up to that time the Israelites had been burning incense to it" (2 Kings 18:3, 4).

There was a revival in Hezekiah's time—the chief factor in God's decision to spare the city from Sennacherib. The interesting thing about this is that Micah is not mentioned in the story of Hezekiah's reign as found in 2 Kings. Isaiah, the well-known prophet of the aristocracy, is there. He is the one who brought the Lord's message to the king. But Micah? Micah is not mentioned! Yet we know from a later incident during the days of Jeremiah that it was because of his preaching that the people repented and Jerusalem was spared.

Jeremiah lived about one hundred years after Micah, but, like Micah, he had also been prophesying the destruction of Jerusalem. He said, "This is what the Lord says: If you do not listen to me and follow my law, which I have set before you, and if you do not listen to the words of my servants the prophets, whom I have sent to you again and again (though you have not listened), then I will make this house like Shiloh and this city an object of cursing among all the nations of the earth" (Jer. 26:4–6). The message offended the priests and other (false) prophets, so they seized Jeremiah and brought him before the officials and people, demanding his death.

Jeremiah gave his defense. Then the elders of the land said: "Micah of Moresheth prophesied in the days of Hezekiah king of Judah. He told all the people of Judah, 'This is what the LORD Almighty says:

" 'Zion will be plowed like a field,
Jerusalem will become a heap of
    rubble,
the temple hill a mound overgrown
    with thickets.'

"Did Hezekiah king of Judah or anyone else in Judah put him to death? Did not Hezekiah fear the LORD and seek his favor? And did not the LORD relent, so that he did not bring the disaster he pronounced against them? We are about to bring a terrible disaster on ourselves!" (vv. 18, 19). As a result of the elders' testimony the life of Jeremiah was spared.

It was because of the memory of Micah! He was heard in the days of Hezekiah. A revival followed. Then, one hundred years later, his words were still remembered, and the memory of what happened earlier was used of God to spare the life of Jeremiah.[1]

WHO WAS MICAH?

Who was Micah? He was not from a distinguished family as his better-known contemporary Isaiah seems to have been. On the contrary, he came from an undistinguished, small, country village called Moresheth—which is why he was later called "Micah of Moresheth" by the Jerusalem elders. Archaeologists have identified Moresheth with the ruins of Tell-el-Judeideh. It was so small that it was usually called Moresheth Gath (Mic. 1:14). That is, it was identified by its proximity to the larger, well-known city of Gath. Obvi-

ously, Micah was a rural person, and he was a stranger in Jerusalem when he first went to the capital to give his prophecies.

He reminds us of Amos, who also had a rural background and appeared as a stranger in Bethel, the shrine city of the northern kingdom.

Micah is like Amos in another way too. It is a notable feature of Amos that the opening chapters pronounce judgments on a variety of nations—Syria, Philistia, Tyre, Edom, Ammon, Moab, Judah, and Israel—and these are arranged in such a way that the net of judgment closes in surely but unexpectedly upon Israel. Syria is northeast. Philistia is southwest. Tyre is northwest, Edom southeast. (The first four nations thus mark out the four points of the compass.) After that come Ammon and Moab to the east, Judah due south, and then Israel. In constructing his book in this way it is as if Amos surrounds the people of the north and catches them off guard. Micah's approach is not nearly so elaborate, but the pattern is the same. He announces that his prophecy concerns Samaria (that is, Israel) and Jerusalem (that is, Judah). He takes the first section (vv. 2–9) to deal with the northern kingdom. But after that his message is entirely for the kingdom of the south where he was then living and prophesying. In other words, there was judgment for others, but his message was primarily for the people of Judah.

We need to take this personally. Quite often when we read the Bible we apply what we read to other people. When we read of judgments on others, we almost sigh in relief, assuming wrongly that if judgment is spoken against them it is therefore not spoken against us. But this is wrong. God is no respecter of persons. Consequently, if

---

[1] Micah was also remembered six hundred years after this in the time of Christ. He was the source of the prophecy that the Messiah would be born in Bethlehem (cf. Matt. 2:3–6; John 7:42).

we are going our way and not God's way, as the people of Jerusalem were doing, then we must do as they eventually did and turn back to God. It is the way we ourselves will escape God's judgment.

AN AVALANCHE OF DISASTER

The first chapter has three main parts, which are highlighted by the paragraph divisions in the New International Version of the Bible: (1) the descent of the Lord in judgment, (2) the fall of Samaria, and (3) the effect of the sin of Samaria on Jerusalem and a call for a proper response to this infection.

The first of these sections is quite moving. Here Micah portrays the Lord as swooping down from heaven to do battle on earth. Micah's language describes precisely what the judgment will do, namely, sweep away everything before it. Notice the movement in verses 2–4. Micah begins with a picture of God in "his holy temple" (v. 2); from here He speaks against the people. Next we see God "coming forth" from His dwelling place (v. 3). Then "He comes down and treads the high places of the earth." At the touch of God's foot the mountains melt beneath Him and thus also accompany His descent (v. 4). Micah imagines the valleys split apart to accommodate this new mass, which, he says, comes down "like wax before the fire, like water rushing down a slope" (v. 4).

This is intended to be terrifying, and it is. It is like the description the Romans gave of the Celtic warriors they encountered in their early conquests in central Europe. To the Romans the Celts were barbarians. In battle they wore no clothes at all. They painted themselves with bright colors and greased their hair so that it stood up fiercely from their heads, as though they had been electrocuted. Before battle they would be out of sight. Then suddenly they would come swooping down the hillsides, shrieking loudly in their unknown languages, and fall upon the enemy ranks. It scared the Romans witless.

Micah paints a similar picture. Only here it is not a mere horde of barbarians with whom we must deal. The attacking foe is God, the sovereign Lord of the universe, and He is so angered at the wickedness He sees that He leaves His holy temple to do battle Himself.

The second part of this chapter concerns the fall of Samaria, here pictured as a close future event. (The city actually fell during the years of Micah's ministry.) In this description the downward-moving imagery of the opening sections continues, for Micah sees the stones of Samaria's great fortifications tumbling down the ridge of Samaria into the valley. In the same way "all her idols will be broken to pieces" and will fall. Amos denounced the kingdom of Israel for its sexual immorality, especially its cultic prostitution (Amos 2:7, 8). This same theme emerges again in Micah: "Since she gathered her gifts from the wages of prostitutes, as the wages of prostitutes they will again be used" (v. 7).

The third section begins with verse 8 and describes the passing of the evils of the northern kingdom to the south. Verse 9 is still speaking of Samaria, but already the transition is apparent: "Her [that is, Samaria's] wound is incurable; it has come to Judah. It has reached the very gate of my people, even to Jerusalem itself." The same thought appears in verse 12: "Disaster has come from the LORD, even to the gate of Jerusalem." In these verses Micah is arguing that even as the sin of Samaria has spread to Jerusalem, so too the judgment befalling the northern kingdom will reach the southern one as well.

In this last section we see something of the inner heart of Micah and perhaps get an insight into why he was so successful. The chapter has only sixteen verses. But despite the fact that he is covering a variety of subjects and is tracing the picture of judgment from the throne of heaven through Samaria to Jerusalem, Micah takes six verses (more than one-third of the whole) to list the cities of Judah that will participate in the coming disaster. He lists ten, including his own town of Moresheth Gath (v. 14). He does this because he feels pity for the people in these smaller cities. The national leaders are insensitive to the plight of their own people, and perhaps that is why Micah has particularly harsh words for the capital cities (v. 5). But Micah knows these people—he is one of them—and he doesn't want them to suffer the consequences of their rulers' sins.

The prophet sets the tone for this section by an introductory quotation from David's elegy over Saul and Jonathan after the Israelite defeat on Mount Gilboa. David laments:

"Your glory, O Israel, lies slain on your heights,
How the mighty have fallen!

Tell it not in Gath,
proclaim it not in the streets of Ashkelon,
lest the daughters of the Philistines be glad,
lest the daughters of the uncircumcised rejoice"
(2 Sam. 1:19, 20).

In verse 10 Micah says that his lament for the fallen cities of Judah is as intense as the mourning of David for Jonathan and Saul.

In his dismay at what is coming, Micah looks over the Judean cities and reflects on the sinister destinies suggested by their names. These reflections are puns. To us puns hardly seem serious, but this is not the way an ancient Jew would have taken them. A name handled in this way became an omen, for names were significant in any case, and a name suggesting disaster would have lingered over the city as a cloud, awaiting fulfillment. As Leslie Allen writes, "Names are treated as omens which, once observed, haunt the localities until they are fulfilled. They are revealed as clues to the curse that is to come upon the country."[2]

The first of the cities is *Beth Ophrah* (v. 10). To Micah the second part of the name sounded like '$\bar{a}p\bar{a}r$, which means "dust." So he told the citizens of this city to "roll in the dust." That is, they will cover themselves with dust in a traditional rite of mourning.

The next city, *Shaphir* (v. 11), sounds like the word for "beautiful." But it will not be beautiful for long, said Micah. Instead its citizens will be marched away naked and in shame, as will others of the southern kingdom.

Zaanan (v. 11) sounds like the Hebrew word for "exit" or "go out" (*yātsā*). But just like the beautiful city, which will not be beautiful, so this city will not go out to face its enemies. The citizens will be shut up inside their city like animals, and they will remain there until the city falls.

Beth Ezel (v. 11) means "the nearby city." But it will not be near in that day. It will be so taken up with its own mourning that it will be of no help to the other cities.

The citizens of *Maroth* ("bitterness") will writhe in bitterness (v. 12).

Lachish (v. 13), a well-known military city about thirty miles southwest of Jerusalem, was famous for its chariot horses. Micah says that in the Day of Judgment these will be harnessed up, but the implication is that they will be harnessed to flee, not to fight. This important city was taken years later at the time of Sennacherib's invasion.

---

[2]Leslie C. Allen, *The Books of Joel, Obadiah, Jonah and Micah* (Grand Rapids: Eerdmans, 1976), p. 278.

Sennacherib considered its conquest significant, for he used scenes from the city's encirclement and fall to decorate his great palace at Nineveh. Today these reliefs are in the British Museum.

Moresheth (v. 14), Micah's home town, sounds like *me'ōreshet* ("betrothed"). So he speaks of giving the city wedding gifts as she passes from the rule of her own family to the authority of her cruel new husband, the invader.

Aczib (v. 14) sounds like *'aksāb* ("deceitful, disappointing"). Micah says she will "prove deceptive to the kings of Israel" (v. 14).

Mareshah (v. 15) is related to the word *yōrēsh* ("possessor, heir"). She will be possessed by someone else.

Adullam (v. 15) was the place of refuge to which David had gone during the dismal days when he was in flight from King Saul. It will happen again, says Micah, for the aristocracy of Israel will be forced to take refuge in this area.

The chapter closes with an appeal to Jerusalem as the father or mother of the outlying villages, her children. The people of Jerusalem are to shave their heads in mourning, for the children in whom they delight are to be taken away into exile. Exile! This is the climax of the chapter. For although Micah has been moving his readers in this direction, he has nevertheless not used this word until now. Now that he does, nothing could be more dreaded or more severe. To go into exile was to become a slave, and to have an entire people exiled was the death of the nation.

Can we feel the force of this? Allen acknowledges that "the impact of this powerful poem upon the modern reader is unfortunately marred by a cultural rift. Anyone who despises puns and prizes emotional restraint as a virtue has a long bridge to cross before

he can enter this particular section of the heritage God would have him make his own. Micah is not playing clever word games for the amusement of his listeners. Words for him and his audience are a web of associations for good or ill, a prey of mystic spells, which in the adverse sense are akin to the irrational superstition that surrounds the number thirteen for many today. The prophet is exploiting this cultural susceptibility, surrounding each place in turn with an aura of doom and evoking feelings of dread and despair. In the middle of this rhetorical *tour de force* he reveals to wide-eyed hearers, aghast and ready to hear the worst, that behind the grim future stands the person of Yahweh, no longer a safe stronghold but his people's enemy . . . Micah whips up his hearers' emotions and pushes them into inconsolable grief in order to dispel their complacency and arouse in them a sense of their own sin and liability to punishment."[3]

Never Give Up

Micah was successful in his ministry to Jerusalem. The people repented, and the turnabout was so significant that it was remembered in Jerusalem one hundred years later. But we are not to think that Micah's success came easily, as if he only needed to sow the seed and then reap the harvest.

There are two important matters. First, when he appealed to the citizens of Jerusalem ("Shave your heads in mourning," v. 16), he was not asking them to do something he refused to do himself. On the contrary, in verse 8 he says that he was already leading them in this repentance: "Because of this I will weep and wail; I will go about barefoot and naked. I will howl like a jackal and moan like an owl." Without doubt, one of the reasons for Micah's

---

[3] Ibid., pp. 283, 284.

success as a witness for God is that he genuinely identified with the people to whom he was speaking and genuinely grieved for what was coming to them. Do you want to be successful in your witness? Then do not give the impression that your sole duty is to announce a disaster and that, you "couldn't care less" what happens to those to whom you speak. More people have been won by honey than by thunder. Many who have rejected a Christian's logic have been won by his tears.

Second, it is hard to miss the fact that, although a revival did come to Jerusalem and Judah during the reign of Hezekiah, Hezekiah's was not the only reign during which Micah prophesied. In fact, he tells us at the beginning of his book that the Lord spoke to him during three succeeding reigns: those of Jotham, Ahaz, and Hezekiah. The first two reigned for sixteen years each. So at the very least, assuming that Micah began his work in the very last months of Jotham's reign and that the revival came in the very first months of Hezekiah's reign, Micah preached for sixteen years without succeeding. It is more likely, indeed highly probable, that there were twenty or twenty-five years of work before the awakening.

That is a long time, but at the end of it success came. Have you prayed for anybody even half as long as that? Have you mourned for a son or daughter, a husband or wife, a relative or neighbor for even ten years? Have you grieved for our country for even five? God does not count time as we do, and with Him a thousand years is as a day. Has He not said to us, "Let us not become weary in doing good, for at the proper time we will reap a harvest if we do not give up" (Gal. 6:9)? Has God not said, "Let nothing move you. Always give yourselves fully to the work of the Lord, because you know that your labor in the Lord is not in vain" (1 Cor. 15:58)?

If we cannot learn from that, at least let us learn from Winston Churchill. He was asked to speak at the English school where he had been educated and give the reason for his success as commander-in-chief of the British forces during World War II. Churchill's answer came in three words: "Never give up." Then he elaborated: "Never give up. Never give up. Never, never give up."

If Churchill triumphed with such a philosophy, why cannot we, who serve the sovereign God of history?

2

Many Are the Plans

(Micah 2:1–13)

Woe to those who plan iniquity,
to those who plot evil on their beds!
At morning's light they carry it out
because it is in their power to do it.
They covet fields and seize them,
and houses, and take them.
They defraud a man of his home,
a fellowman of his inheritance.
Therefore, the LORD says:
"I am planning disaster against this people,
from which you cannot save yourselves.
You will no longer walk proudly,
for it will be a time of calamity.
In that day men will ridicule you;
they will taunt you with this mournful song:
'We are utterly ruined;
my people's possession is divided up.
He takes it from me!
He assigns our fields to traitors.' "

Not many people study Latin today, so we do not often see the old Latin phrase *Deo Volente* (abbreviated D.V.) that Christians used to include in their letters and other writing. It is a pity, for *Deo volente* means "God willing" or "if God wills" and is therefore a useful reminder that our plans are not always the plans of God and that it is God's determinations rather than ours that prevail.

I think of Jesus' parable about the rich fool. This man had such a good crop at harvest time that he did not have a place to store it. He had no thoughts about God or of giving some of what he had harvested to the poor. So he decided to tear his barns down and build bigger ones, thinking that then he would be able to sit back, take life easy, and be merry. In Jesus' story, God said to him, "You fool! This very night your life will be demanded from you. Then who will get what you have prepared for yourself?" The man planned a self-indulgent future—a glorious retirement. But God's plans for him were quite different. Jesus said, "This is how it will be with anyone who stores up things for himself but is not rich toward God" (Luke 12:16–21).

20

We find the same truths in Proverbs, where wise King Solomon wrote: "Many are the plans in a man's heart, but it is the LORD's purpose that prevails" (Prov. 19:21).

MAN'S PLANS AND GOD'S

This is what we find as we begin the second chapter of Micah. The rich of his day were working dishonestly to increase their wealth. In itself there is nothing wrong with prosperity; in fact, it is a blessing of God. But these people were increasing their wealth through force and fraud. They were not even able to wait until daybreak to form their evil strategems. They lay awake plotting. Then, when daylight came, they immediately rushed out to put their plans into effect. Micah says they had forgotten that God had plans too and that His plans rather than theirs would prevail. They "plan iniquity" (v. 1), he writes, but God says, "I am planning disaster against this people, from which you cannot save yourselves" (v. 3).

We saw in our last study that Micah was similar to his contemporary Amos, the prophet who went to the northern kingdom of Israel some years before its fall. Both came from the country. Both went to the city. Both had a way of gradually narrowing down their words from judgments on other nations to judgments on those to whom they were speaking. We have another similarity here. For Micah's words against those who were plotting evil in Jerusalem were similar to Amos's words against the wicked of Samaria. In Samaria people had grown rich at the expense of those less fortunate than themselves. They had built winter houses and summer houses (Amos 3:15). Their furniture was of the finest quality (Amos 6:4). They had lush vineyards (Amos 5:11). They ate the best food and drank the most abundant wine (Amos 6:4–6). But it was all acquired by fraud, oppression, and corruption.

Amos wrote:

> They sell the righteous for silver,
>   and the needy for a pair of
>   sandals.
> They trample on the heads of the
>   poor
>   as upon the dust of the ground
>   and deny justice to the oppressed
>   (Amos 2:6, 7).

> You . . . turn justice into bitterness
>   and cast righteousness to the
>   ground (Amos 5:7).

> You hate the one who reproves in
>   court
>   and despise him who tells the
>   truth (Amos 5:10).

> You oppress the righteous and take
>   bribes
>   and you deprive the poor of
>   justice in the courts (Amos
>   5:12).

> Hear this, you who trample the
>   needy
>   and do away with the poor of the
>   land,

> saying,

> "When will the New Moon be over
>   that we may sell grain,
> and the Sabbath be ended
>   that we may market wheat?"—
> skimping the measure,
>   boosting the price
>   and cheating with dishonest
>   scales,
> buying the poor with silver
>   and the needy for a pair of
>   sandals,
>   selling even the sweepings with
>   the wheat (Amos 8:4–6).

Micah found the same horrible practices going on in Jerusalem.

Those who were planning iniquity rose with the earliest light to carry it out by force ("At morning's light they carry it out because it is in their power to do it," v. 1) and fraud ("They defraud a man of his home, a fellowman of his inheritance," v. 2). Were the people of Jerusalem to think that they would be spared by God any more than the people of Samaria? Since they were doing the same things, were they not to expect the same fate?

In talking about this evil Micah uses a very important word: "covet." It comes from the last of the Ten Commandments, in which God says, "You shall not *covet* your neighbor's house. You shall not covet your neighbor's wife, or his manservant or maidservant, his ox or donkey, or anything that belongs to your neighbor" (Exod. 20:17). Micah accuses the people of breaking this tenth commandment. Their covetousness has led them into the plotting and violence they are blamed for.

What does coveting mean? It means to want earnestly something you do not have, particularly something belonging to another person. It means not to be satisfied with what God has already given you. It means to be materialistic and greedy. The tenth commandment reveals that sin is essentially a matter of the heart, for coveting is something that exists internally long before it expresses itself in any outward action. It is conceivable—barely conceivable—that a person could read the first nine commandments and because of a blindness of heart suppose that he or she had observed them. "After all," one might argue, "I do worship the God of the Bible; I do not worship idols; I keep the Sabbath; I do not kill or steal; I have not committed adultery; I do not even lie." But it is hard to see how even such a person could claim to have observed the tenth commandment. All of us are guilty at this point.

Not long ago I was talking with my daughter about the law, and she asked why God gave it. I pointed out that it was to show that we were sinners and needed to believe on Jesus Christ as our Savior.

She said, "But most of us don't do those things. We don't kill people or steal or worship images."

I said, "What about the last one? When you see someone who has a better bicycle than you have, don't you wish it were yours? When people are in someone else's house and think that it is better than theirs, don't they wish they could have it? Don't we wish we were as rich as someone else who has more money?"

She said, "Of course. But everybody does that. That's natural."

"That's just the point," I replied. "Everybody does it."

How modern this all is! How keenly it strikes at the roots of our materialistic Western culture! We object to the sexual innuendos and come-ons in advertising. But even more pernicious is the ceaseless pitch for materialism, the constant temptation to covetousness. It comes in subtle forms, as in the suggestion that buying a particular car or home will make you a more attractive person or allow your children to grow up benefiting from a higher level of society. It comes in more vulgar forms, as in the advertisement for an expensive hair conditioner that says, "I don't care if it is more expensive, because I'm worth it."

We are a generation of people never at peace with what we have, always seeking more. We are as guilty of coveting our neighbor's fields or houses or inheritance as were the citizens of Jerusalem.

POETIC RETRIBUTION

The disaster God plans against such people is an example of what we call poetic justice or having "the punishment fit the crime." There is a song about this in Gilbert and Sullivan's comic operetta *The Mikado*. The chorus goes:

My object all sublime I shall achieve
     in time
To make the punishment fit the
     crime,

The punishment fit the crime.

My favorite verse is the one about billiard players.

> The billiard shark, whom anyone
>   catches,
>   His doom's extremely hard.
> He's made to dwell in a dungeon
>   cell
>   In a spot that's always barred.
> And there he plays extravagant
>   matches
>   In fitless finger stalls,
> On a cloth untrue with a twisted
>   cue
> And elliptical billiard balls.

At this point the singer bursts into a rousing laugh, because a punishment like that is not only appropriate, it is humorous as well. Unfortunately, there is nothing humorous about the poetic justice meted out by God.

As Micah describes it, this justice could have two parts. First, the possessions and fields of the guilty materialists would be taken from them when the invaders came. They had used violence to take those fields from the poor originally (v. 2). Now they would suffer the same fate.

> In that day men will ridicule you;
>   they will taunt you with this
>   mournful song:
> "We are utterly ruined;
>   my people's possession is divided
>   up.
> He takes it from me!
>   He assigns our fields to traitors"
>   (v. 4).

Second, their ruin would be so complete that when the time came, as it did periodically, for the land to be redistributed and portions returned to those who had lost their inheritance, they would have no one to represent them and their place in the nation would be lost forever. In the Old Testament there were two ways the land could be returned. One was by the jublilee principle described in Leviticus 25. Every

fifty years the land was to be returned to its original owners—regardless of what had happened in the meantime. By this principle even the poorest families could hope for a better future. The second way was by lot. This is the way land was originally divided among the tribes when Israel first entered Canaan (Josh. 14:2), and the procedure seems to have been followed in later years as well (Ps. 16:6). Micah refers to this second custom. But, he says, when the lot is drawn there will be no one left from the wicked to draw their straw.

> Therefore you will have no one in
>   the assembly of the LORD to
>   divide the land by lot (v. 5).

The coming destruction was to be a thorough one indeed.

RELIGIOUS OPPOSITION

As might be predicted, Micah's preaching aroused opposition, just as Amos's preaching had in the northern kingdom. We would expect opposition from the greedy rulers Amos and Micah were denouncing, but that was not the original source. Instead, the religious leaders spoke up to defend their rulers and denounce God's spokesmen. They had been working hand-in-glove with the wealthy and had benefited from this association, so they too were guilty, and they flailed out against the prophets' honesty.

Amos was oppressed by Amaziah, the priest of the cult city of Bethel. Amaziah regarded Amos's words as treason and wrote to King Jeroboam, accusing the prophet of attempting to raise a conspiracy against him. We have no record that Jeroboam even took notice of Amos (or of Amaziah). But Amos pronounced a terrible judgment against Amaziah: his sons and daughters would be killed in the invasion, his wife would become a prostitute in the city, and he would die an exile in a foreign land (Amos 7:10–17).

Amaziah had told Amos, "Do not prophesy against Israel, and stop preaching against the house of Isaac" (Amos 7:16). The prophets of Judah were now telling Micah the very same thing.

> "Do not prophesy," their prophets say.
> "Do not prophesy about these things;
> disgrace will not overtake us."
> Should it be said, O house of Jacob:
> "Is the Spirit of the LORD angry?
> Does he do such things?"
> (Mic. 2:6, 7).

These false prophets devilishly called into question God's pronouncement by an appeal to the supposed character of God. They claimed that God could not have said what He in fact did say, because "the Spirit of the LORD [does not get] angry" and does not "do such things." But He does! That is the point. Those who claimed otherwise were doing the Devil's work and not God's.

I came upon a particularly fine example of this recently. The town of Lynchburg, Virginia, considers itself a fairly Christian community. So it was with a kind of religious appeal that the town's newspaper, the *Daily Advance,* carried an editorial in the fall of 1981 against some words of its best-known citizen, the Reverend Jerry Falwell. Falwell had been speaking somewhere and had suggested—not prophesied but merely suggested—that: "God could judge America, perhaps with Soviet" military might, unless the nation repented of its sin and turned to Him. The editors were outraged. The editorial said: "The implication that God would use the Soviet Union as an instrument of punishing America is rather difficult to imagine, since Russia is the great Godless Society." This is a "church-oriented society," they said. "Great churches

and many good works . . . abound throughout this land." The *Daily Advance* concluded that Falwell should retract his statement.[1] Like the prophets of Jerusalem, the editors of Lynchburg were saying, "Do not prophesy about these things; disgrace will not overtake us" (Mic. 2:6). "How can God possibly bring judgment when we are so good?"

The false prophets insisted that God would not judge His people, because it was against His nature. In verses 7 and 8, God answered them. He acknowledged that He did indeed do good to those "whose ways are upright," but that lately His people had "risen like an enemy" against Him.

> "You strip off the rich robe
> from those who pass by without a care,
> like men returning from battle.
> You drive the women of my people
> from their pleasant homes.
> You take away my blessing
> from their children forever"
> (Mic. 2:8, 9).

They had become God's enemy by their treatment of other people. They were so hardened in their sin that they treated men, women, and children alike, exploiting them all. They robbed men of their clothes, women of their homes, and children of their inheritance. Was God not right to send judgment against such wicked individuals?

We make a mistake in thinking that we can have one relationship to God and a totally different relationship to other people. God declares that this is impossible. If we make others our enemies, we make God our enemy too.

This is the principle Jesus enunciated so clearly in His sermon on the Mount of Olives. He told of people who had fed the hungry, given water to the thirsty, taken in strangers, clothed the

---

[1] The story was reported in *The Presbyterian Journal,* October 7, 1981, p. 3.

naked, cared for the sick, and visited those in prison. When they appeared before Christ on Judgment Day, they learned that they had been feeding and clothing and caring for Christ all that time. He told them, "I tell you the truth, whatever you did for one of the least of these brothers of mine, you did for me." Then there were others who had turned their backs on the hungry, did not share their water with the thirsty, did not welcome strangers, clothe the naked, tend the sick or visit the ones who were in prison. They were sent to hell. When they protested that they had never seen the Lord in any of these conditions, He replied, "I tell you the truth, whatever you did not do for one of the least of these, you did not do for me" (Matt. 25:31–46).

Micah is thinking of exile from the land but his declaration of God's judgment on the people of his day is the equivalent of Jesus saying, "Then they will go away to eternal punishment, but the righteous to eternal life" (Matt. 25:46).

> "Get up, go away!
> For this is not your resting place,
> because it is defiled,
> it is ruined, beyond all remedy"
> (v. 10).

Canaan was meant to be a resting place for God's people. It is referred to this way in Deuteronomy 12:9 and Psalm 95:11. But those who have ruined it by taking away the rest others should have enjoyed are now to suffer restlessness themselves. They are to be driven out of Judah to become exiles in a foreign land.

Micah makes one last point—a throwback to the false prophets. The people of Judah would not listen to true prophets. "What prophecies will they listen to?" he asks. The only prophet fit for them is one who foretells an abun-

dance of alcohol (v. 11). For this is what the people want: oblivion until disaster comes.

HOPE FOR THE HOPELESS

The first important section of Micah ends with chapter 2, which is now rounded off with a message of hope for a better day. This is common in the Minor Prophets. No matter how absolute their messages of judgment, they always seem to end with a balancing note of promise. Hosea, Joel, Amos, and Obadiah all end this way.

The change of tone between Micah 1:1–2:11 and 2:12, 13 is so extreme, however, that many commentators have argued that it cannot be taken at face value, that it is merely another false quotation taken from Micah's rivals, or that it is the work of an editor who obviously included it in the wrong place, if indeed it should be included at all. Even Calvin said, "I see not how the prophet could pass so suddenly into a different strain."[2] In my judgment the difficulties are resolved by relating these words to what has gone before, rather than by seeing them as a later or different message entirely. Micah has pronounced a judgment on those who have exploited the poor of the land. The city will fall and they will go into exile. This is just. But what, we may ask, of the poor whom they have exploited? If the city falls and the wicked are punished, will not the poor be punished too? Will the innocent not suffer with the guilty? Micah seems to say that they will. But he has good news for them too: for the remnant of the upright, there will be a restoration.

> "I will surely gather all of you, O Jacob;
> I will surely bring together the remnant of Israel.

---

[2]Quoted by Leslie C. Allen, *The Books of Joel, Obadiah, Jonah and Micah* (Grand Rapids: Eerdmans, 1976), p. 300. Allen also gives examples of those who seek to avoid the passage in the ways indicated.

I will bring them together like sheep
    in a pen,
  like a flock in its pasture;
  the place will throng with people.
One who breaks open the way will
    go before them;
  they will break through the gate
    and go out.
Their king will pass through before
    them,
  the LORD at their head"
    (Mic. 2:12, 13).

Today it is much the same. We live in an evil world in which the innocent do suffer for the sins of wicked men. The sins of the fathers are visited upon the children "to the third and fourth generation" (Exod. 20:5). But what we see today is not the whole of reality, nor is our history the end of all things. The One who rules the future is coming. The King will reign. So regardless of the present, the way is bright for those who wait for that coming and that kingdom.

3

Cry Justice!

(Micah 3:1–4:5)

Hear this, you leaders of the house of Jacob,
*   you rulers of the house of Israel,*
who despise justice
*   and distort all that is right;*
who build Zion with bloodshed,
*   and Jerusalem with wickedness.*
Her leaders judge for a bribe,
*   her priests teach for a price,*
*   and her prophets tell fortunes for money.*
Yet they lean upon the LORD and say,
*   "Is not the LORD among us?*
*   No disaster will come upon us."*
Therefore because of you,
*   Zion will be plowed like a field,*
Jerusalem will become a heap of rubble,
*   the temple hill a mound overgrown with thickets.*

A good feature of American government (and other governments too) is what we call "balance of powers." We mean by this that our government is composed of three semi-independent branches, each of which has unique privileges, including a check on the others. The *executive* branch is directed by the president of the United States. It has power to originate programs, but its power here is balanced by Congress, the *legislative* branch, which must fund them. If Congress does not fund the president's programs, the programs never come into existence. Congress has the right to make laws. But its powers are not absolute; the *judicial* branch, the Supreme Court, has power to declare those laws unconstitutional. To round out the picture, the president has power over the court through his right to appoint justices, and Congress has power over the president and Supreme Court justices through its right to impeach them if a situation warrants this action.

In recent years Watergate provided a working demonstration of this system of checks-and-balances. The executive branch had become corrupt, engaging in illegal spying activities against American citizens and then attempting to cover them up. The situation was righted when Congress began an investigation leading to a possible impeachment proceeding against the president.

That is how the branches of government should operate. But what if all three branches were corrupt and worked hand in hand to oppress the country's citizens? In a situation like that little could be done, except to overthrow the corrupt government entirely.

And No Justice for All

This was the situation that confronted Micah as he entered the capital city of Jerusalem to bring the word of God to the corrupt leadership of Judah. Though there was sin in the outlying areas of the country and among the common people in the capital, it was nothing compared to the evil among the ruling classes. What troubled Micah (and God far more) was the sin in the courts, palaces, and temple. All three branches of government were corrupt. Worse yet they worked hand in hand. The politicians got their way in the courts, and the judges were paid for their destruction of justice. The prophets also benefited from this arrangement and supported the government in turn. "Is not the LORD among us?" they said. "No disaster will come upon us" (Mic. 3:11).

This is not a new theme. It was already hinted at in chapter 2. There Micah describes people who seize property belonging to others, "because it is in their power to do it." They "defraud a man of his home," presumably through "legal" means (vv. 1, 2). Later Micah mentions prophets who speak what the leaders want to hear rather than what God wants them to hear. This suggests the interlocking corruption of the nation's upper classes. Still, it is not until chapter 3 that we see the full picture.

Chapter 3 has three sections. Section 1 (vv. 1–4) concerns judges and the corruption of their courts. Section 2 (vv. 5–8) concerns prophets who speak well for those who pay them. Section 3 (vv. 9–12) concerns politicians who gain support from the others for money.

The word that ties the chapter together is "justice." Justice has departed from Judah. That accusation dominates the chapter. But the word itself is also prominent, occurring in all three sections (vv. 1, 8, and 9). These verses say:

"Listen, you leaders of Jacob,
    you rulers of the house of Israel.
Should you not know *justice*,
    you who hate good and love
        evil. . . ?"

But as for me, I am filled with
        power,
    with the Spirit of the LORD,
    and with *justice* and might,
to declare to Jacob his transgression,
    to Israel his sin.
Hear this, you leaders of the house
        of Jacob,
you rulers of the house of Israel,
who despise *justice*
    and distort all that is right. . . .

Micah wanted to see justice triumph in Judah. But instead he saw each branch of government supporting the others in overturning justice and pulling the highest standards down.

Judgment for the Judges

Sections 1 and 3 both begin with similar wording: "Listen, you *leaders* of Jacob, you *rulers* of the house of Israel" (v. 1); "Hear this, you *leaders* of the house of Jacob, you *rulers* of the house of Israel" (v. 9). This seems to suggest that Micah is addressing the same people in both sections. But as we read the chapter carefully we find that he is speaking to different people (or at least to the same people exercising different areas of responsibility).

In the first section he is obviously referring to perversion in the courts. In the last he is speaking of political perversion involving a different kind of leadership. Undoubtedly, it was common to use the words "leaders" and "rulers" for administrators of justice, as well as political figures. These justices were probably the leaders of houses or families. In Exodus 18 Moses appointed leaders from the various tribes, houses, and families to be a system of courts for minor crimes. No doubt Judah had a similar court system.

Justice is difficult to establish and maintain and even harder to define. I know a Christian who served twenty years in the police department of the city of Philadelphia. On different occasions we have talked about justice, often in the context of the Bible's teaching about it. His experience has made him cynical. When I speak of the need for establishing justice, he replies, "What's justice?" He knows of innumerable cases where the guilty have gone free and the innocent have been punished. "On earth there is no such thing as justice," he says.

Our desire for justice is one reason why we regard justices so highly. A judge should be above reproach.

Micah recognized this too, and he brought charges against the judges of Judah. His complaint was not that the justices were unequal to their task, nor did he fault them with the mere neglect of justice, serious as that would be. Micah's charge was far worse. He accused them of perverting justice. The courts had been established to protect the innocent and punish the guilty, but these men had used them to oppress the innocent and reward the guilty. For this the judgment of God was to come.

Here Micah uses one of the most piercing images in Scripture. He says that these corrupt justices "tear the skin from my people and the flesh from their bones." They "eat my people's flesh" (vv. 2, 3). Micah is saying that these men have become cannibals. They are feeding on those it is their responsibility to defend.

The charge is far worse than those in chapter 2. There Micah described the activity of those who took "the rich robe" from men who passed by, took "their pleasant homes" from women, and took God's "blessing" (that is, their inheritance) from children. Here it is not merely a matter of taking away possessions—clothes or home or inheritance; the judges were attacking the people themselves. They were feeding upon the lifeblood and sinews of the nation.

What is the judgment upon these individuals to be? Micah has a fine sense of poetic justice. He sees the irony in things. So he says that the day is coming when these judges are going to "cry out to the LORD" for mercy. They are going to appeal to the Chief Justice of all. But what is going to happen? He will not answer them! He is going to treat them the way they treated the innocent people of Jerusalem. He will hide his face from them, and judgment will come.

PROPHECY FOR THE PROPHETS

The second group Micah talks about are prophets. He says, "As for the prophets who lead my people astray, if one feeds them, they proclaim 'peace'; if he does not, they prepare to wage war against him" (v. 5).

We need to put this in the same kind of framework we used to talk about the corruption of the judges, dealing first with what Micah does not say. Suppose the problem was merely that there was no word from God. Amos mentions such an eventuality when he talks about God's coming judgment.

"The days are coming," declares the Sovereign LORD,
  "when I will send a famine through the land—
not a famine of food or a thirst for water,
  but a famine of hearing the words of the LORD.
Men will stagger from sea to sea and wander from north to east,

searching for the word of the
   LORD,
   but they will not find it"
      (Amos 8:11, 12).

A situation like that is terrible. Not to hear God is to be cut off. But that is not the problem Micah faces. He is not complaining that the prophets are silent.

In Micah's day the prophets were speaking. There were plenty of oracles, much preaching. But their words were all wrong! They were speaking, but everything they said led people astray. They prophesied peace when there was no peace, and prosperity when the city was about to fall.

It is better to remain silent than to speak words that lead someone else astray in spiritual matters. Jesus talked about people who led others astray, saying, "If anyone causes one of these little ones who believe in me to sin, it would be better for him to have a large millstone hung around his neck and to be drowned in the depths of the sea" (Matt. 18:6). In this matter we are dealing with more than temporal justice. We are dealing with the eternal destiny of the souls of men and women. For a person to be led astray in this area, to be encouraged to perish without faith in Christ as God's way of salvation, is damnable. Yet according to Micah, the prophets of Judah were guilty of this.

We can hardly imagine anything worse. Yet Micah added two more charges. First, these prophets not only led others astray, they did it for money. It is terrible to make an error in the matter of salvation. It is more terrible to teach others your error. It is even worse to do it for personal gain. It grieves me to say this, but I see it happening today. Ministers and other religious leaders speak, write, and establish sects for money. They deceive millions. What is God's judgment of such people

to be? What will happen in the day when the Judge of all the earth does right?

Second, these prophets knew better. They were not prophets of Baal. Micah considered them to be prophets of the living God, who knew the truth and preferred to speak lies. He warned that their judgment would be appropriate. They have prophesied falsely, so when the destruction of the city comes and they cry out for a sure word from God for their people,

"The sun will set for the prophets,
   and the day will go dark for
      them.
The seers will be ashamed
   and the diviners disgraced.
They will all cover their faces
   because there is *no answer from
   God*" (vv. 6, 7).

CHAOS FOR THE RULERS

The political leaders of Judah make up the third group. They are judged because they have distorted "all that is right" (v. 9). It is true that the judges distorted justice, and the prophets distorted the word of God. But Micah speaks of distortion here particularly, because these political leaders had a unique responsibility to order things correctly. They had a managerial role. In terms of God's directions for the proper functions of government, they were to see that justice was established through the courts and were to protect the nation against the encroachment of other nations. But Judah's leaders had failed to carry out their responsibilities. Micah repeats in this section what he said earlier concerning the judges and prophets: "Her leaders judge for a bribe, her priests teach for a price, and her prophets tell fortunes for money" (v. 11). He repeats those charges here because the political leaders were responsible for overseeing the other branches and eliminating such practices. Yet, not only had they allowed it to happen, they had even encouraged it by creating a system in which everything was structured for their profit. They used justice and religion to serve their own ends, and they grew richer at the expense of the poor. Micah said that God was going to overthrow them and the system they had created, because they had established a just order.

In each case the judgment is appropriate. The justices were going to cry for mercy and not get it. The prophets were going to call for a word from God, and God was going to be silent. The rulers were going to seek order but find chaos.

FOUR FREEDOMS

If we were to stop at the end of this chapter, we would be ending on the bleakest note possible. But the first five verses of chapter 4 really belong at the end of this section. We have already seen that the first two chapters of Micah form a long section in which the earlier part has to do with justice (Mic. 1:1–2:11) and the very end with hope (Mic. 2:12, 13). Apparently, Micah did not want to end on a negative note. Justice must be done. Judgment must come. But God is still the God of hope. We have the same pattern here. Chapter 3 is about judgment. But then the first five verses of chapter 4 introduce hope.

The second reason why 4:1–5 belongs with chapter 3 is that there is a tie-in between them. When Micah writes at the end of chapter 3 about the judgment to come upon the rulers he says, "Because of you, Zion will be plowed like a field, Jerusalem will become a heap of rubble, the temple hill a mound overgrown with thickets" (v. 12). Chapter 4 begins, "In the last days the mountain of the LORD's temple will be established as chief among the mountains." Micah is saying that by their mismanagement and sin these corrupt rulers had made the mountain

of God into a little mound, overgrown with thorns. But even so, Jerusalem was still to be God's mountain, the place of His justice where He demonstrates the righteousness of His name. So Micah says that God is going to raise it up to become a mountain again. In fact, it will be the mountain of mountains, the chief mountain. People will stream into it to worship the God who has done these things.

What happens then? This is really wonderful; for, as Micah begins to talk about it, he shows that under God's management all that had been corrupted in Judah will be overcome, and men and women will be set free to worship Jehovah.

On January 6, 1941, Franklin Delano Roosevelt gave a speech on the four freedoms. He talked about freedom of speech, freedom of religion, freedom from want, and freedom from fear. Micah 4 mentions two of them: freedom from want ("Every man will sit under his own vine and under his own fig tree") and freedom from fear ("No one will make them afraid, for the LORD Almighty has spoken"). Though Micah does not mention Roosevelt's first two freedoms they must come first if the others are to be established.

Micah's own list of freedoms begins with freedom from ignorance (v. 2). He does not mean your ABC's nor does he mean classical literature; he does not mean Latin or even Hebrew. He is talking about ignorance of the law of God. He is saying that in the day when God establishes His rule in Jerusalem, all will learn the law of God and become missionaries of it. The first freedom will be freedom from ignorance of that law.

Second, there will be freedom from war (v. 3). This text is familiar. "They will beat their swords into plowshares and their spears into pruning hooks. Nation will not take up sword against nation, nor will they train for war anymore" (cf. Isa. 2:4; Joel 3:10). It is significant that this freedom follows freedom from ignorance of God's law. The basis for a true peace is not a balance of arms, though in a corrupt world that probably has its place. The basis for a true peace is knowledge of the law of God and obedience to that law and the gospel. When that takes place, people's hearts are changed and they desire peace and pursue it.

Third, it follows that there will now be freedom from want, because the resources that go into war will be turned to other ends (v. 4).

Finally, where there is freedom from want, in the end there will also be freedom from fear. This is a glorious prophecy. It is a prophecy to people everywhere as to how the Golden Age, the age of God's full blessings in truth and righteousness, will be found.

There is one more interesting thing. In verse 2 Micah writes, "Many nations will come and say, 'Come, let us go up to the mountain of the LORD." Then, toward the end of that same verse, he says, "The law will *go out* from Zion." People will go up, and the law will go out. Most of us are all for getting the law out. The question is: Have we first gone up to God to learn it from Him ourselves? We do not stand on any pinnacle of privilege as if we could speak from wisdom in ourselves. We cannot say, "I know what you must do, and you must do it because I say so." Rather, we must first go up to God, look to Him, and seek His instruction. You and I cannot remake this world. But we can be agents of renewal—of justice, truth and order—if God first instructs us, transforms us, and empowers us.

4

A King for Judah

(Micah 4:6–5:5)

"But you, Bethlehem Ephrathah,
    though you are small among the clans of Judah,
out of you will come for me
    one who will be ruler over Israel,
whose origins are from of old,
    from ancient times."

Therefore Israel will be abandoned
    until the time when she who is in labor gives birth
and the rest of his brothers return
    to join the Israelites.

He will stand and shepherd his flock
    in the strength of the LORD,
    in the majesty of the name of the LORD his God.
And they will live securely, for then his greatness
    will reach to the ends of the earth.
    And he will be their peace.

The Book of Micah is a little-known portion of the Word of God, but if there is any part of Micah likely to be known to the average person, it is that which foretells the birth of the Lord Jesus Christ in Bethlehem (Mic. 5:2). It was the part quoted by the chief priests and teachers of the law at the time of the birth of Christ, as recorded in Matthew 2. Jesus had already been born in Bethlehem when the Magi came to Jerusalem seeking Him; and Herod, who had not the slightest idea where Jesus might be but worried about any budding pretender to the throne, asked the priests and teachers: "Where is the Christ to be born?"

They replied, "In Bethlehem in Judea, for this is what the prophet has written:

"But you, Bethlehem, in the land of Judah,
    are by no means least among the rulers of Judah;
for out of you will come a ruler
    who will be the shepherd of my people Israel" (Matt. 2:5,6).

In their response the priests and teachers combined Micah 5:2 and 5:4 and predicted rightly that the coming divine king of Judah would be born in Bethlehem.

This prophecy is the climax of the

next section, running from Micah 4:6 (introduced by the phrase, " 'In that day,' declares the LORD") to Micah 5:5 (which completes the prophecy of the coming King of Judah). The section is tied together by pungent imagery—of sheep and their shepherd (in Mic. 4:8 and 5:4) and of a woman in labor (Mic. 4:10 and 5:3)—and by increasingly hopeful oracles on current judgment joined to future blessing.

THEMATIC VERSES

It is difficult to fit the first two verses (Mic. 4:6, 7) into any neat outline, but they are probably best taken as a statement of a theme which the following three oracles develop. It is a hopeful theme in contrast to the dominant note of dismay and grief expressed thus far in the prophecy.

Quite obviously, these verses follow from what has gone before, particularly the verses on which the preceding section ended. Micah had been castigating the leaders of the people for their failure to do what they had been commissioned to do. Judges had failed to give justice. Prophets had failed to speak a true word from God. Rulers had ceased to rule. As a result the kingdom was in chaos, and an even greater judgment was coming. But this was not the final word, and the section ended with the prophecy of a golden age to be marked by four freedoms: freedom from ignorance of God's law, freedom from war, freedom from want, and freedom from fear. In this section Micah continues the thought to say that the golden age will also be a time of regathering. It is true that judgment will come. Jerusalem will fall. The people will be scattered. But God is going to regather the people and rule over them again from Mount Zion.

Micah introduces a beautiful image at this point, saying that the Lord will rule over His people as a shepherd watches over his sheep. It is a theme found elsewhere in the Old Testament.

> The LORD is my shepherd, I shall lack nothing.
> He makes me lie down in green pastures,
> he leads me beside quiet waters,
> he restores my soul.
> He guides me in paths of righteousness
> for his name's sake.
> Even though I walk
> through the valley of the shadow of death,
> I will fear no evil,
> for you are with me;
> your rod and your staff,
> they comfort me (Ps. 23:1–4).

Even though the fall of Jerusalem and the ensuing captivity would be a "valley of the shadow of death" for the people, God would nevertheless be with them and eventually restore them to their land.

Later in the Psalms we find the same image.

> Know that the LORD is God.
> It is he who made us, and we are his;
> we are his people, the sheep of his pasture (Ps. 100:3).

The prophet Isaiah wrote:

> See, the Sovereign LORD comes with power,
> and his arm rules for him.
> See, his reward is with him,
> and his recompense accompanies him.
> He tends his flock like a shepherd:
> He gathers the lambs in his arms
> and carries them close to his heart;
> he gently leads those that have young (Isa. 40:10, 11).

Micah is saying that this is what God will do with the captives of Judah. He will gather them as a shepherd gathers limping sheep, assemble them into a flock, and eventually return them to their capital city.

What a difference such a shepherd makes! Philip Keller writes in his book on the Twenty-third Psalm, "The lot in life of any particular sheep depended on the type of man who owned it. Some men are gentle, kind, intelligent, brave and selfless in their devotion to their stock. Under one man sheep would struggle, starve and suffer endless hardship. In another's care they would flourish and thrive contentedly."[1] Micah is telling his readers that even in times of judgment it is good to be in the gentle care of Israel's good shepherd.

THE FIRST TWO ORACLES

The first of the three oracles found in Micah 4:8–5:5 is the least hopeful, but it starts the transition from judgment to restoration. Micah writes with scorn, looking ahead to the time of deportation: "Have you no king? Has your counselor perished?"

> Writhe in agony, O Daughter of
>   Zion,
>   like a woman in labor,
> for now you must leave the city
>   to camp in the open field.
> You will go to Babylon (v. 10).

Such language may seem cruel to us. It may be difficult to see any good motive in it or imagine any good coming from it. But, of course, Micah's motive is good, and good will come. His concern is to awaken people to the true gravity of their situation and lead them to repentance, and as we learned earlier, he was successful.

Micah's procedure reminds me of a similar tactic employed once by Donald Grey Barnhouse. In the early days of his ministry he met a man who lived not far from the church to whom he would occasionally speak about salvation. Each time he did this the man would laugh him off, saying that he was not the kind who needed church. He was a member of a lodge and said that if a person lived up to the high

principles of that particular lodge he would be all right. The day came when the man was stricken with a serious illness and was not expected to live out the day. Barnhouse went to see him. A member of the man's lodge was already there on what was called the deathwatch, the point being that no member of their organization should be allowed to die alone. This death-bed companion was sitting across the room reading a magazine, and Barnhouse had scarcely entered when his replacement came. It was a desperate situation, and it called for a desperate remedy.

Barnhouse sat down by the dying man's bedside. He said, "You do not mind my staying here a few minutes and watching you, do you? I have wondered what it would mean to die without Christ, and I have known you for several years now as a man who said he did not need Christ but that his lodge obligations were enough. I would like to see a man come to the end of his life that way to see what it is like."

The stricken man looked at him like a wounded animal and said slowly, "You . . . wouldn't . . . mock . . . a . . . dying man . . . would you?"

Barnhouse then wondered aloud what he would answer when God asked what right he had to enter His holy heaven. Great tears ran down the man's pale, wrinkled cheeks as he looked back in agonized silence. Quickly Barnhouse told him the way of salvation through faith in the merits of Christ. The man replied that his mother had taught him those things as a child but that he had abandoned them. Then, in those moments at the very end of life, the man came back to those truths and to faith. He believed, prayed, and soon asked that the members of his family be brought in to hear his testimony. He asked that his story might be

---

[1] Phillip Keller, *A Shepherd Looks at Psalm 23* (Grand Rapids: Zondervan, 1970), p. 17.

told at his funeral, which was a few days later.

Micah employs the same shock tactics. He mocks the people for their unbelief, but not out of cruelty. He speaks in love. Moreover, even as he foretells Jerusalem's fall and the ensuing deportation, he cannot help but speak of the nation's deliverance. "You will go to Babylon," he says. "[But] there you will be rescued. There the LORD will redeem you out of the hand of your enemies" (v. 10).

In the first of the three oracles appearing in this section there are nine lines of judgment as compared to three lines of hope (NIV). In the second oracle the proportion shifts in the direction of hope, four lines of judgment as compared to ten lines of hope. In these verses (vv. 11–13), Micah begins with the situation that confronted the nation as he spoke ("But now many nations are gathered against you. They say, 'Let her be defiled, let our eyes gloat over Zion!' "). But he immediately passes on to say that these nations do not know the Lord's plan and that God will yet give Judah "horns of iron" to drive them out and break their armies into pieces.

Verse 12 takes us back to 2:1–3, where Micah first contrasted those who plot iniquity with God who plans judgment. In the earlier passage he was referring to the corrupt rulers of Judah. Here he refers to the pagan nations who are planning to overthrow Jerusalem.

There is a problem here that is evident to anyone who reads the chapter carefully. Micah has been telling of the fall of Jerusalem throughout his prophecy and has apparently been thinking along these lines even as late as verse 11. But in verse 12 he writes of deliverance from the very enemies who were then gathering against the city. This seems contradictory and may well have been puzzling to Micah's hearers. How

can the nation fall to the Babylonians and be delivered at the same time? How can Jerusalem win and yet lose? At the time he uttered these words it was probable that no one (maybe not even Micah) had answers to these questions. But in view of the history of the nation we can see what was involved. When Micah wrote, the city was threatened by the armies of Sennacherib. This threat, plus the prophecies of Micah and Isaiah, drove King Hezekiah and the other leaders of Jerusalem to their knees. A revival followed, and God delivered Jerusalem. God's angel killed 185,000 Assyrian soldiers. When Sennacherib saw the carnage, he was appalled and withdrew (cf. 2 Kings 18, 19; 2 Chron. 32; Isa. 36, 37).

This is probably what Micah is referring to. As a result of his preaching there was a true but temporary deliverance. The people did repent. But soon after they returned to their sin, and the judgment pictured in the bulk of the prophecy came on them.

THE SHEPHERD-KING

If we are right in suggesting that the oracle of Micah 4:11–13 refers to Sennacherib's invasion, then it is also in view at the start of the well-known verses that predict the birth of Christ. Micah 5:1 speaks of a siege in which the invading forces symbolically "strike Israel's ruler on the cheek with a rod." It suggests public humiliation, which the invasion of Sennacherib certainly was. "Is this to continue forever?" someone might ask. "Is Judah always to be humiliated?" Micah replies that this will not be the case, for there will be a time of permanent triumph and greatness when the divine ruler prophesied for Israel comes.

Micah has two points of emphasis. First, he stresses that the one to be born in Bethlehem "will be a *ruler* over Israel" (v. 2). This is not a theme unique to Micah, of course. We think of

2 Samuel 7:16, in which God promised King David, "Your house and your kingdom will endure forever before me; your throne will be established forever." In his response David recognized that an eternal kingdom is not the destiny of mere men. A prophecy like this requires a divine king for its fulfillment. "So it shall be," says Micah. The one who is coming will be He "whose origins are from of old, from ancient times [literally, 'from days of eternity']."

Isaiah intensified the promises. He said,

For to us a child is born,
  to us a son is given,
  and the government will be on
    his shoulders.
And he will be called
  Wonderful Counselor, Mighty
    God,
  Everlasting Father, Prince of
    Peace.
Of the increase of his government
    and peace
  there will be no end.
He will reign on David's throne
    and over his kingdom,
establishing and upholding it
with justice and righteousness
  from that time on and forever
    (Isa. 9:6, 7).

This is not the way with human kings and kingdoms. On the contrary, history shows the kingdoms of this world rising and falling across the centuries. Historians like Arnold Toynbee tell us that the world has known twenty-one great civilizations, but all of them have endured only for a time and then have passed away. Babylon was mighty. Today it is gone. Greece and Rome have fallen. Even the United States of America and the Soviet Union, although now at the pinnacle of world power, will not be able to escape that inexorable law of God for history: "Righteousness exalts a nation, but sin is a disgrace to any people" (Prov. 14:34).

The normal course of the kingdoms of this world is described in a striking way in Daniel. Belshazzar, the king of Babylon, had given a party during which he defiled the vessels taken from the temple of God at Jerusalem. In the midst of the party, handwriting appeared on the wall of the palace, and Belshazzar was frightened. The writing was: "MENE, MENE, TEKEL, PARSIN." It meant: "God has numbered the days of your reign and brought it to an end; . . . you have been weighed on the scales and found wanting; . . . your kingdom is divided and given to the Medes and Persians" (Dan. 5:26–28).

Daniel told Belshazzar: "The Most High God gave your father Nebuchadnezzar sovereignty and greatness and glory and splendor. . . . But when his heart became arrogant and hardened with pride, he was deposed from his royal throne and stripped of his glory. He was driven away from people and given the mind of an animal; he lived with the wild donkeys and ate grass like cattle; and his body was drenched with the dew of heaven, until he acknowledged that the Most High God is sovereign over the kingdoms of men and sets over them anyone he wishes. But you his son, O Belshazzar, have not humbled yourself, though you knew all this" (Dan. 5:18, 20–22).

All human kings and kingdoms follow this course. God lets a man rise above his fellows in power, he is overcome with pride, and eventually God brings him down. It is not this way with Christ. His kingdom is forever. As we sing in Handel's *Messiah:* "And he shall reign for ever and ever. Hallelujah!"

We can imagine a king who would rule like this and yet be undesirable because he was a tyrant. But this is not the way it will be, according to Micah. The one to come will be a *ruler* in Israel who "will stand and *shepherd* his flock" (v. 4). In using this image Micah stresses the compassion and gentle care of the divine King and thus ties the closing prophecy of the section to the statement with which he began.

OUR GOOD SHEPHERD

It is impossible for one who lives on our side of the birth, death, and resurrection of Jesus Christ to read this and not think of Jesus' claim to be "the good shepherd" (John 10:11, 14). There have been other shepherds, of course. In ancient times most kings were considered shepherds to some degree. But Jesus is not like those other shepherd-kings. Which of them could possibly be called a "*good* shepherd," much less "*the* good shepherd"? Yet Jesus is both the unique and good shepherd of all who are His people.

In John 10, where Jesus calls Himself "the good shepherd," there are two explanations of why He is so designated. First, Jesus is the good shepherd because He laid down his life for the sheep (vv. 11, 15, 17, 18). Christ's death was voluntary. Peter spoke of Christ, saying, "This man was handed over to you by God's set purpose and fore-knowledge" (Acts 2:23). As the angel told Joseph, Jesus was born for this: "You are to give him the name Jesus, because he will save his people from their sins" (Matt. 1:21). Jesus did not have to come to this earth, any more than anyone has to be a shepherd. He did not have to die. Nevertheless, He willingly gave His life for our salvation.

Christ's death was vicarious; that is, Jesus died not for His own sin—He had none—but for our sins and in our place. He indicates this by saying, "The good shepherd lays down his life *for his sheep.*"

I cannot understand why so many have been urged to deny this. The words are plain enough, both here and elsewhere. They tell us that Jesus died, not only for others in the sense of "on their behalf," but (even stronger than this) in the sense of "in their place." The Greek preposition is *hyper,* and its meaning is given beyond any doubt in Romans 5:6–8, where the word occurs three times: "When we were still powerless, Christ died *for* the ungodly. Very rarely will anyone die for a righteous man, though *for* a good man someone might possibly dare to die. But God demonstrates his own love for us in this: While we were still sinners, Christ died *for* us."

The second explanation of why Jesus is the good shepherd is that He knows His sheep and is known by them (John 10:14). Friends know one another: parents know their children. A husband and wife know each other in a special and beautiful way. In spite of these things, there is in each of us a deep inner hunger to be known better, to be known for what we really are and to share a corresponding and similar knowledge of another. This exists on the spiritual level. For though we are sinners and in rebellion against God, there is, nevertheless, a certain hunger to know God and to be known of Him. Augustine called it restlessness, adding, "Our hearts are restless until they find their rest in thee." Jesus is a good shepherd, because He satisfies that deep longing of the human soul and mind.

Moreover, Christ knows us as "his sheep." To be known by Jesus is to be a member of His flock and therefore to be one for whom He died. It is to be one who will never be snatched from His hand, as He says later. Nothing about us will ever suddenly rise up to startle our divine Shepherd-King and diminish His love.[2]

---

[2] Cf. "Our Good Shepherd" in James Montgomery Boice, *The Gospel of John,* vol. 3 (Grand Rapids: Zondervan, 1977), pp. 98–105.

5

God's Call to the City

(Micah 5:5–6:16)

He has showed you, O man, what is good.
And what does the LORD require of you?
To act justly and to love mercy
and to walk humbly with your God.

Listen! The LORD is calling to the city—
and to fear your name is wisdom.

In one important way Micah was an eminently modern man. He came from the country, but he went to the city. He saw that the sins of the city, committed by the leaders who lived and worked there, were the chief sins of the nation for which the judgment of God was coming. Micah had concern for the city. His prophecy begins on this note: "the vision he saw concerning Samaria [the capital of the northern Jewish kingdom of Israel] and Jerusalem [the capital of the southern Jewish kingdom of Judah]" (Mic. 1:1). Throughout his book he keeps coming back to these cities, particularly Jerusalem. Now, as he comes to the end, he calls out to the capital of the southern kingdom again. "Listen!" he says, "The LORD is calling to the city" (Mic. 6:9). His call is for justice, for mercy, and for walking humbly with God. It is a call very much needed in our time.

Strange to say, however, in an age which boasts of thriving evangelical churches and more than fifty million persons who identify themselves as having had a "born again" experience,

American church leaders have had very little to say to the city and its sins. Even stranger, some of the secular writers are beginning to note and bemoan this fact.

On April 1, 1977, the New York columnist William Reel wrote a piece for the *Daily News* called "Mean Street . . . X-rated Streets" in which he had some very harsh words for New York City. He noted recent statistics showing that there were 400,000 alcoholics, 500,000 narcotics users, and 300,000 compulsive gamblers; that there had been 658,147 felonies during the previous year (assaults, robberies, muggings, rapes, and murders); that the pornographers of Times Square had reached new lows in featuring sex films involving children. He called Times Square the "sewer of the universe." He reported the experience of one citizen who had been the victim of violence, had been brushed off by the authorities, and was about to leave the city.

He came to this conclusion: "Of course, you gave up on New York politicians long ago. They are pathetic and embarrassing. But what is worse than the abdication of political leadership in New York is the abdication of spiritual leadership. There is no one willing to speak the truth, to call the Neros to account, to warn of the wrath of God.

"When was the last time a Catholic leader said anything more forceful than 'God bless you'? New York needs a John the Baptist and Catholicism gives us Caspar Milquetoasts. The Protestant leadership is effete and insipid, debating Holy Orders for lesbians at a time when grandmothers are regularly and brutally assaulted by muggers and rapists. The Jewish establishment is moribund. Jeremiah must weep when, looking down from above, he contemplates these sad sacks sitting in their studies composing Passover messages that have no more spiritual content than a press release from the Liberal Party."

He concluded somewhat wistfully, "New York was a great city when it put a great emphasis on spiritual values. Maybe we can get back to this."

The Late Great Nation

Micah must have been thinking similar thoughts as he composed the indictment we find in chapter 6. In form, it is a legal summons and proceeding—the same kind of call and accusation already found in Hosea 4 and 5 and Amos 3. In it God enters into a legal proceeding against His people, calling them to remember what He has done for them and what they have done.

In Micah there is a special background to this judicial proceeding in which the future glory of the nations is pictured (Mic. 5:5–15). This section follows the prophecy of the coming divine King of Israel and is therefore set in a future tense. It is a reminder of what the nation could be. It could be victorious, for one thing (vv. 5, 6). As Micah wrote, the kingdom of Hezekiah was being humbled under the hand of Assyria. But the nation had been victo-

rious in the past. It would be again. What a contrast between the possibilities open to those who love and serve God and Judah's present misery.

Second, the nation could be a source of blessing and even a corrective judgment for others (vv. 7–9). Here Micah uses two images.

> The remnant of Jacob will be
> in the midst of many peoples
> like *dew* from the LORD,
> like showers on the grass. . . .
>
> The remnant of Jacob will be among
> the nations,
> in the midst of many peoples,
> like a *lion* among the beasts of the
> forest,
> like a young lion among flocks of
> sheep (vv. 7, 8).

Dew is an image of blessing, as it literally was in Judah's dry land. A lion is a symbol of destruction and fierce judgment. Israel had been both in the past and would be both again. But what was she now? Neither! How great the contrast between her potential and her present reality.

Third, Micah writes of a day when the nation would be purified of its sin and maintained in an attitude of pure and intense devotion to God. She would give up trust in foreign military alliances (vv. 10, 11), the occult (v. 12), and false gods (vv. 13, 14). But at the present the opposite was the case, and the people were the people of God in name only.

God builds His case against Israel against this important background. First, Israel (particularly the city of Jerusalem, which stood at the spiritual heart of the nation) had forgiven God. That is, the people had forgotten the mighty acts of God toward them in past days. God had made them a nation by redeeming them when they were slaves in Egypt. He had given them leaders— Moses, Aaron, and Miriam—and had brought them into their own land.

"I brought you up out of Egypt
　and redeemed you from the land
　　of slavery.
I sent Moses to lead you,
　also Aaron and Miriam. . . .

Remember your journey from
　　Shittim to Gilgal,
　that you may know the righteous
　　acts of the LORD" (vv. 4–5).

The people had forgotten this. They had forgotten it in the sense that it no longer made any difference in their lives.

The second part of God's accusation is that, having forgotten Him, the people had become increasingly corrupt, and dishonesty and violence had become marks of their civilization. This was particularly true of their city. God asks:

"Am I still to forget, O wicked
　　house,
　your ill-gotten treasures
　and the short ephah, which is
　　accursed?
Shall I acquit a man with dishonest
　　scales,
　with a bag of false weights?
Her rich men are violent;
　her people are liars
　and their tongues speak
　　deceitfully" (vv. 10–12).

We must ask whether Micah's description of his nation is not also an apt description of our own and whether God's call to the city of Jerusalem is not a call to our own cities too. In making this comparison we acknowledge that the Jews were God's people in a way different from God's use of any other people in history. God had entered into a special covenant with them and had promised to be their God nationally. They were bound together by worship of the one true God. No other nation

has ever had precisely this experience. At the same time, while not erring on the side of overly comparing the United States of America with Israel, we do not want to err on the side of missing our unique experiences of God's blessings either. We are not God's covenant nation. But we were a godly nation once. We have been richly blessed by God. We are in danger of judgment for having forgotten both God and those blessings.

We live in such a secular age that our spiritual roots are even willfully suppressed and forgotten. We have been told repeatedly that Christopher Columbus, the pathfinder to the New World, discovered this new continent almost accidentally and that his sole concern in sailing westward was for gold. But this was not the way Columbus himself told it. He confessed a deep faith in Christ and believed that God had put it into his mind to convey the light of the gospel of Jesus Christ to new lands.[1]

Among the founders of this nation were the Puritans who settled New England. Modern history has portrayed them as narrow-minded, self-righteous fanatics whose ways were quickly and rightly forgotten. But these were actually godly men and women who endured great hardship to establish a Christian society in America. They called their venture an "errand into the wilderness."[2]

George Washington has been portrayed as little more than a deist, whose struggle was for personal fame rather than for any genuine moral ends. But Washington was a devout believer in Christ. In a small prayer book written when he was about twenty years old Washington implored: "O most

---

[1] Peter Marshall and David Manuel, *The Light and the Glory* (Old Tappan, N.J.: Fleming H. Revell, 1977), pp. 17, 25–66.

[2] This was the topic of a sermon preached by Samuel Danforth in 1670 and subsequently used by Perry Miller as the title of his classic book on the New England experiment (Cambridge: Harvard University Press, 1956).

glorious God . . . remember that I am but dust, and remit my transgressions, negligences and ignorances, and cover them all with the absolute obedience of thy dear Son, that those sacrifices (of sin, praise and thanksgiving) which I have offered may be accepted by thee, in and for the sacrifice of Jesus Christ offered upon the cross for me. . . . Direct my thoughts, words, and work; wash away my sin in the immaculate blood of the Lamb; and purge my heart by thy Holy Spirit."[3]

At the time of the American Revolution, John Witherspoon, then president of the College of New Jersey (Princeton), wrote, "He is the best friend to American liberty who is most sincere and active in promoting true and undefiled religion, and who sets himself with the greatest firmness to bear down on profanity and immorality of every kind."

Samuel West, a minister from Dartmouth, New Hampshire, said, "Our cause is so just and good that nothing can prevent our success but only our sins. Could I see a spirit of repentance and reformation prevail throughout the land, I should not have the least apprehension or fear of being brought under the iron rod of slavery."[4]

It is true that Jefferson was a deist. Benjamin Franklin was a skeptical unbeliever. Nevertheless, there was at this time and for many years both before and after the Revolution, a rich core of people who so knew Christ and so desired His will and glory in this land that they actually infused the theology and morality of Christianity into the nation's cultural and political fabric. Their buildings bore inscriptions to God's glory. Their money, which we still use, stated "In God We Trust." Even Franklin, who, as I have said, was an utter unbeliever, did not hesitate to speak of the value of sincere prayer at the crucial turning point of the Constitutional Convention in Philadelphia in May, 1787. He said: "In the beginning of the contest with Britain, when we were sensible of danger, we had daily prayers in this room for Divine protection. Our prayers, Sir, were heard, and they were graciously answered. . . . I have lived, Sir, a long time, and the longer I live, the more convincing proofs I see of this great truth: 'that God governs in the affairs of man.' And if a sparrow cannot fall to the ground without his notice, is it probable that an empire can rise without his aid?" He then called for regular, imploring prayer to begin each of the Convention's sessions.[5]

We do not need to pretend that every pious thought recorded from those past days was genuine. Even if they were only partially genuine, we have still fallen a long, long way. Is our case so much different, then, from Israel's? Is it not true that we too have forgotten God and become increasingly corrupt and violent in our lives?

FRUSTRATION

In case we are not quite convinced of our culpability at this point, let me place in evidence the present tone of our national life and show that this is precisely what God foretold as the nature of His judgment upon Judah. God said:

> "Therefore, I have begun to destroy you,
>   to ruin you because of your sins.
> You will eat but not be satisfied;
>   your stomach will still be empty.
> You will store up but save nothing,
>   because what you save I will give to the sword.

---

[3] William J. Johnson, *George Washington, the Christian* (Nashville: Abingdon Press, 1919), pp. 23–28.

[4] The quotations from Witherspoon and West are in Marshall and Manuel, *The Light and the Glory*, pp. 296, 297.

[5] Ibid., pp. 342, 343.

You will plant but not harvest,
  you will press olives but not use
    the oil on yourselves,
  you will crush grapes but not
    drink the wine. . . .

Therefore I will give you over to
  ruin
  and your people to derision;
  you will bear the scorn of the
    nations" (vv. 13–16).

There are several emphases to this judgment. First, it is gradual. God says, "I *have begun* to destroy you," that is, He was not doing it all at once. Second, it is expressed in frustration. The people will eat but not be satisfied, store up but save nothing, plant but not harvest. Third, it will result in derision and scorn of the once favored nation by other peoples.

Each of these elements can be seen in contemporary America. But of the three, the most evident of all is frustration. Within the memory of at least half the Americans living today there is remembrance of this land as the land of opportunity and high ideals. Here was freedom's home. Here were unending personal possibilities. Here was progress, measured in such tangible things as safe homes, good schools, abundant jobs, and fair prices. An individual could plot our advance year by year and decade by decade. In those days we were proud to be Americans. But things have changed. In less than a lifetime the conditions of our national life have been so altered that nothing seems to work any longer. Our economy is struggling. Our military has proved to be inadequate to several challenges. Prestige abroad has plummeted. And within, a national life once marked by moral standards and high aspirations has become a cesspool. People do what they wish without regard either to God or man. Our cities are dirty and unsafe. Crime abounds. Structures collapse. Perversions flaunt

their evils in our faces. This is precisely what God told Israel would happen to that favored nation. Israel's case is our own.

TEARS FOR THE CITY

We are tempted to write culture off at this point, particularly the culture of our cities. But desperate though the situation may be, we are not yet right in doing that. There is a famous sermon by the great Scottish preacher Thomas Guthrie (1803–1873) entitled "Sins and Sorrows of the City." Guthrie bemoans the decline of Scotland's cities. But he says that however much we must cry over our cities, our tears are not like those of Jesus when He wept over Jerusalem but rather like Jesus' tears shed at the tomb of Lazarus. Jerusalem was doomed beyond redemption. But our cities are not necessarily doomed. So long as we have the case of Nineveh and its repentance, and so long as the return of Christ in final judgment is postponed, we have always before us the possibility of a spiritual and moral resurrection.

What must we do? The answer is in Micah 6:8, a verse which contains what are probably Micah's best-known words, even though most people would not know they are from Micah.

He has showed you, O man, what
  is good.
  And what does the LORD require
    of you?
To act justly and to love mercy
  and to walk humbly with your
    God (v. 8).

This is a word for people who are willing to do all sorts of religious things but are not willing to do what is needful. The verses before this (vv. 6, 7) contain four questions asked by the ungodly but religious inhabitants of Jerusalem to the effect that they were more than willing to do anything God might require—if only He would make

His wants known. Does He want "burnt offerings . . . calves a year old"? They are willing to bring those. Does He want "thousands of rams," perhaps "ten thousand rivers of oil"? That can also be arranged. Perhaps He wants the "firstborn" children? They suggest that they might even offer their children. This has to be seen against God's criticism of them for their forgetfulness of His great acts. God is faulting them. But what do they come back with? They are arrogant enough to suggest that the fault is not theirs but God's. "Tell us what we haven't done," they say. "We are far more ready to serve you than you are to tell us your requirements."

God answers quietly that He is not asking for anything new. He is not laying down further religious ordinances. All He asks is what has been asked from the beginning. And it is not ritual or routine! It is the reality, not the form. It is: (1) to act justly, (2) to love mercy, and (3) to walk humbly with God.

To act justly is most important, for it does not mean merely to talk about justice or to get other people to act justly. It means to do the just thing yourself. I am impressed by something I heard from Dr. Anthony Campolo, a professor at Eastern College and the University of Pennsylvania. He was speaking to a group of businessmen on the Christian's responsibility in the area of social justice, and he said that experience had caused him to change the way he was going about such matters. When he was younger he thought that the way to produce change was to buy shares in an offending company, go to the stockholders' meetings and demand changes. But he found that, having done that, nothing happened. Having endured his outbreaks, the executives of the companies merely went about their business and ignored him. Moreover, he was getting a reputation for being a loudmouth who disrupted

things. So he took a different tack. Instead of demanding changes in others he began to work as one who was on the inside. Instead of coming in as one who knows in advance what needs to be done, he now says simply, "I think what we are doing does not please God. There must be something else we can do." This approach produces favorable responses, and results have exceeded anything he had anticipated.

There is one more thing about acting justly. It is not only something we must *do*. It is also something we must do over a considerable period of time. That is, we must be persistent. Each of us is only one person. With the blessing of God another person may join us, so that there will then be two—or five or ten. That is good. It does not take a large number of people to produce change. But it does take time! So we must hang in there even when things are frustrating and no change seems to come.

I spoke to a student group at the University of Pennsylvania along these lines, stressing the kind of Christian leadership needed in today's cities. After I finished, a student approached me to object that he had been working in city politics and had found the work so frustrating that he had quit. He thought I was being too optimistic, too naive. I asked what year he was in school. He said he was a senior. I asked how old he was. He was twenty-two. I asked how long he had been working in the political system. He answered that he had been involved for about a year and a half. Then I said, "You are not old enough nor have you worked in the system long enough to have the right to be frustrated." I say the same thing to myself. He had been working in the city for eighteen months. I have been working in Philadelphia for sixteen years, but I have no more right to be frustrated than this student. God takes a long view, and our responsibility is to work and act justly, however long it takes.

The second requirement is that we love mercy. This does not mean simply that we should act in a merciful way here and there or from time to time. It means that we are to love mercy consistently. We are to love it in others, and we are to love it as God develops that characteristic in ourselves. It is easy for us to be judgmental of city life and of those who live in urban areas. We say, "Look at those people, how bad they are!" Or, "Look at that irresponsible behavior!" We are proud of the fact that we are not like that, and we remain aloof. We have to love such people and show mercy in our dealings with them. The presence of Christians in a sinful city can be just and merciful at the same time.

The final requirement is to walk humbly with God. Have you known Christians who are anything but humble in the way they go about business? I am sure you have. Such people think they have all the answers, and they rightly bring the world's scorn upon themselves. We do *not* have all the answers. At best we are part of the solution, and we may even be part of the problem. How can we who are sinners be anything but humble? How can we not desire above all things to walk humbly with God? I think of Enoch, whose walk is described in Genesis 5:21–24. He began to walk with God when he was 65 years old, and he was still walking with God when, at the age of 365, God took him. He had a three-hundred-year walk! That is what God calls us to do and be. We are to act justly, love mercy, and walk humbly with our God.

The World Is Watching

The world is waiting for us to do just that. It is waiting for Christian people to be Christian people. You say, "I don't believe that. I try to witness to my non-Christian friends, and they don't even want to hear about Christianity." Well, that is true. They do not want to be urged to become like you, but they do expect you to be what you profess to be. The world looks for far more from us than we give them credit for.

Some time ago the Gallup Poll organization conducted a survey of urban residents, ages eighteen and over, asking what city entities they perceived as trying to improve city life. They were asked to indicate whether they thought they "are trying" or not. It was a great list: the mayor, city council, local newspapers, local service groups, neighborhood groups, the Chamber of Commerce, local retail merchants, local television stations, district councilmen, local Jaycees, local radio stations, local women's groups, city banks, small companies, major companies, the League of Women Voters, public utilities, local builders, local real estate people, the company "you work for," local labor unions, the advertising industry, city insurance agents. Do you know what organization topped the list of those perceived of trying hardest to improve city life? The local churches! They received mention by 48 percent of the more than three thousand urban residents interviewed. The next highest on the list was the mayor, who only got 39 percent.

There are times in history when it takes a thousand voices to be heard as one. But there are other times, like our own, when one voice can be heard as a thousand. Today people are desperate for leadership. They are expecting those who speak in the name of God to act justly and mercifully for the good of all.

6

No One Like God

(Micah 7:1–20)

Shepherd your people with your staff,
*   the flock of your inheritance,*
which lives by itself in a forest,
*   in fertile pasturelands.*
Let them feed in Bashan and Gilead
*   as in days long ago.*

"As in the days when you came out of Egypt,
*   I will show them my wonders."*

Nations will see and be ashamed,
*   deprived of all their power.*
They will lay their hands on their mouths
*   and their ears will become deaf.*
They will lick dust like a snake,
*   like creatures that crawl on the ground.*
They will come trembling out of their dens;
*   they will turn in fear to the Lord our God*
*   and will be afraid of you.*
Who is a God like you,
*   who pardons sin and forgives the transgression*
*   of the remnant of his inheritance?*
You do not stay angry forever
*   but delight to show mercy.*
You will again have compassion on us;
*   you will tread our sins underfoot*
*   and hurl all our iniquities into the depths of the sea.*
You will be true to Jacob,
*   and show mercy to Abraham,*
as you pledged on oath to our fathers
*   in days long ago.*

The most important verse in the last chapter of Micah is verse 18, which asks, "Who is a God like you, who pardons sin and forgives the transgression of the remnant of his inheritance?" It is a theme verse and appropriately

46

ends the book. For it is a play on Micah's name. Micah means "Who is like Yahweh?" It is fitting that the book that bears his name should end by answering the question posed by his name, saying in effect, "There is no one like Yahweh; there is no god like the God of Israel."

This question is not uncommon in the Old Testament. It is asked in Exodus 15:11, for example. This chapter contains the "Song of Moses," in which God is praised following His deliverance of the Jews from Egypt. The song delights in the defeat of Israel's enemies. It describes how God hurled both the horse and its rider into the sea, drowning Pharaoh's soldiers and officers. It describes how He caused the waters to pile up while the people of Israel passed through and then caused them to descend again on the pursuing enemy. It then asks: "Who among the gods is like you, O LORD? Who is like you—majestic in holiness, awesome in glory, working wonders?" The point is that no one can match the acts of Israel's God. Psalm 71:19 asks the same question: "Who, God, is like you?" The psalm answers the question in personal terms, describing how God delivered the author from his enemies and accusers, from ruin, shame, and confusion. Indeed, it is almost always like that. There is no one like God, because there is none that can do the mighty acts that Israel's God does.

Yet in Micah we have something different. Micah rehearses the ways in which the true God is unlike all others. Deliverance by mighty acts is among those ways. Yet his emphasis is on God's willingness to forgive sin and show mercy, which he concludes is the supreme measure of God's surpassing excellence.

Supreme in Judgment

The last chapter of Micah suggests four ways in which God is unsur-

passed. The first is judgment. It is the emphasis of verses 1–7. The matter of God's judgment is hardly a new theme at this point in the book, and yet Micah handles it in a new way. Until now God's judgment has been thought of mainly as the impending military overthrow of the city, which was indeed the end to which God brought it. Jerusalem did fall to the armies of Nebuchadnezzar in 587 B.C. However, in the verses immediately preceding this chapter Micah quoted God as saying that He was even then beginning to destroy the people because of their sins. This was described as a time in which the people would "eat but not be satisfied, . . . store up but save nothing, . . . plant but not harvest, . . . press olives but not use the oil, . . . crush grapes but not drink the wine" (6:14, 15). In chapter 7 Micah seemed to pick up on this imagery, saying that although the city had not fallen, judgment had nevertheless come.

> What misery is mine!
> I am like one who gathers summer fruit
>   at the gleaning of the vineyard;
> there is no cluster of grapes to eat,
>   none of the early figs that I crave
>   (v. 1).

What he means by this is soon made clear. Micah means that the fruit of righteousness, which God had every right to expect from His people, were not present. In fact, the opposite was the case. Instead of righteousness there was a striking increase of evil.

Micah is describing a monumental breakdown of society. It is seen, first, in a breakdown of morality. No society is ever entirely upright or godly; there are always evil people in it. But in a well-functioning society the evil are suppressed and those of good character are prominent and rule the land. In times of moral breakdown this is inverted. The evil triumph, and the good are driven out. Micah says, "The godly have been swept from the land; not one upright man remains" (v. 2). Therefore, "All men lie in wait to shed blood; each hunts his brother with a net. Both hands are skilled in doing evil" (vv. 2, 3). In my judgment this is happening in our own time. I was talking with the principal of one of our city schools. He is an excellent man, but he was resigning because of the irrational and impossible demands being made of him by the school administration. He said that he felt he was working in an insane asylum run by inmates. It is a case of the upright being swept from the land.

The second area of breakdown is the nation's leadership. This is an old theme for Micah, but it is fitting that it is brought back as the book draws to a close. As in chapter 3, Micah accuses the rulers of taking bribes and conspiring together for their own advancement at the expense of the poor: "The ruler demands gifts, the judge accepts bribes, the powerful dictate what they desire—they all conspire together" (v. 3).

We do not need to look far to see this in our land. The Watergate era was full of revelations of precisely this kind of corruption, even including payoffs to a vice president of the United States. Not long after, the Federal Bureau of Investigation began its Abscam probes in which numerous congressmen, senators, and others were caught receiving bribes to give special treatment to imaginary Arab oil interests. Not long ago a New Jersey judge was arrested going up the courthouse steps with $12,000 in his pocket that he had been given to waive or reduce sentence on a convicted arsonist. These are just a few recent examples of people in high places who have been caught! Are we to believe that this is all the corruption there is? Are these the only felons?

The third area of breakdown is the family. Human relationships are failing,

says Micah. As a result, a time has come when one cannot trust his neighbors, his friend, or even his wife (v. 5). Sons dishonor their fathers. Daughters rebel against mothers, daughters-in-law against mothers-in-law. Micah's classic statement is in verse 6: "A man's enemies are the members of his own household."

I wonder if this is not being fulfilled in our own time in many instances. Externally, people appear successful and happy. They have good jobs. They have good relationships with their friends. They have no real enemies. But often there is something gnawing away inside, and that inner agony is often a case of heartbreak or even hatred at home. Not long ago I had a Jewish man come to see me. He was not interested in Christianity. He would never have turned to me under normal circumstances. He was married to a nominally Christian wife who was an alcoholic. Outwardly they were a beautiful couple. Professionally he was riding on the crest. But the wife was slipping downhill quickly, and for the husband every moment on the job was filled with desperate thoughts about what might be happening at home either to his wife or their children.

I know another couple who are distressed over their teenaged daughter. They are marvelous parents who have struggled to make a good life for her. They have worked hard to see that she is instructed and fed in Christian things. But the girl has utter disregard for their feelings and for the turmoil she is causing. She wants her own way without responsibility. I could reproduce more examples but the point is clear. We are experiencing the same kind of decline in our own time as occurred in Micah's times. Morality, leadership, and family are crumbling. But notice this: it is not just a meaningless decline. It is part of God's judgment. For God has decreed that whenever a society departs from Him, the effects of that departure will be seen in every aspect of the life of that society. Paul talks about that in Romans 1:18–32, where he says that once men and women give up on God, neither glorifying Him nor giving Him thanks, God also gives them up to various sins and perversions, and to depraved minds. God is a moral God; He is faithful in doing this. There is no one like God in such judgments.

Supreme in Deliverance

The next section of the chapter is easier for most of us to appropriate and understand. In these verses Micah praises God for His great acts of deliverance (vv. 8–13; 15–17) and concludes that there is no one like God in this way either.

This section of Micah is most like those other passages of the Bible that exalt God, with which we began. The difference here is that Micah is looking forward rather than back. True, he does this in reference to the past: "As in the days when you came out of Egypt, I will show them my wonders" (v. 15). But his praise is not so much for a past redemption as it is for an anticipated future deliverance. In other words, this chapter is fully in line with the earlier message of the book. The prophet has been writing about judgment to come: he is not retracing that now. Judgment will come. The people will be carried off to Babylon. But as the book draws to a close, he looks beyond the deportation to another deliverance and regathering into the Promised Land. In that day the enemies of the people will be defeated, Jerusalem will be rebuilt, and the borders of the nation will be extended as they were previously.

> The day for building your walls will
> come,
>   the day for extending your
>   boundaries.

> In that day people will come to you
>   from Assyria and the cities of
>   Egypt,
> even from Egypt to the Euphrates
>   and from sea to sea
>   and from mountain to mountain.
> The earth will become desolate
>   because of its inhabitants,
>   as the result of their deeds (vv.
>   11–13).

God's role in delivering Israel from her captivities is not paralleled in our case. But all who have believed in Jesus as Savior have experienced an even greater spiritual deliverance. Micah speaks of having been plunged into darkness and then brought out into the light. That is true of us as well. We have been lost in sin's darkness but have been brought into the glorious light of Christ. Micah speaks of being subjected to the enemy but of being raised up again. We have been cursed by sin but have been raised to newness of resurrection life in Christ. Charles Wesley wrote about that in his great hymn "And Can It Be That I Should Gain?"

> Long my imprisoned spirit lay
> Fast bound in sin and nature's
>   night;
> Thine eye diffused a quick'ning ray,
> I woke, the dungeon flamed with
>   light;
> My chains fell off, my heart was
>   free,
> I rose, went forth, and followed
>   thee.

If we have known this quickening power of Christ, we will agree with Micah that there is no one like God in His ability to deliver from sin and restore a fallen one to usefulness.

Supreme in Pastoral Care

The third area in which God is without equal is pastoral care. He is the supreme shepherd. The theme reappeared here for the third time in Micah. It has appeared every time the hope of better days has broken through the clouds of pending judgment: Micah 2:12; 4:6–8; 5:4; and now here.

> Shepherd your people with your staff,
>   the flock of your inheritance,
> which lives by itself in a forest,
>   in fertile pasturelands.
> Let them feed in Bashan and Gilead
>   as in days long ago (v. 14).

Certainly there is no shepherd like the good Shepherd-King of Israel.

Under the care of this shepherd the contented sheep will lack nothing. David knew that. In the Twenty-third Psalm he compares himself to a sheep. He begins with the statement: "The LORD is my shepherd, I shall lack nothing." Then he lists what he will not lack.

First, he will not lack rest. For, "He makes me lie down in green pastures, he leads me beside quiet waters, he restores my soul" (vv. 2, 3). In *A Shepherd Looks at Psalm 23,* Phillip Keller tells how difficult it is to get a sheep to lie down. Sheep do not easily lie down, he says. In fact, "It is almost impossible for them to be made to lie down unless four requirements are met. Owing to their timidity they refuse to lie down unless they are free from all fear. Because of the social behavior within a flock, sheep will not lie down unless they are free from friction with others of their kind. If tormented by flies or parasites, sheep will not lie down. . . . Lastly, sheep will not lie down as long as they feel in need of finding food. They must be free from hunger."[1] To rest, a sheep must be free from fear, tension, aggravation, and hunger. So the psalm begins with a picture of a sheep who has found its shepherd to be a good shepherd, able to meet its physical needs and provide release from anxiety.

Second, he does not lack guidance, for "he leads me beside quiet waters" and "guides me in paths of righteousness for his name's sake" (vv. 2, 3). Sheep are among the stupidest animals on earth. For one thing, they stray easily. Their shepherd may lead them to good grazing land with an abundant water supply, but they still will wander away to barren fields with undrinkable water. Or again, they are creatures of habit. Their shepherds may find them good grazing land, but having found it, they will continue to graze upon it until every blade of grass and even every root is eaten and the fields ruined. It has happened to sheep lands in many parts of the world—Spain, Greece, Mesopotamia, North Africa, parts of the western United States, and New Zealand.

No other class of livestock requires more careful handling and more detailed directions than do sheep. Therefore, a shepherd who is able to give good guidance is essential for their welfare.

Third, the sheep in this psalm do not lack safety, even in the presence of great danger: "Even though I walk through the valley of the shadow of death, I will fear no evil, for you are with me; your rod and your staff, they comfort me" (v. 4). This verse has been used, quite appropriately, to comfort the dying. But it chiefly speaks of the shepherd's ability to protect the sheep in danger. It is a reference to the passage from the lowlands where sheep spend the winter through the valleys to the high pastures where they go in summer. The valleys are the places of richest pasture and of the abundant water. But they are also places of danger. Wild animals lurk in the broken canyon walls to either side. Sudden storms sweep down the val-

---

[1] Phillip Keller, *A Shepherd Looks at Psalm 23* (Grand Rapids: Zondervan, 1970), p. 35.

leys. There may be floods. The sun does not shine so well into the valleys. So there really is shadow that at any moment might become death's shadow. Our Lord leads us in safety through such experiences.

Fourth, the psalm speaks of the shepherd's provision for the physical need of each sheep: "You prepare a table before me in the presence of my enemies. You anoint my head with oil; my cup overflows" (v. 5).

Keller thinks that preparing a table refers to the shepherd's advance preparation of the high tablelands or mesas where the sheep graze in summer. If so, it implies the elimination of hazards, the destruction of poisonous plants, the driving away of predators— all before the sheep arrive. Alternately, it may refer to God's provision of peace and pasture even when enemies lurk nearby. In such a time, says David, God anoints him with oil and fills his cup of wine to overflowing.

In biblical imagery oil and wine speak of joy and prosperity, for the growing of olives and grapes and their transformation into oil and wine took time and gentle care. In times of domestic turmoil or war these tasks were forgotten. Moreover, oil and wine well suited the inhabitants of a dry, barren land and were therefore highly valued. In Palestine, where the sun shines fiercely most of the year and temperatures continually soar well above one hundred degrees, the skin quickly becomes cracked and broken and throats become dusty and parched. Oil soothes the skin, particularly the face. Wine clears the throat. Therefore, when a guest arrived at the home of a friend in Palestine in ancient days, hospitality demanded that oil and wine be provided. David alluded to this elsewhere when he prayed, "Let your face shine on your servant" (Ps. 31:16). A shining face was the face of a friend. In another psalm he thanks God for "wine that gladdens the

heart of man" and "oil to make his face shine" (Ps. 104:15). David knew that his Good Shepherd provided for him abundantly, and his face shone and his heart was merry because of it.

Finally, having spoken of these provisions, David adds no less gladly that he does not lack for a heavenly home: "Surely goodness and love will follow me all the days of my life, and I will dwell in the house of the LORD forever" (v. 6). This is a great promise. It causes us to look forward with joy to that day when we will stand

. . . before the throne of God
and serve him day and night in his temple.

It is said of us in that day,

Never again will they hunger;
   never again will they thirst.
The sun will not beat upon them,
   nor any scorching heat.
For the Lamb at the center of the throne will be their shepherd;
   he will lead them to springs of living water.
And God will wipe away every tear from their eyes (Rev. 7:16–17).

SUPREME IN FORGIVENESS

Great as our God is in each of these three preceding characteristics—supreme in judgment, deliverance, and guidance—He is greatest in the characteristic Micah mentions last: forgiveness. Indeed, it is in reference to this characteristic specifically that he asks his thematic question:

Who is a God like you,
   who pardons sin and forgives the transgression
   of the remnant of his inheritance?
You do not stay angry forever
   but delight to show mercy.
You will again have compassion on us;
   you will tread our sins underfoot
   and hurl all our iniquities into the depths of the sea.
You will be true to Jacob,

and show mercy to Abraham,
as you pledged on oath to our
    fathers
in days long ago (vv. 18–20).

The people who join Micah in praising God for His forgiveness here are quite different from the arrogant, self-righteous people who have appeared throughout the book. These earlier people could not imagine how they had offended God and actually blamed Him for their failures, claiming they had not been told clearly enough what to do. The people who speak here have been humbled under God's hand and are now quite willing to acknowledge their sins. Moreover, it is precisely because they know themselves to be sinners that they are so aware of God's mercy. Because they know Him as a God of mercy, they are anxious to avoid sinning again.

This is a great biblical principle. We might think that assurance of God's forgiveness might encourage us to go on sinning; but actually the opposite is the case, as John says clearly in his first epistle. He makes this promise: "If we confess our sins, he is faithful and just and will forgive us our sins and purify us from all unrighteousness" (1 John 1:9). But no sooner has he said this than he adds, "My dear children, I write this to you so that you will not sin" (2:1). In other words, the most important truth to keep us from sinning is the knowledge that God is unsurpassed in His forgiveness and will have mercy on us even if we do.

Donald Grey Barnhouse has written of an incident that is an excellent illustration of this truth. He had been holding meetings on a college campus and had been approached by one of the young professors at the close of a meeting. The man had a sad story to tell. During the First World War, before he had become a Christian, he had fallen in with bad companions and while living in Paris had fallen into sexual sin. Now he had returned home, become a Christian, and fallen in love with a Christian girl who also loved him. However, he hesitated to tell her of his love, because he was afraid his past sin might lead him to sin again and thus wound her. What should he do? He stated his problem and waited for an answer.

Barnhouse advised him that if he was to share his life with the girl he must do so completely, telling her the whole story so that there would be no barriers between them. Besides, he said, her knowledge of his weakness would help him at every step of the way. Then he told him this story.

Some time before, two other people had come into Barnhouse's life and had shared a similar set of experiences. The man had also lived a life of great sexual sin but had been converted and eventually had come to marry a fine Christian woman. He had confided to her the nature of his past life in a few words. After he had told her these things, the wife kissed him and said, "John, I want you to understand something. I know my Bible well, and therefore I know the subtlety of sin and the devices of sin working in the human heart. I know you are a thoroughly converted man, John, but I know that you still have an old nature and that you are not yet as fully instructed in the ways of God as you soon will be. The Devil will do all he can to wreck your Christian life, and he will see to it that temptations of every kind will be put in your way. The day might come—please God that it never shall—but the day might come when you will succumb to temptation and fall into sin. Immediately the Devil will tell you that it is no use trying, that you might as well continue on in sin and that above all you are not to tell me because it will hurt me. But, John, I want you to know that here in my arms is your home. When I married you I married your old nature as well as your new nature. And I want you to know there is full pardon and forgiveness in advance for any evil that may ever come into your life."

While Barnhouse told this story to the college professor, the man kept his face covered with his hands. However, at this point in the story, he lifted his eyes and said reverently, "My God! If anything could ever keep a man straight, that would be it."[2] God is the God of forgiveness, and He excels in this, as in all His other attributes. Moreover, He wants you to know it precisely so you might be kept from sinning.

A stanza from a hymn by Martin Luther aptly summarizes the entire last chapter of Micah's prophecy. If we have understood and responded to the prophecy, we should be able to join in his sentiments.

> Though great our sins and sore our
>   wounds
>   and deep and dark our fall,
> His helping mercy hath no bounds,
>   his love surpassing all.
> Our trusty living Shepherd he,
>   Who shall at last set Israel free
> from all their sin and sorrow.

---

[2]Donald Grey Barnhouse, *God's Methods for Holy Living* (Grand Rapids: Eerdmans, 1951), pp. 72–74.

NAHUM

7

God Against Nineveh

(Nahum 1:1–2:13)

An oracle concerning Nineveh. The book of the vision of Nahum the Elkoshite.

> *The LORD is a jealous and avenging God;*
> *the LORD takes vengeance and is filled with wrath.*
> *The LORD takes vengeance on his foes*
> *and maintains his wrath against his enemies. . . .*

> *"I am against you,"*
> *declares the LORD Almighty.*
> *"I will burn up your chariots in smoke,*
> *and the sword will devour your young lions.*
> *I will leave you no prey on the earth.*
> *The voices of your messengers*
> *will no longer be heard."*

There is something disturbing about the fall of great cities. We think of the fall of Rome to the advancing horde of barbarians at the beginning of the fifth century or the fall of Saigon to the Viet Cong after the American withdrawal in 1975.

The minor prophecy of Nahum is about the fall of Nineveh. The destruction of Nineveh was far greater than that of the cities I have mentioned—in fact, probably greater than that of any city in the entire history of the world. But unlike Saigon or even Rome, Nineveh's existence lies so far in the past that it is largely unknown to us and its fall means little.

How are we to overcome this problem? How are we to appreciate this prophecy?

NINEVEH THE GREAT

One way is by learning something about Nineveh. So far as secular sources are concerned, the founding of Nineveh lies hidden in the past. But Genesis 10:11 assigns the building of the city to Nimrod, the first "mighty warrior on the earth" (v. 8). Nimrod was the despot responsible for the first world empire, its principalities being Babylon, Erech, Akkad, Calneh, Nineveh, Rehoboth-Ir, and Resen. Of course, Babylon and Nineveh were the two most prominent. Babylon emerged as the archetypal secular city. Nineveh became the embodiment of human violence and conquest. Babylon stands for the warfare of man against God. Nineveh stands for the warfare of man against his fellow human beings.

In secular sources Nineveh is first mentioned in the Code of Hammurabi (c. 2200 B.C.). Hammurabi calls himself the king who made the name of the goddess Ishtar famous in the temple of Ishtar in Nineveh (IV, 60-62). Still, for centuries after this, little is heard about the city. We have the name of a Ninevite king from about 1900 B.C. and other scattered references. But not until the middle 800s (when Israel came into contact with the expanding empire of Assyria) are there significant historical records.

Shalmaneser III, who reigned from 858–824 B.C., made Nineveh the base for his campaign to subjugate the northern Jewish kingdom. He relates that he met "Ahab the Israelite" with two thousand chariots and ten thousand soldiers. In the account of his fourth campaign (824 B.C.), he declares that "at that time I received tribute . . . of Jehu, son of Omri." This scene is represented on the famous Black Obelisk in the British Museum. On it Jehu is seen on his knees before the king of Assyria, and the inscription reads: "Tribute of Jehu, son of Omri. Silver, gold, a golden bowl, a golden beaker, golden goblets, pitchers of gold, lead, staves for the hand of the king, javelins, I received from him."[1] Significantly, this first great humbling of the Jews was effected by an Assyrian king setting out from Nineveh.

Tiglath-pileser III (745–727 B.C.) invaded Judah and received tribute of Azariah. In 733–732 B.C. he invaded Israel, deposed Pekah, placed Hoshea over the nation as an Assyrian vassal, received tribute, and deported many of the people.

The final blow against Israel came in 722 B.C. when Tiglath-pileser's son, Shalmaneser V, returned and besieged Samaria. He died early in this campaign and was succeeded by Sargon II (721–705 B.C.), the founder of a new dynasty. Samaria fell to Sargon, and the history of the northern Jewish kingdom ended. The conqueror recorded: "At the beginning of my rule, in my first year of reign . . . I carried away 27,290 people of Samaria. I selected 50 chariots for my royal equipment. I settled there people of the lands I had conquered. I placed my official over them as governor. I imposed tribute tax upon them, as upon the Assyrians."[2]

In 701 B.C. occurred the well-known invasion of Judah by Sennacherib (705–681 B.C.), Sargon's son (2 Kings 18–19; Isa. 36–37). Sennacherib's account is as follows: "As for Hezekiah, the Jew, who did not submit to my yoke, 46 of his strong, walled cities, as well as the small cities in their neighborhood, which were without number—by leveling with battering rams and by bringing up siege engines, by attacking and storming on foot, by mines, tunnels and breaches—I besieged and took 200,150 people, great and small, male and female, horses, mules, asses, camels, cattle and sheep without number, I brought away from them and counted as spoil. Himself, like a caged bird, I shut up in Jerusalem, his royal city. . . . As for Hezekiah, the terrifying splendor of my majesty overcame him, and the Urbi (Arabs) and his mercenary troops which he had brought in to strengthen Jerusalem, his royal city, deserted him."[3]

The Bible tells this story differently, as we know. It acknowledges the force of Sennacherib's invasion. But it tells

---

[1] Walter A. Maier, *The Book of Nahum* (Grand Rapids: Baker, 1980; original edition, 1959), p. 89. See also F. W. Farrar, *The Minor Prophets* (New York: Anson D. F. Randolph, n.d.), p. 145. The quotations in Maier are from David Daniel Luckenbill, *Ancient Records of Assyria and Babylonia* (1926, 1927), I, pp. 222, 223.

[2] Maier, *The Book of Nahum*, p. 90.

[3] Ibid., pp. 90, 91.

how Sennacherib's field commander stood before the walls of Jerusalem and uttered the blasphemous boast that Assyria's gods were stronger than the God of Judah. He demanded the surrender of the city. After this the emperor himself sent Hezekiah a letter, saying, "Do not let the god you depend on deceive you when he says, 'Jerusalem will not be handed over to the king of Assyria.' Surely you have heard what the kings of Assyria have done to all the countries, destroying them completely. And will you be delivered? Did the gods of the nations that were destroyed by my forefathers deliver them?" (2 Kings 19:10–12). Hezekiah spread this letter before the Lord in the temple and prayed for deliverance. Isaiah sent a message saying that God would deliver the people, and that night "the angel of the LORD went out and put to death a hundred and eighty-five thousand men in the Assyrian camp" (v. 35). This so weakened Sennacherib's army that he returned to Nineveh without achieving the capitulation of Jerusalem.

The Assyrian monarch may have been checked by God in 701 B.C., but these were still great days for Nineveh. Sennacherib more than doubled the city's size, making it the world's largest city for that time. The inner city was surrounded by a wall eight miles in circumference. It was one hundred feet high and so wide that three chariots could race around it abreast. It had twelve hundred towers and fourteen gates. Beyond this was a much longer, outer wall. There was an inner city, an outer city, and what we would call extensive suburbs beyond that. In Jonah this wide expanse was termed a "three days' " journey (Jonah 3:3).

Sennacherib's palace was called "The Palace With No Rival." It was of cedar, cypress, and alabaster. Lions of bronze and bulls of white marble guarded it. Its great hall measured forty by one hundred and fifty feet. Sennacherib's armory, where he kept his chariots, armor, horses, weapons, and other equipment, covered forty-six acres and took six years to build.

What a magnificent city this was! Yes, but what a wicked city! And with what cruelty and violence was it constructed! Nineveh grew rich at the expense of the nations she had plundered. In his exhaustive study of Nahum, Walter A. Maier writes, "To Nineveh came the distant chieftains who kissed the royal feet, rebel leaders paraded in fetters, distant and deceitful kings tied with dog chains and made to live in kennels. To Nineveh were sent gifts of far-off tribute, heads of vanquished enemies, crown princes as hostages, beautiful princesses as concubines. In Nineveh rulers who experienced rare mercy carried brick and mortar for building operations. There recalcitrant captives were flayed, obstinate opponents crushed to death by their own sons. The Nineveh against which the prophet thunders divine denunciation had become the concentrated center of evil, the capital of crushing tyranny, the epitome of cruelest torture. Before the beginning of the seventh century and Sennacherib's reign, other cities had been royal residences: Calah, Ashur, Dur Sharrukin; but Sennacherib made Nineveh his capital, the world metropolis, the source of unmeasured woe for Judah, as for other, far greater nations.[4]

This great city had existed almost from the beginning of time. Under Sennacherib it rose to unparalleled strength and splendor. But it was to end. Within ninety years of Sennacherib's encampment before Jerusalem's

---

[4] Ibid., pp. 92, 93.

walls, Nineveh, the largest city in the world, was overthrown—never to be inhabited again.

THE AVENGING GOD

Historians give varied reasons for Nineveh's fall—internal corruption, the rise of Babylon, external and otherwise unpredictable factors. But however these may have contributed, the true answer is given by Nahum at the start of his prophecy. The avenging wrath of God destroyed it.

Many people do not like to think of God as a God of wrath. They prefer to think of Him as a God of sickly love and sentimental indulgence. What a weakening of the biblical concept of the only true God this is! It is true that God is a God of love and mercy—a holy love and an utterly undeserved and sovereign mercy. But it is also true that God is a God of wrath against sin. Peter describes Him as being "patient . . . not wanting anyone to perish" (2 Peter 3:9), but even this welcome description is set in the context of God's sure, though postponed judgment: "The day of the Lord will come like a thief. The heavens will disappear with a roar; the elements will be destroyed by fire, and the earth and everything in it will be laid bare" (v. 10).

This is the point at which Nahum begins his prophecy. Nahum means "comfort," but there is no comfort for Nineveh in what he speaks. For Nineveh, God is to be a God of vengeance. The city is to fall.

The idea of God's vengeance is developed in verses 1–6. First, there is an emphasis upon vengeance itself. The word is repeated three times in verse 2: "The LORD is a jealous and *avenging* God; the LORD takes *vengeance* and is filled with wrath. The LORD takes *vengeance* on his foes and maintains his wrath against his enemies." Vengeance is retaliatory punishment for wrong done. The Ninevites had committed great wrongs. Now they were to be repaid for those wrongs by the one who had solemnly declared, "It is mine to avenge; I will repay. In due time their foot will slip; their day of disaster is near and their doom rushes upon them" (Deut. 32:35; cf. Rom. 12:19).

The second point is the Ninevites' guilt. When we think of God taking vengeance we instinctively react against it, as if this is unjust and uncalled for. But this only shows how insensitive we are to sin both in ourselves and others. God's wrath is not capricious, but He will take vengeance. Nineveh was guilty. Thus, although God is "slow to anger, . . . he will not leave the guilty unpunished" (v. 3). Justice would be done. Numerous commentators on this book have criticized Nahum for failing to condemn the corresponding sins of Israel. Since the prophecy is directed against Nineveh, this is hardly a valid criticism of Nahum. But while *he* does not reflect on the sins of any others than the ancient inhabitants of Assyria (and may be excused for his procedure), *we* must not stop at this point. We must recognize that Nahum's words apply to us and our sins too. We need only think here of Paul's condemnation of the entire race in Romans. In that epistle Paul speaks of the revealed wrath of God, much as Nahum does at the beginning of his prophecy. He goes on to show, as Nahum also does, that it is due to our wickedness.

"There is no one righteous, not
    even one;
  there is no one who understands,
  no one who seeks God.
All have turned away,
  they have together become
    worthless;
there is no one who does good,
  not even one."
"Their throats are open graves;
  their tongues practice deceit."
"The poison of vipers is on their
  lips."

"Their mouths are full of cursing
and bitterness."
"Their feet are swift to shed blood;
ruin and misery mark their ways,
and the way of peace they do not
know."
"There is no fear of God before
their eyes" (Rom. 3:10–18).

In making this comprehensive denunciation Paul quotes from Psalms 14:1–3;
53:1–3; Ecclesiastes 7:20; Psalms 5:9;
140:3; 10:7; Isaiah 59:7, 8; and Psalm
36:1, in that order. But there is nothing
that is said of us here that is any less
damning than what is said in Nahum
about Nineveh. They had turned from
the one true God. So have we! Their
tongues practiced deceit. So have ours!
Their mouths were full of cursing and
bitterness. Are ours more pure? They
were swift to shed blood. Is our society
not equally guilty at this point? Can it
not also be said of many today that
there is "no fear of God" before their
eyes?

God's wrath is poured out against the
perpetrators of just such things, against
the guilty: "He will not leave the guilty
unpunished." How then shall we escape? We shall not, unless we flee to
Christ, as Paul indicates we must do in
the next section of his epistle.

The third point of Nahum's opening
verses is the certainty of God's judgment. This theme occurs throughout
the prophecy, but it is developed in
particularly powerful language here.
Nahum looks at nature, noting that
God dries up seas and makes the rivers
run dry. There are times when even
Bashan, Carmel, and Lebanon (prover-
bial sites of lush vegetation) wither
(v. 4). Mountains quake before God;
hills melt away; earth trembles (v. 5). If
this is true of nature, what mere mortal
can stand against God's fierce indigna-
tion? Who can endure when "his wrath
is poured out like fire [and] the rocks
are shattered before him"? (v. 6).

GOD AND GOD'S PEOPLE

There are three reasons why God was
going to destroy Nineveh, according to
this prophecy. Two have already been
suggested: first, God is a jealous God
(He will have no other gods before
Him, Exod. 20:3–6), and second, He is
an avenging God (the God of all the
earth will do right, Gen. 18:25). The
prophet gives another reason in the
second half of chapter 1 (vv. 7–15):
God's goodness to His people. They
have been abused by Nineveh. Now
God is going to rise up and make an
end to the oppressor.

This passage was especially meaningful to Martin Luther, who undoubtedly
found it a source of comfort in his own
difficulties during the Reformation. He
called verse 7 ("The LORD is good, a
refuge in times of trouble") "an outstanding statement, overflowing with
consolation." He said, "We must relate
and apply it not merely to that trial of
Judah but to absolutely every day of
our trials and adversities, so that we
may learn to flee for refuge in any trial
at all to this sweetness of the Lord as if
to a holy anchorage. Many psalms are
filled with statements of this sort. Thus
Psalm 9:9 has 'a stronghold in times of
trouble.' The Lord is a sweet stronghold
at the very time when we are greatly
afflicted, when we hunger, when we
suffer adversity, when our consciences
trouble us, as he says elsewhere in the
psalm (Ps. 50:15): 'Call upon me in the
day of trouble; I will deliver you.' He
commands us to flee to him for refuge,
to call upon him. Yet such is the
weakness of the human heart that even
if it is ordered to seek out and escape to
this sweetness, it fears and loses faith
in temptation. In this way, clearly the
Lord comforts in tribulation. That is,
even when temptation presses us hard,
yet he will not allow us to succumb.
Paul says the same thing in every detail
(1 Cor. 10:13): 'God is faithful, and he

will not let us be tempted . . . but with the temptation will also provide the way of escape.' "[5]

Not only is the Lord going to punish Nineveh, He is going to destroy it completely. Nahum announced this as a comfort to Judah at least seven times.

1. "With an overwhelming flood he will make an end of Nineveh; he will pursue his foes into darkness" (v. 8). The "overwhelming flood" has been interpreted as an invading military force, but it may actually mean what it says. According to secular accounts, during the final siege of Nineveh by a rebel army of Persians, Medes, Arabians, and Babylonians, unusually heavy rains caused the rivers to flood and undermine the city's walls, which then collapsed over a length of twenty-one furlongs. The invading armies entered the city through this breach in its defenses. Moreover, although some of the Ninevites managed to escape and set up a continuing city-state at Haran, this lasted only a few years after which they, like the rest of the city's great population, disappeared from history—"into darkness," as Nahum says.

2. "Whatever they plot against the LORD he will bring to an end; trouble will not come a second time" (v. 9). The force of this verse is in its repetition of the words "an end" from verse 8. There will be no need for trouble to come a second time; God will have finished His work in the first attack.

3. "They will be consumed like dry stubble" (v. 10). Stubble is consumed by fire. This may seem a contradiction of the prophesied destruction by water, mentioned just a verse before. Nevertheless, that is what happened. After the city was overrun, due to the destruction of part of the wall by flood, the armies burned the city thoroughly. The excavators of Nineveh have re-

marked on the large deposits of ash, which are evidence of a gigantic conflagration.

4. "Although they are unscathed and numerous, they will be cut down and pass away" (v. 12). Judah was aware of how numerous the Assyrian troops were; she had seen them during Sennacherib's invasion in 701 B.C. Bas-reliefs of the assault of Lachish during that campaign, now in the British Museum, show large numbers of carefully positioned armies—archers, spearsmen, slingers, and others—all supplied with ladders, battering rams, and other assault equipment. But numbers do not impress God. Although the hosts of Assyria were unscathed and numerous, they would soon pass away. Already 185,000 had been cut down when Sennacherib's army lay encamped before Jerusalem.

5. "You will have no descendants to bear your name" (v. 14). Not only were these people lost from history, even the city was lost until it was discovered and excavated by archaeologists, beginning in the 1840's.

6. "I will preserve your grave, for you are vile" (v. 14). Nineveh was not merely to be humbled for a time. She was to die and be buried. In this verse the word "vile" actually means "light" in the sense of being morally "insubstantial." It is the word used of Babylon in Daniel 5:27: *Tekel*—"You have been weighed on the scales and found wanting."

7. "No more will the wicked invade you; they will be completely destroyed" (v. 15). The invasion of Judah by Sennacherib was suggested in verse 11 and is referred to again here. But it will not occur again! The nation that launched it will be annihilated.

In the first half of verse 15 Nahum seems to quote a text from Isaiah, who

[5]Martin Luther, *Luther's Works*, vol. 18, *Lectures on the Minor Prophets*, I, Hilton C. Oswald, editor (Saint Louis: Concordia, 1975), p. 288.

had prophesied in Judah for a long time, including the days of the Assyrian invasion. Isaiah had written, "How beautiful on the mountains are the feet of those who bring good news, who proclaim peace, who bring good tidings, who proclaim salvation" (Isa. 52:7). In Isaiah this seems to be a prophecy of the arrival and reign of the Messiah. The apostle Paul interpreted the passage that way in Romans 10:15. But in Nahum it refers to the announced fall of Nineveh. Just as Isaiah saw the prophesied release of the people of God from their Babylonian captivity to be a token of that final and perfect release from sin and its bondage through Christ, so does Nahum see the fall of Assyria's capital as a promise of the ultimate defeat of all wickedness by the triumph of Christ.

THE FALL OF NINEVEH

The second chapter of Nahum describes the actual fall of Nineveh. In it the prophet turns from a broad forecast of Nineveh's destruction to specific details, and from Judah, whom he had been addressing previously, to Nineveh, to whom he now speaks. This chapter is a masterpiece of ancient literature, unsurpassed for its graphic portrayal of a military assault. It gives us: (1) Nineveh's preparations for the coming invasion, (2) the first sighting of the armies, (3) the overrunning of the city's suburbs by enemy chariots, (4) defense of the walls, (5) use of the river to undermine the city's foundation, and (6) the plunder. The chapter ends with the statement: " 'I am against you,' declares the LORD Almighty" (v. 13).

Ancient sources give a remarkably consistent picture of the destruction of Nineveh. There had been rebellions in the Assyrian empire for some time.

Many of them were repulsed by the armies of Nineveh supported by her allies. But in the year 612 B.C. the doom of the city arrived. Combined armies of Babylonians and Scythians marched up the left bank of the Tigris River and surrounded the city. It happened in early spring at the time of the annual rainfalls. Since the rains were especially hard that year, the Tigris and other rivers flooded and apparently washed away a portion of the walls, leaving a breach for the armies to enter the city.

The Greek historian Diodorus Siculus (c. 20 B.C.) says that the river not only broke down the walls of the city, it also inundated part of it. At this point, the king, Sardanapalus, remembering an oracle to the effect that Nineveh would only fall when the river itself declared war against it, believed that the oracle was fulfilled and abandoned any hope of saving himself. He built a gigantic funeral pyre in the royal precincts, heaped up large quantities of gold and costly clothes, shut his concubines and eunuchs in a chamber he had made in the midst of the pyre, and then burned himself, his family, his concubines and eunuchs, and the palace.

Whatever had not been burned in this conflagration was destroyed by the entering armies. There was a terrible slaughter. Diodorus said, "So great was the multitude of the slain that the flowing stream, mingled with their blood, changed its color for a considerable distance."[6]

There was unparalleled looting. For centuries the wealth of the ancient world had been pouring into Nineveh as a result of the Assyrian conquests. Now it poured out. Diodorus says, using a phrase which he did not employ in any other description of a city's

---

[6]Maier, *The Book of Nahum*, p. 127. Diodorus's work is called the *Chronicles*. The material on the fall of Nineveh is taken in turn from *Persica*, a chronicle of Assyria and Persia in twenty-three books by a Greek physician named Cresias, of which only fragments survive.

fall, "They plundered the spoil of the city, *a quantity beyond counting.*"[7] This seems literally to have been the case. The royal reports of Nineveh speak again and again of its unmeasurable wealth. On the Black Obelisk of Shalmaneser III are listed:

> Tribute of Sua, the Gilzanite: silver, gold, lead, copper vessels, staves for the hand of the king, horses, camels. . . .
>
> Tribute of Iaus (Jehu), son of Omri: silver, gold, a golden bowl, a golden beaker, golden goblets, pitchers of gold, lead. . . .
>
> Tribute of Karparunda of Hattina: silver, gold, lead, copper, copper vessels, ivory, cypress. . . .

The Nimrud slab of Adad-nirari (805–782 B.C.) lists:

> 2,000 talents of silver, 20 talents of gold, 3,000 talents of copper, 5,000 talents of iron, colored woolen and linen garments, an ivory bed, an ivory couch. . . .

Sargon lists this booty:

> His [Aramaens'] royal tent, his golden palanquin, his royal throne, golden scepter, golden couch, golden footstool, his weapons, his implements of war. . . . The great hosts of Assur plundered for three days and nights and carried off countless spoil: 90,580 people, 2,500 horses, 610 mules, 854 camels.[8]

What would the plunder of a city like this be like? Nahum tells us: "Nineveh is like a pool, and its water is draining away. 'Stop! Stop!' they cry, but no one turns back. Plunder the silver! Plunder the gold! The supply is endless, the wealth from all its treasures! She is pillaged, plundered, stripped! Hearts melt, knees give way, bodies tremble, every face grows pale" (Nah. 2:8–10). It

is an impressive confirmation of this prophecy that nothing of all this gold and silver has been discovered in the ruins of Nineveh by archaeologists. Nineveh was indeed stripped bare.

The agreement between Nahum's prophecy and the details of Nineveh's fall are so great that some commentators have declared it a *vaticinium ex eventu* (a "prophecy" made after the event). But Nahum did not write after Nineveh's fall. He wrote at the height of her power, shortly after the invasion of Judah by Sennacherib. That a Judean author, writing at a time when the invincible armies of Assyria were running unchecked across Asia, plundering all in their path, should predict the sudden destruction of the Assyrian capital and do so in such minute detail is surely another evidence of the divine origin of the Word of God.

BENEATH CHRIST'S CROSS

The last verse of chapter 2 says, " 'I am against you,' declares the LORD Almighty. 'I will burn up your chariots in smoke, and the sword will devour your young lions. I will leave you no prey on the earth. The voices of your messengers will no longer be heard.' " This is a dreadful thing. It is terrible to have the great God of the universe say, "I am against you." But it is not only to Nineveh that He speaks those words. He speaks them to all who sin against Him, whether in Nineveh, Rome, New York, Philadelphia, or wherever the sinner may be. If God says that to you, you should know that it is a terrible thing to fall into the hands of such an angry God.

These judgments, recorded so vividly in the pages of the Word of God, are not given to us to titillate our minds by comparing them with their eventual fulfillment in history. God records

[7] Ibid., p. 128.
[8] Maier lists these and other records of Nineveh's spoil on pp. 268–70.

these judgments to show us that He is a God of judgment as well as of love and that judgment upon the wicked will surely come. The Judge of all the earth does right. What is right where you are concerned? If you have gone your way, spurned God's law, sought out your own corrupt devices—justice demands your eternal condemnation. God must and will judge you. In terms of that great judgment, which is hell, the fall of Nineveh is almost insignificant.

Yet God tells you this so you might turn from your sin and seek His face at the cross of His Son, the Lord Jesus Christ. Deliverance is to be found at this cross, because God poured out His judgment there. The cross is your shelter, if you will have it so. It is only as we stand beneath it that we are protected from that greatest of all judgments, which is yet to come.

8

Applause! Applause!

(Nahum 3:1–19)

"I am against you," declares the LORD *Almighty.*
"I will lift your skirts over your face.
I will show the nations your nakedness
and the kingdoms your shame.
I will pelt you with filth,
I will treat you with contempt
and make you a spectacle.
All who see you will flee from you and say,
'Nineveh is in ruins—who will mourn for her?'
Where can I find anyone to comfort you?" . . .

Everyone who hears the news about you
claps his hands at your fall,
for who has not felt
your endless cruelty?

In the eighteenth chapter of Revelation there is a moving description of the fall of "Mystery Babylon." Babylon had been a sister city of Nineveh, both having been founded by Nimrod according to Genesis 10:11. It had become a symbol of secular man united in opposition to God, just as Nineveh had become a symbol of man united in opposition to other men and women. By the time Revelation was written, earthly Babylon had fallen. So the Babylon mentioned here is termed "Mystery Babylon" (Rev. 17:5), and is a symbolic representation of all cities of all ages of human history that have opposed God in wickedness. The text says, "Fallen! Fallen is Babylon the Great!" (Rev. 18:2).

It is a striking feature of this chapter that Babylon's fall is marked by three mournful dirges, each beginning with the words: "Woe! Woe!" The kings of the earth express their grief (v. 10):

"Woe! Woe, O great city,
O Babylon, city of power!
In one hour your doom has come!"

Then the merchants join in (vv. 16–17):

"Woe! Woe, O great city,
dressed in fine linen, purple and
scarlet,
and glittering with gold, precious
stones and pearls!
In one hour such great wealth has
been brought to ruin!"

At last the sea captains, sailors, passengers, and traders exclaim (v. 19):

"Woe! Woe, O great city,
    where all who had ships on the
        sea
    became rich through her wealth!
In one hour she has been brought
    to ruin!"

This grief is so poignant that an angel even adds his words, commenting that "the music of harpists and musicians, flute players and trumpeters, will never be heard in you again" (vv. 10, 16, 17, 19, 22).

Then something tremendous happens. These sounds die away, and the scene shifts to heaven, where the people of God are singing God's praises. Their words are not words of woe, though the fall of Babylon is still on their minds. Instead, the word that comes to their lips is "Hallelujah!" A great multitude cries out:

"Hallelujah!
Salvation and glory and power
    belong to our God,
    for true and just are his
        judgments.
He has condemned the great
    prostitute
    who corrupted the earth by her
        adulteries.
He has avenged on her the blood of
    his servants."

"Hallelujah!
The smoke from her goes up for
    ever and ever."

At this the twenty-four elders exclaim:

"Amen, Hallelujah!"

Again the multitude cries out:

"Hallelujah!

For our Lord Almighty reigns.
Let us rejoice and be glad
    and give him glory!" (Rev.
    19:1–4, 6, 7).

What is mourned on earth is applauded in heaven. On earth the fall of Babylon is judged an unmitigated tragedy. In heaven it is cause for rejoicing before God.

CITY OF BLOOD

The third chapter of Nahum reminds us of this heavenly perspective as it describes the fate of Nineveh. Like Revelation 18, it begins with a cry of woe for the city. It will fall. It will become a spectacle of desolation. But no one will mourn for such a city. In fact, the end of the chapter suggests that the opposite will occur: those who hear will actually applaud Nineveh's destruction. "Everyone who hears the news about you claps his hands at your fall" (v. 19).

Up to this point, the sins of Nineveh have not been spelled out, probably because they were all too well known. However, at the beginning of chapter 3 the prophet cites Nineveh's crimes: violence, deception, plunder, and witchcraft. The first of these, *violence*, gets the most attention, being the characteristic vice of Nineveh: "Woe to the city of blood . . . never without victims! The crack of whips, the clatter of wheels, galloping horses and jolting chariots! Charging cavalry, flashing swords and glittering spears! Many casualties, piles of dead, bodies without number, people stumbling over the corpses" (vv. 1–3).[1]

When Nahum calls Nineveh a "city of blood," his words are a massive

[1] Walter Maier regards verses 2 and 3 as a return to a preview of the final assault of the Babylonians and their allies on Nineveh, which Nahum had already described in 2:1–10. This is a possibility. In fact, there is an obvious parallel between the two passages, each being followed by a section beginning, " 'I am against you,' declares the LORD Almighty" (2:13; 3:5). However, since the third chapter begins with a denunciation of Nineveh for its violence, it is better to see the description of casualties as those inflicted by Nineveh rather than upon it. The parallelism is in the appropriate nature of the judgment. As Nineveh had done, so should it be done to her.

understatement. In all the ancient world no single city had matched the Assyrian capital for its calculated cruelty. Indeed, none had boasted about it as the rulers of Assyria had done. On a monument commemorating the first eighteen years of his reign, Ashurnasirpal II (885–860 B.C.) declared: "Great number of them in the land of Kirhi I slew . . . 260 of their fighting men I cut down with the sword. I cut off their heads, and I formed them into pillars. . . . Bubo, son of Buba, I flayed in the city of Arbela and I spread his skin upon the city wall.

"I flayed all the chief men [in the city of Suru] who had revolted, and I covered the pillar with their skins; some I walled up within the pillar, some I impaled upon the pillar on stakes, and others I bound to stakes round about the pillar; many within the border of my own land I flayed, and I spread their skins upon the walls; and I cut off the limbs of the officers, of the royal officers who had rebelled. Ahiababa I took to Nineveh, I flayed him, I spread his skin upon the wall of Nineveh.

"600 of their [the people in the city of Hulai] warriors I put to the sword; 3,000 captives I burned with fire; I did not leave a single one among them alive to serve as a hostage. . . . Their corpses I formed into pillars; their young men and maidens I burned in the fire. . . .

"3,000 of their [the people in the city of Tela] warriors I put to the sword. . . . Many captives from among them I burned with fire. From some I cut off their hands and their fingers, and from others I cut off their noses, their ears, and their fingers, of many I put out the eyes. I made one pillar of the living, and another of heads, and I bound their heads to posts (tree trunks) round about the city."[2]

The utter fiendishness of impaling defeated soldiers on stakes, skinning commanders alive, cutting off limbs, noses and ears, putting out eyes, heaping up skulls in the city squares, and burning vast numbers alive was without parallel in the ancient world.

The second crime for which Nineveh is to be brought into judgment is *deceit*, for, as Nahum writes, the city is "full of lies." We have a particularly clear example of this in 2 Kings in the story of Sennacherib's threats against Jerusalem. The emperor's field commander appeared before the wall and employed the technique so often adopted by those engaged in interrogating prisoners: alternating threats with promises. On the one hand, he threatened the swift destruction of the city, arguing that the gods of the other captive peoples had been unable to protect them. On the other hand, he declared, "Make peace with me and come out to me. Then every one of you will eat from his own vine and fig tree and drink water from his own cistern" (2 Kings 18:31). We know from the records what actually happened to such conquered people.

Third, Nineveh is indicted for its *plunder*. It had grown rich, but it had done so at the expense of other nations. Nineveh was not in the business of producing its own wealth. It simply stole it. Its wealth was now to be taken from Nineveh in precisely the same way (Nah. 2:8–10).

Nahum elaborates on Nineveh's fourth crime: *witchcraft*. He says that Nineveh was "the mistress of sorceries, who enslaved nations by her prostitution and peoples by her witchcraft" (v. 4). Archaeologists have confirmed that the people of Nineveh practiced witchcraft. Maier reports: "Thousands of tablets uncovered in the Mesopotamian valley show abysmal superstition. Hundreds of sorcery incantations have

---

[2] Walter A. Maier, *The Book of Nahum* (Grand Rapids: Baker, 1980; original edition, 1959), p. 291. Maier has taken the material from Daniel D. Luckenbill, *Ancient Records of Assyria and Babylonia* (Chicago: University of Chicago Press, 1926), vol. 1, pp. 142ff.

been brought to light. Astrology flourished widely as a means of foretelling the future. For the Assyrians the world was filled with omens to be found in moths, swallows, pigs, scorpions, wild oxen, sparrows, doves, cows, rats, crows, worms, dogs, hens, grasshoppers, lambs, sheep, foxes, fish, snakes, jackals. Amulets of stones, plants, bones, and insects were worn to ward off evil spirits."[3] The pantheon of hideous, destructive deities was similar to today's Hindu pantheon. Most of these were imagined to hate and persecute human beings.

In response to these crimes God declares that He is against the Ninevites (v. 5) and that He will expose them to the contempt of the nations they have plundered (vv. 6, 7). No doubt Nineveh had actually treated others in this fashion: exposing their nakedness, pelting them with filth, mocking them in great public spectacle. Now she is to be treated in like fashion. And none will grieve for her, so great have her atrocities been! She is to vanish from history—friendless and unmourned.

The Fall of Thebes

Thus far no place other than Nineveh has been named. But now another city is brought in. In Hebrew the name is *No Amon*. To the Assyrians the place was *Ni'u*. The Greeks called it *Dios Polis*, that is, the "City of Zeus." We know it as Thebes. Today Thebes is represented by the impressive ruins of Karnak and Luxor on the east side of the Nile River and by the abandoned residences of the Egyptian kings on the west.

Like Nineveh, the origins of Thebes have been lost in antiquity, but the city rose to prominence as the capital of the Eighteenth Dynasty (about 2100 B.C.) at about the time Nineveh first appears in historical records. What happened at Thebes during the eighteenth dynasty and the two that followed is evidenced by the massive ruins that may still be seen at Karnak and the surrounding sites. Forests of columns stretching forty to sixty feet into the air, avenues bordered by statues, immense palaces, treasures of gold and silver form the burial sites in the Valley of the Kings— all these testify to Thebes's wealth and political prominence. Homer spoke of Thebes's wealth. The city was probably the leading metropolis of the Nile Valley during these important centuries.

Like Nineveh, Thebes was also well situated for defense. It was on the Nile, as Nineveh was on the Tigris. But in addition to this, Thebes was also largely surrounded by the Nile's waters, which divided into several parallel channels at this point. The Karnak channel on the right bank and the Fadiliyah channel on the left flanked the central portion of the city.

Like Nineveh, the city on the Nile also gained support from her allies. Nahum names Cush, Egypt, Put, and Libya. Cush is Ethiopia, an area including most of the territory south of Aswan. It embraced parts of modern-day Sudan, Nubia, and Ethiopia. For a time it was called Abyssinia. In this context Egypt refers to Lower Egypt, meaning the country farther down the Nile from Thebes. The identification of "Put and Libya" is difficult for the reason that Put is usually identified as Libya. Libya is the region of North Africa west of Egypt. Put may have been part of it at one time or, as Maier argues, it may have been the Red Sea coast country as far south as Somaliland. Either way, the four names seem to denote the major land blocks south, north, west, and (possibly) east of Thebes. The point is that Thebes was surrounded by allies. Not only did she have her impressive

[3] Maier, *The Book of Nahum*, p. 303.

natural defenses, she also was supported by the military alliances and rich resources of the surrounding countries.

Yet Thebes fell. And no one should know this better than the people of Nineveh, for it was to the armies of Ashurbanipal, who had set out from Nineveh, that Thebes capitulated. Sometime between 668 and 662 B.C. Ashurbanipal marched through Egypt's delta country, leaving a trail of fire, ruin, and death behind him. He surrounded Thebes and took it after minimal delays. Convinced that he could not properly govern a city so far removed from Nineveh, Ashurbanipal determined to make an example of it so that the terrifying memory of what he had done would deter future uprisings. He took captive everyone he could and killed the rest. The children were massacred in the streets. Nahum brings this memory before Nineveh:

> Are you better than Thebes,
>   situated on the Nile,
>   with water around her?
> The river was her defense,
>   the waters her wall.
> Cush and Egypt were her boundless
>   strength;
>   Put and Libya were among her
>   allies,
> Yet she was taken captive
>   and went into exile.
> Her infants were dashed to pieces
>   at the head of every street.
> Lots were cast for her nobles,
>   and all her great men were put in
>   chains (vv. 8–10).

Obviously, the Lord is drawing a lesson for mighty Nineveh from Thebes. Thebes had been an equally great city, Nineveh's rival. Yet Thebes had fallen. Who were the Ninevites to think that they should be spared?

The same lesson applies to us. We see the fall of others but somehow imagine that our Western world and cities are different. They are not. They are part of the same world ruled by the same unchanging God, and the moral laws that operated in the destruction of Thebes and Nineveh will also destroy us unless we repent and seek God's blessing. The great English historian Herbert Butterfield wrote, in a chapter specifically commending the concerns of the Hebrew prophets, "Though some offences may pass at first without a reckoning, yet if men presume on such immunity, those old debts may accumulate at compound interest and may still have to be met when the moment comes for the final settlement of the account."[4] If God does not settle the account in our lifetimes, we can be sure that He is going to close the books on that final day when we must all stand before Him to be judged.

Last Days of Nineveh

In the final days of a declining civilization everything seems to fly apart, and the fall, when it finally comes, often comes quickly. This is what Nahum says about Nineveh in the final verses of the prophecy. She had been mighty for centuries. For much of her life she had seemed invincible. However, when the final assault came, she was to fall as easily as ripe figs when the tree that has been supporting them is shaken. As he develops this striking image, the prophet adds a particularly grim thought: the figs will fall, not onto the ground, as one might expect, but into the mouth of the one who shakes the tree (v. 12).

Nahum prophesies three failures of Assyrian life at this period. First, there would be a failure of the army. Earlier, in chapter 2, Nahum described the failure of courage that would overtake everyone when the city fell: "Hearts melt, knees give way, bodies tremble,

---

[4]Herbert Butterfield, *Christianity and History* (New York: Scribner, 1949), p. 50.

every face grows pale" (2:10). Then he describes the effect of the assault on the soldiers. "Look at your troops—they are all women," he declares. This image is not unknown to the other prophets (cf. Isa. 19:16; Jer. 50:37; 51:30), but it is particularly forceful in describing a city that by this time was noted for its homosexual effeminacy. History reports that by the time of the assault the Assyrian armies were unable to acquit themselves like men.

Nahum mocks this army, as he had every right to do. He utters five terse imperatives: (1) "Draw water for the siege." Though surrounded by water, the rivers of Nineveh were largely undrinkable and the first actions of the besieged people would have been to store up this precious commodity. (One of the first acts of the invaders was to cut off the water which came into the city from a distant reservoir built by Sennacherib.) (2) "Strengthen your defenses!" This refers to the fortified walls of the city. These would need to be repaired and thickened. Archaeologists have found traces of a counterwall raised by the inhabitants in their last extremity. It stood inside the outer wall, where the city's defenses had been before the final rebuilding by Sennacherib. (3) "Work the clay." Huge quantities of brick would have been necessary for this feverish rebuilding. The taunt is to dig into the soil to prepare the needed clay. (4) "Tread the mortar." While some dug the clay and prepared the necessary bricks, others would be engaged in mixing the mortar that was to join these bricks together. (5) "Repair the brickwork!" While new walls were being constructed, the old would be repaired. Maximum efforts would be made. But it was all to be of no use. "There the fire will devour you; the sword will cut you down and, like grasshoppers, consume you" (v. 15).

The second group to fall in the crisis would be the *merchants*. Every great city thrives on commerce. Dominant nations are always trade nations. According to Nahum, Nineveh had increased its merchants until they were more numerous than the stars (v. 16). Yet the commerce of Nineveh would be of no help to it in its last days.

Finally, Nahum refers to the failure of the officials or *civil service*. These will fly away "like locusts" (v. 17). Numbed by the massive governmental bureaucracy of our day, we may think the comparison of civil servants to locusts quite apt—their large numbers, their utter sameness, their devouring but unproductive habits. But Nahum's point is rather that in anticipation of the attack the bureaucracy would flee from the city in masses, as locusts do when the sun rises in the morning and warms their wings. Tradition has preserved testimony to the fact that this happened. Thousands fled. Later many of these attempted to set up a continuing kingdom in Haran, but this was short-lived.

So great would be the slaughter ("your shepherds slumber; your nobles lie down to rest") and scattering ("your people are scattered on the mountains with no one to gather them"), that the city would never rise again. Other oriental cities have fallen and have been rebuilt. Not so Nineveh. Her fall would come quickly. Her destruction would be final. And all who heard of her would clap their hands in glee.

I close with these thoughts. First, Nahum's prophecy was intended to be a source of comfort to God's people and can be a similar source of comfort to us today. We are surrounded by evil. But evil does not go unjudged. Though delayed, God's vindications of His own and condemnation of the wicked are both full and certain. Luther saw this and wrote in his closing words on Nahum: "These consolations ought also to fill us all with courage in any need, so that we may have confidence and trust absolutely that the Lord will not allow foes of God's Word to prevail against us. You see, He had promised Judah freedom and a safe kingdom from which Christ was to be born. He stood by His promises. He did make them superior to all their foes, which the prophet has very clearly shown here in the case of the very powerful and wealthy realm of the Assyrians. In the same way, may we also have no doubts that He will be near us in every need, physical or spiritual. Indeed, our God is still the same One who redeemed Judah, who said that a hair of our head would not fall without His will."[5]

My second thought is this. Earlier in the collection of Minor Prophets there is another book concerned with Nineveh: Jonah. Jonah was told to go to Nineveh and preach a message of utter and lasting destruction (Jonah 1:1, 2; 3:1, 2). On that occasion the city turned from its sin, and Nineveh was spared.

If you are not yet a believer in the Lord Jesus Christ, you are in a position similar to Nineveh on the earlier occasion. Judgment hangs over you because God is a God of justice, and justice will be done. But this is the day of God's grace. Judgment, though imminent, has not yet come. There is still time to turn from your sin and embrace Him who said, "Come to me, all you who are weary and burdened, and I will give you rest" (Matt. 11:28). But let it be a firm and permanent decision. And remember that although Nineveh appeared to turn from her sin for a time, she was not really changed and eventually fell back into that pattern of cruelty and repine for which God eventually wiped her from the surface of the earth. The Bible says, "Therefore . . . be . . . eager to make your calling and election sure" (2 Peter 1:10), and "he who stands firm to the end will be saved" (Matt. 10:22).

---

[5] Martin Luther, *Luther's Works*, vol. 18, *Lectures on the Minor Prophets*, I, Hilton C. Oswald, editor (Saint Louis: Concordia, 1975), p. 135.

HABAKKUK

9

Problems of a Puzzled Prophet

(Habakkuk 1:1–11)

The oracle that Habakkuk the prophet received.

> *How long, O LORD, must I call for help,*
>   *but you do not listen?*
> *Or cry out to you, "Violence!"*
>   *but you do not save?*
> *Why do you make me look at injustice?*
>   *Why do you tolerate wrong?*
> *Destruction and violence are before me;*
>   *there is strife, and conflict abounds.*
> *Therefore the law is paralyzed,*
>   *and justice never prevails.*
> *The wicked hem in the righteous,*
>   *so that justice is perverted.*

The first time I preached on Habakkuk a man told me that in all the years he had been going to church he had never heard a sermon on this book and had come to hear me especially for that purpose. I suppose his experience is not at all unusual. But it is unfortunate, because Habakkuk is so eminently contemporary. For a book written in Judah more than 2,500 years ago, it deals with surprisingly modern problems.

At the beginning of this century, Christians had to face the challenge of the new understandings of reality opened up by nineteenth-century scientific discoveries. On the one hand, the universe was much bigger and more complex than we had previously imagined. But on the other hand, it now seemed uniquely within the knowledge and grasp of mankind. The battles that were fought at this time focused on the existence of God and the relationship of revelation to scientific discoveries.

This is no longer the case. True, there are still people who wrestle with these problems: for example, those who argue the case for creationism against evolution and press for the right to teach this in the public schools. But the ground has shifted. Einstein's discovery of relativity and similar insights in other areas have made science less sure of itself. It is far less inclined to speak in absolutes.

Besides, the concerns of Christianity have also changed. Again, there are remnants of the old wars. It is still necessary to argue for the complete truthfulness of the Word of God, including those areas where the Bible touches on scientific concerns. But for the most part the questions have shifted, and the problems bothering most thinking people today are what we would call personal and historical. They boil down to the individual's involvement in history. On the personal level, they express themselves in such questions as: Who am I? Why am I here? What is the meaning of life? On the historical level, they emerge as: What is the meaning of history? What is God's involvement with history? Why is there evil in history? Why doesn't God do something about wickedness? How can I believe in a loving, personal God when He allows bad things to happen to me?

Habakkuk raises these questions too. He asks, "Is God in charge of history?" and, "If He is, why do things happen as they do?" In dealing with these questions he speaks as directly to our own times as any comparable portion of the Word of God.

THE PROBLEM OF HISTORY

We do not know much about Habakkuk personally, for he is mentioned nowhere else in the Old Testament. But it is evident from the situation described in his book that he must have been writing sometime after the fall of Nineveh to the Babylonians in 612 B.C. (as prophesied by Nahum) and before the fall of Jerusalem to the Babylonians in 587 B.C. Habakkuk probably wrote somewhere in the middle of that twenty-five-year period, because the dreaded Assyrians have already faded from view and the Babylonians, or Chaldeans, are spoken of as *"being* raised" up.

Again, we do not know how old Habakkuk was when he wrote. But if he was a mature man, as we would expect him to have been, he must have spent his childhood in Judah during the reign of the boy king Josiah. Josiah was one of the two later Judean kings that the chronicles considered righteous. He

had been crowned at the age of eight (in 639 B.C.), and when he was sixteen he began a religious reform that changed the nation's life. The chronicler tells us, "In the eighth year of his reign, while he was still young, he began to seek the God of his father David. In the twelfth year he began to purge Judah and Jerusalem of high places, Asherah poles, carved idols and cast images. Under his direction the altars of the Baals were torn down; he cut to pieces the incense altars that were above them, and smashed the Asherah poles, the idols and images. These he broke to pieces and scattered over the graves of those who had sacrificed to them. He burned the bones of the priests on their altars, and so he purged Judah and Jerusalem. In the towns of Manasseh, Ephraim and Simeon, as far as Naphtali, and in the ruins around them, he tore down the altars and the Asherah poles and crushed the idols to powder and cut to pieces allthe incense altars throughout Israel" (2 Chron. 34:3–7).

In the eighteenth year of his reign Josiah began to repair the temple, which had been allowed to fall into ruin. In the process of this repair, Hilkiah the priest found the book of the Law of the Lord and had it brought to Josiah. When it was read, Josiah and those with him were convicted of their sin. A national revival followed, and the observance of the Passover was revived.

This was a real reform, but it must have been from the top down. After the death of Josiah (in battle against Pharaoh Neco of Egypt on the plain of Megiddo in 609 B.C.), disillusionment with the reform set in and Judah reverted to its former evil ways. Jeremiah and Ezekiel describe this age in detail. It continued until the fall of Jerusalem in 587 B.C.

This was the age in which Habakkuk lived and wrote, and it is against this background that we must understand the questions the puzzled prophet raised. The first verses describe the period of marked spiritual and moral decay after the brighter period under Josiah:

How long, O Lord, must I call for
    help,
    but you do not listen?
Or cry out to you, "Violence!"
    but you do not save?
Why do you make me look at
    injustice?
Why do you tolerate wrong?
Destruction and violence are before
    me;
    there is strife, and conflict
        abounds,
Therefore the law is paralyzed,
    and justice never prevails.
The wicked hem in the righteous,
    so that justice is perverted (Hab.
    1:2–4).

It is clearly an anguished cry from a man who loved justice. He had seen justice perverted and had cried out to God against the evil. It is the kind of cry we might utter over the deplorable state of the church in our days or the equally deplorable moral decline of America.

Habakkuk must have waited for the Lord's answer for some time, because he begins his complaint with the words "How long, O Lord, must I call for help, but you do not listen? Or cry out to you, 'Violence!' but you do not save?" At last the Lord did answer, but the answer was an unexpected one and gave Habakkuk new and even greater problems. The Lord replied:

"Look at the nations and watch—
    and be utterly amazed.
For I am going to do something in
    your days
    that you would not believe,
    even if you were told.
I am raising up the Babylonians,
    that ruthless and impetuous
        people,
who sweep across the whole earth

to seize dwelling places not their
    own.
They are a feared and dreaded
    people;
they are a law to themselves
and promote their own honor
(Hab. 1:5–7).

The verses go on to describe the fierceness of the Babylonian armies and their scorn of all who resist them.

No doubt, Habakkuk had expected the Lord to intervene graciously and to send revival like the one in Josiah's day. But when God answered it was to say that He would send the Babylonian nation to scourge His people.

This raised a second dilemma for Habakkuk, which we will treat more carefully in the next chapter. The first had been God's inactivity while injustice increased in Judah. God resolved it with His promise of judgment. But then Habakkuk faced a situation in which a most ungodly nation, Babylon, was going to be used to judge Israel, God's special people. Habakkuk cries out, "Wait! Wait! Hold on just a minute! I understand why you are judging us. We deserve it. But what I cannot understand is how you can use the Babylonians as agents of that judgment. They are even more wicked than we are." Habakkuk's own words are:

Your eyes are too pure to look on
    evil;
    you cannot tolerate wrong.
Why then do you tolerate the
    treacherous?
Why are you silent while the
    wicked
swallow up those more righteous
    than themselves? (Hab. 1:13).

The answer to this second question constitutes the heart of the prophecy and leads to 2:4, the great text that meant so much to the apostle Paul. God's answer is that He will judge the Babylonians too but that in the meantime His people are to live by faith in

Him and His control of history (Hab. 2:4). This leads to a lament upon all who resist God and practice unrighteousness (the remainder of chapter 2) and to a great prayer of personal faith by Habakkuk (chapter 3). He ends by looking ahead to the coming invasion by the Babylonians, and saying:

> Though the fig tree does not bud
>   and there are no grapes on the vines,
> though the olive crop fails
>   and the fields produce no food,
> though there are no sheep in the pen
>   and no cattle in the stalls,
> yet I will rejoice in the LORD,
>   I will be joyful in God my Savior
> (Hab. 3:17, 18).

FOUR LESSONS

Shortly after World War II, the great Welsh preacher Dr. D. Martyn Lloyd-Jones preached a series of sermons on Habakkuk in response to the anguish arising from that conflict. They were later published in a book called *From Fear to Faith*. It was a classic study of Habakkuk, and I have used Lloyd-Jones's analysis in what follows.

He showed that four lessons emerge in the opening exchange between God and His questioning prophet. First, *history* (regardless of how it seems to us) *is under God's control*. We see this in God's reply to Habakkuk, for He tells him: "I am going to do something in your days. . . . I am raising up the Babylonians" (Hab. 1:5, 6). Lloyd-Jones writes: "Every nation on earth is under the hand of God, for there is no power in this world that is not ultimately controlled by him. Things are not what they appear to be. It seemed to be the astute military prowess of the Chaldeans that had brought them into the ascendancy. But it was not so at all, for God had raised them up. God is the Lord of history. He is seated in the heavens, and the nations to him are 'as grasshoppers, as a drop in a bucket, or as the small dust of the balance.' The Bible asserts that God is over all. He started the historical process, he is controlling it, and he is going to end it. We must never lose sight of this crucial fact."[1]

Second, *history follows a divine plan*. The events of history are not accidental, though they may appear so to us. They follow God's plan. "There is a purpose in history, and what is now happening in this twentieth century is not accidental. Remembering that the church is at the center of God's plan, let us never forget the pride and arrogance of the church in the nineteenth century. Behold her sitting back in self-satisfaction, enjoying her so-called cultured sermons and learned ministry, feeling just a little ashamed to mention such things as conversion and the work of the Holy Spirit. Observe the prosperous Victorian comfortably enjoying his worship. Note his faith in science and his readiness to substitute philosophy for revelation. How constantly he denied the very spirit of the New Testament! Yes, the church needed chastisement, and it is not at all difficult to understand this twentieth century when we consider the story of the nineteenth."[2]

Third, *history follows a divine timetable*. This comes out at several places in Habakkuk's prophecy. In chapter 1 God says, "I am going to do something in your days," that is, not before or after but precisely when He wanted it to happen. In chapter 2 the point is made even stronger: "The revelation awaits an appointed time; it speaks of the end and will not prove false. Though it linger, wait for it; it will certainly come and will not delay" (Hab. 2:3).

---

[1] D. Martyn Lloyd-Jones, *From Fear to Faith* (London: InterVarsity Press, 1966), p. 22. Original edition 1953.

[2] Ibid., pp. 22, 23.

Fourth, *history is bound up with the divine kingdom.* "The key to the history of the world is the kingdom of God. The story of the other nations mentioned in the Old Testament is relevant only as it bears upon the history of the Christian church. What really matters in the world is God's kingdom.

"Let us not therefore be stumbled when we see surprising things happening in the world. Rather let us ask, 'What is the relevance of this event to the kingdom of God?' Or, if strange things are happening to you personally, don't complain, but say, 'What is God teaching me through this? What is there in me that needs to be corrected? Where have I gone wrong and why is God allowing these things?' There is a meaning in them if only we can see it. We need not become bewildered and doubt the love or the justice of God. If God were unkind enough to answer some of our prayers at once, and in our way, we should be very impoverished Christians. Fortunately, God sometimes delays his answers in order to deal with selfishness or things in our lives that should not be there. He is concerned about us, and intends to fit us for a fuller place in his kingdom. We should therefore judge every event in the light of God's great, eternal and glorious purpose."[3] When we approach the events of our time with that outlook, we are following the advice Jesus gave His disciples: "Watch out that no one deceives you. For many will come in my name, claiming, 'I am the Christ,' and will deceive many. You will hear of wars and rumors of wars, but see to it that you are not alarmed. Such things must happen, but the end is still to come" (Matt. 24:4–6).

Europe in Wartime

In the summer of 1939, the war on which Martyn Lloyd-Jones was later to

reflect in his study of Habakkuk was just around the corner, and Donald Grey Barnhouse, a former pastor of the church I now serve, was in Scotland preaching. His family had been staying at a little summer resort on the coast of Normandy in France. It was a summer full of meetings in Scotland with more scheduled in September for Belfast, Ireland. But there was a week between the close of the first set of meetings and the beginning of the second, and Barnhouse decided to join his family in France for the interval.

Leaving Edinburgh on the night train, Barnhouse arrived in London in the early morning and immediately took a taxi across the city to the old airport of Croyden so he could fly across the channel to the little town of Deauville. At the airport a young official questioned him about his travel plans. Barnhouse answered that he planned to go over that day and return toward the end of the week for meetings in Belfast starting on Saturday night. The official looked at him earnestly and said, "If you want to be in Belfast on Saturday I strongly urge you not to go to France today." Barnhouse knew that Europe was in political turmoil. Hitler had just signed his perfidious treaty with Russia and was threatening to march into Danzig. Still the possibility of actual war seemed remote. He decided to go, and the young man stamped his passport. But he shook his head and said, "Don't forget that I warned you."

The flight over the channel was even more beautiful than the ride across London, and the joy of seeing his family pushed the possibility of war from Barnhouse's mind. Oh, there were French soldiers everywhere. The airport buildings had been turned into military barracks. When he stopped at

---

[3] Ibid., pp. 23, 24.

the desk to check on his return accommodations for Friday, he was told that no one was sure there would be a return flight on Friday. All flights might be canceled. The threat, however, seemed unreal with the joy of reunion uppermost in Barnhouse's mind.

Leaving the airport, the family drove down the coast for a few miles to a calm and peaceful village. There were hundreds of families there, for it was the height of the French vacation season, and the children played while their mothers watched them with pride. From time to time an airplane would appear in the distance, and the whole beach would suddenly become still as it drew closer. Then someone would say, "It's one of ours," and activity would resume again. The pictures Barnhouse took on that beach were later used by United States Naval Intelligence as a small part of the information gathered in preparation for the Normandy invasion. Monday went by . . . Tuesday . . . Wednesday. Finally, on Thursday morning word came that there would be no more flights back to England. If Barnhouse wanted to return to England, he would have to go by train to Paris and then travel back across France to the coast and London. A decision had to be made at once. Barnhouse left on the next train.

While he traveled, the French ordered mobilization. No one who lives in a country defended year in and year out by a professional army can really understand it. Every man in France must do military service and is therefore part of the army and knows what to do in case of an emergency. Every mayor in every little hamlet and village of the country has posters prepared beforehand that can be posted as soon as the order is received from Paris. All France knows about the mobilization within moments of the issue of the order, and there is instant response.

Moreover, the tocsin is sounded. In the Middle Ages, when few people knew how to read, Europe developed a bell-ringing code to alert the countryside of important events or dangers. The bells would tell when young people were being married, when a child was being baptized, when death had occurred. They also told of war.

This was the bell that sounded from every tower and steeple in France as Barnhouse's Paris-bound train moved across the green fields. At every stop there were tragic scenes. Men by the thousands were leaving their weeping wives and children to board the trains that would take them to war. Many would never return, and the villages and towns through which the train was passing would later crumble under the bombs of the Allies as the Western armies came with their own terrible liberation years later. At this point, however, there was only the tragedy of separation and a pervasive, gripping fear.

Hours later the train reached Paris, and Barnhouse made his way through the streets. The first blackout was in effect, and everything was oddly different. Music came from the bars and restaurants as Paris, the city of lights, tried hard to be festive. An hour later Barnhouse was again on a train, this time speeding toward the coast. Later he learned that it was the last train to carry civilians. In the darkness the train swung alongside the steamer, and within a few minutes the steamer—the last to transport civilians across the channel for many years—moved out of the harbor toward England.

On board, the Belfast-bound preacher made his way to the bridge and introduced himself to the captain. Together they listened to the radio reports. Hitler had moved into Danzig. The bombing was frightful. Chamberlain had called a meeting of his cabinet. If the Germans were not out of Danzig by eleven o'clock on Sunday morning,

Chamberlain had said, war would be declared.

The captain, with British calmness, said, "This time there will be no turning back. This is it." Barnhouse went to his cabin for a few fitful hours of sleep and then got up again to go ashore in England. It was Friday, September 1, 1939.

Once again it was a beautiful day as the English train carried the steamer passengers across Kent to London. That little bit of sky above was soon to be the theater for the battle of Britain in which a handful of England's bravest pilots would thwart Hitler's bid for mastery of the English skies. From Victoria Station, Barnhouse took a taxi across the city to the great complex of stations serving northern England and Scotland. As he drew near the stations, he saw thousands of children lined up for immediate evacuation from London. There was some time before the departure of the next train, so Barnhouse walked among the children. It was a pitiful sight. In all the fear and commotion of the moment, children were already victims of the war. One little child's plight seemed to sum up the whole picture. He had been given some chocolate to eat and had managed to smear it all over the lower part of his face. He had wet his pants. And he had begun to cry, his cries the expression of great misery and mixed with terror. His case was but one little island in the midst of a great nation of misery.

In time the train to the north left London, but it stopped constantly to allow troop trains and trains full of children to go past. At last, about midnight, the travelers reached Carlisle. They spent the night in the crowded lobby of the station hotel. Then there was another train, which took most of Saturday to push on to the coast of Scotland. That night, when he should have been sitting at a formal dinner in Belfast, Barnhouse stood at the edge of the water at Stranraer and gazed at Ireland across the gray-blue sea.

After dark—much after dark—the little ship that was to take him to Ireland set off across the sea. The only visible light came from an automatic lighthouse, and one man remarked with a curse that the navy should shoot the thing out. The Germans could have used it for a landmark if they had been ready to fly over and bomb.

The little steamer docked at Larne on the Irish coast. Another train made the run to Belfast, arriving just after three o'clock in the morning. The committee that had arranged the Belfast meetings was waiting, having judged rightly that Barnhouse would make every effort to arrive on time. For a moment they prayed, then they made their way carefully through the lightless streets to the hotel. The hotel was heavily curtained inside, so it was possible to turn on a dim light there. The committee said goodnight. Church was at 11:00 and they would be by to pick him up at 10:30. One of them added, "I hope you will have a good sermon. It may well be the last that some of the men will ever hear." Then they were gone.

Barnhouse stood alone in the room with baggage piled around him. Slowly he picked up a piece of paper lying on the desk and walked over to the mantelpiece to write the outline of his sermon for that morning. It had to be a sermon hammered out on the anvil of life, not one that smelled of the study in any way. Barnhouse later declared, "I stood there and prayed, and suddenly I thought of the perfect text for that hour. With great rapidity I wrote down the text and three or four thoughts that would be my subheads and then went to sleep."

In the morning his friends came to drive him to St. Enoch's, perhaps the largest church in Ireland. There the minister, who was quite beside himself, greeted him. It was a few minutes before 11:00. Chamberlain had announced that he would speak on the radio at that hour, and everyone sensed that he would declare war on Germany. The minister thanked Barnhouse over and over again for being there. "The church will be full of lads who will never come back," he said. "I pray God will give you something for them."

As the little group started into the church, the thought occurred to Barnhouse that everyone would be home listening to the radio. He was wrong. The auditorium was full. There was not a vacant seat. The service began. They sang hymns. An elder slipped a note to the pastor, who then handed it to Barnhouse. It read, "No reply from Hitler. The prime minister has declared war." A moment later Barnhouse was introduced to preach.

Barnhouse began by telling how he had outlined his sermon in the dim light of his hotel room at 4:00 that morning but that, in spite of the circumstances, he had a text for them that was the most wonderful text in the Bible for such a day, September 3, 1939. It was spoken first by the Lord Jesus Christ, and it was a command: "You will hear of wars and rumors of wars: *see that ye be not troubled.*"

He then recounted the series of experiences he had had on his way to Belfast. He told of the horrors and after each succeeding horror he stopped and repeated the text: *Do not be troubled!* The tocsin will sound; mobilization will take place. *Do not be troubled!* Millions of homes will be broken up. *Do not be troubled!* Thousands of children will be torn from their mothers and will represent in their cries all the wails that have

been going up from the world. Christ said, *"Do not be troubled!"*

The tension was mounting in the church. But then when monstrous grief had been piled on agonizing horror, Barnhouse stopped and said: "These words are either words of a madman or they are the words of God." He shook his fist toward heaven and said, "God, unless Jesus Christ is God, then these words are the most horrible that could be spoken to men who have hearts which can weep and bowels which can be gripped by human compassion and sympathy. Men are dying. *Do not be troubled?* Children are crying in their naked loneliness with no beloved face in sight. *Do not be troubled? O God! How can Jesus Christ say such a thing?"*

But then came the answer. Jesus Christ is God. Jesus Christ is the Lord of history. Jesus Christ is the God of detailed circumstance. Nothing has ever happened that did not flow in the channel God dug for it. No event has ever flamed up in spite of God or left Him astonished, bewildered, or confused. He is our God. The sin of man has reduced the world to an arena of passion and fury. Like wild beasts, men tear at each other's throats. Yet in the midst of the history of which Jesus Christ is Lord, each individual who has believed in Him as the Savior and as the Lord of life will know the power of His resurrection and will learn that events, however terrible, cannot separate us from the love of God.[4]

This is the lesson that God taught Habakkuk: God is Lord of history, He controls history, and He accomplishes His purposes in history for those who are His own.

---

[4] I have retold this story from Donald Grey Barnhouse's original studies of the "Epistle to the Romans," part 55 (Philadelphia: The Bible Study Hour, 1955), pp. 4–12. It does not appear in the later, bound edition of the Romans series. I have told it myself in *The Last and Future World* (Grand Rapids: Zondervan, 1974), pp. 132–39. That book is now out of print.

10

Habakkuk's Second Question

(Habakkuk 1:12–2:3)

O LORD, are you not from everlasting?
  My God, my Holy One, we will not die.
O LORD, you have appointed them to execute judgment;
  O Rock, you have ordained them to punish.
Your eyes are too pure to look on evil;
  you cannot tolerate wrong.
Why then do you tolerate the treacherous?
  Why are you silent while the wicked
  swallow up those more righteous than themselves? . . .

I will stand at my watch
  and station myself on the ramparts;
I will look to see what he will say to me.
  and what answer I am to give to this complaint.

Then the LORD replied:

  "Write down the revelation
    and make it plain on tablets
    so that a herald may run with it.
  For the revelation awaits an appointed time;
    it speaks of the end
    and will not prove false.
  Though it linger, wait for it;
    it will certainly come and will not delay."

Habakkuk is a profound book, one which delves deeply into the mysteries of God. Not all the Bible's books are like this. The apostle Paul's pastoral letters, for example, are quite straightforward in their presentation of truth. Habakkuk is profound because it raises deep questions about the workings of God in history—why God does what He does, why He does it in the way He does, and why He sometimes does nothing. It is also profound because of the answers God gives. God says that although the righteous may not understand everything He is doing in history, they nevertheless should live by faith in Him (Hab. 2:4). This statement is so important that it is picked up and quoted three times in the New Testament: twice by Paul (Rom. 1:17; Gal. 3:11) and once by the author of Hebrews (Heb. 10:38).

Habakkuk had a problem. He had lived through a period of national revival followed by a period of spiritual decline, and when he cried out to God about it, God replied that He was sending the Babylonians to be an agent of judgment on His people. This was not what Habakkuk wanted. He had been looking for another revival. But in addition to not getting what he wanted, he now had the further problem of reconciling God's actions with what he knew of God's moral standards.

It would be like crying out to God about the state of the visible church in America and hearing that God is going to destroy it by a Communist invasion. At first we would have been quite critical of the failures of God's people. We would have pointed to lax theological standards and even open heresy in some places, to lack of discipline and open immorality. We would have been asking for a renewing movement of God's Spirit and would have been distressed that our prayers had gone unanswered for such a long time. But then, after God had replied that He was going to destroy the church by an invasion of utter unbelievers, we would find ourselves protesting. The church may be in a deplorable state, we would argue, but surely it is not as bad as all that. Even if it were, it would not seem right that it should be destroyed by an utterly godless nation. We might ask at this point, as Habakkuk does: "Why . . . do you tolerate the treacherous? Why are you silent while the wicked swallow up those more righteous than themselves?" (Hab. 1:13).

We encounter this on a personal level too. Suppose you lose your job because a person who "has it in for you" misrepresents something you have done. Why did God allow this very bad person to succeed? Suppose you are sick and a doctor misdiagnoses your case so that you get worse. Why has this happened? Suppose you experience some great disappointment—the death of a child or spouse, the breakup of a marriage or an engagement, a failure to get into the right graduate school or residency. Doesn't God care? You are not perfect, but why should someone who is not even a Christian have it good while you lose out?

A Proper Procedure

When we face problems like this it is important that we follow a proper procedure in dealing with them. When things go wrong, some people tend to withdraw. They drop out of Christian activities, stop going to church, pull back into their spiritual corner, and pout. Others repudiate their past. They conclude that they must have been wrong about God and renounce all belief in Him. I have counseled people in each category. Both are wrong ways to deal with such problems.

How should we deal with them? Martyn Lloyd-Jones suggests four steps in his classic study of Habakkuk.

First, *stop to think*. Most of us have a tendency to talk first and think afterward, if we think at all. But James tells us, "Everyone should be quick to listen, slow to speak" (James 1:19). When we speak first, we often muddle ourselves by fanning the flames of our own unbelief or muddying the water of our ignorance. When we shut up and think, we begin to sort things out and allow the light of God to shine into our situation.

Second, *restate basic principles*. Lloyd-Jones says, "When you start to think you must not begin with your immediate problem. Begin further back. Apply the strategy of the indirect approach. . . . Such an approach is sometimes of vital importance in the spiritual life."[1] This is the principle of finding sound footing.

Were you ever on a sidewalk in the winter when the snow was cleared off but there were still treacherous icy spots? How did you walk? If you are like most people, you kept your eyes down and placed your feet carefully on safe ground. You must do the same thing spiritually. Your problem is a slippery spot, but surely not all your experience with God is like that. Get onto the parts that are firm. Remind yourself of things you know. Then you will find that the problem begins to fall into proper perspective and principles for solving it emerge.

Third, *apply the principles to the problem*. "The fact of the matter is that all problems are capable of solution only if they are put into the right context. The way to interpret a difficult text of Scripture is to consider its context. We often mistake the meaning of a phrase because we take it out of its context; but when you put your problem text into its context, the context will generally interpret the text for you. The same is also true of the particular problem that is causing you concern."[2]

Fourth, *if still in doubt, commit the problem to God in faith*. This is the most important point of all. Suppose you have stopped to think. Suppose you have gone back to basic principles. Suppose you have tried to apply these to the specific problem that is confronting you. What should you do if you are still as puzzled as you were at the beginning? Should you give up? Should you go back to withdrawing or repudiating what you had professed before? Not at all! At this point you must leave the matter with God. In other words, you must say, "Lord, I have done everything I know to do with this problem. I have faced it on the basis of everything I know, and I still don't understand it. From here on it's your problem, not mine anymore." That is what God wants you to do. He wants you to make your problems His problems, because He knows that then you will grow in faith and your knowledge of Him will deepen. In time God will give you a proper answer to the problem you are facing.

So here are the four points: (1) stop to think, (2) restate basic principles, (3) apply the principles to the problem, and (4) if still in doubt, commit the problem to God in faith. That is the biblical method of dealing with problems you do not seem able to cope with on the basis of your limited experience.

THE THINKING PROPHET

Having pointed out what we should do to solve personal and historical problems, I show now that this is precisely what Habakkuk did when confronted by the Lord's prophecy of a Babylonian invasion. First, *Habakkuk stopped to think*. Habakkuk did not write much, but he was a great thinker. He wrestled through his problems and thought about them deeply before writing anything. We know because of what he has written down.

Second, *he reminded himself of first principles*. What principles were they? As we read Habakkuk 1:12 and the following verses we find that they are the most basic of all theological principles, namely, the attributes of God. Habakkuk begins with the statement, "O, LORD, are you not from everlasting?" We can imagine his train of thought. In the previous two verses God had been talking about the Babylonians He was going to send to invade Israel, and He had said: "They laugh at all fortified cities; they build earthen

---

[1] D. Martyn Lloyd-Jones, *From Fear to Faith* (London: InterVarsity Press, 1966), pp. 26, 27. Original edition 1953.
[2] Ibid., pp. 27, 28.

ramps and capture them. Then they sweep past like the wind and go on—guilty men, whose own strength is their god" (vv. 10, 11). Habakkuk must have reflected on the nature of this "god" of the Babylonians. He must have asked himself, "Who is this 'god' anyway? Why, the 'god' of the Babylonians is only an idol; he is nothing at all. He is even less of a reality than the Babylonians." Then he must have compared him to the God of Israel, Jehovah, whose name begins verse 12 and who is an "everlasting" God. He must have reminded himself that Jehovah was before anything came into existence and would be long after Babylon faded away. Even if Habakkuk could not understand all that God did, he would have found comfort in knowing that he served the everlasting God.

His second sentence refers to another of God's attributes: holiness. Habakkuk says, "My God, my Holy One, we will not die." This is a most important characteristic of God. In the Bible it is the attribute stressed more than any other. We do not find the Bible speaking often of God's "sovereign name," "loving name," or "wise name," but again and again God reminds us of His "holy name." It is the only attribute thrice repeated: "Holy, holy, holy is the LORD Almighty" (Isa. 6:3; Rev. 4:8).

This attribute of God is also of special importance for the matter Habakkuk is raising. Habakkuk asks, "Is it right for God to allow the wicked to destroy those more righteous than themselves?" He is really asking, "Does God act rightly?" In the context of this set of questions it was important for Habakkuk to remind himself that God is the Holy One.

Habakkuk also refers to God's sovereignty. He writes, "O LORD, you have appointed them to execute judgment" and "O Rock, you have ordained them to punish." God controls history. The Babylonians did not simply rise up on

their own. God raised them up. Moreover, He was raising them up *when* He wanted and to operate *in the precise geographical sphere* He wanted. This is something David would have understood immediately, for in his great prayer at the dedication of the goods collected for the construction of the temple in Jerusalem, he prayed:

> Yours, O LORD, is the greatness and
>   the power
>   and the glory and the majesty
>   and the splendor,
>   for everything in heaven and
>   earth is yours.
> Yours, O LORD, is the kingdom;
>   you are exalted as head over all.
> Wealth and honor come from you;
>   you are the ruler of all things.
> In your hands are strength and
>   power
>   to exalt and give strength to all
>   (1 Chron. 29:11, 12).

The fourth characteristic of God that Habakkuk mentions is faithfulness. He expresses it by saying that God is a place of security for His people. He calls Him his Rock. A rock provides firm footing. It is a foundation on which a person can build a secure dwelling. It is often a fortress to which a soldier can run and be safe. God is all these things to us.

The personal relationship of the prophet to God is stressed repeatedly: "*My* God, *my* Holy One."

What did Habakkuk do once he had reminded himself of these great attributes of God? He had stopped to think. He had restated his basic principles. Next he took the third step and *applied these basic principles to his problems.* I think his reasoning must have been along these lines. If God is the everlasting God—if He was here before anything we know came into existence and will be here after all our problems and enemies have faded away—then the Babylonian invasion is not His last word, however final that invasion may seem. His relationship to us is more important and more lasting. Again, if God is holy, as I know Him to be, then the outcome of this invasion (since it is being caused by God) will not be evil but good in the final analysis. It will accomplish some good purpose. If God is sovereign, then the invasion is not the result of mere chance. God is still in control. Finally, if God is faithful, then the victory of the Babylonian armies must be for the good of God's people. It does not indicate that God has changed His mind. He has not abandoned us. We are still His people.

Think what Habakkuk has accomplished by this reasoning. If the Babylonian invasion is not the last word in God's relationship to His people, it is not to be evil in the final analysis, if it is not the result of mere chance, if it does not indicate a change of mind on God's part—then what must the invasion be? The answer is: it must be a tool in God's hand for the correction and purification of His people. It is to do them good. Habakkuk expresses his conclusion by saying: "O, LORD, you have appointed them to execute judgment; O Rock, you have ordained them to punish."

THE WAITING PROPHET

What we have at this point is an answer to the first half of Habakkuk's problem. He has stopped to think; he has restated basic principles; he has applied them to his problem; and he has arrived at the answer: the invasion must be a tool in God's hand for the correction and purification of His people. But Habakkuk is not yet satisfied. He can see the ultimate purpose of the coming invasion, but he is still troubled by the moral dimensions of using the Babylonians, an ungodly people, to punish Israel. Israel is far from righteous, but the Babylonians are even less righteous. They are actually terribly wicked. Isn't it wrong for God to exalt

such a wicked people? Is this not an endorsement of evil?

At this point Habakkuk seems to be doing exactly what he did with the first half of his problem. Once again he stops to think, restates his principles, and then applies them to the problem. In verse 13 he writes: "Your eyes are too pure to look on evil; you cannot tolerate wrong." But this time the procedure does not work because the difficulty is bound up with the principles. It is precisely because God is too pure to look on evil and cannot tolerate wrong that the problem of God's using the Babylonians as a tool arises.

What is Habakkuk to do now? He still does not have the answer. At this point he comes to step four and does what was mentioned in the summary of these points earlier: *he commits the problem to God in faith.* That is, he leaves it with Him. That is how he begins chapter 2:

> I will stand at my watch
> and station myself on the
> ramparts;
> I will look to see what he will say
> to me,
> and what answer I am to give to
> this complaint (Hab. 2:1).

Habakkuk has gone as far in his reasoning as he can. Now he needs to know more if he is to make progress. So he waits for that instruction. He says that he is going to wait to see what God will say to him.

This is worth looking at in detail, for it answers the question: *How* do we leave a problem with God? What should our frame of mind be?

First, we should *detach ourselves from the problem.* Habakkuk suggests this when he says he will go to a watchtower. A watchtower was often built in a grain field or vineyard to provide a place for a guard to keep an eye on the harvest. It could also be a tower in the city or on the walls of the city from which a watchman could keep a sharp eye out for an enemy. In view of Habakkuk's mention of "ramparts" in this verse, he is probably thinking of the second kind of watchtower. But in either case the idea is the same. A tower is something set apart from or detached from the common press of life. So when Habakkuk says that he is going to stand at his watch and station himself on the ramparts, he is saying, "I have been down in the valley with my problem and have not been able to solve it. Now I am going to draw apart for a while and leave it with God. I am going to detach myself from the difficulty."

Martyn Lloyd-Jones says this is "one of the most important principles in the psychology of the Christian life." But he adds that it is often precisely where we go astray. "We have a perplexity, and we have applied the prophetic method of laying down postulates and putting the problem in the context of those propositions which we had laid down. But still we do not find satisfaction, and we do not quite know what to do. It may be the problem of what we are to do with our lives; or it may be some situation that is confronting us which involves a difficult decision. Having failed to reach a solution, despite seeking the guidance of the Holy Spirit, there is nothing more to do but to take it to God in prayer. But what so frequently happens is this. We go on our knees and tell God about the thing that is worrying us; we tell Him that we cannot solve the difficulty ourselves, that we cannot understand; and we ask Him to deal with it to show us His way. Then the moment we get up from our knees we begin to worry about the problem again."[3]

We also tell other people about it, and from what is probably a very wrong motive. Actually, it is often the case that we are proud of our problem: it shows that we are serious Christians and that we are wrestling with deep, spiritual things. We want to let other people know about it. If we are doing this, we have not left the problem with God. If you have a problem like this, leave it with God. You do not have the right to talk about it or brood over it any longer.

Second, we should *expect God's answer*. Just because we have left something with God and have ceased worrying about it does not mean that we should forget about it entirely. Here again Habakkuk's image of the watchtower is helpful. The tower is detached from the crowds of people below, but the person who enters it does so in order to keep an eye on the landscape. He is on duty, as it were. He has work to do, and that work is to watch to see what will happen. Habakkuk says that he "will stand at" his watch and "look to see" what God will say to him.

How do we look for God's answer? How does God speak? The primary way is through Scripture. Sometimes God directs us by what used to be called "intimations," deep personal feelings concerning the way we should go. He frequently directs us by what we call "open or closed doors." That is, God provides an opportunity for service or takes it away. These things occasionally enter in. Still, the primary (and ultimately the only fully reliable) way of knowing God's direction or answer to our perplexities is through Scripture. Anyone who has made a habit of reading the Word of God regularly knows how that happens. We have a problem, have been unable to solve it, and have left it with God. It may be that we have even forgotten about it temporarily. But one day we

³ Ibid., p. 37.

are reading a passage of the Bible and suddenly a verse leaps out at us and we recognize at once that it contains the solution to what has troubled us. It is God's answer to the problem we previously left with Him.

The final point is that we should *be persistent in our expectation.* Habakkuk also implies this by his image. He says that he is going to stay in his watchtower until God answers his question. God likes that kind of tenacity. I think that is the kind of persevering attitude God honors.

God honored it in the case of Habakkuk, for the entire second chapter is God's answer, expressed in a series of judgments upon those who are not upright and who do not live by faith in the true God. The answer, which we are going to look at in the next chapter, is this: God says, "I have heard your prayer, Habakkuk, and I understand perfectly what is bothering you. Here is my answer. It is true that I have raised up the Babylonians to punish my people, but this does not mean that I am endorsing their evil or sin. On the contrary, I will judge them in due course. I have raised them up; I will bring them down again. They will suffer the full outpouring of my wrath. Meanwhile my people will be purified of their sin and restored to my favor. And while this is happening, the one who is truly righteous must live by faith in me. Write this down. Make it plain, so that anyone who reads it may live by it." This is what Habakkuk did. He wrote it down in his prophecy. We are called to read it and live by faith in our great God.

11

Living By Faith

(Habakkuk 2:4–20)

> *"See, he is puffed up;*
>   *his desires are not upright—*
>   *but the righteous will live by his faith—*
> *indeed, wine betrays him;*
>   *he is arrogant and never at rest.*
> *Because he is as greedy as the grave*
>   *and like death is never satisfied,*
> *he gathers to himself all the nations*
>   *and takes captive all the peoples."*

Habakkuk 2:4 is the central revelation of this important and quite contemporary prophecy. The verse is God's answer to the questions Habakkuk raised in the opening sections of his book. Habakkuk was troubled by ungodliness in Israel. But when God revealed that He was about to use the Babylonians to punish His people, Habakkuk asked how God could use the ungodly to punish those more righteous than themselves. It was a daring moral question, for Habakkuk was asking whether God was doing right. The prophet waited intently and apprehensively before the answer came.

The answer, which begins with 2:4 and continues to the end of the chapter, has to do with God's judgment upon the Babylonians. Just because the foreign army would pride itself on its strength and have a moment of triumph over Israel in its conquests did not mean that the Babylonians were justified in God's sight. They were not. So judgment was going to fall on them too.

The wonderful thing about this chapter, however, is not the large part of it that speaks of judgment on the Babylonians (vv. 6–20) but rather the one verse (v. 4) that speaks of the life of the believer in a time of crisis: "The righteous will live by his faith." This is a great text. It could even be called *the* great text of the Bible. To understand it is to understand the Christian gospel and the Christian life. It is so important that it is picked up by the New Testament writers, twice by Paul (Rom. 1:17; Gal. 3:11) and once by the author of the Book of Hebrews (Heb. 10:38).

MARTIN LUTHER'S TEXT

It is not possible to go on with a discussion of this verse without acknowledging the impact it has had on history, particularly the way it gripped the heart and mind of Martin Luther and thus led in a very direct and obvious way to the Protestant Reformation.

In Luther's day the glory of the

90

gospel—that a man is justified before God on the basis of what God has done and that he receives this by faith and not by works—had been clouded over by the traditions of medieval Catholicism, much as the truth of the gospel has been covered over by traditions in many Protestant and Catholic churches today. Luther, who grew up under the medieval system, felt the burden of his sin and did not know how to free himself of it. He was not sick or crazy, as some have claimed. He simply recognized God's just standards expressed in His law and knew that he fell short of them. As Luther read the Decalogue and other ethical portions of the Bible he knew that he was condemned by those standards and trembled because of it.

Determined to seek his salvation, Luther entered the Augustinian monastery at Erfurt and in that monastery had opportunity to study the Bible carefully. He was encouraged in this by a wonderful spiritual father, his superior, who directed him to important portions of the Word of God. As Luther studied the Word he came upon this text— "The righteous will live by his faith"— and it began to take root in his mind. At this point Luther did not understand the verse, as he later would come to understand it, but he recognized its importance. He recognized that somewhere in these words was a revelation of a different way of pleasing God than by fastings, self-immolations, prayers, charity, and good works.

There was a second period in his life when this text also spoke to him. He had begun a pilgrimage to Rome, and on that journey he had crossed the Alps and had fallen sick at Bologna. He was deathly ill. During this sickness he was tenderly cared for by the monks. But Luther was overcome with the utmost darkness and dejection, reflecting on how horrible it was to die thus—under the burning sky and in a foreign land. His physical condition reflected the inner turmoil of his soul and was an image of what he imagined it would be like to stand before the burning wrath of God. While he lay thus the words that had earlier pressed themselves upon his thinking returned to his mind, and he found himself repeating in growing belief: "The righteous will live by his faith. The righteous will live by his faith."

When Luther recovered from his illness he went to Rome. In that capital, in the church of St. John's Lateran, there is a staircase that is said to be from Pilate's judgment hall. The existing stairs are in four parts: the special inner two, said to have been transported there miraculously from Jerusalem, and the ordinary outer two. The inner steps are not walked on. Here pilgrims mount painfully on their knees, a step at a time, saying prayers as they go. At different points on these stairs there are stains that have been covered with pieces of glass. They are said to have been caused by the blood of Christ, spilled when he was taken in and out of Pilate's hall. As the pilgrims go up the stairs they stop at these places and kiss the glass, praying constantly. Luther came to the Lateran church to perform this rite. The pope had promised an indulgence to all who would do it. What happened to him there is told by his son Dr. Paul Luther in a manuscript preserved in the library of Rudolstadt: "As he repeated his prayers on the Lateran staircase, the words of the prophet Habakkuk came suddenly to his mind: 'The just shall live by faith.' Thereupon he ceased his prayers, returned to Wittenberg, and took this as the chief foundation of all his doctrine."[1] Luther's turnabout on

---

[1] Quoted by F. W. Boreham in *A Bunch of Everlastings or Texts that Made History* (Philadelphia: Judson Press, 1920), p. 20.

those stairs marked the beginning of the Reformation that was soon to sweep Europe.

Luther himself said of this text, "Before those words broke upon my mind I hated God and was angry with him because, not content with frightening us sinners by the law and by the miseries of life, he still further increased our torture by the gospel. But when, by the Spirit of God, I understood those words—'The just shall live by faith!' 'The just shall live by faith!'—then I felt born again like a new man; I entered through the open doors into the very Paradise of God."[2]

NEW TESTAMENT INTERPRETATION

We have an easy way of approaching this text, because the places where it is quoted in the New Testament (once in Romans, once in Galatians, and once in Hebrews) are explanations of the three main parts of the verse. In the original language, Hebrew, the important part of the verse has only three words: "the justified man" (Who is he? What is justification?), "by his faith" (What is faith? How does it function?), and "will live" (What is the Christian life? How does one live before God?). Romans is our commentary on the justified man. Hebrews is our commentary on faith. Galatians is our commentary on the Christian life. We turn to these books to understand what Habakkuk 2:4 means.

The revelation to Habakkuk shows that a person can be righteous (or justified) before God. In ourselves we are not righteous. This is what bothered Luther so deeply. Instead of being righteous, as we ought to be, we are sinners and therefore under God's just wrath and condemnation. How can a person who is a sinner and under God's condemnation attain righteousness? How can such a one become

perfect? The answer is that nobody can attain to righteousness. No one is capable of perfect goodness.

How do we get it then? It is God's gift to us in Jesus Christ. This is what Romans explains. It shows that the justified person is the one who has ceased trying to please God by his own efforts and who has turned to Jesus instead for the righteousness that God gives freely. This is what it means to be a Christian. It means to stop trying to attain heaven by our own good works and instead to receive what God has done for us in Christ. The foundation of our Christian life is not what we can do for God but what God has done for us. Therefore, the entrance into that life is not by working but by receiving. It is opening our hands to God's gift. Paul speaks of this by saying at the very beginning of Romans, "I am not ashamed of the gospel, because it is the power of God for the salvation of everyone who believes: first for the Jew, then for the Gentile. For in the gospel a righteousness from God is revealed, a righteousness that is by faith from first to last, just as it is written: 'The *righteous* will live by faith' " (Rom. 1:16, 17).

We next ask: How do we receive God's gift? The answer is found in the second word in Habakkuk 2:4: "by faith." The Book of Hebrews is the New Testament commentary on it. What is faith? According to Hebrews, particularly Hebrews 11, faith is believing God and acting upon that belief. In the long list of the heroes of the faith in chapter 11, each is shown to have done something as an expression of belief. Abel believed God and *offered a better sacrifice* than Cain did (v. 4). Enoch believed God and *pleased* Him by his long and faithful life (v. 5). Noah believed God and *built an ark* to the saving of his

---

[2]Ibid., p. 27.

family (v. 7). Abraham, the author's chief example, did four things. He believed God and *obeyed* Him in setting out for the Promised Land; he *made his home in the land* like a stranger in a foreign country; he *was enabled to become a father* in the engendering of Isaac; later he *offered Isaac* as a sacrifice at God's command (vv. 8, 9, 11, 17). Isaac believed God and *blessed* Jacob and Esau according to God's direction (v. 20). Jacob believed God and *blessed* Joseph's sons (v. 21). The list goes on, in each case showing how faith expressed itself in activity.

It is important to stress faith's action, because we have a definition of faith in our day which reduces it to mere intellectual assent and which is therefore far less than what the Bible means by belief. We can meet somebody on the street today and say to him, "Do you believe in God?" and have the person answer, "Of course I do. What do you think I am, an atheist?" He does not want to be an atheist, so he believes in God. But this does not necessarily mean that he is a Christian or that this faith makes any difference in his life. Belief includes intellectual assent. We must believe that there is a God and that He rewards those who diligently seek him (Heb. 11:6). But faith is more than this. In salvation matters it means trusting the Lord Jesus Christ as the one who died in our place and thus also turning from sin to follow Him.

This is the context of the use of Habakkuk 2:4 in Hebrews. It occurs just before Hebrews 11, in chapter 10, where the author writes: "In just a very little while,

'He who is coming will come and
   will not delay.
But my righteous one will live by
   faith.
And if he shrinks back,
I will not be pleased with him.'

But we are not of those who shrink back and are destroyed, but of those who believe and are saved" (Heb. 10:37–39). Clearly, the faith Hebrews is talking about involves commitment.

This commitment carries on throughout life, which is what the third word in Habakkuk 2:4 is all about. The word does not say that the righteous shall begin by faith and then proceed on some other principle. It does not say that the righteous shall draw on faith from time to time as faith is needed. It says "the righteous will *live* [continuously] by his faith." That is, the righteous will operate on this principle twenty-four hours a day, seven days a week, fifty-two weeks a year—so long as life lasts.

The Book of Galatians stresses this principle. Paul had gone to Galatia during his early missionary travels and had taught the people of Galatia the whole counsels of God. He had taught that the Lord Jesus Christ had died for them and had explained the meaning of His death. He had taught the truth of the resurrection and had explained that they could have newness of life in Christ. He had taught them about the Holy Spirit and Christ's expected return. He had taught them about Christian ethics and the necessity of studying the Bible. As he unfolded this, the church grew, prospered, and was soundly established. However, some time after he had gone away he heard that those who had begun by faith were now ceasing to live by it. They had begun to adopt Jewish ordinances and say to themselves, "Faith may have been all right as a beginning when we were new Christians, but now we must add works to faith. We will have productive, healthy, obedient, blessed Christian lives only when we observe the feasts, perform circumcision, and add other ceremonies." When he received this news Paul was aghast. Immediately he wrote back to warn them that they had adopted a different gospel, one that could truly enslave them.

Paul uses Habakkuk 2:4 to challenge living by the law. He says, "All who rely on observing the law are under a curse, for it is written, 'Cursed is everyone who does not continue to do everything written in the Book of the Law.'" (Gal. 3:10, 11). The only way to live is to "live by faith." This world may crumble about our ears. All that we know and love may vanish. "But the righteous will live by his faith." He will live by faith in the One who keeps us, not only in the moment of our initial belief in Jesus Christ as Savior, but in every later moment of life as well.

WOES OF THE WICKED

The life of faith mentioned in this key verse is nevertheless only one of two distinct paths the chapter sets before us. One is the way of faith. The other is the way of "un-faith" or unbelief. The contrast is seen in Habakkuk 2:4 itself. Even the most casual reader can see that the greater part of this verse deals with the wicked. It begins, "See, he is puffed up; his desires are not upright. . . ." Then there is a dash, followed by the part of the verse we have been studying ("but the righteous will live by his faith"), followed by another dash. Then the passage continues, "indeed, wine betrays him; he is arrogant and never at rest. Because he is as greedy as the grave and like death is never satisfied . . ." (vv. 4, 5).

The way of the righteous is the way of faith in God. The way of the wicked is the way of drawing back from faith in God. The first submits to God and trusts God. The second submits to no one. The person who chooses the second way is arrogant. He says, "I don't need religion. I can take care of myself. I can do without God." The bulk of this chapter shows the course and dismal end of the ungodly.

In 2:6–20 we find what scholars call a "taunt song." It is the kind of song that a once-oppressed people might direct against its former oppressor. Often taunt songs begin with the word "woe" or "alas." In this case, there are five occurrences of the word "woe," each of which marks a stanza within the song. The first woe is in verse 6; the stanza it introduces is in verses 6–8. The second woe introduces verses 9–11. The third woe introduces verses 12–14. The fourth woe introduces verses 15–17. The final stanza encompasses verses 18–20, but the woe comes in the middle in verse 19. These five stanzas show the misery of the person or nation that thinks it can do without God.

The first stanza begins, "Woe to him who piles up stolen goods and makes himself wealthy by extortion!" The problem here is *greed*, as the preceding verse indicates. Greed is a natural but destructive characteristic of the one who will not trust God. If a person trusts God, he does not need to be covetous of more and more material possessions. The Lord is the portion of the righteous. Besides, the Lord amply supplies his need. The Lord Jesus Christ spoke of God's provision for the birds of the air and the flowers of the field and asked: "If that is how God clothes the grass of the field, which is here today and tomorrow is thrown into the fire, will he not much more clothe you, O you of little faith? . . . Seek first his kingdom and his righteousness, and all these things will be given to you as well" (Matt. 6:30, 33). If a person trusts God, he does not need to acquire more and more possessions, since he knows God will provide what he needs. If he does not trust God, then the need for things becomes a burden. This world is an insecure place, and the individual is insecure within it. So he works to get more and more in the hope that if he only has a little more land or stocks or capital, he may get by.

It does not work. This is what the

verses say clearly. For one thing, they talk about "stolen goods" and things acquired "by extortion." In the beginning, the person who is trying to build security with things probably intends to be quite honest in doing it. But, somehow, what is acquired is never enough, and he therefore finds himself resorting to questionable and eventually to dishonest practices in the quest for more. The verses also talk about this person's "debtors," suggesting that a person like this easily overextends himself and eventually falls prey to the collectors. This is quite contemporary. The people of the Western world are more in debt than they have ever been, and many are losing houses or other tangibles to the collectors. Many are going into personal bankruptcy. These facts are testimonies to the truthfulness of God's Word and proof of what happens when a person or nation rejects God and lives without Him.

Verse 9 begins, "Woe to him who builds his realm by unjust gain to set his nest on high, to escape the clutches of ruin!" The problem here is *injustice.* Here is a man who has tried to accumulate as much as he can by more or less honest means, but when he finds he cannot get enough, resorts to unjust means to enlarge his portfolio and place himself beyond the possibility of ruin. But ruin comes. The text says that even what he has accumulated will cry out against him: "You have plotted the ruin of many peoples, shaming your own house and forfeiting your life. The stones of the wall will cry out, and the beams of the woodwork will echo it" (vv. 10, 11).

Picture a nobleman in the Babylonian army. He wants to rise to a high position and enjoy its rewards—to have an opulent house and to be secure in it. So he cuts down a forest that belongs to somebody else and from the trees of that forest makes great beams for his home. Then he destroys some-

one else's home and takes the beautiful stone blocks it was made of for himself. When he finishes he has a beautiful house, a "nest on high" (v. 9). But everyone who looks at it knows where the stones and beams came from, and his pride and joy become a cause for shame. When the opportunity arises they will see that the nobleman is treated as he treated others.

Verse 12 introduces *violence:* "Woe to him who builds a city with bloodshed and establishes a town by crime!" This was a vice particularly observable among the Babylonians, but it is characteristic of our time as well. Here are people who have gone from greed to injustice to violence. Not content with what their injustices can procure, they are now adding crimes of violence to their vices, so great is their desire to have things.

The specific setting of this stanza concerns building, in this case building a city. Building is not wrong itself, though the desires that motivate it may be. There is nothing wrong with building a city or a company or a house—if the motives and means are right. But here is an example of building by wrong means, and the decreed result is that the work will not endure. That which exalts man will pass away: "For the earth will be filled with the knowledge of the glory of the LORD, as the waters cover the sea" (v. 14).

We can even apply this to building a church. It is possible to build a large church by secular means. That is, you can prosper externally by using good marketing, advertising, and other secular techniques. Find out what the people want, then give it to them—that is the secret. If they want bowling alleys and gymnasiums, give them bowling alleys and gymnasiums. If they want classes on how to fulfill themselves as individual people and get ahead in business, give them those classes. If they want soothing, reassuring sermons, give them such sermons. Give them anything they want. Above all, do not confront them with the harsh statements or demanding standards of the Bible. A church built along these lines will grow, as I have said. But it will not endure! When hard times come or tastes (including tastes in religion) change, it will fade away. On the other hand, a church that seeks to do things God's way will endure, even though its way may be harder and the growth quite slow. Floods may come upon a church like this. The winds of adversity may blow upon it. But it will stand and be a source of blessing.

The fourth stanza of Habakkuk's taunt song says, "Woe to him who gives drink to his neighbors, pouring it from the wineskin till they are drunk, so that he can gaze on their naked bodies" (v. 15). These are indelicate words. They are referring to *seduction*, and seduction is fairly far along the slippery slope of moral decline that this chapter highlights. We can note the progression. First there is greed. Then there is mild injustice, followed by more serious injustice. Next comes violence. Now there is seduction and perversion. You say, "How does this concern the secular man's quest for security?" In this way: having sought for security in things and being disappointed there, the God-despising man now turns to personal relations, hoping to find security through love. But he does not know how to love. He does not know what a true, intimate relationship is. All he can do is seduce another person. So he does! And that which should be a thing of glory becomes shame.

Many view seduction as power. Habakkuk sees it as sin. He says that the one who seduces another becomes a seducer; the one who corrupts, a corrupter. People who do this have their reward.

The final stanza of this chapter concerns *idolatry:* the "woe" is in verse 19. "Woe to him who says to wood, 'Come to life!' Or to lifeless stone, 'Wake up!' Can it give guidance? It is covered with gold and silver; there is no breath in it." In the context of the references to the Babylonians, it is clear that this involves not merely simple idolatry, a case of an individual bowing down to a wooden or stone idol. It involves the Babylonians' whole religious system with its divination, sorcery, spiritism, and demonism. Babylon was a center for such practices.

Unfortunately, we also have this in our time. It is hard to understand why an educated, scientifically minded, modern people such as we imagine ourselves to be should be so intrigued by spiritism and the occult; but our chapter explains it perfectly. It is simply the end condition of a people who will not walk by faith in God but who trust to their own devices instead. We trust ourselves, but we are not adequate for the trust. So, finding no help in mere human beings and having rejected the true God, we turn to superstition.

The most widespread American version of occult practices is astrology, and I have often asked myself why astrology is so popular in our "enlightened" age. I have found three explanations. First, astrology offers religion without moral responsibility. This is inherent in the very axioms of astrology which substitute a casuality of stars and planets for human free will, liberty, and responsibility. It is fatalism, and fatalism absolves man from duty. This outlook is also evident in other forms of occult practices where nothing is taught or said that might possibly make an individual feel guilty for something he or she has done. Second, astrology offers revelation without the disconcerting doctrines of the Bible. It pretends to give a word from beyond, but it does not speak of sin, death, or judgment. The Bible does. It says, "We must all appear before the judgment seat of Christ, that each one may receive what is due him for the things done while in the body, whether good or bad" (2 Cor. 5:10). Third, astrology offers salvation without a real Savior. The popular song from the musical *Hair* claims,

When the moon is in the Seventh
    House
And Jupiter aligns with Mars,
Then peace will guide the planets,
And love will steer the stars.

But this is not true. God guides the planets, just as God guides history. If there is to be peace and love in the world, then the Lord Jesus Christ, who alone is the embodiment of peace and love, must provide it.[3]

AS FOR ME AND MY HOUSE

If what we need is God, as the Bible claims, and if we turn to things instead of God, as we so often do, these other things will inevitably disappoint us no matter how much we have or how fervent our misplaced devotion to them may be. What do you turn to for strength and security in life? Is it money? Do you think that if you only have enough money you will be all right? Is it other people? Do you think that somehow your friends will help you get by? Is it success? Fame? Your own strength and ability, whatever it may be? Do you think that if you get all these in order, somehow you will manage?

They will not be enough! You and I are made in the image of God, destined for fellowship with God. If we will not have God, then there will always be a vacuum—a terrible, hellish vacuum—in our lives.

The challenge presented to us in this chapter is that choice. Will it be the world's way, the way of the ungodly with its emptiness, frustration, and eventual ruin? Or will it be God's way, the way of faith in Him who alone is worthy of that faith? Joshua presented the choice to the people of his day. He had come to the end of his life and was soon to die. But before he died, he brought the people together and reminded them of all God had done for them from the time He first called Abraham out of Ur of the Chaldeans to the day He brought them out of Egypt into the Promised Land. At the end he said, "If serving the LORD seems undesirable to you, then choose for yourselves this day whom you will serve, whether the gods your forefathers served beyond the River, or the gods of the Amorites, in whose land you are living. But as for me and my household, we will serve the LORD " (Josh. 24:15).

Joshua was saying what Habakkuk later said in other language. He was affirming what Martin Luther found. Though the world should rise up against us, the righteous will live by faith. It is by faith in the righteous God alone that we can stand against it.

---

[3]I have analyzed the current manifestations of astrology and the occult at greater length in *The Last and Future World* (Grand Rapids: Zondervan, 1974), pp. 73–80.

12

The Secret of Effective Prayer

(Habakkuk 3:1, 2)

A prayer of Habakkuk the prophet. On shigionoth.

> LORD, *I have heard of your fame;*
>   *I stand in awe of your deeds, O* LORD.
> *Renew them in our day,*
>   *in our time make them known;*
>   *in wrath remember mercy.*

The third chapter of Habakkuk is a prayer. It is one of the great prayers of the Bible, to be placed alongside Abraham's intercession for Sodom, David's prayer at the dedication of the materials for the temple, and the Psalms. But it is a prayer in context and cannot properly be understood apart from the entire prophecy.

Habakkuk began his book by asking God why He was so slow in answering his prayer for revival in Israel. Then when God did answer He said He was going to send the Babylonians to punish His people Israel. This was not the answer Habakkuk wanted, and he asked God how He could do such a thing. How could He use a wicked people to punish those more righteous than themselves? These questions were asked in chapter 1. God's answer came in chapter 2, summarized in verse 4: "See, he is puffed up; his desires are not upright—but the righteous will live by his faith." In the remainder of chapter 2 God describes how the one who is "puffed up" will be brought low. The Babylonians will themselves be punished. In the meantime, the one who knows God will live by faith in God. Times may be bad. The future may become worse. But the righteous will live by faith in Him who alone is worthy of that faith.

Chapter 2, which contains this revelation, ends by saying: "The LORD is in his holy temple; let all the earth be silent before him" (v. 20). It is an appropriate and solemn ending. All that remains is for Habakkuk to worship this God and lay his petitions before Him.

THE NATURE OF PRAYER

Prayer is speaking to God. If you can talk to your wife or husband, you can talk to God. If you can talk to your brother or sister, you can talk to God. Anything that obscures the simplicity and spontaneity of prayer as conversation should be avoided, for prayer is a very simple thing. We must not think that we need a special time or place or mood to pray.

But having said that and having emphasized it as much as I know how, let me also say that prayer can also be formal. The last chapter of Habakkuk is such a prayer. It is a carefully structured, formal composition. In fact it is a poem. This suggests that after Habakkuk had received the revelation of God's coming judgment on the Babylonians and the instruction to live by faith, he collected his thoughts and composed this chapter as a beautiful and careful expression of what his heart wanted to say to God. (Mary's Magnificat may be another example of such a careful composition.)

If the thought of a carefully composed prayer bothers you, disregard this thought until later in your Christian walk. It is far more important that prayer be a simple thing in which you truly utter the deep thoughts of your heart and pour out your petitions to God. If prayer is not a simple thing for you yet, do not be led astray by the truth that it can also be more complex. Still, if you are one who prays naturally and if you know that you can come to God at any place and at any time, you can learn something additional from this prayer of Habakkuk. There is also room for composed prayer in which we put down in writing the deepest expression and clearest insights of our hearts and minds.

Habakkuk's prayer can be divided into three parts. The first part is an approach to God; we find it in verse 2. The second part is the prayer itself, consisting largely of rehearsal of God's mighty acts; we find it in verses 3–15. The third and final part is Habakkuk's personal testimony; we find this in verses 16–19. The first of these (verse 2) will occupy our thoughts in this chapter.

Approaching Humbly

Habakkuk's prayer begins in this way: "LORD, I have heard of your fame; I stand in awe of your deeds, O LORD. Renew them in our day, in our time make them known; in wrath remember mercy." In many ways this is a very simple verse. Still, it contains all the essential elements of an effective approach to God and teaches us how our prayers can be effective.

What are the elements of effective prayer? The first and most essential is humility. We cannot succeed in prayer if we come into God's presence demanding things because of who we are. We cannot succeed if we think that somehow we deserve to be there and deserve to be heard. Habakkuk's approach to God is a very humble prayer. Some might say, "How do you get humility from that verse? Is it because the prophet claims to stand in awe of God's deeds?" That is part of it. But the true measure of Habakkuk's humility in this prayer is seen by comparing Habakkuk 3:2 with the prophet's earlier prayers. Place them side by side. Here he says: "I stand in awe of your deeds, O LORD. Renew them in our day, in our time make them known; in wrath remember mercy." Earlier the prophet's prayers went: "How long, O LORD, must I call for help, but you do not listen? Or cry out to you, 'Violence!' but you do not save?" (Hab. 1:2); "Your eyes are too pure to look on evil; you cannot tolerate wrong. Why then do you tolerate the treacherous? Why are you silent while the wicked swallow up those more righteous than themselves?" (Hab. 1:13). Can you not hear the difference? The prayers of chapter 1 are complaints. The final prayer assumes a different attitude.

The first prayers were not entirely bad. If we are free to come to God at any time of the day or night on any day of the week to voice what is on our hearts and minds, then we are certainly free to ask the kind of questions Habakkuk asks in these verses. Habakkuk was grieved by Israel's sin. He was disturbed that revival had not come. The prophet had every right to ask God why there was no revival and what God was going to do about the situation.

But something happened in the interval between the prayers of the first chapter and the prayer of the third, and it changed Habakkuk. Quite simply, Habakkuk had taken his mind off himself, the Israelites, and the Babylonians and focused on God. So long as he was operating merely on the human level the difference between the relative goodness of Israel and the relative badness of the Babylonians seemed great. He could ask, "Why are you silent while the wicked swallow up those more righteous than themselves?" But once he had looked to God—once he saw the righteousness of God and reminded himself of the eternal and sovereign God he worshiped—these differences faded into insignificance and the relative goodness of Israel seemed unimportant. Habakkuk saw that all, including himself, fall short of God's standards and require God's mercy to be saved.

Lloyd-Jones puts it this way: "How was Habakkuk brought to such a position? It would seem that it was when he stopped thinking of his own nation, or of the Chaldeans, and contemplated only the holiness and justice of God against the dark background of sin in the world. Our problems can nearly all be traced to our persistence in looking at the immediate problems themselves, instead of looking at them in the light of God. So long as Habakkuk was looking at Israel and the Chaldeans, he was troubled. Now he has forgotten Israel as such, and the Chaldeans, and his eyes are on God. He has returned to the realm of spiritual truth—the holiness of God, sin in man and in the world—and so he is able to see things in an entirely new light. He is now concerned for the glory of God and for nothing else. He had to stop thinking in terms of the fact that the Chaldeans were worse sinners than the Jews and that yet God was going to use them, perplexing though this problem was. That attitude made him forget the sin of his own nation through concentrating on the sin of others which happened to be greater. As long as he remained in this attitude he remained in perplexity, unhappy in heart and mind. But the prophet came to the place where he was lifted entirely out of that state, to see only the wonderful vision of the Lord in His holy temple, with sinful mankind and the universe beneath Him. The distinction between the Israelites and the Chaldeans became relatively unimportant when things were seen like that. It was no longer possible to be exalted either as an individual or as a nation. When things are seen from a spiritual viewpoint, there can only be an acknowledgment that 'All have sinned and come short of the glory of God,' and 'The whole world lieth in the evil one.' The holiness of God and the sin of man are the only things that matter."[1]

This is what needs to happen if we are to learn to pray effectively. As long as we come into God's presence saying, "Well, I am not perfect, God, but I am a good deal better than Bill Smith or Mary Jones; and therefore, you should listen to me because, after all, I am a Christian and I am pretty good and, well, I did put five dollars in the collection plate last Sunday instead of a quarter, and . . . "—as long as we come with that attitude we are going to have an exceedingly ineffective prayer life. But on the other hand, if we can say, as Habakkuk himself learned to say, "It is only by grace that I am even led to pray, only on the basis of grace that I can come; I do not deserve

---

[1]D. Martyn Lloyd-Jones, *From Fear to Faith* (London: InterVarsity Press, 1966), pp. 59, 60. Original edition 1953.

anything from you, but I come because you have invited me to come; I lay my petitions before you"—if we pray like that, God will hear our prayer and will answer.

Sometimes this error can be quite subtle. R. A. Torrey tells how on one occasion when he was speaking on prayer a note was put into his hands that read: "Dear Mr. Torrey: I am in great perplexity. I have been praying for a long time for something that I am confident is according to God's will, but I do not get it. I have been a member of the Presbyterian church for thirty years, and have tried to be a consistent one all the time. I have been a superintendent in the Sunday school for twenty-five years, and an elder in the church for twenty years; and yet God does not answer my prayer and I cannot understand it. Can you explain it to me?"

Torrey replied, "It is perfectly easy to explain it. This man thinks that because he has been a consistent church member for thirty years, a faithful Sunday school superintendent for twenty-five years, and an elder in the church for twenty years, that God is under obligation to answer. He is really praying in his own name, and God will not hear our prayers when we approach him in that way. We must, if we would have God answer our prayers, give up any thought that we have any claims upon God. If we got what we deserved, every last one of us would spend eternity in hell. But Jesus Christ has great claims on God, and we should go to God in our prayers not on the ground of any goodness in ourselves, but on the ground of Jesus Christ's claims."

At the close of the meeting a man stepped up to him and said, "You have hit the nail square on the head. I did think that because I had been a consist-ent church member for thirty years,a Sunday school superintendent for twenty-five years, and an elder in the church for twenty years, that God was under obligation to answer my prayers. I see my mistake."[2]

So long as we approach God feeling that we are owed something because we are better or more faithful than someone else, we are making this mistake too. It is only when we abandon all thoughts of being better that we begin to approach God with a genuine and proper humility.

This is necessary when we pray for our church, particularly if we are Evangelicals. We Evangelicals tend to look at the liberal church and condemn it for its obvious departure from biblical truth. We say, "The liberal church no longer believes the Bible to be the authoritative and inerrant Word of God. It no longer believes in the virgin birth of Christ. It has doubts about the Resurrection. It may even question the Lord's divinity. Isn't that terrible? Isn't it good that we still believe these doctrines?" Well, it is terrible that a professedly Christian church should deny such doctrines, even in part. It is good that the evangelical church still holds to them. But if we approach God on the basis of that distinction, thinking that we therefore have some special claim upon God because of it and that He must answer our prayers because of it, we are repeating the error of the man who talked to Torrey. The only way we dare approach God is humbly, and the only way we can rightly present our petitions is with the utterance "God be merciful to me a sinner." We may be relatively better than the liberal church, but we are also relatively worse than the church of other generations. We do not have the convictions of the martyr church, nor the sensitivity to sin of the church of

---

[2] R. A. Torrey, *The Power of Prayer and the Prayer of Power* (Grand Rapids: Zondervan, 1955), pp. 138, 139.

the Great Awakenings. If there is to be a revival, it will not start with the liberal establishment. It will begin with us. It is only when the *people of God* humble themselves and pray and seek God's face and turn from their wicked ways that He hears from heaven, forgives their sins, and heals their land (2 Chron. 7:14).

ADORATION

The second element in Habakkuk's approach to God (the second secret of effective prayer) is worship or adoration. This is also seen in the opening half of the verse: "LORD, I have heard of your fame; I stand in awe of your deeds, O LORD." Worship is acknowledging God's true worth, His "worthship." It is rehearsing His attributes so that we might have a true mental image of Him. Habakkuk does precisely that in the central part of his prayer.

Most of us have a problem at this point. Often our prayers have very little worship or adoration in them. We have an acrostic for prayer based on the word ACTS: "A" for adoration, "C" for confession of sin, "T" for thanksgiving, and "S" for supplications or petitions. In this acrostic, adoration rightly comes first and should dominate any normal prayer, with each of the other items (particularly the last) taking progressively less time. But what often happens is quite different. We rush through the first part of our prayer ("Oh, Lord, we thank you that you are a wonderful God and that you sent Jesus to die for us . . .") but then settle down on the requests ("Lord, here are sixteen things I want from you"). This is how Habakkuk prayed at the beginning. It is not very effective. Our requests will not be God's desires for us and most will go unanswered. On the other hand, if we focus first on God's great characteristics and His acts in past and present history, then our requests will change—they will be more in line

with God's desires—and we will receive what we are praying for now quite properly.

PRAYER FOR GOD'S WORK

This leads to the third and final secret of effective prayer, namely, petitions that are in accord with God's desires. After Habakkuk had approached God humbly and had recognized His true worth and great deeds, he was ready to make his petitions; but now, as we suggested would be the case, they are different from what he was uttering a chapter or two earlier. There are two petitions: first, that God would renew His deeds in the prophet's day and, second, that God would remember mercy in the midst of the anticipated outpouring of His wrath.

The first request deserves special study. Notice how Habakkuk prays that *God's* deeds, not his own deeds or desires, might be renewed. This is what "them" in the phrase "renew *them* in our day" refers to. Usually, when we pray to God for some specific project, we are asking God to renew our work. It is like building a castle of dominoes. So long as the structure goes up unhindered we seldom think of God. We do not need Him. But suddenly something jars the table a bit, and the dominoes tumble. Now we become alert to prayer. We say, "Oh, God, renew the work; the structure is tumbling." Our interest is really on what we are building and not on what God may desire. We need to learn that God may not be interested in our little piles of dominoes. We need to come to the point where we say, "Renew *your* deeds; revive *your* work."

We notice too that Habakkuk prays for revival. That is what the word "renew" or "renewal" means. To renew is not merely to refurbish something, like refinishing an antique. It is to do a new work. It is to make a new creature in Christ out of one who was an old sinner. Revival means to make alive. Formerly the people were spiritually dead. Now they are being made alive through God's Spirit.

Earlier Habakkuk might have prayed for God to change His mind regarding the Babylonian invasion. So long as Habakkuk was thinking of his own work, he would have been concerned for that. Since the Babylonian invasion threatened the work he knew, he would have wanted God to turn the invasion aside. However, he has gotten his mind off his own work now and desires the establishment of God's work instead. He knows that if God is sending the Babylonian invasion, He will build a new work out of the disaster of that invasion. At this point he is ready to write off the relative goodness of Israel and anticipate nothing less than a whole new beginning.

Notice, finally, that the prayer is for God to renew His work "in our day, in our time." What day is that? What time is he referring to? Clearly, it is the day of the invasion. Habakkuk is asking for renewal in the midst of bad times.

The 1982 meetings of the Philadelphia Conference on Reformed Theology were on the theme of revival, and John Richard de Witt made the point that revivals usually begin in bad times. He used the text, "I will pour water on the thirsty land, and streams on the dry ground" (Isa. 44:3) and then illustrated it from revival periods. "One thinks of what took place in the Reformation period, the greatest time of revival and reformation in all the history of the church. We know the condition of the church before the ministry of Martin Luther. Alexander VI, the Borgia pope, was in the Vatican. He filled the palace with his own illegitimate children and did not hesitate to lift them to positions of esteem and influence. (It was a far more reprehensible thing in those days for a minister of religion to be married than to keep a concubine.) Alexander VI was succeeded by Julius II, the warrior pope so pillared by Erasmus. Then came Leo X, the Medici pope who said, 'God has given us the papacy; let us enjoy it.' That was the attitude of the leadership of the church of Christ in those days. All across Europe the church was in a ruinous condition. People were superstitious and ignorant. They were looking here and there for answers to their spiritual problems. They sought answers in mysticism, the relics of the saints, holy days and the purchase of indulgences—but to no avail.

"There had been the distant rolling of revival thunder and dimly perceptible flashes of lightning in the ministries of men like John Wycliffe of England and John Hus of Bohemia, but it was not until the early sixteenth century that God had mercy on his church. Martin Luther arose, groping through the dry land of the religious teachings of his time with a thirst that would not be satisfied with anything short of the pure water that only the Lord Jesus Christ can give. Luther had been terrified by the righteousness of God. 'I could not love a righteous God,' Luther said. 'I hated him.' But Luther persisted in study of what he called 'the dear Paul' until he came to understand that 'the just shall live by faith.' Then he bestrode the Europe of his day like a colossus. With the mighty hammer of the Word of God he shattered the corrupt ecclesiastical establishment and held high the banner of the cross of the Lord Jesus Christ and his sole sufficiency to deliver his people from their sins. It was on dry ground that the water of God's reviving Holy Spirit fell in the sixteenth century.

"Jonathan Edwards has something to say about this as well. Edwards succeeded his grandfather Solomon Stoddard as minister of the church in Northampton, Massachusetts. In Stoddard's long ministry there had been five periods of quickening, but for many years after the fifth of those quickenings there was barrenness and aridity. Edwards speaks of the licentiousness which prevailed among the young people, the breakdown in family structure, the failure of family worship, the contentions, jealousies and divisions which marked the community. The situation of Northampton was marked by a spiritual need that only the Holy Spirit could remedy. And he did remedy it! There too the Holy Spirit of God came down and did his reviving work.

"The same was true of England in the eighteenth century, Bishop J. C. Ryle, in his *Christian Leaders of the Eighteenth Century*, tells of the great lawyer Blackstone, whose name will be familiar to any who have studied law. Early in the reign of King George III Blackstone visited the principal churches of London to see what was being preached. His report was that there was no more Christianity in the discourses he heard than in the writings of Cicero and that it was impossible to discover from what he heard whether the preachers were followers of Mohammed, Confucius or Jesus Christ. This was the scene upon which revival burst through the ministries of George Whitefield and John and Charles Wesley. God came down on a spiritual desert."[3]

This is the way God usually operates. So Habakkuk was in line with God's normal way of acting when he prayed for renewal in the time of invasion and destruction soon to come upon Israel. Are our times bad? Is ours a spiritual desert? If so, it is now particularly that we can cry out for revival and be heard.

REMEMBER MERCY

The last of Habakkuk's requests is a simple one, but it goes to the heart of all we have been saying: "In wrath remember mercy." What a great request to leave with God! What an effective request! What an appropriate way to win and be assured of God's favor! God is the God of mercy, so to pray for mercy (even in the day of His wrath) is to plead for that which is central to His character.

If we would see a mighty working of the Spirit of God in our time, we must get to the point where we desire and earnestly pray for His mercy. We must pray for His mercy on us as a nation. On one occasion the Lord Jesus Christ told a story about a Pharisee and a tax collector. The Pharisee was proud of his spiritual achievements, so when he went up to the temple to pray he prayed like this: "God, I thank you that I am not like all other men—robbers, evildoers, adulterers—or even this tax collector. I fast twice a week and give a tenth of all I get." The tax collector was aware of his failures and would not even look up to heaven. He prayed, "God, have mercy on me, a sinner."

This is precisely what the second and third chapters of Habakkuk are about. The Pharisee? He is the man who is "puffed up," whose "desires are not upright" (Hab. 2:4). The tax collector? He is the "righteous" man who lives "by his faith." He prays, "In wrath remember mercy." It is this man who, so the Lord says, goes home "justified" (Luke 18:14; cf. vv. 9–14).

[3] John Richard de Witt, "Repentance: The Fruit of Revival" in *Tenth: An Evangelical Quarterly*, vol. 12, no. 3 (July 1982), pp. 44, 45.

13

Joy in the God of Salvation

(Habakkuk 3:3–19)

I heard and my heart pounded,
my lips quivered at the sound;
decay crept into my bones;
and my legs trembled.
Yet I will wait patiently for the day of calamity
to come on the nation invading us.
Though the fig tree does not bud
and there are no grapes on the vines,
though the olive crop fails
and the fields produce no food,
though there are no sheep in the pen
and no cattle in the stalls,
yet I will rejoice in the LORD,
I will be joyful in God my Savior.

The Sovereign LORD is my strength;
he makes my feet like the feet of a deer,
he enables me to go on the heights.

Habakkuk is one of the shortest of the Minor Prophets, surpassed in brevity only by Obadiah, Nahum, and Haggai. But in spite of its brevity, it deals with profound issues. In chapter 1 Habakkuk is concerned with sin in Israel. He is troubled by God's apparent inactivity in history, a problem linked to what we would call "unanswered prayer." Later in the same chapter, when God does answer, the prophet is perplexed by the moral dimensions of God's proposed action. In chapter 3 still another problem emerges: fear. God has revealed what is to happen. He has told Habakkuk to live by faith in the coming

troublous times. Habakkuk will do it. Still he is afraid as he contemplates these judgments. He says,

I heard and my heart pounded,
my lips quivered at the sound;
decay crept into my bones,
and my legs trembled (v. 16).

This is a brilliant description of intense, bone-shattering fear, and Habakkuk is honest enough to say that this is how he felt when God spoke to him about the Babylonian invasion. The last chapter of the prophecy deals with this fear.

Is fear common enough to demand this degree of attention? It probably is, though we usually try not to admit it.

David was a man of great strength and faith. Yet he speaks of fear as he faced his enemies. Paul also possessed great courage. He bore up wonderfully in hardships, beatings, imprisonments, and riots. But he confesses that at times he "despaired even of life" (2 Cor. 1:8).

Strong faith is not incompatible with fleshly weakness, even that intense weakness that expresses itself in great anxiety. But how can we deal with it? How can we make sure that fear does not make a shambles of our lives?

Victory Over Weakness

Fortunately, the third chapter of Habakkuk is not only a confession of weakness and fear on the part of this embattled prophet. Habakkuk did fear as he anticipated the violence that would occur at the time of the Babylonian invasion. But he did something else too. He turned to God, and turning to God gave him victory over this weakness. It is significant that the book does not end on the note of fear. Fear is mentioned, but it is surpassed by faith as Habakkuk comes to rejoice in the God of salvation.

> Though the fig tree does not bud
>   and there are no grapes on the
>   vines,
> though the olive crop fails
>   and the fields produce no food,
> though there are no sheep in the
>   pen
>   and no cattle in the stalls,
> yet I will rejoice in the LORD,
>   I will be joyful in God my Savior
>   (vv. 17, 18).

This victory is available to all God's people, whatever they are called upon to go through. Sometimes it is an operation or a separation. Eventually, for all, it is death. In precisely these situations it is possible to rejoice in God and have joy in Him bring victory.

This is entirely different from the world's approaches to fear—for, of course, the world faces fearful things too. One of the world's reactions is resignation. A person will say, "If this is going to happen to me, I suppose there is just nothing that can be done about it. Everybody suffers. Everybody dies. I might as well be resigned to it." This may be better than screaming in the face of misfortune, but it is not the Christian way. At best it is a grim Stoicism.

A second reaction of the world is detachment. A person will say, "I don't want to think about such things. Every time I think about them I get depressed—when I think about my own personal future, when I think about the future of the country. The stock market depresses me. International news depresses me. The best solution is not to think about these things at all." A person who reacts this way may try to fill his life with amusements or even work hard to keep his mind occupied. But this view refuses to face reality, and reality, whether we like it or not, is still there. Moreover, it usually leaves its impact anyway. We try to detach ourselves from our problems, but they remain with us subconsciously and inevitably disturb the activities we are using to escape them.

A third approach is sheer bravado. People will tell us, "Pull yourselves together and face this with your chins up. Don't let the future depress you. Don't let anything get you down." That would be all right if we could do it, but in the situations I am talking about our knees are already knocking together and our lips are quivering. Nobody would be in this state if he or she could help it. When you are terrified, all the pep talks in the world avail little.

The Christian way of dealing with fear is to rejoice in the God of salvation. Someone might wonder if this is not also impossible. "You have acknowledged that it is often impossible to overcome fear by mere courage," such a person might say. "In the same situation, isn't it also impossible to rejoice in God?" No, it is not impossible. When we try to overcome fear with courage, we are relying on our own inadequate resources. When we rejoice in God, we are placing our confidence in one who acts powerfully and effectively on our behalf.

That is the solution Habakkuk arrives at in this chapter. Earlier, when he was puzzled about the reason for God's sending the Babylonians to invade Israel, Habakkuk used the process of: (1) stopping to think, (2) restating basic principles, and (3) applying basic principles to the problem. When that did not work, he left the problem with God. In this case, he reminded himself of God's attributes—that God was everlasting, holy, sovereign, and faithful—and concluded that if God was sending the Babylonians to invade Israel, it would be for the ultimate good of His people and not for their harm. Here he does the same thing. Faced with fear, he reminds himself of what he knows. He knows that he worships a mighty God, and he remembers the powerful acts of God in past days. A God like that is a joy forever. Remembering Him restores his joy and brings him victory over fear of the future.

It is important to emphasize knowledge, for there are situations in life in which only knowledge will help us. Emotion will not save us. Reason will not save us. The only thing that can save us is knowledge of what we know to be true.

Imagine a situation in which a Christian young man goes away to college and falls in love with a girl who is not a Christian. He is wondering if he should marry her. The Word of God is very clear about this. We are not to be unequally yoked together with unbelievers (2 Cor. 6:14); Christian marriage is a marriage of two Christians. But he is wrestling with this matter, and it is a big problem for him. What is going to save him in this situation? Emotion will not save him. It is emotion that has gotten him into trouble in the first place. Reason will not save him. Every time he thinks of a reason why he should not marry the girl, ten more reasons occur to him why he should. The human mind is quite subtle, and it has a marvelous ability to select only those facts we want to hear. What will save the young man in this situation? Only one thing: knowledge of what the Word of God says and what God desires. If he is to have victory, he must know God's teaching and pray along these lines: "Lord God Almighty, I certainly don't want your will in this, and I can find ten reasons why I am right and you are wrong. But I can't escape what you say. I know that you have told me not to marry an unbeliever, and for that reason alone I won't marry her." Only knowledge of the Word of God saves him.

In Matthew 5:10–12, the Lord Jesus Christ gave some instructions about persecution in which He said, "Blessed are those who are persecuted because of righteousness" and "blessed are you when people insult you, persecute you and falsely say all kinds of evil against you because of me" (vv. 10, 11). The word "blessed" means deeply happy. So he is telling those who are insulted, slandered, and persecuted for His sake to be happy. How? How are we to rejoice in persecutions? It is by knowledge of two things: that ours is "the kingdom of heaven" (v. 10) and that we have a "reward in heaven" (v. 12). Knowledge of God leads to joy in Him, and joy overcomes fear.

OUR MIGHTY GOD

This is precisely the path Habakkuk took to overcome his fears of the coming invasion. Notice what Habakkuk knew.

First, Habakkuk had knowledge of

God's mighty acts. Indeed, this whole chapter is a rehearsal of them, beginning with verse 3. These verses are a bit hard to understand. They are poetic, not written in the most obvious terms that Habakkuk could have used. It is not the way the authors of 1 and 2 Chronicles or 1 and 2 Kings would have told the story. Still, the verses are clear enough. They deal with God's defense of the Jewish people when He led them out of Egypt, through the wilderness, and into the Promised Land. Verse 3: "God came from Teman, the Holy One from Mount Paran. His glory covered the heavens and his praise filled the earth." Teman and Paran are mountain ranges in southern Israel bordering on the Sinai. So Habakkuk is saying that God came out of the Sinai, where He had met with Moses, in order to deliver the people from Egypt. Habakkuk is looking back to that great deliverance.

Verse 4 goes further: "His splendor was like the sunrise; rays flashed from his hand, where his power was hidden." This is probably speaking of the shekinah glory, the cloud by which God manifested His presence. That cloud stood between the people of Israel and the Egyptians on the night of their deliverance to give them time to cross the Red Sea, and later it led them during the years of their desert wandering.

Verse 5: "Plague went before him; pestilence followed his steps." Habakkuk is speaking of the plagues on Egypt at this point. "He stood, and shook the earth; he looked, and made the nations tremble." These sentences refer to the conquest of Canaan.

Verse 8: "Were you angry with the rivers, O LORD? Was your wrath against the streams?" This refers to the parting of the Red Sea and later the Jordan.

Verse 11: "Sun and moon stood still in the heavens at the glint of your flying arrows, at the lightning of your flashing spear." This reference is to the incident related in Joshua 10. The Jewish armies had fallen on the forces of the Amorite kings before the walls of Gibeon and had routed them. As the Amorites fled, the Lord struck many of the soldiers with large hailstones, and when Joshua prayed for the sun and moon to stand still while he and the army pursued and completely destroyed the Amorite armies, the Lord obliged by answering his prayer. The story says, "Surely the LORD was fighting for Israel" in that day (Josh. 10:14).

We acknowledge that this intervention was an extreme, supernatural event. But it is the essence of God's acts on His people's behalf. The religion of the Old and New Testaments is not a religion of ideas, essentially, though it contains many great ideas. It is essentially a religion of acts—God's mighty acts. These alone provide the kind of deliverance from fear and provision of inner moral fortitude we need in bad times.

I think here of the testimony of Joseph Ton, an exiled Romanian pastor who is director of the Romanian Missionary Society based in the United States. He became a Christian in Romania in his youth before entering college, and during his college days he grew in faith through Christian fellowship and Bible study—in spite of strenuous Communist attempts at indoctrination in the Marxist world view. During his college years he felt a call to the ministry, so he enrolled in the Baptist seminary in Bucharest for theological study after college. One day a friend gave him a book by an English-speaking, liberal theologian: *A Plain Man Looks at the Cross*. Ton knew nothing about this man, but he was delighted to have a theological book, any book. Books were scarce in his homeland. He began to read eagerly. There he found arguments demolishing the doctrines of the vicarious atonement of Jesus Christ.

The writer was calling the biblical teaching metaphors.

Ton went to his professor and asked, "Can you give me an answer to this?"

The professor said he could not. "This man is a great theologian," he said. "If he says something is so, it is so." Ton later wrote, "At that moment I saw my faith, like scaffolding in my insides, going down in pieces. Everything in me was demolished. I went to my room and said, 'It is risky to preach the gospel here. I was ready to risk my life for the truth, but for metaphors I will risk nothing.'" He left the ministry and got a job as a teacher.

Today, of course, Ton is an effective voice for the true Christian gospel, as he was for many years in Romania before his exile. I tell his story for the sake of his statement about metaphors. "For metaphors I will risk nothing," he said. He was right! Who in his right mind would risk freedom, health, and life for fantasies? But for the truth, for facts, a man can die and, what is perhaps at times even more difficult, live victoriously, even in the midst of Communist persecutions and other brutal circumstances.[1]

Christianity is fact. The first issue any inquirer needs to settle is whether it is truly fact or only fiction. Is the biblical faith only a collection of beautiful and inspiring stories? Or did God actually deliver the Jewish people from Egypt by miracles at the time of the Exodus? Did He actually bring plagues upon Egypt? Did He divide the waters of the Red Sea and later the waters of the Jordan? Did He stop the sun and moon in the days of Joshua at Gibeon? Above all, did He really send His only begotten Son, the Lord Jesus Christ, to die for the sins of His people—His death for their death—and then triumphantly rise again from the dead?

If these things are true, we have a great God in whom we can indeed rejoice. We can rejoice in even the worst of times, as Habakkuk did.

OUR FAITHFUL GOD

There is a second characteristic of God that Habakkuk reminds himself of and which he finds to be a help in his distress over the impending Babylonian invasion. It is God's faithfulness, expressed in verse 13: "You came out to deliver your people, to save your anointed one." This verse is in the train of the earlier verses that recount God's mighty acts in history, but it adds another dimension. The phrase "your anointed one" refers to one or more of the kings of Israel. Indeed, the second half of the verse and the next (v. 14) probably refer to David's victory over Goliath ("With his own spear you pierced his head when his warriors stormed out to scatter us"). But whatever the specific reference, the central point is clear. It is God's faithfulness to *His* people and *His* anointed one.

God's mighty past acts in history amply demonstrate that He is *able* to save those who look to Him in faith. But He has also *promised* to save His people and therefore *will* save them. The God who makes promises stands by His promises. The God who makes oaths keeps them.

I remind you of some of the promises the Lord Jesus Christ has given for living in hard times. Matthew 6:25–33: "Therefore I tell you, do not worry about your life, what you will eat or drink; or about your body, what you will wear. Is not life more important than food, and the body more important than clothes? Look at the birds of the air; they do not sow or reap or store away in barns, and yet your heavenly Father feeds them. Are you not much

---

[1]Joseph Ton, "The Beast and the Lamb" in *Tenth: An Evangelical Quarterly*, vol. 12, no. 4 (October 1982), pp. 2–8.

more valuable than they? . . . And why do you worry about clothes? See how the lilies of the field grow. They do not labor or spin. Yet I tell you that not even Solomon in all his splendor was dressed like one of these. If that is how God clothes the grass of the field, which is here today and tomorrow is thrown into the fire, will he not much more clothe you, O you of little faith? So do not worry, saying, 'What shall we eat?' or 'What shall we drink?' or 'What shall we wear?' For the pagans run after all these things, and your heavenly Father knows that you need them. But seek first his kingdom and his righteousness, and all these things will be given to you as well."

John 14:1–3: "Do not let your hearts be troubled. Trust in God; trust also in me. In my Father's house are many rooms; if it were not so, I would have told you. I am going there to prepare a place for you. And if I go and prepare a place for you, I will come back and take you to be with me that you also may be where I am."

John 14:25–27: "All this I have spoken while still with you. But the Counselor, the Holy Spirit, whom the Father will send in my name, will teach you all things and will remind you of everything I have said to you. Peace I leave with you; my peace I give you. I do not give to you as the world gives. Do not let your hearts be troubled and do not be afraid."

Matthew 28:18–20: "All authority in heaven and on earth has been given to me. Therefore go and make disciples of all nations, baptizing them in the name of the Father and of the Son and of the Holy Spirit, and teaching them to obey everything I have commanded you. And surely I will be with you always, to the very end of the age."

SUPPOSITIONS

The last section of this chapter contains some of the most moving verses in all the Bible. On one occasion it was used by Benjamin Franklin, who was not a Christian, to confound some of the sophisticated, cultured despisers of the Bible whom he met in Paris when he was serving as United States Plenipotentiary to that country. The skeptics were mocking him for his admiration of the Bible. So he decided to find out how well they knew the book they professed to scorn. One evening he entered their company with a manuscript that contained an ancient poem he said he had been reading. He said that he had been impressed with its stately beauty. They asked to hear it. He held it out and read this great third chapter of Habakkuk ending with:

> Though the fig tree does not bud
> and there are no grapes on the
> vines,
> though the olive crop fails
> and the fields produce no food,
> though there are no sheep in the
> pen
> and no cattle in the stalls,
> yet I will rejoice in the LORD
> I will be joyful in God my Savior.
>
> The Sovereign LORD is my strength;
> he makes my feet like the feet of
> a deer,
> he enables me to go on the
> heights (vv. 17–19).

The reading was received with exclamations of extravagant admiration. "What a magnificent piece of verse!" they cried. Where had Franklin found it? How could they get copies? They were astonished when he informed them that it was the third chapter of Habakkuk's prophecy.

What is it that makes this chapter, and particularly the final verses, so forceful? In my judgment it is the courageous way in which Habakkuk embraces all the calamities he can imagine and nevertheless triumphs over them in the knowledge and love of his Savior.

In one of his volumes on texts that made history, Frank W. Boreham tells of a conversation he once had with a parishioner named Jeanie McNab. She was a bit of a Pollyanna, and he was led to say to her one day, "But, supposing, Jeanie. . . . "

"Now don't you have anything to do with supposings," she exclaimed. "I know them all. 'Suppose I should lose my money!' 'Suppose I should lose my health!' And all the rest. When those supposings come knocking at your heart, you just slam the door, and bolt it, and don't let any of them in!"[2]

It was good advice from a worldly point of view, certainly a better procedure than worrying over a list of calamities that would probably never happen. But it was not as good as Habakkuk's procedure. When the supposings came knocking at his door Habakkuk did not slam the door and bolt it. He opened the door and cried, "Come in!"

"Suppose the fig tree does not bud?"

"Suppose there are no grapes on the vines?"

"Suppose the olive crop fails?"

"Suppose the fields produce no food?"

"Suppose there are no sheep in the pen?"

"Suppose there are no cattle in the stalls?"

"Come in, come in!" cried Habakkuk. He did not fear the supposings, because One greater than these or any other supposings was in the room. That greater One was the Lord. He was Habakkuk's own personal Savior (v. 18). He was the One who, he knew, would give him the necessary strength even in the most threatening times.

William Cowper, the English poet who suffered from acute mental distress and illness, knew this personally, for he cast Habakkuk's testimony into these great lines:

Though vine nor fig tree neither
Their wonted fruits should bear,
Though all the fields should wither,
Nor flocks nor herds be there;
Yet, God the same abiding,
His praise shall tune my voice;
For, while in him confiding,
I cannot but rejoice.

[2]F. W. Boreham, *A Handful of Stars: Texts That Have Moved Great Minds* (Philadelphia: Judson Press, 1922), pp. 140, 141.

ZEPHANIAH

14

Once More the Judgment

(Zephaniah 1:1–2:3)

The word of the LORD that came to Zephaniah son of Cushi, the son of Gedaliah, the son of Amariah, the son of Hezekiah, during the reign of Josiah son of Amon king of Judah:

> *"I will sweep away everything*
> *from the face of the earth,"*
> > *declares the LORD.*
>
> *"I will sweep away both men and animals;*
> *I will sweep away the birds of the air*
> *and the fish of the sea.*
> *The wicked will have only heaps of rubble*
> *when I cut off man from the face of the earth,"*
> > *declares the LORD.*

Of all the Minor Prophets, Zephaniah has suffered most from obscurity and from an academic "bad press." He is so obscure that he is often confused with Zechariah, whose much longer book occurs just pages later in the Bible. In the scholarly world Zephaniah is often dismissed as dull or derivative. One writer says, "With the prophet Zephaniah we meet for the first time a considerable diminution of prophetic originality."[1] Another writes, "Zephaniah can hardly be considered great as a poet. He does not rank with Isaiah, nor even with Hosea in this particular. He has no great imaginative powers; no deep insight into the human heart is reflected in his utterances; nor any keen sensitiveness to the beauties of nature. His harp is not attuned to the finer harmonies of life like that of Jeremiah."[2]

Comments like this are probably unfair. It is true that Zephaniah depends on some of the earlier writings and specifically alludes to a number of them. The call for silence before the sovereign Lord in 1:7 reminds the reader of Habakkuk 2:20. The statement that the Lord had prepared a sacrifice to be made up of His own people, which occurs in the second half of the same verse, seems drawn from Isaiah 13:3 and 34:6. Most notable are the descriptions of the coming day of the Lord in Zephaniah 1:14–18. They echo the

---

[1]Ewald, quoted by F. W. Farrar, *The Minor Prophets* (New York: Anson D. F. Randolph, n.d.), p. 155.

[2]J. M. Powis Smith in Smith, Ward, and Brewer, *A Critical and Exegetical Commentary on Micah, Zephaniah, Nahum, Habakkuk, Obadiah and Joel* (Edinburgh: T. & T. Clark, 1911), p. 176.

language of Joel and Amos. ("That day will be a day of wrath, a day of distress and anguish, a day of trouble and gloom, a day of clouds and blackness. . . ." See Joel 2:1, 2 and Amos 5:18–20.) The opening verses seem reminiscent of the account of the Flood. But this is not evidence of Zephaniah's weakness as a poet or prophet. Rather, it is a deliberate device of one whose work stands as a summation and recapitulation of the pre-exile prophecy.

This is the key to understanding Zephaniah: to see that his book is a summary of the prophets who have preceded him. His position in the corpus of the Minor Prophets may be meant to indicate this. The Minor Prophets belong to two main divisions: (1) the first nine, ending with Zephaniah, who prophesied before the exile to Babylon, and (2) the last three, who prophesied after the return of the Jews to Judah. Habakkuk and Zephaniah were the latest of the first group. Habakkuk actually wrote later than Zephaniah, so the fact that Zephaniah is put last in the grouping of the first nine prophets probably indicates that he is to be understood as summarizing them.

Carl Friedrich Keil puts it well: "There are many respects in which Zephaniah links his prophecy to those of the earlier prophets, both in subject matter and expression; not, however, by resuming those prophecies of theirs which had not been fulfilled or were not exhausted during the period of the Assyrian judgment upon the nations, and announcing a fresh and more perfect fulfillment of them by the Chaldeans, but by reproducing in a compendious form the fundamental thoughts of judgment and salvation which are common to all the prophets, that his contemporaries may lay them to heart."[3]

THE MAN AND HIS TIMES

Of Zephaniah himself we know virtually nothing, except what he tells us in the first verse, namely, that he was the son of Cushi who was the son of Gedaliah who was the son of Amariah who was the son of Hezekiah. This is a rare instance of an introductory genealogy being pushed back four rather than merely three generations. This has led some to read special significance into the inclusion of the fourth name. Since Hezekiah was an earlier king of Judah it is assumed by such people that King Hezekiah is meant and that this is Zephaniah's way of identifying himself as a member of the royal family and hence as being among the aristocracy. This is possible, of course. But Hezekiah was a common name, and it is a puzzle why, if King Hezekiah is meant, he is not identified as king specifically, especially since Amon is identified as "king of Judah" just a few words later. All we can say is that we really do not know anything for sure about Zephaniah.

He does tell us when he prophesied. It was "during the reign of Josiah," the king who had assumed the throne in 639 B.C. at the age of eight and who died in battle against Pharaoh Neco of Egypt after a thirty-year period.

We can narrow the dates even further. In Zephaniah 2:13 the destruction of Nineveh is prophesied (in terms similar to those used by Nahum). Nineveh fell in 612 B.C., so the work of Zephaniah which prophesies its fall must be before this date. To go even further, the great revival which took place during Josiah's reign began when the king was eighteen, which was the year 629 B.C. Since nothing in Zephaniah indicates an awareness of that revival, it is reasonable to think that the book was written in those early years, that is,

[3]C. F. Keil and F. Delitzsch, *Biblical Commentary on the Old Testament: The Twelve Minor Prophets*, vol. 2 (Grand Rapids: Eerdmans, 1949), pp. 123, 124.

between 639 and 629 B.C. If that is the case, it may be that this book, so despised by some of its critics, was a factor in that important though short-lived revival.

It would be good if it could have that effect in our time also. The Day of the Lord is coming, and the message "Seek the LORD, . . . seek righteousness, seek humility; perhaps you will be sheltered on the day of the LORD's anger" is one we also need to take to heart.

WARNING OF JUDGMENT

Zephaniah falls into a number of clearly defined parts: (1) an opening prophecy focusing on the coming Day of the Lord (1:2–2:3), (2) a series of judgments against the surrounding gentile nations, ending with an oracle against Jerusalem (2:4–3:8), and (3) a closing anticipation of a bright new day of God's blessing (3:9–20). The first of these sections is a classic little prophecy, which follows the general pattern so common in the prophets: (1) an announcement of God's wrath, (2) an explanation for God's anger, (3) a prophecy of the coming destruction, and (4) a call to repentance, that the judgment might be averted and the people spared.

The significant thing about this opening announcement of God's wrath is that its extreme and exaggerated language seems to go beyond any mere reference to the coming Babylonian invasion. Zephaniah quotes God as saying, "I will sweep away everything from the face of the earth" (v. 2). And again, "I will sweep away both men and animals; I will sweep away the birds of the air and the fish of the sea. The wicked will have only heaps of rubble when I cut off man from the face of the earth" (v. 3). This language immediately reminds one of God's warnings to Noah of the coming world flood: "I will wipe mankind, whom I have created, from the face of the

earth—men and animals, and creatures that move along the ground, and birds of the air" (Gen. 6:7; cf. 7:4, 17–23). But in Zephaniah the words are even stronger than in Genesis. Here even the fish are included, and there is no reference to survivors, as was the case with God's words to Noah and his family.

Does this mean that Zephaniah is not thinking of the Babylonian invasion? Not necessarily. For one thing, the prophet indicates that he is using hyperbole, for the same sentence that speaks of cutting man off from the face of the earth also says that "the wicked will have only heaps of rubble." If the wicked are present to possess the heaps of rubble, they at least will not be obliterated by what is coming. Besides, the rest of the prophecy shows that Zephaniah is actually thinking of specific historical judgments upon certain specific cities and countries, including Jerusalem. This is precisely what occurred.

At the same time, the extreme language of these opening verses is not without purpose in warning the Jews of his day as well as all subsequent readers of the book that a greater, final judgment is still pending. This is where Zephaniah speaks to us. God is still the righteous Judge of the universe, and He will no more tolerate sin in us than was the case with His chosen people in Old Testament times. If we do not become new creatures through faith in Jesus Christ, we will be swept away with all the ungodly at the final judgment.

CORRUPTION MOST FOUL

The second part of this classic opening prophecy (in Zeph. 1:2–2:3) is an explanation of why the wrath of God is coming against the nations. It is an important part, perhaps the most important part of what the prophet has to say—for the simple reason that people are so ready to protest their innocence and proclaim that any judgment of God, however mild, is unjust.

Early in this century there was a well-known gangster in New York City named Two-Gun Crowley. He killed without any apparent qualms. One day when he was in a car by the side of the road a policeman walked up to him and asked to see his license. Instead of showing it to the policeman, Crowley pulled out a gun and shot him. Then he leaped from the car and fired five more shots into the officer's body. Crowley was a difficult man to be around. At length he was captured in his girl friend's apartment in a fashionable part of the city and was sent to Sing Sing Prison. What do you suppose a man like this thought about himself? Surely he must have known what he was like! He must have thought, "I am a bad man; I kill people." This was not the case. We know what Crowley thought of himself because of a note he wrote while shooting it out with the police at the time of his capture: "Under my coat is a weary heart, but a kind one—one that would do nobody any harm."

Another man once said, "I have spent the best years of my life giving people the lighter pleasures, and all I get is abuse, the existence of a hunted man." The speaker was Al Capone, one of the most vicious gangsters of the Chicago gangland era.

The situation was no different in Zephaniah's time. His people were quick to proclaim their innocence whenever any mention was made of God's judgment. Consequently, Zephaniah now gives a capsule version of the reasons for it. He talks of four classes of people: priests, princes, merchants, and the masses. In terms of the nation's life, he speaks of religious activity, social customs, commerce, and the common life of those who tried to remain indifferent to what was happening.

1. *Religion.* Zephaniah begins his de-nunciation of the religious activities of the people by a reference to "idolatrous priests" (v. 4), but it is soon evident that he has both priests and people in mind. He writes:

> I will cut off from this place every
> remnant of Baal,
>   the names of the pagan and the
>   idolatrous priests—
> those who bow down on the
> housetops
>   to worship the starry host,
> those who bow down and swear by
> the LORD
>   and who also swear by Molech,
> those who turn back from following
> the LORD
>   and neither seek the LORD nor
>   inquire of him (vv. 4–6).

Some scholars read into "every remnant of Baal" and "idolatrous priests" the idea that Josiah's reform was already underway and that the Book of Zephaniah must therefore be dated rather late. But this is not what is involved here. This is a picture of a very corrupt period in the religious life of the people. Indeed, there are no true priests at all. There are men who are called priests, but they are idolatrous. That is, they are actually worshiping false gods and are therefore rightly placed in the category of "pagan" priests. In addition to these, there are many who mix worship of Jehovah with worship of Molech and other false gods and others who have nothing to do with Jehovah either in word or deed.

There are three categories of religious offenses in the verse just quoted: (1) idolaters, who worship false gods regardless of the name they use in worshiping them, (2) adulterers, who worship the true God but other false gods too, and (3) apostates, who have fallen away from worshiping God entirely. All are condemned. The Lord makes no difference among these offenses.

I think of a verse from an Irish folk song popularized by the Clancey brothers: "There was an old woman in Wexford, in Wexford town did dwell; she loved her husband dearly, but another man twice as well." This is the case of many in their so-called worship of God. They profess to love Jesus. Indeed, they profess their love loudly. But they love others or other things more. They love their sexual sins more than they love Jesus. They love their money more than they love Jesus. They love their reputation with the beautiful people too much to attempt to tell them about the Savior. Is it possible to love the Lord like that? It is not! In God's opinion, such spiritual adultery is as offensive as outright idolatry or indifference. The utter apostate is no worse than the one who trifles thus with the divine affection.

Jesus said that the first and greatest commandment was: "Love the Lord your God with all your heart and with all your soul and with all your mind" (Matt. 22:37; cf. Deut. 6:5). The Ten Commandments say, "You shall have no other gods before me" (Exod. 20:3). Anything less than this is an offense against God and merits judgment.

2. *Social customs.* The second reason given for the wrath of God in Zephaniah 1:4–13 is Judah's social customs or practices. The text says:

On the day of the LORD's sacrifice
  I will punish the princes
  and the king's sons
and all those clad
  in foreign clothes.
On that day I will punish
  all who avoid stepping on the
    threshold,
who fill the temple of their gods
  with violence and deceit (vv.
    8, 9).

It is not so easy to know what the references to being "clad in foreign clothes" or avoiding "stepping on the threshold" refer to, and scholars are divided. Some think that foreign clothes were vestments worn by the idolaters in their worship. Some refer to the prohibition in Deuteronomy 22:5, 11 against men wearing women's clothes and vice versa. Still others go back to Amos and think of these as clothes taken from the poor as pledges (Amos 2:8). Each of these explanations has appeal because of relating it to some other portion of Scripture, but none explains the really unique element in the phrase, namely, that the clothes are "foreign." Probably it is merely an unparalleled reference to a practice which had grown up unexpectedly at this time, namely, of imitating other nations in their dress. The problem would be as Laetsch states it: "The Jews were unwilling to be recognized by their manner of dress as the people of Jehovah. . . . As the people of Judah had adopted the idols of the surrounding nations largely in the hope of gaining political or business advantages, so they adopted also their dress and were eager to parade the latest fashions from the millinery and tailor shops of Babylon, Nineveh, Memphis."[4]

I wonder what Zephaniah would say of our customs. We imitate the world in so many ways. Could it be that we do not want to be identified too closely as God's people? Luther saw this among the Germans of his day and rightly identified it as proof of "great levity and of inconsistent minds."[5]

The second phrase, "avoid stepping on [or leaping over] the threshold," is also problematic. In 1 Samuel 5:5 there is a reference to this practice among the pagan priests of Dagon, and some have

---

[4] Theo. Laetsch, *Bible Commentary: The Minor Prophets* (Saint Louis: Concordia, 1956), p. 360.

[5] Martin Luther, *Luther's Works,* vol. 18, *Lectures on the Minor Prophets: I* (Saint Louis: Concordia, 1975), p. 327. Luther calls it "monkeys see, monkeys do."

supposed that the worship of Dagon was therefore practiced in Judah, though there is no real evidence for it. Others have linked it to the following lines in the sense of leaping over the threshold of houses in a sudden rush to plunder them; but the reference is to "the temple of their gods," not houses. Probably this is just a silly foreign custom to be placed in the same category as wearing foreign clothes. At the best it was an indication of immaturity. At the worse it was spiritually treasonous.

3. *Commerce.* The third reason for God's coming judgment is not at all difficult to understand. It concerns the merchants, and although it does not say so explicity, it undoubtedly concerns the injustices and corruption that were then current in the business world (cf. Amos 5:11, 8:3–6; Micah 2:1, 2, 8, 9; 6:10–12). The rich were stripping the poor of possessions, even necessities, and they were aided in this by a corrupt political system and corrupt courts. Zephaniah says, "Wail, you who live in the market district; all your merchants will be wiped out, all who trade with silver will be ruined" (v. 11).

4. *The common life of the indifferent.* When hearing a series of denunciations like this it is easy to excuse oneself, saying, "I am not doing any of those things, and I am not to blame for those who do. I'm just going to keep quiet and go on doing my own thing." In Zephaniah's opinion such people are not without guilt; and, however many they may be, the Lord is going to search them out and punish them also.

Zephaniah's reference to the complacent reminds one of Amos where a special judgment is spoken against those who are "complacent in Zion" (Amos 6:1). Surrounded by a corruption so great that it is bringing on the judgment of the almighty God, they are nevertheless quite unconcerned. According to Amos, they are unconcerned for several reasons. Some are presumptuous; they argue that they are God's people, that Jerusalem is God's city, and that God will therefore preserve both them and the city at all costs. Some are procrastinators; they recognize the evil, but for personal convenience's sake they put off doing anything about it. Some are self-indulgent; they may not be directly responsible for the corruption of their society, but they profit from it all the same and do not want anything to disturb their creature comforts. Still others are indifferent to what is happening.

Zephaniah may have noted these types of complacency, but they are not the kind he refers to in his prophecy. The complacency he refers to is spiritual. It is the kind that discounts God, saying, "The LORD will do nothing, either good or bad" (v. 12). It is the worst kind of all.

Unfortunately, this kind of complacency is widespread in our society today. Generally our society does not presume on God's protection, though some disobedient Christians do. It discounts God entirely. Live for today, it says. There is no day of reckoning.

Do you think this way? Are you continuing in sin because you suppose that there is no God or that, if there is one, He will do nothing? This is not the teaching of the Bible or the lesson of history. After World War II the English historian Herbert Butterfield wrote of the judgments of God in his day, concluding that there is a moral order in the universe and that there is a day of reckoning. He saw judgments in the fall of Rome, the horrors of the French Revolution and, of course, the destruction of Nazi Germany. He said, "There is a judgment embedded in the fabric of history."[6] That is what the Bible says too, though it goes on to argue from historical to individual judgments. People may scoff at such things, but if they do, it is only because they are willfully ignorant of them.

The apostle Peter reminds such persons both of the earlier examples of God's judgment and of the warnings of a day of judgment upon all men yet to come, concluding: "Since everything will be destroyed in this way, what kind of people ought you to be? You ought to live holy and godly lives as you look forward to the day of God and speed its coming" (2 Peter 3:11, 12).

DIES IRAE

In my own conclusion to this section of Zephaniah, I have anticipated the prophet's next point. For, having shown that the wrath of God is justified, Zephaniah next prophesies the day of the outpouring of that wrath. The section begins:

The great day of the LORD is near—
near and coming quickly (v. 14).

In verse 15 Zephaniah begins to describe the day of wrath, using words which, taken from the Latin text of the Old Testament, form the basis of the hymn commonly called the *Dies Irae.* The hymn is attributed to Thomas de Celano, an assistant to Francis of Assisi, and it has been translated into more languages than any other hymn. Here, in just two verses, Zephaniah crowds together a host of powerful words designed to impress his readers with the horrors of that judgment. It will be a day of "wrath," of overflowing, crushing wrath (cf. v. 18). It will be a day of "distress and anguish," of "trouble and ruin." Like Amos before him, Zephaniah describes the judgment as

"a day of darkness and gloom, a day of clouds and bitterness." Like Joel, he describes it as "a day of trumpet and battle cry against the fortified cities and against the corner towers." The end is that "the whole world will be consumed" and that God "will make a sudden end of all who live in the earth" (v. 19).

It is an interesting feature of this description that Zephaniah mingles words that seem to refer to an immediate historical catastrophe ("shouting of the warrior . . . a day of trumpet and battle cry against the fortified cities and against the corner towers") with words that seem to refer to a final, all-inclusive world judgment ("the whole world will be consumed . . . a sudden end of all who live in the earth"). This is deliberate, for it carries us back to the opening verses of the chapter with their similar references. In those verses "the wicked" will remain to enjoy their "heaps of rubble." Yet the Lord is going to "cut off man from the face of the earth" (v. 3).

This means that there was to be an immediate outpouring of wrath in the coming Babylonian invasion, but there was also to be a final judgment of all men and women of which the earlier judgment was to be merely a type and warning. This brings the prophecy home to us. As Judah was judged, so will we be judged. As they were warned, so are we.

SEEK GOD AND LIVE

This is the point at which the classic prophecy of Zephaniah 1:2–2:3 ends: with an appeal to the humble of the land to seek God. A century earlier, when Amos was crying out to the people of Israel to turn from their wicked ways, the prophet said, "Seek the LORD and live, or he will sweep

---

[6]H. Butterfield, *Christianity and History* (New York: Scribner, 1949), p. 59. See the chapter on "Judgment in History," pp. 48–67.

through the house of Joseph like a fire" (Amos 5:6). That was a direct and unqualified promise. If the people would seek God, then the fire of judgment would not come and they would live. In Zephaniah, one hundred years later, the promise is not so unqualified. The people are to "seek the LORD, . . . righteousness, . . . humility." But the promise is only, "*Perhaps* you will be sheltered on the day of the LORD's anger" (Zeph. 2:3). In the case of God's destruction of Judah and Jerusalem by means of the Babylonians there was no guarantee that even the righteous would be kept from the calamity.

How much greater is the promise to those of us who seek God's face today! We may have difficulties in life, but we are assured of God's favor in the day of wrath—if we have truly sought Him and do what He commands. Have we? Have you sought God and His right-eousness? Are you among the humble of the land?

You say, "But what does it mean to seek God?" It means to seek Him where alone He can be found, namely, in the person of the Lord Jesus Christ, who was crucified for your sin, buried, and raised again from the dead for your justification. You say, "What does it mean to do what God commands?" Jesus answered that question for the people of His day. They had asked, "What must we do to do the works God requires?" Jesus answered, "The work of God is this: to believe in the one he has sent" (John 6:28, 29). The person who does that has not merely sought the Lord. He has found Him, and he is already on the way to living that life of practical obedience, righteousness, and humility, which is pleasing both to others and God.

15

God of the Nations

(Zephaniah 2:4–3:8)

Gaza will be abandoned
and Ashkelon left in ruins.
At midday Ashdod will be emptied
and Ekron uprooted. . . .

"I have heard the insults of Moab
and the taunts of the Ammonites,
who insulted my people
and made threats against their land.
Therefore, as surely as I live,"
declares the LORD Almighty, the God of Israel,
"surely Moab will become like Sodom,
the Ammonites like Gomorrah. . . .

"You too, O Cushites,
will be slain by my sword."

He will stretch out his hand against the north
and destroy Assyria,
leaving Nineveh utterly desolate
and dry as the desert. . . .

Woe to the city of oppressors,
rebellious and defiled!
She obeys no one,
she accepts no correction.
She does not trust in the LORD,
she does not draw near to her God.

The second part of Zephaniah (Zeph. 2:4–3:8) summarizes a second major theme of the Minor Prophets, just as the first section of Zephaniah summarized their first and central message. The first section is a warning to Judah of God's judgment, coupled with a call to repentance. The second section contains an announcement of God's rule over the entire world and a warning that all nations are answerable to Him.

This truth runs counter to every

secular tendency. One tendency in our day is toward pluralism, even in the churches. Today's pluralism is not merely the recognition that people are different, have different religions, and must be given the right to live and worship differently if they so choose. It is the erroneous belief that reality itself is pluralistic and that therefore there can be no one true God or true religion. Edward Gibbon, the author of *Decline and Fall of the Roman Empire*, wrote that in the days of the declining empire all religions were regarded by the people as equally true, by the philosophers as equally false, and by the magistrates as equally useful. In our irrational day many persons could embrace all three, the bottom line being that no one religion can have a claim on everybody.

A second tendency of our age is toward compartmentalism. This is the conviction that various areas of life need to be kept in separate places and that one area not only need not but should not have bearing on another. The religious application of this principle is to put faith on a reservation. A person can believe whatever he wants to believe or do there—out of sight, where he will cause no trouble. But he must not bring his conviction off the reservation into the "real" world of the schools, commerce, or national and international politics.

The prophets of Israel were utterly opposed to these outlooks. So opposed were they that they could not even conceive of a fragmented world where the claims of religion would have no bearing upon anything. Quite the contrary! The God of the prophets is the God of the entire universe, and this makes Him God of all life and all people, whether this is acknowledged by the individuals involved or not. The prophets took no cognizance of whether an individual was or was not religiously inclined. They did not care what gods or goddesses another nation worshiped. They were convinced of the truth that there is only one God, the God of Israel, who is also the God of the Bible, and that all people must and will render account to Him.

We see a true universalism in the prophets. A prophet like Joel, though writing to Judah on the occasion of a great natural disaster, nevertheless speaks of a gathering of all nations to judgment:

> "Let the nations be roused;
>   let them advance into the Valley
>   of Jehoshaphat,
> for there I will sit
>   to judge the nations on every
>   side" (Joel 3:12).

Obadiah is written against Edom. Nahum condemns Nineveh. Amos throws the widest net of all, for he cries out against six of the surrounding gentile nations—Syria, Philistia, Tyre, Edom, Ammon, and Moab—before turning his attention to the two Jewish states.

LAND OF THE PHILISTINES

In the structure of his writing Zephaniah comes closest to Amos and may actually be imitating his approach. As we noted, Amos wrote against Syria, Philistia, Tyre, Edom, Ammon, and Moab, but in a way which gradually brought the accusations he was making to bear most forcefully against his own people. Syria, the first nation mentioned, was located to the northeast of Israel. Philistia, the second, was to the southwest, that is, directly opposite Syria. Tyre was to the northwest. Edom was southeast. Ammon and Moab complete the list of the immediately surrounding nations by filling in the gap between Syria and Edom on the east. After condemning these surrounding nations, which would no doubt have delighted his Jewish listeners, Amos denounced the sins of Judah (to the south) and Israel (which he was primarily addressing).

Zephaniah follows this pattern with slight changes in nations that reflect the altered historical circumstances of his day. He begins with Philistia, which he must have been thinking of as lying largely to the west of Judah. He continues with Moab and Ammon taken together, lying to the east. Third, he looks to the far south in a short word against Ethiopia. Fourth, he utters a judgment against Assyria, which although it lay to the northeast of Judah, always invaded from the north. Finally, Zephaniah turns to the "city of oppressors," Jerusalem and the country it controlled.

Philistia was the lowland area along the Mediterranean coast dominated by the five "chief cities" of Gaza, Ashkelon, Ekron, Ashdod, and Gath. The early history of the people is unknown, but they were already established on the seacoast by the time of Abraham—that is, about 2000 B.C. (Gen. 21:32; 26:1). They were known for their seagoing trade and commerce.

It is an interesting feature of Zephaniah's prophecy that he does not say why the judgment of God is to fall on these people. Perhaps this is because Amos had already made the case well. Amos had condemned Philistia, "because she took captive whole communities and sold them to Edom" (Amos 1:6). This is a condemnation of slavery, but not necessarily of slavery in and of itself. It is rather a matter of how the Philistines pursued it. The custom of the times allowed for soldiers who had been taken in battle to be sold as slaves, but the fault of the Philistines was that they had used their military supremacy to enslave whole populations—soldiers and civilians, men and women, adults and children—for commercial profit. The Philistines did not need more slaves. They merely sold the captured peoples to Edom for more money.

Zephaniah does not mention this. He assumes it, or assumes that the other offenses of the Philistines (Amos speaks of "three sins" and "four") were well known. What he does say is that the word of the Lord was against Philistia and that a destruction from God was coming, after which none would be left.

MOAB AND AMMON

Zephaniah next takes up the case of Moab and Ammon (vv. 8–11). They are taken together, in part because of their proximity to each other east of Jerusalem and in part because of their common origin and history. Their origins go back to the days of Lot and Abraham. After the destruction of Sodom and Gomorrah, Lot and his two daughters settled in the mountains where the unmarried daughters conceived the idea of having children by their father. They got him drunk and then had sexual relations with him. Two sons were born of this incest, one to the older daughter and one to the younger. The older daughter called her son Moab, which means "from Father"—a most brazen name. The second called her son Ben-Ammi, which means "son of my people." He gave his name to the Ammonites.

With this beginning, it is not surprising that the Moabites and Ammonites became a great problem for the Jews in later years. The relationship of the descendants of Abraham to the descendants of Lot was not all bad. Ruth was a Moabitess. She followed Naomi to Bethlehem and then married Boaz, becoming an ancestor of King David and of the Lord Jesus Christ. Namah was an Ammonite who became one of Solomon's wives. She was the mother of King Solomon. Still, when the people of Israel were traveling from Egypt to Canaan through the desert, the Moabites opposed their march, and Balak, the king of Moab, tried to bribe the prophet Balaam to curse the people (Num. 22–24). In later years there were frequent wars between Israel and these brother nations.

Amos condemns Ammon and Moab for cruelty. Ammon "ripped open the pregnant women of Gilead in order to extend his [the country's] borders" (Amos 1:13). Moab "burned . . . the bones of Edom's king" (Amos 2:1). These were crimes against the helpless. Moreover, they were crimes against both the future and the past. Ammon killed the pregnant women of Gilead to eliminate unborn future generations, thus making the task of assimilating Gilead easier. Moab burned the bones of the king of Edom to insult one of the nation's heroes and its history.

Zephaniah does not mention these offenses. But unlike his handling of Philistia, where he does not mention any specific crimes, in this case he focuses on the taunts of the Moabites and Ammonites against the Jewish people and traces this to the base sin of pride:

> This is what they will get in return
>   for their pride,
>   for insulting and mocking the
>   people of the LORD Almighty
>   (v. 10).

So long as verse 9 stands in Zephaniah's second chapter it will never be entirely correct to accuse the prophet of lacking all poetic imagination or originality. This verse speaks of the coming judgment of God on the two eastern nations, saying that they will be made like Sodom and Gomorrah—"a place of weeds and salt pits, a wasteland forever." When it is remembered that the births of the two sons, Moab and Ben-Ammi, were connected historically with the destruction of the cities of the plains—when God "rained down burning sulfur on Sodom and Gomorrah" and "overthrew those cities and the entire plain, including all those living in the cities—and also the vegetation in the land" (Gen. 19:24, 25)—it is appro-

priate that the destroyed cities should be mentioned again in this judgment. Moab and Ammon emerged out of destruction and would return to it. For trying to destroy others their own land would be devastated.

ETHIOPIA AND ASSYRIA

The Cush of Zephaniah 2:12 is Ethiopia; but it does not get much mention, only the passing, "You too, O Cushites, will be slain by my sword." Cush was one of the sons of Ham, the son of Noah, and is therefore mentioned several times in the genealogies of Genesis 10 (vv. 6–8) and 1 Chronicles 1 (vv. 8–10). But aside from that there are few additional references. A certain "land of Cush" is mentioned in Genesis 2:13. Psalm 68:31 speaks briefly of a day when "Cush will submit herself to God." The only extensive passage is Isaiah 18, which pronounces a "woe" against Cush without giving much more reason for it than Zephaniah does. Isaiah notes only that the people of Cush were aggressive and greatly feared.

In speaking of Ethiopia, Zephaniah may have a particular offense in mind. On the other hand, he may be citing the most distant known nation to the south and intimating that the judgments of God are going to extend over the entire earth.

Assyria was a nation somewhat closer at hand and certainly the major threat to Judah at this time. Nineveh, the capital city of Assyria, was destroyed by the combined forces of the Babylonians and Scythians in 612 B.C. So it was to Babylon rather than to the armies of Nineveh that Jerusalem finally fell in 587 B.C. But at this time (probably between 639 and 629 B.C.) Nineveh was still strong, and the judgment pronounced against her by Zephaniah (and Micah before him) must have seemed an exceedingly remote possibility. The city was the world's largest. It had an inner city and an outer city, and these were probably augmented greatly by suburban development. The inner city was surrounded by a wall eight miles in circumference. It was 100 feet high and was so wide that three chariots could have raced around it abreast. It had twelve hundred towers and fourteen gates. Another mighty wall surrounded most of the outer city. At the heart of the city was King Sennacherib's "Palace with No Rival." Lions of bronze and bulls of white marble guarded it. Its great hall measured 150 by 40 feet. Nearby was a forty-six-acre armory where the king kept his chariots, armor, horses, and other military equipment. Nineveh was an awesome and seemingly impregnable metropolis. Yet it was overthrown suddenly and was left utterly desolate, as Zephaniah said.[1]

In Nahum, which is written against the sins of Nineveh exclusively, the capital is condemned for its idolatry (1:14), violence (3:1–3), and sorceries (3:4). Zephaniah blames it for being "carefree," for saying, "I am, and there is none besides me" (2:15). This latter boast is the theme song of our secular, self-satisfied age. We cry, "I am the master of my soul; I am the captain of my fate." We boast that we do not need God. We do not need anybody. How foolish! It is a lesson of history that those who exalt themselves are brought low (Isa. 14:12–15).

JERUSALEM

This second section of Zephaniah ends with a strong word against Judah. It makes us sad when we think of the company into which those who were called to be the "people of God" had fallen.

There was a farmer who used to go out in his field with a shotgun and shoot crows. He had a pet parrot, but he kept it in the house because whenever it got out it used to fly with the crows and he was afraid that one day it might get hurt. On one occasion he shot at some crows. A number fell, and when he walked forward to see how many he had hit, he found his parrot, which must have gotten out of the house without his being aware of it. The bird was fatally wounded but still alive. He talked to it sadly. "What bad company you got into, Polly. Whatever brought you to this sad state?"

The parrot answered, "Bad company! Bad company!"

It was the same with Judah. As Zephaniah said in chapter 1, the people of Judah had turned from the Lord to follow the pagan gods of their gentile neighbors. They had even adopted their neighbors' foreign clothes and foolish superstitions. Inevitably, they were also in their neighbors' company when judgment was meted out.

The indictment is an old story by now. Verse 2 lists four faults of God's people: (1) they obeyed no one, certainly not God; (2) because they obeyed no one, they certainly did not accept correction; (3) they did not trust God; and (4) naturally they did not draw close to the God they distrusted. As God's people they should have done precisely the opposite, but they were as vain as Moab and Ammon, and as arrogant as Nineveh. Verses 3 and 4 carry the indictment further, implicating the leaders. Jerusalem's *officials* are condemned as "roaring lions." Her *rulers* are described as "evening wolves." The *prophets* are "arrogant" and "treacherous." The *priests* "profane the sanctuary and do violence to the law." What can be done with a people like this? The Lord has done no wrong (v. 5). He even warns of judgment,

---

[1] There is a much fuller discussion of Nineveh, its history, and its fall in the chapters on Nahum, pp. 57–72.

reminding Judah of other peoples He has destroyed (v. 6). Judah has even seen God's judgment fall on Israel to the north, and still it persists in its ways.

What more could God do? There was nothing left to do. "Therefore," says God,

> "I have decided to assemble the
>   nations,
>   to gather the kingdoms
> and to pour out my wrath on
>   them—
>   all my fierce anger.
> The whole world will be consumed
>   by the fire of my jealous anger"
>   (v. 8).

We cannot miss seeing that this is the case with countless millions in our day. On one occasion the Lord Jesus Christ told the story of a landowner who planted a vineyard and rented it to tenant farmers. He went away, but when harvest time came he sent servants to collect his fruit. The tenants seized the servants, beating one, killing another, and stoning a third. He sent more servants, and the tenants did the same to them. At last the owner sent his son, saying, "They will respect my son." But they did not. Instead, they killed the son, thinking that they would now seize the inheritance. As the Lord finished the story He asked, "Therefore, when the owner of the vineyard comes, what will he do to those tenants?" (Matt. 21:33–40).

His hearers replied properly, "He will bring those wretches to a wretched end" (v. 41).

The story presents no mystery. The owner is God. The servants are the prophets. Those who beat and killed them are the leaders of Judaism. The son is Jesus. In fact, so clear is the story that those who heard Jesus tell it immediately perceived that He was speaking about them and soon set about doing the very thing Jesus was foretelling; that is, they began to look for a way to arrest Him and have Him crucified.

In that day Jesus had not yet been killed. But we stand on the far side of His cross, and when God asks today, as He does, "What more can I do? I have sent my Son, and they have killed even Him," there is far more cause for His judgment on us than there was for Judah. You have heard the gospel. You know Christ's teaching and have been told of His life and death for sinners. If with all that you still will not turn back from your own way and seek the Lord, what more can be done? Must judgment not fall on you just as surely and fiercely as it fell on the inhabitants of Jerusalem?

Fortunately, the patience of God is long. His grace is great. You can still come to Him while His wrath tarries.

16

New Day Dawning

(Zephaniah 3:9–20)

Sing, O Daughter of Zion;
shout aloud, O Israel!
Be glad and rejoice with all your heart,
O Daughter of Jerusalem!
The LORD has taken away your punishment,
he has turned back your enemy.
The LORD, the King of Israel, is with you;
never again will you fear any harm.
On that day they will say to Jerusalem,
"Do not fear, O Zion;
do not let your hands hang limp.
The LORD your God is with you,
he is mighty to save.
He will take great delight in you,
he will quiet you with his love,
he will rejoice over you with singing."

I do not know if your experience in studying the Minor Prophets has been the same as mine, but I suspect it has, at least in this respect: the prophets' reiterated message of coming judgment is oppressive, so that any serious attempt to understand and apply it often leaves a person depressed. I have felt this particularly in my study of Joel, Amos, Obadiah, Micah, and Nahum. I feel it also in the greater part of the Book of Zephaniah.

But I have had this experience, too. I have noticed that no matter how depressing the message of judgment in the Minor Prophets becomes, it is never the final word of God to God's people. Usually even the judgments themselves offer some hope. They threaten destruction only if people will not repent, though expectation of that repentance becomes less and less as the history of the period develops. But more than that, after even the worst of these judgments there is always some word of ultimate and unqualified blessing. Amos is a prime example. The message of judgment is so pervasive in Amos that some scholars find the last five verses, which speak of a future hope, too out of character for Amos to have written.[1] Yet the words are there. There

---

[1]See, for example, James Luther Mays, *Amos: A Commentary* (Philadelphia: Westminster, 1976),p. 165.

is no manuscript evidence to suggest a different hand or later addition. And the book does end: " 'I will plant Israel in their own land, never again to be uprooted from the land I have given them,' says the LORD your God" (Amos 9:15).

The Bible as a whole is like that too. Many of its books end depressingly. Genesis ends, "So Joseph died at the age of a hundred and ten. And after they embalmed him, he was placed in a coffin in Egypt" (Gen. 50:26). The Old Testament concludes with the words: ". . . or else I will come and strike the land with a curse" (Mal. 4:6). But these are not the ultimate words. They are only the penultimate words. The Bible as a whole ends by saying:

He who testifies to these things says, "Yes, I am coming soon."
Amen. Come, Lord Jesus.
The grace of the Lord Jesus be with God's people. Amen (Rev. 22:20–21).

If this book were only a human book, it would never end this way. Or if it did, its note of optimism would ring false. Nothing in life encourages us to think that all will turn out well in the end and that the judgments of history will not be the final word. But this is not a human book. Consequently, the promise of a new day of blessing rings true and is believable for the simple reason that the sovereign and gracious God says it.

What a joy that is! Sin will not have the final word. Evil will not triumph. The Devil will be judged. It is an encouraging word for our depressed and despairing civilization.

GOD'S NEW DAY

In Zephaniah the encouragement comes in the last twelve verses (3:9–20), which is what we should expect if Zephaniah is a summation of the pre-exilic prophets. His first section conveyed the prophet's basic message:

God's gathering wrath and the threat of judgment, coupled with a call to repentance. His second section carried this same theme to the surrounding nations: God is not the God of Israel or Judah only but of all people. His third and last section shows that although the judgment of God will fall on Judah, this will not be the last word. It will be a prelude to a regathering and blessing of God's people.

The text says:

"Then will I purify the lips of the peoples,
    that all of them may call on the name of the LORD
    and serve him shoulder to shoulder.
From beyond the rivers of Cush
    my worshipers, my scattered people,
    will bring me offerings.
On that day you will not be put to shame
    for all the wrongs you have done to me,
because I will remove from this city those who rejoice in their pride.
Never again will you be haughty on my holy hill.
But I will leave within you the meek and humble,
    who trust in the name of the LORD.
The remnant of Israel will do no wrong;
    they will speak no lies,
    nor will deceit be found in their mouths.
They will eat and lie down
    and no one will make them afraid" (vv. 9–13).

This promise probably relates to a literal regathering of the people in their own land, as the ending verses of Amos also do. But like the opening sections of Zephaniah, which refer to a limited historical judgment upon Judah as well as to a universal eschatological judgment upon all persons, this text too undoubtedly has a double meaning. On the one hand, there is the historical regathering. The prophet speaks of "this city," and later on of "Zion," "Israel" and "Jerusalem" (v. 14). On the other hand, there is reference to a greater gathering of people of God in the heavenly Jerusalem, for in this company there will be no one who does not worship and serve the Lord, no one who is proud and not humble, no one who deceives another or lies. In this life there is always a mixture, even in the most sanctified of gatherings. But the mountain of the Lord will be occupied only by those who have "clean hands and a pure heart, who [do] not lift up [their] soul[s] to an idol or swear by what is false" (Ps. 24:4).

Another way of saying this is that the blessings of God's new day are not for everybody. True, there is a new day dawning. But that day is to be characterized by truth and righteousness, and only those who are true and righteous will enter it. Zephaniah indicates this when he speaks of "the *remnant* of Israel" which will then do no wrong.

The question is: Are you part of that remnant? Are you one who will actually rejoice at the dawning of this new day of God?

You may say, "I do not know the answer to that question. I do not know whether I am part of that remnant. How can I know?"

Zephaniah gives three ways by which you can know whether you are one of God's spiritual children. The first is in verse 9. The second is in verses 11 and 12. The third is in verse 13.

First, you can know whether you are among the people of God or not by asking whether you "*call on the name of the* LORD *and serve him shoulder to shoulder*" with other Christians (v. 9). It should be evident by now that calling

on the name of the Lord is not a casual thing. It means a wholehearted trust in and worship of Him to the exclusion of all others. This is what the phrase "purify the lips" means in this same sentence. Some commentators have mixed this up by saying the pure lips are God's and then translating the sentence, "I will cause the nations to be preached to with friendly lips that they may all call upon the name of the LORD."[2] But "friendly lips" is a mistaken translation, and the sentence can only mean that God "turns the nations to a *pure* lip by purifying their lips; i.e., He converts them, that they may be able to call upon Him with pure lips" and serve Him.[3]

This is the desired contrast to what we have seen earlier in God's condemnation of the idolatrous priests and people. The priests claimed to be the Lord's servants, but they also served Baal. The people would swear by the Lord, but they would also swear by Molech (Zeph. 1:4, 5). They were as bad as those who did not serve God at all. The only hope for such people is that they might be converted and thus call upon the name of the Lord sincerely out of lives given over entirely to Him.

That is the first test. Have your lips been purified and your nature transformed so you can worship and serve God only?

Second, you can know whether you are among the people of God by asking whether God has conquered your "pride" and left you "*meek and humble*" before Him (vv. 11, 12). This does not mean that you must have achieved perfection now, though a perfection of spirit must be yours before you enter finally into God's presence in heaven. It means that there must be a profound

[2]For a discussion of this view, see Carl Friedrich Keil, *The Twelve Minor Prophets*, vol. 2, from the series C. F. Keil and F. Delitzsch, *Biblical Commentary on the Old Testament* (Grand Rapids: Eerdmans, 1965), pp. 155, 156.
[3]Ibid., p. 156.

and pervasive change in your inner life. Before, you were as proud as Satan. You were not going to bow down before God. On the contrary, you were going to be your own god and have others bow to you (Isa. 14:13, 14). You regarded life as for your own benefit. Then you met Christ. You saw Him as the true King and Lord of your life, and with that new recognition you also saw your sinful rebellion for what it was, and you repented of it. You turned from sin, yielding your pride, and humbly called not for justice but for mercy from Him who is your Savior.

Is that the case with you? Has that been your experience? If not, you are no true child of God. You are no Christian. "For it is by grace you have been saved, through faith—and this not from yourselves, it is the gift of God—not by works, so that no one can boast" (Eph. 2:8, 9).

The third test for knowing whether you are among the people of God is whether you are *living a holy life*, for, as Zephaniah says, "The remnant of Israel will do no wrong; they will speak no lies, nor will deceit be found in their mouths" (v. 13). Again, this does not mean a moral perfection, though a perfect holiness provided by God must be yours before you enter heaven. But it does mean the beginning of and progress in a life of obedience to God.

A New Testament parallel to Zephaniah 3:13 is 1 John 2:3: "We know that we have come to know him if we obey his commands." John is writing to Christians in this letter, and he is giving them tests by which they can know that they truly know God. One test is obedience. This does not mean perfect obedience, for immediately before this John has argued, "If we claim we have not sinned, we make him out to be a liar and his word has no place in our lives" (1 John 1:10). He is simply saying that there must have been a change in us so that we are henceforth not

trying to please and serve ourselves, but God whom we claim to love. If we love Him, we will obey His commandments (John 14:15).

There is no escaping this test. A number of years ago when the "new morality" was at the peak of its popularity, a group of theologians met at a large seminary to discuss it. Most were in favor. So the discussion centered on the value of being free of all regulations. "But there must be some guidelines," someone said. This was debated. At length it was decided that the only acceptable guideline was love. Anything that flowed from love was permissible. Anything was allowed so long as it did not hurt anybody.

While the discussion was going on along these lines a Roman Catholic priest, who had been invited to the discussion and was in the room, became very quiet. At length the silence was noticeable. The others turned to him and asked what he thought. "Don't you agree that the only limiting factor in any ethical decision is love?" they asked him.

The priest replied, "If you love me, you will keep my commandments" (John 14:15).

That is what Zephaniah is saying. If you are among those who have been touched and changed by God and who therefore love Him, you will be striving to do what God says. You will want to obey Him. You will be succeeding more and more, for wanting to obey Christ is the most important factor in a life of holiness.

I reiterate what Zephaniah is saying. There is a new day for the people of God, a day marked by peace, joy, and security. But it is only for those who are really God's children. You can know that you are a child of God if: (1) you are calling on the name of the Lord and desiring to serve Him only, (2) your pride has been broken and you are taking up a meek and humble stance in

His presence, and (3) you are growing in holiness by obeying His commandments. If that is not true of you, you need to get your relationship to God straightened out now while there is still time to do it.

SING A NEW SONG

I have taken a good bit of time with these primary matters because the issue involved is all-important. It is of utmost importance to know whether you are among the people of God or not. If you are not, you must stop and settle the matter; it would be fatal to neglect it. But now, assuming that you are God's child and are growing in holiness, what follows? In this chapter, what follows is a song of joy. That is, you are invited to sing and shout aloud, because

> The LORD has taken away your
>   punishment,
>   he has turned back your enemy.
> The LORD, the King of Israel, is with
>   you;
>   never again will you fear any harm
>   (v. 15).

There is a double cause for singing in that statement. First, if you are one who has come to serve the Lord only and who is going on with Him in holiness and service, you can know that your sins have been forgiven and that God has turned back your great enemy, the Devil. The Lord said something like this when His disciples had returned from one of their itinerant preaching trips, rejoicing that God had given them power over sickness. Jesus replied, "Do not rejoice that the spirits submit to you, but rejoice that your names are written in heaven" (Luke 10:20). Second, if you are truly the Lord's then you can know that He is with you and that you will never again need to fear any harm. This makes us think of Psalm 23:6: "Surely goodness and love will follow me all the days of my life, and I will dwell in the house of the LORD forever." Or Matthew 28:20: "Surely I will be with you always, to the very end of the age."

I know of nothing greater to sing about than that, because it is God's reversal of the Fall, which opened the sluice gate of misery on the human race. When Adam and Eve sinned, the first thing they were aware of (in addition to their own psychological nakedness) was that a barrier now existed between themselves and God. Before this they had been willing to meet with Him. No doubt the times of such meeting were the most blessed of their existence. But when they sinned and then later heard God walking in the garden in the cool of the day, they hid from Him. When God called them and began to confront them with their disobedience, they tried to hide behind excuses. Adam blamed Eve, and she blamed the serpent. As punishment for their sin, God sent them from the garden, which in a certain sense was also sending them away from Himself.

What joy to have that reversed! What joy to have our sin forgiven and the lost relationship between ourselves and the holy God restored!

WORD TO THE REMNANT

The last verses of Zephaniah 3 come down a bit in their emotional tone, but they are not less positive. They are encouragement for the remnant of the Jews as they wait for the consummation of God's kingdom.

The most striking thing about these verses is their emphasis upon God's ability, surely a fitting close to a book that has had so much to say about human inability. Seven times in these verses we find the words "I will" as God promises to do all that needs to be done for His people's restoration:

> "The sorrows for the appointed
>   feasts
>   *I will* remove from you. . . .

At that time I will deal
  with all who oppressed you:
I will rescue the lame
  and gather those who have been
    scattered.
I will give them praise and honor
  in every land where they were
    put to shame.
At that time I will gather you;
  At that time I will bring you
    home.
I will give you honor and praise
  among all the peoples of the earth
when I restore your fortunes
  before your very eyes,"
            says the LORD (vv. 18–20).

As I read these verses I sense that the prophet's thoughts are primarily on the coming Babylonian invasion and on the restoration of the people to their own land following the Exile. If this is the case, the "sorrows for the appointed feasts" are the sorrows of the exiles who were unable to observe the feasts in Babylon. They will be removed because God will bring the people to the land where they will be established. This has already happened by the time we get to Haggai, the next book in the Bible. Similarly, God's dealing with "all who oppressed you" is His punishment on the Babylonians and their allies. The rescue of "the lame" and the regathering and bringing home of the people is a literal regathering of the people under the leadership of Ezra and Nehemiah. "Praise and honor" is that given to Israel as reconstituted in the land. It took a sovereign God to do it. If God

had not pronounced His "I will," the people would not have been regathered and the Jews would have vanished from the earth.

But as has been the case elsewhere in Zephaniah, these words also have application to all God's people and to an even greater gathering of these into God's church. The oppressors are the enemies of the righteous at all times and in all places. The lame are the spiritually impotent. The regathering is a gathering of the entire people of God into Christ's flock.

This too takes the power of God for its accomplishment. Indeed, it requires even more of God's power than a mere earthly regathering. It requires the new birth and the transformation of rebellious hearts. I am glad God has said He will do this. If He had not said it, I for one would despair of any new day. If God cannot or will not change hearts, what hope do you and I have of changing them? None whatever! We can argue or plead or cajole. We can present the truths of the gospel as being in the sinner's best interest. We can warn of destruction. But this will be utterly worthless unless God intervenes to say, "I will rescue the lame and gather those who have been scattered. . . . I will bring you home."

That is what God does. He is doing it at this moment as He presses the claims of Jesus upon rebellious sinners' hearts. That can be your story too. What joy to find your way back to the Father's household!

HAGGAI

17

Call to God's Remnant

(Haggai 1:1–15)

In the second year of King Darius, on the first day of the sixth month, the word of the
LORD came through the prophet Haggai to Zerubbabel son of Shealtiel, governor of Judah,
and to Joshua son of Jehozadak, the high priest:
This is what the LORD Almighty says: "These people say, 'The time has not yet come for
the LORD's house to be built.' "
Then the word of the LORD came through the prophet Haggai: "Is it a time for you
yourselves to be living in your paneled houses, while this house remains a ruin?"
Now this is what the LORD Almighty says: "Give careful thought to your ways. You have
planted much, but have harvested little. You eat, but never have enough. You drink, but
never have your fill. You put on clothes, but are not warm. You earn wages, only to put
them in a purse with holes in it."
This is what the LORD Almighty says: "Give careful thought to your ways. Go up into the
mountains and bring down timber and build the house, so that I may take pleasure in it and
be honored," says the LORD. "You expected much, but see, it turned out to be little. What
you brought home, I blew away. Why?" declares the LORD Almighty. "Because of my house,
which remains a ruin, while each of you is busy with his own house. Therefore, because of
you the heavens have withheld their dew and the earth its crops. I called for a drought on the
fields and the mountains, on the grain, the new wine, the oil and whatever the ground
produces, on men and cattle, and on the labor of your hands."

There is a conviction, shared by various writers, that history is a series of key moments in the otherwise undistinguished flow of human life. According to this view, years may go by with little of importance happening. But suddenly there will be a crisis. A challenge will emerge, and the nature of the next period of history will be determined by how the leaders of the day react to that challenge. Hitler's invasion of Danzig on the last days of August 1939 was one such moment. Would England go to war as she had threatened to do? Or would Hitler be allowed to continue in his announced course of aggression? That England did go to war marked out the course of Western history for decades.

The year 520 B.C. was like that. It would not appear so to most secular historians or even to many biblical historians, but it was important enough for God to have sent a prophet to deal with it and to record what happened in the Word of God.

Sixteen years earlier, in 536 B.C., the Persian emperor Cyrus had issued a decree permitting the Jewish exiles in Babylon to return to Jerusalem to rebuild the temple (cf. Ezra 1:2–4). In response to this decree, about fifty thousand people returned under the leadership of the newly appointed governor of Judah, Zerubbabel, also called Shesbazzar (cf. Ezra 1:11; 5:14, 16), and Joshua, the high priest. These people settled in or near Jerusalem and began the restoration. They cleared the temple court of rubble and replaced the altar of burnt offerings on its base, thus making it possible for the daily sacrifices to begin again. This was in the fall of 536 B.C. By the spring of the next year they had laid the foundations of the temple.

Then troubles began. The people experienced hostility from various neighboring tribes, especially the Samaritans, whose help in rebuilding they had earlier declined. Moreover, Cyrus died in battle, and his successor Cambyses, also called Ahasuerus (cf. Ezra 4:6), was pushed to stop the work. When the work ceased, the people turned to private affairs and gradually became used to worshiping among the ruins of the once great temple. Desire to rebuild died out, and fifteen years passed. The people were on their way to becoming merely the secular occupants of an impoverished land. Then came the year 520 B.C. In that year God sent the prophet Haggai with his challenge to the people to get on with God's work and build the temple. That they listened to Haggai and started rebuilding was a significant turning point in their history, as important in its own way as the building of the temple in the first place or the fall of Jerusalem to Babylon.

Prophets of the Restoration

We know very little about Haggai himself, as has been true with others of the prophets. His name is based upon the Hebrew word *hag* ("festival") and means "my feast" or "my festival." It may indicate that he was born on a feast day, but we cannot be certain. We do not even know who his father was, since he is merely referred to as "the prophet," both in his own book and in Ezra (Hag. 1:1; Ezra 5:1).

Haggai is one of the three last prophets of the Old Testament period, the prophets of the restoration: Haggai, Zechariah, and Malachi. The others came to Israel or Judah before the fall of those nations, the former to the armies of Assyria in 721 B.C., the latter to the armies of the Babylonians in 586 B.C. The earlier years saw great giants of prophets, chief among them Isaiah and Jeremiah. Later there were prophets whose words were spoken mainly against the gentile nations: Obadiah, Jonah, and Nahum. There were prophets to the northern kingdoms: Hosea and Amos. Others carried on their ministries in the south: Joel, Micah, and Zephaniah. During the Exile, Ezekiel and Daniel had made their contribution. But those periods were past now, and it was a radically different age that confronted these last spokesmen for God in the Old Testament. Gone was the glory of the former kingdom and temple. Gone was the great population. All that was left was the rubble of Jerusalem, the remnant of the people, and the task of restoration.

There are five biblical books that may profitably be read together in studying this period: the three prophets of the restoration, which we have already mentioned (Haggai, Zechariah, and Malachi), and two historical books: Ezra and Nehemiah. Of the three prophets, Haggai and Zechariah come rather early in the period. (Zechariah began his work just two months after Haggai.) Malachi comes approximately one hundred years later, in years of decline.

The People and Place

We are not going to get very far in studying Haggai (and later Zechariah) unless we realize that this was not an unredeemably bad period in Judah's history. In our studies so far we have become accustomed to prophetic warnings of God's judgment on a sinful and self-righteous people. But the last three prophets spoke to a different situation. Their audience was the remnant. These people were not at all like those who had lived in Israel and Judah previously. True, they were neglecting to build the temple and this was serious in God's sight. It was an indication that their spiritual priorities were not right. They were living for themselves rather than for God's glory. But they were still the right people, living in the right place, wanting to do the right work for the right reasons.

These points are worth looking at in detail. First, in Haggai we are dealing with the *right people*, select people whose devotion to and zeal for God were evident. This is summed up in the spiritual meaning of the word "remnant" which we have already used to describe them. It means that they were not the entire body of the Jewish people at this time. Many thousands had been carried away to Assyria. Others had been deported to Babylon. In fact, when Cyrus issued his decree permitting the Jews to return to their homeland and rebuild the temple, most of the exiled Jews remained in Babylon, where they had settled down and prospered during the Exile period. It was only these few 42,360 (plus 7,337 servants and 200 singers) who actually left Babylon and made the long journey back to Judah with Zerubbabel. One commentator says, "The 'remnant' to whom the message was given was composed of Israelites who were distinguished by special devotion to the Lord. It was their devotion to him, and their zeal for his house, that was the cause of their separation from the mass of their brethren who remained behind

in Babylon. They were, therefore, a choice company of people. They had been separated for a purpose of great importance; for the direct line of God's dealings was to continue with them to the coming of Christ."[1]

Second, the people to whom God directs His word through Haggai were in the *right place*. That is, they were in Jerusalem and its environs at the call of God and not in Babylon among those who had preferred their fixed way of life to the rigors of a return.

This is not insignificant. Today God does not restrict His work to a particular place. When the Samaritan woman asked Jesus whether the mountain of Gerazim in Samaria or Jerusalem was the proper place to worship, Jesus replied, "Believe me, woman, a time is coming when you will worship the Father neither on this mountain nor in Jerusalem. . . . Yet a time is coming and has now come when the true worshipers will worship the Father in spirit and truth" (John 4:21, 23). That time came with His own death and resurrection. But it was not yet true in the days of Haggai and the other Old Testament figures. In the Old Testament period God had placed a special value on Jerusalem and had required that the sacrifices for sin be made there and not elsewhere. He had punished the people by exile, but He had also promised to bring them back after the years of their exile were finished. This was the hope of the people while in Babylon. The people who had returned with Zerubbabel and Joshua were sensitive to these promises and wanted to be in the place of God's blessing. When the call to return came, they left Babylon and got back to Jerusalem as soon as possible.

A moment ago I said that God's commitment to a particular place has

[1]Philip Mauro, *The Last Call to the Godly Remnant: A Study of the Five Messages of Haggai* (Swengel, Pa.: Reiner, 1976), p. 3.

been altered to a concern for the whole world in our day. That is true in one sense, but it is misleading in another. It is true that God has sent His people into the whole world with the gospel, and in this sense Christianity has become universalistic rather than particularistic. But it is equally true that God does not send the individual believer into "all the world." He sends him to a particular place and to a specific group of people where he is to live for Christ and share the gospel. In other words, our response to God as individuals must be as related to a place as was God's call to the Jewish remnant. If we are to be the right people, we must be in the right place also.

Third, the remnant to whom Haggai spoke also wanted to be about the *right work*. There were many things they needed to do. They needed to provide homes for their families. They needed to make a living, in their case largely through farming. They needed to establish schools, shops, commerce, trade. These were all valid and necessary pursuits. But in addition to these and chief among them, the people also wanted to rebuild the temple, which is what God had put into the heart of Cyrus to decree (cf. Ezra 1:2ff.).

As Ezra tells it, the first thing the people did when they arrived in Jerusalem was take a freewill offering toward the rebuilding of the house of God. It was a substantial offering. Ezra says, "According to their ability they gave to the treasury for this work 61,000 drachmas of gold, 5,000 minas of silver and 100 priestly garments" (Ezra 2:69). In our weights the gold was 1,100 pounds or 13,200 ounces (Troy weight), for a value somewhat in excess of five million dollars. The silver weighed three tons and was worth more than half a million dollars at our current rates of exchange. The people used this money to pay masons and carpenters and to buy and transport cedar logs from Lebanon. Then, in the second month of their second year in Judah (after they had established themselves and presumably brought in the first harvest), they began the work and progressed as far as laying the foundation of the great temple. These people clearly wanted to serve God and put His work above their own interests.

Finally, the people were working for the *right reasons*. We could imagine them rebuilding the temple to assert themselves with some sense of distorted national pride: "The Babylonians destroyed our temple; but we'll show them who will have the last word. We'll build it again." We can imagine them attempting to construct a monument to their own fierce independence, like the Tower of Babel. These were not their motivations. So far as we are told, their sole desire was to please God.

Philip Mauro, whom I quoted earlier, writes correctly: "They were characterized by affection and zeal for God's house, and this is a great thing in his sight. Not only so, but, in pursuit of that object, they had voluntarily turned away from all the magnificence, grandeur and luxury of Babylon, where, after a long residence, the people of God had become thoroughly domesticated. They had faced trials and difficulties in crossing the intervening territory, and the result of all their efforts and hardships was but to bring them to a desolated land and a ruined city. So their devotion and zeal for the Lord's interests had been fully proved. There was nothing to attract them to that land and to that city except the fact that it was God's holy land, and the city which he had chosen to put his name there."[2]

---

[2] Ibid., p. 4.

So I repeat, the people to whom the prophet Haggai spoke were the right people, living in the right place, trying to do the right work for the right reasons. Yet the years had gone by, and they were sufficiently caught up in their own pursuits to let the work for which they had come to Jerusalem slide.

Many in our day are like that. They are not unbelievers. They are not even unconcerned believers. These people want to know the will of God and do it. At least they did at one time—perhaps when they were in a Youth for Christ group in high school or in Campus Crusade or InterVarsity Fellowship during their years in college. Perhaps they were zealous for God in the years immediately following their conversion. But life has moved on. Now there is a job or a wife or children (or any one of a dozen other things) to think about, and somehow they have let the work of God slide. They have left the work to younger or older or newer or merely other Christians.

The word of God by Haggai comes to such people—to you, if you are one. God says: What is the condition of my house? What is the condition of my work in your home, your church, your neighborhood, your city, your land? He says: What are you doing to fulfill the purpose for which you have been set apart by Jesus Christ?

"CONSIDER YOUR WAYS"

In a certain sense there is only one message in this book: "Give careful thought to your ways." It is found twice in chapter 1 (vv. 5, 7) and three times in chapter 2 (vv. 15, 18). In the first chapter it comes about like this. Apparently the people had not only ceased work on the temple, they had also done what many Christians who become lazy in the Lord's work also do. They had begun to make excuses. This is a clue to underlying guilt. If there is no wrongdoing, there is no need to

make excuses. But here there was guilt, and excuses were being made. The people said: "The time has not yet come for the LORD's house to be built" (v. 2).

How many times have you heard that?

"Yes, I believe in foreign missions, but with our economy the way it is, this is just no time to expand our missionary budget."

"Well, of course every Christian is to be a witness where he lives and works. But witnessing to my co-workers is a delicate business. I don't think it's time to tell them about Jesus Christ."

"I know I should tithe, but I can't do it this year. I have too many family obligations."

"I'm flattered that you think my talents might help in that particular area of the church's work, but I don't have time to serve just now. Perhaps later when the pressures of my job let up a bit or when I retire."

I am glad David Livingstone did not think that way when he was being called by the Lord to set out on his missionary journeys to Africa. He had applied to a mission society in Scotland, but they had told him, "Young man, when God sees fit to evangelize Africa He will do it without your help." Livingstone rightly recognized that every time is the right time to evangelize and that the work of missions is every Christian's job.

In the first chapter of Haggai, God challenges this excuse and the inactivity behind it with two arguments. First: "Is it a time for you yourselves to be living in your paneled houses, while this house remains a ruin?" (v. 4). That was a very biting argument. God was accusing the people of having plenty of time for themselves while pleading a lack of time for God. It was an accusation of having plenty of money to spend on their own comfort and pleasures while claiming not to have enough for God's service. The people were prospering. How could it be, then, that they were unable to get on with the work God had given them to do?

When I read this I think of the evangelical church in America. It fits the pattern of the Jewish remnant perfectly. Evangelicals are orthodox; in that sense they are the right people. They are in the right place; they attend good, Bible-believing fellowships. They are trying to do the right things; they want to share the gospel and do works honoring God. They are even trying to do it for the right reasons; that is, they really want to please God rather than man and see Christ honored. But something is wrong. Their intentions do not come to fruition, and the reason is their failure to put God first. Instead of having God first, they put affluence first.

A generation ago Harry Ironside wrote in his study of Haggai: "Alas, how much is sacrificed for money! Christian fellowship, the joys of gathering at the table of the Lord, gospel work, and privileges of mutual edification and instruction in divine things—all are parted with often simply because the opportunity arises of adding a few paltry dollars to the monthly income and savings. Brethren with families even will leave a town or city where the spiritual support and fellowship of their brethren is found, and where their children have the privilege of the gospel meeting and the Sunday-school, simply because they see, or fancy they see, an opportunity to better their earthly circumstances. Alas, in many instances, they miss all they had hoped for, and lose spiritually what is never regained!"[3]

At this point we are beginning to see why the failure of the people to build the Lord's house was so tragic, and

why similar failures are so tragic for ourselves. It is not that any particular temple is in itself all that important—though the temple in Jerusalem was special and anything God commands is of importance simply because He commands it. But the failure to proceed with the temple was the result of inverted priorities, and in the final analysis all inverted priorities are idolatry. They put the creation before the Creator.

God says, "You shall have no other gods before me" (Exod. 20:3). He says, "Love the LORD your God with all your heart and with all your soul and with all your strength" (Deut. 6:5).

The second argument with which Haggai challenges the people's inactivity is an observation on what has actually transpired in their lives. They had put other things before God, and God, who will have no other gods before Him, sent leanness. This is where the reference to giving careful thought comes in. "Give careful thought to your ways. You have planted much, but have harvested little. You eat, but never have enough. You drink, but never have your fill. You put on clothes, but are not warm. You earn wages, only to put them in a purse with holes in it" (vv. 5, 6). Later on the word of God continues in the same vein: "You expected much, but see, it turned out to be little. What you brought home, I blew away. Why? . . . Because of my house, which remains a ruin, while each of you is busy with his own house. Therefore, because of you the heavens have withheld their dew and the earth its crops. I called for a drought on the fields and the mountains, on the grain, the new wine, the oil and whatever the ground produces, on men and cattle, and on the labor of your hands" (vv. 9–11).

---

[3]Harry A. Ironside, *Notes on the Minor Prophets* (Neptune, N.J.: Loizeaux, 1966), pp. 329, 330. Original edition 1909.

I do not know of any passage in the Bible that better describes the feverish yet ineffective activity of our own age. Haggai's first remark (in v. 6) is that the people had "planted much" but had "harvested little." Since farming was their chief occupation, it is the equivalent of saying that they were always working. They were like the people in our day who take on extra jobs, who work through lunch and stay at the plant to work nights, who are always rushing around to get ahead. Yet little had come of it. They were like the person in the Pennsylvania Dutch expression: "The hurrier I go, the behinder I get." They were so concerned about working every possible moment that they were upset if they missed one turn of the revolving door. Yet they seemed on a treadmill. They were running up the escalator two steps at a time while it was coming down faster than they were climbing.

Not only were they falling behind in their push to get ahead—a picture of frustration—they were also dissatisfied, even in the midst of their apparent abundance. A number of the phrases speak of this: "You eat, but never have enough. You drink, but never have your fill. You put on clothes, but are not warm." I do not think this means that there was insufficient food or drink—though the next verses do speak of a drought which affected the fields. The people were eating, after all. They were drinking. They did have clothes to wear. But they were not satisfied by these things and therefore always went about with a sense of longing for what was not there.

Is this not a picture of our age? More cars, more houses, more furniture, more food, more television sets, more games, more vacations. . . . Yet people are wretchedly unsatisfied. People have everything, but they are miserable. And some of those miserable people are so-called evangelical Christians. What

is the cause of this? It is the work of God. God has sent emptiness so that His people might awake from their idolatry and turn back to Him. The psalmist says, "He gave them their request, but sent leanness into their soul" (Ps. 106:15, KJV).

The last phrase is a classic description of inflation, the scourge of the latter third of our century: "You earn wages, only to put them in a purse with holes in it." We save, but our savings dribble away, eaten up by taxes and the progressive devaluation of our currencies through government overspending.

What is the solution? It is not a few more government programs. It is not prayer in Congress or the schools. It is not a crusade or a demonstration or a campaign to mail letters to our senators. It is obedience! It is getting on with what God has given us to do. In the context of Haggai's situation, it was the command: "Go up into the mountains and bring down timber and build the house, so that I may take pleasure in it and be honored" (v. 8). In our context it is to set spiritual matters first and get on with serving God to the best of our ability.

The Result and God's Promise

It is one of the discouragements of the Christian ministry that so often a pastor will preach the Bible with as much power as he possesses and then be greeted with yawns by his parishioners as they go back to doing what they had been doing all along. Still, from time to time there is something quite different. The Word of God strikes home, and a life is genuinely changed. When that happens in large numbers you have a revival.

This happened under Haggai's preaching. We recall from our study of the earlier prophets that the warnings given to the Jewish people before God's judgment by the Assyrian and

Babylonian invasions generally went unheeded. Micah had some success.[4] But for the most part the people could not have cared less for the prophets' warnings. To our joy we see a different kind of response from the people of Judah under Haggai's ministry. They had been negligent of God's work. They had invented flimsy excuses as to why they were inactive. But they were not basically hostile to God or His commandments as the people living before the Exile had been. They really wanted to please God. So when the word of the Lord came to them by Haggai, they recognized it as a true word of God and did what God commanded. The prophecy says, "Then Zerubbabel son of Shealtiel, Joshua son of Jehozadak, the high priest, and the whole remnant of the people obeyed the voice of the Lord their God and the message of the prophet Haggai, because the Lord their God had sent him. And the people feared the Lord" (v. 12).

The chapter concludes, "So the Lord stirred up the spirit of Zerubbabel son of Shealtiel, governor of Judah, and the spirit of Joshua son of Jehozadak, the high priest, and the spirit of the whole remnant of the people. They came and began to work on the house of the Lord Almighty, their God, on the twenty-fourth day of the sixth month in the second year of King Darius" (vv. 14, 15).

There is an interesting note in that last verse, where we are told that the people resumed the work on the twenty-fourth day of the month. If we compare that with the first verse of the chapter, where we are told that Haggai began to preach on the first day of the month, we find that the change came about in just twenty-three days. Haggai spoke on August 30, 520 B.C. The work began on the twenty-first of September.

I wonder if there is a date like that in your life or if today might possibly become that day. I do not mean the day of your conversion; you may or may not have a known day for that. I mean the day in which you finally got the priorities of your life straightened out and determined that from that time on you would put God and His work first in everything. You need to do that. You need to ask yourself these questions: "Is my own comfort of greater importance to me than the work of God? Am I making increasing efforts to get ahead financially but finding greater and greater disappointment in my life?" If the answer is yes, just turn around and get on with God's business. Obey Him. Put Him first in your life.

---

[4]See "A Prophet Who Was Remembered" (Mic. 1:1–16), pp. 13–19.

18

Former Glory, Future Glory

(Haggai 2:1–23)

On the twenty-first day of the seventh month, the word of the LORD came through the prophet Haggai: "Speak to Zerubbabel son of Shealtiel, governor of Judah, to Joshua son of Jehozadak, the high priest, and to the remnant of the people. Ask them, 'Who of you is left who saw this house in its former glory? How does it look to you now? Does it not seem to you like nothing? But now be strong, O Zerubbabel,' declares the LORD. 'Be strong, O Joshua son of Jehozadak, the high priest. Be strong, all you people of the land,' declares the LORD, 'and work. For I am with you,' declares the LORD Almighty. 'This is what I covenanted with you when you came out of Egypt. And my Spirit remains among you. Do not fear.'

"This is what the LORD Almighty says: 'In a little while I will once more shake the heavens and the earth, the sea and the dry land. I will shake all nations, and the desired of all nations will come, and I will fill this house with glory,' says the LORD Almighty. 'The silver is mine and the gold is mine,' declares the LORD Almighty. 'The glory of his present house will be greater than the glory of the former house,' says the LORD Almighty. 'And in this place I will grant peace,' declares the LORD Almighty."

People familiar with George Frederick Handel's great oratorio *Messiah* know that it is not many minutes into the work when the bass soloist sings the recitative containing Haggai's great promise: "Thus saith the Lord of Hosts, yet once a little while and I will shake the heavens and the earth, the sea and the dry land, and I will shake all nations, and the desired of all nations shall come." The recitative is preceded by the words: "The glory of the LORD shall be revealed." It is followed by: "But who shall abide the presence of his coming?" These musical segments rightly present both the glory and terror of Christ's coming.

In the second chapter of Haggai the emphasis is on the glory. God's prom-ise to shake the nations is meant to be an encouragement to God's people.

CALL FOR COURAGE

We have already seen something of the historical situation into which Haggai spoke his message. Fifteen years before, the people had returned to Jerusalem from Babylon and had laid the foundation of the temple that had been destroyed by the earlier Babylonian invasion. As Ezra tells it, there was a celebration of some sort on this occasion. The priests put on their vestments. The people assembled. Together they sang and gave great shouts of praise to God for His goodness in allowing the foundations for His house to be relaid. "But," we are told, "many

145

of the older priests and Levites and family heads, who had seen the former temple, wept aloud when they saw the foundation of this temple being laid" (Ezra 3:12). The older people remembered the temple that had been and realized that nothing they could do in this later day would ever make their temple equal to the earlier one.

Something like this must have happened in Haggai's day too, on the occasion of the people's return to the building. As the people returned to their task they must have been overcome with depression as they realized that their new structure would never equal the one that had been lost.

We go through moods like this ourselves. We begin the Lord's work with joy, but the time comes when we compare what we are doing with something that seems to us to be or have been greater, and we become discouraged. In light of the other work our own work seems paltry, and we find ourselves in the same slump the people of Haggai's day were in.

Sometimes we compare the church of our day with that of previous ages. We look to the apostolic age, for example. Acts says that the early Christians "were together and had everything in common. . . . Every day they continued to meet together in the temple courts. They broke bread in their homes and ate together with glad and sincere hearts, praising God and enjoying the favor of all the people" (Acts 2:44–47). The Lord blessed that church, adding to it "daily those who were being saved." But our churches are not like that, we reason. The apostolic church was united; we are divided. They were filled with joy and were often praising God; we are discouraged and depressed. They had favor with the people; we are despised by the people. They had many converts; often we seem to have none. We say, "This is a bad age; no matter how hard we work, our days are never

going to equal the days of the apostles."

Or we look at the Protestant Reformation. There were great men of God in those days, and the people of Europe gave unprecedented attention to the gospel. The doctrine of justification by faith literally swept across the continent. We say, "Where is the power of that gospel today? Where are those leaders?" By comparison our century seems to be one of small things. We are discouraged.

Or again, we look at the Great Awakenings in England and America. We say, "Where are the Whitefields? Where are the Wesleys of our time? Where are the gatherings of twenty, forty, or even fifty thousand people to hear the gospel, not just on a rare occasion, but regularly?" We do not see that, so we get depressed.

Even if we do not look to the past to compare our situation with that of some former age of church history, we often do the same thing by comparing our work with other contemporary works. We look at another church and say, "Look at that congregation. Twenty-five years ago they were only ten people meeting in a house. Now there are five thousand people, and they have a magnificent new building. All sorts of projects have been launched through that ministry." Or we look at an organization that has so much money it does not seem to know what to do with it, while our organization just struggles along. Or we look at another person's life and say, "That person seems to be so joyful, so victorious in everything. He doesn't seem to have any problems at all. Every time he opens his mouth somebody seems to become a Christian. I have been struggling with my neighbor, talking about the gospel for years, but there is nothing to show for it. What's wrong with me?"

Situations like this get us down emotionally, and we find ourselves thinking that our efforts are useless. We think we might as well give up.

God has a word for any who think like that, the word spoken to the returned exiles through Haggai. It has several parts. First, God says that He knows how we feel and that it is true that the work we are doing does not compare with what was done previously or with what is going on elsewhere. In Haggai's day the people had been working for approximately three and a half weeks, from the twenty-fourth day of the sixth month (Hag. 1:15) to the twenty-first day of the seventh month (Hag. 2:1), and already discouragement had set in. So God said, "Speak to Zerubbabel son of Shealtiel, governor of Judah, to Joshua son of Jehozadak, the high priest, and to the remnant of the people. Ask them, 'Who of you is left who saw this house in its former glory? How does it look to you now? Does it not seem to you like nothing?' " (vv. 2, 3). In these words God is acknowledging the situation as they saw it. He is not trying to cover it up. He is not telling them that they have overly idealized those earlier days or that they are putting themselves down too much. He begins by acknowledging that things really were bad. That is, God begins with realism.

The second part builds on this realism. It is a message to "be strong" in precisely this dismal situation: " 'Now be strong, O Zerubbabel,' declares the LORD. 'Be strong, O Joshua son of Jehozadak, the high priest. Be strong, all you people of the land,' declares the LORD" (v. 4).

Have you ever noticed how often God or one of His messengers has to tell someone to be strong? When Moses delivered his final charge to Israel before they crossed the Jordan to enter the Promised Land, he told them to be strong before their enemies: "Be strong and courageous. Do not be afraid or terrified because of them, for the LORD your God goes with you; he will never leave you nor forsake you" (Deut. 31:6).

Shortly thereafter, Joshua, Moses' successor, stood on the far side of the Jordan to begin the conquest. God appeared to him with a threefold repetition of the charge Moses had given the people earlier: "Be strong and courageous, because you will lead these people to inherit the land I swore to their forefathers to give them. Be strong and very courageous. . . . Be strong and courageous. Do not be terrified; do not be discouraged, for the LORD your God will be with you wherever you go" (Josh. 1:6, 7, 9). Then even the people joined in, saying to Joshua, "Only be strong and courageous" (v. 18).

Later, Joshua spoke to the people: "Do not be afraid; do not be discouraged. Be strong and courageous" (Josh. 10:25).

David gave a charge like this to his son Solomon in regard to building the temple: "Be strong and courageous, and do the work. Do not be afraid or discouraged, for the LORD God, my God, is with you. He will not fail you or forsake you until all the work for the service of the temple of the LORD is finished" (1 Chron. 28:20).

In the New Testament we find the apostle Paul saying, "Finally, be strong in the Lord and in his mighty power" (Eph. 6:10).

Repetition is characteristic of these verses, as it is in Haggai 2:4, where the words "be strong" are repeated three times: "Be strong, O Zerubbabel. . . . Be strong, O Joshua. . . . Be strong, all you people of the land." God repeats His words precisely because of our discouragement.

The texts in which God or one of His messengers says to be strong have another feature, which explains why God can say this. It is the promise of God's presence. Moses said, "For the LORD your God goes with you; he will

never leave you nor forsake you."
Joshua was told: "The LORD your God
will be with you wherever you go."
David told Solomon, "The LORD God,
my God, is with you. He will not fail
you or forsake you until all the work for
the service of the temple of the LORD is
finished." In Haggai God says, "I am
with you. . . . This is what I covenanted with you when you came out of
Egypt. And my Spirit remains among
you. Do not fear" (vv. 4, 5).

It is the presence of God that makes
God's people strong. In ourselves we
are not strong. That is why God does
not say, as we might say to someone in
order to buck them up, "Go on, I know
you can do it. Just be strong. Give it
your best." That advice might be valuable at a football rally or when a person
is waiting to participate in a talent
contest, but it is not valuable in spiritual things simply because we are not
equal to our spiritual tasks. Like Moses,
we are weak. Like Joshua, we face tasks
that are impossible by normal means.
Like Solomon, we are not the heroes
our forefathers were. But we can be
strong and we can be equal to the task,
because God is with us. In His strength
we can be courageous.

THE GLORY TO COME

In the second half of the message
given through Haggai on the twenty-
first day of the seventh month, the
Lord had an even more encouraging
word. The people were building a temple that they could see was not going to
be glorious, at least when compared
with the temple built by Solomon. They
were looking back, and from that perspective the present looked bleak. But
God spoke again, directing them
toward the future. Compared to the
past, the present was indeed bleak. But
what they could not see was that the
present was leading to a future that
would make even the temple of Solomon look dingy. "This is what the

LORD Almighty says: 'In a little while I
will once more shake the heavens and
the earth, the sea and the dry land. I
will shake all nations, and the desired
of all nations will come, and I will fill
this house with glory,' says the LORD
Almighty. 'The silver is mine and the
gold is mine,' declares the LORD Almighty. 'The glory of this present
house will be greater than the glory of
the former house,' says the LORD Almighty. 'And in this place I will grant
peace,' declares the LORD Almighty"
(vv. 6–9).

This is a great paragraph. It contains
great promises.

1. *I will shake all nations.* There is some
doubt as to how these words should
be taken. They may refer to political
events in Zerubbabel's day or to events
in the distant future, events perhaps
more spiritual than political.

The promise certainly appears to refer to Zerubbabel's own day. It is
repeated further on in a direct word to
Zerubbabel: "Tell Zerubbabel governor
of Judah that I will shake the heavens
and the earth. I will overturn royal
thrones and shatter the power of the
foreign kingdoms. I will overthrow
chariots and their drivers; horses and
their riders will fall, each by the sword
of his brother" (vv. 21, 22). This seems
to refer to a literal shaking of those
kingdoms with which Zerubbabel
would have been familiar.

Moreover, the nations were shaken.
The Ionian Greeks, who had expanded
eastward to the western shore of Asia
Minor, had been subjected to the rule
of Persia by Cyrus the Great about 540
B.C. But in 501 B.C., about twenty years
after the date of Haggai's prophecy,
they rebelled against Persia, bringing
on a Persian invasion of Greece about a
decade later. Darius was king at this
time. He led a great army, but he was
defeated at Marathon in 490 B.C. in a
victory the Greeks still remember with
pride. Shortly thereafter Darius's suc-

cessor Xerxes marshaled an even larger army and a powerful navy. The army contained 1.8 million men. The navy was the largest ever seen. But in 480 B.C. the Greek boats scattered the Persian navy, and the Greek army defeated the Persian army at both Thermopylae and Plataea. A year later the reassembled Persian navy was again defeated. Thus Persian hopes of conquering the Greek mainland were forever crushed.

As the Persian Empire began a gradual collapse, Alexander the Great came to power and led the Greek armies over the Bosperous against Persia. He defeated the Persian armies at Granicus in 334 B.C., Issus in 332 B.C., and Arabela in 331 B.C. At his death the Greek empire broke up and was eventually replaced by Roman rule of the Mediterranean countries. The Romans were in control at the time of Christ. If there was ever a shaking of the nations and a redistribution of power, it was during this period.

Yet there are reasons to think that God was also pointing to more distant events. In the New Testament the author of Hebrews takes Haggai's words and applies them to the shaking that will take place at God's final judgment. He warns that everything that is not firmly established in the kingdom of Christ will be plucked up and blown away: "At that time [God's appearance to give the Law on Mount Sinai] his voice shook the earth, but now he has promised, 'Once more I will shake not only the earth but also the heavens.' The words 'once more' indicate the removing of what can be shaken—that is, created things—so that what cannot be shaken may remain" (Heb. 12:26, 27). In this text the earlier, former shakings are evidence of the greater shaking to come.

2. *The desired of all nations will come.* The second promise in this important paragraph of Haggai is the one for which the text was incorporated into Handel's *Messiah*. In this case, as in popular Christian thinking generally, "the desired of all nations" is assumed to be Jesus and the promise is assumed to be about His birth.

But that is not the correct interpretation. The nations are not desiring Christ. They are actually resisting Him. Also the verb following the Hebrew word translated "desired" is plural in number, so the subject of the verb must also be plural. Thus, it must refer, not to Jesus Christ, but to either the "desired people" or "desired things" that are to come.

Here again there is a division of opinion. Some writers, such as Thomas V. Moore, regard this as the "wealth" or "choice things" of the heathen. This is a probable interpretation, because the passage goes on to speak of the silver and gold that are God's (v. 8). In this context, the verse seems to be teaching that the heathen will bring their silver and gold to Jerusalem so that the temple will regain and even surpass its older glory. This did happen. Under Herod the Great the temple of Zerubbabel was gradually replaced with more elegant buildings, and, when all was completed, the temple enclosure was the glory of the East. The pinnacle was covered with gold, which shone out over the whole city during the time of Jesus Christ.[1]

In my opinion, the "desired of all nations" refers to people, in the sense that "the chosen, the elect out of all nations, those gentiles whom God has

---

[1]Thomas V. Moore, *A Commentary on Haggai, Zechariah and Malachi* (Edinburgh and Carlisle, Pa.: Banner of Truth Trust, 1979), p. 76. Original edition 1856. Moore does not restrict the bringing of the Gentiles' riches to the building of the temple, however. He also applies it to the church's present work of evangelism, saying, "It is the gifts, the gold and the toil of the Gentiles, that are now advancing that kingdom of God" (p. 77).

from eternity foreknown and predestinated,"[2] will increase the glory of the true temple, which is the church. That is, the ultimate glory of God's house will not be a mere physical glory but a spiritual glory that comes from having an increasingly large host of all tongues and nations enter into it.

3. *The glory of the present house will be greater than the glory of the former house.* What we have already said about the "desired of all nations" illuminates this point, but it is worth adding a New Testament passage in which the apostle Paul compares the glory of the old covenant with the greater glory of the new. He is not thinking of this passage in Haggai, so far as one can tell. He is reflecting on the way Moses' face glowed with a transferred glory as the result of his having spent time with God on the mountain. But the contrast is the same. He writes: "What was glorious has no glory now in comparison with the surpassing glory. And if what was fading away came with glory, how much greater is the glory of that which lasts!

"Therefore, since we have such a hope, we are very bold. We are not like Moses, who would put a veil over his face to keep the Israelites from gazing at it while the radiance was fading away. But their minds were made dull, for to this day the same veil remains when the old covenant is read. It has not been removed, because only in Christ is it taken away. Now the Lord is the Spirit, and where the Spirit of the Lord is, there is freedom. And we, who with unveiled faces all reflect the Lord's glory, are being transformed into this likeness with ever-increasing glory, which comes from the Lord, who is the Spirit" (2 Cor. 3:1–18).

4. *In this place I will grant peace.* If this promise concerns peace from physical fighting, it has not been fulfilled yet, because Jerusalem has been anything but the "city of peace" its name suggests. Actually, this refers to the work of Christ who made peace between God and man through His death on the cross in Jerusalem. We are not at peace with God in our natural state. We are at war with God. But Jesus crossed the lines, died as our Mediator, made peace with God, and now lives to grant peace in full measure to all who come to the Father through Him.

CONSIDER YOUR WAYS

The last half of Haggai 2 gets back to practical matters, probably in response to a question that might have gone like this: "You are speaking of a future glory of the temple, which is all well and good. And I grant that there is some encouragement in knowing that. It makes our labor just a little more meaningful. But still, we are living in a most discouraging time. You speak of the future. But we don't have that perspective. We have to live in the present, and day by day as we handle our bricks and apply our mortar and see the walls of the temple slowly rising, we are reminded of how bad things are. What good is a distant future, however glorious, when we live here and now?"

God's word is for any who may be in this condition. It is a word that comes to where we are. The people have been complaining about the grimness of their present days, so God tells them to pay good attention to those days, especially by comparing the days before they began to work on the temple with the days afterward.

The challenge was conveyed in a dramatic way. Haggai was to go to the priests and ask them for a ruling on how an object could become conse-

---

[2]Theo. Laetsch, *The Minor Prophets* (Saint Louis: Concordia, 1956), p. 395.

crated or defiled. He asked the question: "If a person carries consecrated meat in the fold of his garment, and that fold touches some bread or stew, some wine, oil or other food, does it become consecrated?"

The priests answered, "No." That was right. Holiness is an isolated virtue. It is not communicable.

Then Haggai asked: "If a person defiled by contact with a dead body touches one of these things, does it become defiled?"

The priests answered, "Yes." Again they were right. Contamination is communicable. It is far easier to spread evil than virtue.

God explains that it has been like that with Israel. They have been living in a contaminated state due to their inverted priorities, and, as a result, everything they have touched has been contaminated. "Consider how things were before one stone was laid on another in the LORD's temple. When anyone came to a heap of twenty measures, there were only ten. When anyone went to a wine vat to draw fifty measures, there were only twenty. I struck all the work of your hands with blight, mildew and hail, yet you did not turn to me." But now they have turned to God, and therefore from this point on the situation will be different. "From this day on, from this twenty-fourth day of the ninth month, give careful thought to the day when the foundation of the LORD's temple was laid. Give careful thought: Is there yet any seed left in the barn? Until now, the vine and the fig tree, the pomegranate and the olive tree have not borne fruit.

"From this day on I will bless you" (vv. 15–19).

Earlier I pointed out that the phrase "Give careful thought" (vv. 5, 7) is almost the theme statement of the book. It occurs twice in the first chapter and three times in chapter 2 (vv. 15, 18). In each case "give careful thought"

calls attention to the well-being or lack of well-being of the people. They were to look to their state before they began to put the work of God first, and they were to look to their state after they began to put God's work first. By comparing the two they were to see that they had nothing but trouble, frustration, and disappointment when they put their own work first, but that they experienced peace, fulfillment, and blessing as soon as they determined to serve God.

Are you bold enough to accept that kind of challenge? Usually we are not very bold in this area. We are afraid of anything as tangible as this, because we do not really believe that God will bless us if we put Him first and are convinced that if we did act this way, our faith would be shaken. We retreat into a spiritual world over against the "real," material world. We can be utterly down in the mouth. But if someone asks, "How are you?" and we reply, "Well, God has certainly blessed spiritually this week," no one can question that. If you claim that God has blessed you spiritually, who can prove you wrong?

But if you say, "I've determined to put God's interests first, and I am counting on God to bless me in tangible, material ways, because this is what He has promised," then you really put your faith on the line. That is something that both you and others can see, and the issue is whether God is real or not and whether or not His work can be trusted.

This is a very bold challenge. You may have been going your own way, putting yourself first. You may have said, "Well, I have to do that. If I don't look after myself, no one else is going to do it. I have to look out for number one." But God asks you, "How does it work out when you do it that way? You haven't done very well, have you? Things have gotten pretty rough.

You're having trouble with your boss, your family, your wife, your husband. Isn't that the case? Isn't that what you see when you give careful thought to your ways?" You have acknowledged that God is right, and that is indeed true. But now God says, "I want you to change your priorities and put me to the test. I want you to turn from the way you've been living and begin to live as a Christian should live. I want you to 'seek first [my] kingdom and [my] righteousness' and see if 'all these things will [not] be given to you as well' (Matt. 6:33). Three months from now, or a year from now, I want you to look back and ask yourself: 'Was God a God of His word or wasn't He? Does Christianity work or doesn't it? Is it better to follow God or the world?' "

God is not afraid of that kind of test. Are you? He puts the challenge to you directly.

WORD TO THE GOVERNOR

The last words of Haggai are to Zerubbabel, the governor. I am glad they are, because there are special burdens of leadership that not everyone has, and leaders, therefore, need encouragement even more than other people. Zerubbabel lived in difficult, even dangerous times. The work had not been going well. The people were discouraged. The building of the city walls had not even begun. Anyone could invade the city. Zerubbabel could be killed.

God told Haggai to give Zerubbabel this message: "Tell Zerubbabel governor of Judah that I will shake the heavens and the earth. I will overturn royal thrones and shatter the power of the foreign kingdoms. I will overthrow chariots and their drivers; horses and their riders will fall, each by the sword of his brother. 'On that day . . . I will take you my servant Zerubbabel son of Shealtiel . . . and I will make you like my signet ring, for I have chosen you,' declares the LORD Almighty" (vv. 21–23). The signet ring was a stone carved with the symbol of the person in power. It was used by pressing it into clay tablets to authenticate what was written on them. That is, it was much like a signature today. The signet was a precious object. So it was kept on the ruler's finger or on a cord around his neck. It was guarded with his person. God was telling Zerubbabel that he was going to be like that to God. God was going to place the governor on His finger or hang him around His neck so, that though the nations and even heaven and earth should be shaken, Zerubbabel would remain safe. He would be kept secure until God had done all the things spoken about in this prophecy.

I point out one last thing. The closing words of Haggai are "the LORD Almighty." This designation of God occurs fourteen times in the book. It is appropriate, because it focuses on the strength or sovereignty of God. It is as if God is saying, "I, the sovereign God, stand behind these promises." The sovereign God is not just Haggai's God. He is not just Zerubbabel's or Joshua's God. He is our God, if we have come to Him through faith in the Lord Jesus Christ. Our God stands behind His promises.

ZECHARIAH

19

A Great Beginning

(Zechariah 1:1–6)

In the eighth month of the second year of Darius, the word of the LORD came to the prophet Zechariah son of Berekiah, the son of Iddo:

"The LORD was very angry with your forefathers. Therefore tell the people: This is what the LORD Almighty says: 'Return to me,' declares the LORD Almighty, 'and I will return to you.' says the LORD Almighty. Do not be like your forefathers, to whom the earlier prophets proclaimed: This is what the LORD Almighty says: 'Turn from your evil ways and your evil practices. But they would not listen or pay attention to me,' declares the LORD. Where are your forefathers now? And the prophets, do they live forever? But did not my words and my decrees, which I commanded my servants the prophets, overtake your forefathers?

"Then they repented and said, 'The LORD Almighty has done to us what our ways and practices deserve, just as he determined to do.' "

Zechariah is one of the most difficult books of the Old Testament, but one thing is not difficult: the dating of the book. In the very first words of his prophecy, Zechariah says that he received his first revelation from God in the eighth month of the second year of Darius, the emperor of Persia. This places Zechariah within the same time frame—indeed, within the same year—as his contemporary Haggai. Haggai and Zechariah were among the 42,360 Jews who had returned to Judah under the leadership of Zerubbabel the governor and Joshua the high priest to rebuild the temple in Jerusalem, and it was only two months after Haggai had received his first message from God that Zechariah received his. He thereby became the second prophet of the restoration. Since Haggai prophesied until near the end of the ninth month of the second year of Darius, Zechariah and Haggai overlapped as prophets for a short period.

These circumstances, plus the content of the books, encourage us to think of Zechariah's prophecy as supplementary to that of Haggai. The burden of Haggai's book is that the temple of God must be rebuilt, and that God would make it glorious. In speaking of this great but future glory, Haggai pointed forward to, but did not elaborate on, the messianic age. He promised that God would be with His people and would bless them once they began to rebuild the temple. These words must have encouraged the small committed band so overwhelmed by the enormity of the task. Like Haggai, Zechariah's message is one of encouragement. But he was aware that not all the returned remnant were fully sincere in their desires to serve God, and he therefore counseled them to repent of sin and return to God with all their hearts and minds.

Zechariah's encouragement made his

book particularly dear to the reformers. Martin Luther has provided us with two commentaries on Zechariah, one in Latin (prepared by others from careful lecture notes) and one in German. Luther regarded Zechariah as the very "model" or "quintessence" of prophecy (*Ausbund der Propheten*), particularly in its messianic predictions.

John Calvin regarded it as particularly suitable to his age. "This doctrine may be fitly applied to our age: for we see how Satan raises up great forces, we see how the whole world conspires against the Church, to prevent the increase or the progress of the kingdom of Christ. When we consider how great are the difficulties which meet us, we are ready to faint and to become wholly dejected. Let us then remember that it is no new thing for enemies to surpass great mountains in elevation; but that the Lord can at length reduce them to a plain. This, then, our shield can cast down and lay prostrate whatever greatness the Devil may set up to terrify us: for as the Lord then reduces a great mountain to a plain, when Zerubbabel was able to do nothing, so at this day, however boldly may multiplied adversaries resist Christ in the work of building a spiritual temple to God the Father, yet all their efforts will be in vain."[1]

Zechariah should encourage anyone who is trying to do a work for Christ in any age.

WHO WAS ZECHARIAH?

Zechariah is a common name in the Bible—at least twenty-seven Bible characters had it—but the author of the prophecy distinguishes himself as the "son of Berekiah, the son of Iddo" (Zech. 1:1, 7). Apparently his father died young, for he is named as the immediate successor of Iddo in the list of the heads of the priestly families in Nehemiah 12:12–21. Probably for the same reason, he is identified merely as a descendant of Iddo in Ezra 5:1 and 6:14. Since he is called a "young man" (Zech. 2:3), he was probably little more than a child when he returned with the first wave of the regathering exiles.

The only real problem with Zechariah's identity comes from a New Testament saying of Jesus Christ. In Matthew 23:35 Jesus says to the people of His day, "And so upon you will come all the righteous blood that has been shed on earth, from the blood of righteous Abel to the blood of Zechariah son of Berekiah, whom you murdered between the temple and the altar." Since there is a story of the murder of a prophet named Zechariah, son of Jehoiada, by stoning in the courtyard of the temple in 2 Chronicles 24:20–22, it is assumed that Jesus confused the two, thinking that the later Zechariah, the eleventh of the minor prophets, was the earlier Zechariah, who died about 800 B.C. This introduces the additional problem that the earlier Zechariah, who died by stoning in the temple area, was of the last of the Old Testament martyrs, which Jesus' statement implies.

The solution to this problem is to start over again with the assumptions (quite well founded) that Jesus knew what He was talking about, that the Zechariah He was referring to was indeed Zechariah son of Berekiah, and that Zechariah son of Berekiah was also martyred between the temple and the altar in a manner reminiscent of the murder of the earlier prophet of the same name. One writer concludes, "Since Jesus referred to Zechariah as the *last* of the Old Testament martyrs, there can be no legitimate doubt that it was the eleventh of the twelve minor prophets he had in mind. . . . We can

---

[1]John Calvin, *Commentaries on the Twelve Minor Prophets*, vol. 15, lect. 142, trans. John Owen (Grand Rapids: Baker, 1979), p. 114.

only conclude that the later Zechariah died in much the same way the earlier one did, as a victim of popular resentment against his rebuke of their sins. Since there are about twenty-seven different individuals mentioned in the Old Testament bearing the name Zechariah, it is not surprising if two of them happened to suffer a similar fate."[2]

We do not have any biblical or other history of this period, so we do not know what Zechariah's life may have been like between the beginning of his prophetic ministry in 520 B.C. and his death by stoning years later. Because of the scattered time references throughout the prophecy we do know that he continued to prophesy for several years at least.

Did Zechariah write all of Zechariah? This has been questioned because of the differences between the first (chaps. 1–8) and second (chaps. 9–14) halves of the book. These contain different subject matter and are written in different styles. The first half is dated by reference to the years of King Darius; the second is not. These differences lead many scholars to posit two authors and two separate works that have somehow become joined.

These arguments are valid only if it is necessary to believe that a writer must use one and not a variety of styles and deal with one and not a variety of subjects. Many scholars operate on these assumptions, but they are highly questionable for any writer and particularly so for Zechariah who came so near the end of the line of the prophets. It is understandable that Zechariah would write of the conditions of his day, giving encouragement to those who were attempting to rebuild the temple. In this he is at one with his contemporary, Haggai. But it is also reasonable that he (or any prophet) should also be

led of God to look ahead to that future day of full messianic blessing, as in the last six chapters. Since the last half of Zechariah deals with events that will occur largely in the future, how could the subject matter, moral issues, and historical setting not be different from chapters 1–8? Their difference is not fixed proof of separate authorship.

CALL TO REPENTANCE

Zechariah is going to unfold many rich and comforting promises both in the first and also the second sections of this prophecy. But riches like these are for people who have repented of sin and are ready to embrace the will and declarations of God. For this reason, the book opens with a message calling on the people to return to God and not be as their forefathers who refused to listen to Him.

The prophecy says: "The LORD was very angry with your forefathers. Therefore tell the people: "This is what the LORD Almighty says: 'Return to me,' declares the LORD Almighty, 'and I will return to you,' says the LORD Almighty. Do not be like your forefathers, to whom the earlier prophets proclaimed: This is what the LORD Almighty says, 'Turn from your evil ways and your evil practices. But they would not listen or pay attention to me,' declares the LORD. Where are your forefathers now? And the prophets, do they live forever? But did not my words and my decrees, which I commanded my servants the prophets, overtake your forefathers?

"Then they repented and said, 'The LORD Almighty has done to us what our ways and practices deserve, just as he determined to do' " (vv. 2–6).

These verses contain a number of valuable truths that are worth getting in mind at the outset of our study, even as the people of Zechariah's day must have fixed them in their minds.

---

[2] Gleason L. Archer, *Encyclopedia of Bible Difficulties* (Grand Rapids: Zondervan, 1982), p. 338.

1. *God judges sin.* If there is anything past history should have taught the returning exiles, it is that God does indeed judge sin. For hundreds of years the people were unwilling to acknowledge this, even when God gave them ample proof of His displeasure and unrelenting warnings of the destruction that was to come. There were warnings to the people of the northern kingdom of Israel by such prophets as Hosea and Amos. In the south Joel, Micah, Habakkuk, Zephaniah, Isaiah, and Jeremiah warned of judgment. Jeremiah alone prophesied for a period of forty years. During this time, with the exception of a few brief periods of partial revival, the people continued to go their way, arguing that no judgment could come upon them simply because they were the chosen people of God and Jerusalem was God's city. Indeed, for all those years it seemed as though these self-righteous and presumptuous people might be right. God did indeed seem reluctant to destroy their city.

Yet destruction came. Jerusalem was overrun, the people were deported, and both the temple and the walls of the city were destroyed. This was a great and inescapable fact of recent Jewish history, and the evidence of it was fresh on every hand. The walls were still down. The city was still a ruin. The land which had once flowed with milk and honey was now a barren wilderness.

So no one could possibly miss this first point when Zechariah reminded them of it. The prophet said, "The LORD was very angry with your forefathers."

The hearts of the people would have been forced to echo, "Indeed, He was."

Zechariah declared, "Where are your forefathers now?"

The people would have answered, "Gone, dead, scattered."

"And the prophets, do they live forever?"

The people would have been forced to acknowledge that even the prophets had been carried away in the judgment that came upon Jerusalem.

"Did not my words and my decrees, which I commanded my servants the prophets, overtake your forefathers?" Zechariah asked.

The people would have answered that the word of God through the prophets had indeed come true and that the kingdoms of Israel and Judah had indeed been overthrown, as they had said. Could anything be more obvious? God judges all. Although in His patience judgment may be for a time delayed, it does at last come and sinners do have to give an accounting for what they have done, whether good or bad.

2. *Past judgments are a warning to us to turn from sin.* This is the central point of Zechariah's opening message to the remnant. They were aware of what had overtaken their forefathers for their obstinate refusal to heed the word of God. They could hardly escape this knowledge. But the facts of that earlier destruction were not merely items of historical interest. They were examples intended to bring about wholehearted repentance and subsequent obedience.

Some people have imagined a problem at this point. They point out that when Zechariah's contemporary, Haggai, preached his first message just two months earlier, the people "obeyed the voice of the LORD their God," "feared the LORD," and got on with the rebuilding (Hag. 1:12–15). Does this mean that they had relapsed by the time Zechariah started his ministry? Did Zechariah read the situation wrongly? Or is something more involved here? We could point out that obeying one specific instruction from the Lord is not the same thing as a wholehearted turning from all sin, which is what Zechariah is calling for. But that is beside the point and probably is an underestimate of the depths of repentance under Haggai's preaching. What the people needed now was renewed and deeper dedication. As Leupold writes, "Every repentance, every return unto the Lord is imperfect at best. It is an expression that requires deepening; it must be done more sincerely and thoroughly. In a sense, a godly life consists of perfecting repentance, always doing it more effectually. So what Haggai claimed was true: the people had God on their side because they had returned to Him. But what Zechariah claimed was also true: Israel needed to return with more sincere devotion if God's promises for the future were to become a reality."[3]

That is why these stories of God's past judgments are still relevant for us, even though we may have turned from sin to Christ in our conversion. We can be Christ's and still live for a time as the disobedient Israelites. We can go our own way and turn a deaf ear to God's warnings. Are you doing this? If so, you must learn from God's judgments and allow them to turn you back from sin. We must all be warned to follow closer after God.

3. *Obedience brings blessing.* Sin brings judgment, but obedience brings blessing. This is the point most emphasized in Zechariah's message: "This is what the LORD Almighty says: 'Return to me,' declares the LORD Almighty, 'and I will return to you,' says the LORD Almighty" (v. 3). The point is clear: if the people will return to Him, God will return to the people and will bless them. The threefold repetition of the name "the LORD Almighty" underscores its certainty.

We think of what God said through Haggai. In the second chapter of that book, in a message delivered about a month after Zechariah had begun his ministry, Haggai quoted God as saying:

" 'Now give careful thought to this from this day on—consider how things were before one stone was laid on another in the LORD's temple. When anyone came to a heap of twenty measures, there were only ten. When anyone went to a wine vat to draw fifty measures, there were only twenty. I struck all the work of your hands with blight, mildew and hail, yet you did not turn to me,' declares the LORD. 'From this day on, from this twenty-fourth day of the ninth month, give careful thought to the day when the foundation of the LORD's temple was laid. Give careful thought: Is there yet any seed left in the barn? Until now, the vine and the fig tree, the pomegranate and the olive trees have not borne fruit.

" 'From this day on I will bless you' " (Hag. 2:15–19).

This passage is, in a certain sense, a commentary on Zechariah. Up to the twenty-fourth day of the sixth month the people had been disobeying the Lord out of twisted priorities and motives. They had been serving themselves, and their lives and work had not prospered. Their fields had not flourished. Their vines and trees had not borne fruit. But they had responded to Haggai's word and had obeyed God, and God had said that their fortunes would be spared from blight, mildew, and hail. They would see the fig, pomegranate, and olive trees begin to produce fruit in abundance. The vines would flourish, and the wine vats would again be full. This is a remarkable promise of material well-being predicated on a life of obedience by God's people. But it is what Zechariah is saying too, though in perhaps more spiritual terms. If God seems far away, it is because we are removed from Him by our sin. It is not God's fault. If we return to Him, He will return to us and bring blessing.

---

[3] H. C. Leupold, *Exposition of Zechariah* (Grand Rapids: Baker, 1978), p. 23.

4. *Like God Himself, the word of God is inescapable.* The prophecy says, "But did not my words and my decrees, which I commanded my servants the prophets, overtake your forefathers?" (v. 6). The fathers of the remnant thought they could escape God's judgment, but the word overtook them and they perished. So it was with the Flood generation. So it will be at Christ's final judgment. No one escapes God's word. God's word is eternal. It is longer lasting even than the prophets who speak it. They passed away (v. 5), yet the word spoken through them lived on and was fulfilled in the people's experience (v. 6). Jesus said, "Until heaven and earth disappear, not the smallest letter, not the least stroke of a pen, will by any means disappear from the Law until everything is accomplished" (Matt. 5:18).

"RETURN TO ME"

The last sentence of Zechariah's message tells of a past generation: "Then they repented and said, 'The LORD Almighty has done to us what our ways and practices deserve, just as he determined to do'"(v. 6). He is not speaking about the generation that perished in the destruction of Jerusalem, but their successors, those who saw the hand and justice of God in what happened. This is the spirit Zechariah wants to see in the remnant before he begins to unfold the visions that constitute the bulk of his book.

If we had only Haggai to go on, we might assume, however wrongly, that God was interested most of all in the temple, that is, in buildings. But this is not the case. True, God had given instructions about this building. But most of all, God was interested in the people to whom He had given this work, and He was concerned that they be truly surrendered to Him. Luther saw this and wrote: "This, then, is a brief outline of this first sermon of Zechariah: he first wishes to make the people pious and God-fearing by means of threats and promises; and in order to frighten them, he offers them the example of their fathers. For while they are to build the temple and the city of Jerusalem and do good deeds like these, he first wants them to be pious, so that they might not think that God would be satisfied with their work of building the temple and the city, as their fathers had thought that it was good enough if they sacrificed. No, my good man, rather than all good works he wants faith and a heart converted to him. That is all he is interested in. This must come first and be preached first: 'Return to me, and after that build me a temple,' and not, 'First build me a temple, and after that return to me.' Good works inflate us and make us proud, but faith and conversion humble us and make us despair of ourselves."[4]

This is the good beginning God wants. He wants it to be said of us, as it was of the believers of the apostle Peter's day: "You were like sheep going astray, but now you have returned to the Shepherd and Overseer of your souls" (1 Peter 2:25).

[4]Martin Luther, *Luther's Works*, vol. 20, *Lectures on the Minor Prophets: III, Zechariah* (Saint Louis: Concordia, 1973), pp. 165, 166.

20

Three Visions

(Zechariah 1:7–2:13)

During the night I had a vision—and there before me was a man riding a red horse! He was standing among the myrtle trees in a ravine. Behind him were red, brown and white horses. . . .

Then I looked up—and there before me were four horns! . . . Then the LORD showed me four craftsmen. . . .

Then I looked up—and there before me was a man with a measuring line in his hand! . . . "Shout and be glad, O daughter of Zion. For I am coming, and I will live among you," declares the LORD. "Many nations will be joined with the LORD in that day and will become my people. I will live among you and you will know that the LORD Almighty has sent me to you. The LORD will inherit Judah as his portion in the holy land and will again choose Jerusalem. Be still before the LORD, all mankind, because he has roused himself from his holy dwelling."

In our previous study of the Minor Prophets we have not come upon anything quite like the nine visions described in Zechariah 1:7–6:15. The closest parallel is in Amos where, in the seventh, eighth, and ninth chapters, the prophet was shown objects to which God gave prophetic meaning: swarms of locusts, a fire, a plumb line, a basket of ripe fruit, and the Lord standing by the altar. But Amos's visions were essentially word pictures. In one case at least (the basket of ripe fruit), the meaning of the vision consisted of a play on the word "ripe" rather than on the visual element itself. By contrast, in Zechariah we encounter visions similar to those recorded by Daniel. These involve real sights and real people, and they are presented in an ongoing fashion that involves dialogue, response, and development. The

visions are: (1) a man and a troop of horses standing among some myrtle trees (1:7–17), (2) four horns and four craftsmen (1:18–21), (3) a man with a measuring line (2:1–13), (4) a provision of cleansing for Joshua the high priest (3:1–10), (5) a gold lampstand with two olive trees (4:1–14), (6) a flying scroll (5:1–4), (7) a woman representing wickedness seated in a basket (5:5–11), (8) four chariots going out into the whole world (6:1–8), (9) the crowning of Joshua the high priest (6:9–15). Apparently, these visions were all received in one night: the night of the twenty-fourth day of the eleventh month of the second year of King Darius, that is, a night in late February of the year519 B.C.

These visions are hard to interpret in some particulars, and it raises a question about visions. Why should revelations from God be given in this form?

Part of the answer is that it is part of God's diversity of revelation, part of the "various ways" in which God spoke to our forefathers through the prophets (Heb. 1:1). Having spoken through sermons and symbols, through orations and oracles, God now uses apocalyptic visions to drive home His truth.

Yet a more pointed answer may be given. As we study these nine visions, we see that they are largely illustrations—stories or visual pictures—by which the message of encouragement that dominates Zechariah is made memorable and vivid to God's people. Charles Haddon Spurgeon, in *Lectures to My Students*, calls illustrations "windows" that let in "light." They illuminate, interest, enliven, and quicken attention.[1] That is precisely what Zechariah's visions do. It is true that they also puzzle us. At times they are exasperating. But they are still both interesting and vivid, and they serve their chief end of encouragement as much today as they undoubtedly did in the time of Zerubbabel, Joshua, Haggai, and Zechariah.

THE MAN AMONG THE MYRTLES

The visions Zechariah unfolds are said to have been given to him on the twenty-fourth day of the eleventh month of the second year of King Darius. This was five months after the resumption of the work on the temple. In view of Haggai's emphasis on the original twenty-fourth day, when the work began (1:15; cf. 2:10, 18, 20), it may be that the day has special significance in Zechariah also. Since this is the day on which the people resumed their work, God may have singled it out and made it memorable by these revelations.

The first vision was of "a man riding a red horse" standing (presumably,

sitting upon the back of his horse) among the myrtle trees in a ravine. Behind him were other horses, which were red, brown, and white. The picture seems to be that of a troop of heavenly cavalry led by the man at their head. When Zechariah asks the meaning of the vision, he is told that they "are the ones the LORD has sent to go throughout the earth." They report that they have found the earth to be at rest and peace. This created an unfavorable comparison with Jerusalem and the towns of Judah still in ruin. The head of the troop, now identified as "the angel of the LORD," asks God how long He will withhold mercy from Jerusalem. The answer comes back: "Proclaim this word: This is what the LORD Almighty says: 'I am very jealous for Jerusalem and Zion, but I am very angry with the nations that feel secure. I was only a little angry, but they added to the calamity.'

"Therefore, this is what the LORD says, 'I will return to Jerusalem with mercy, and there my house will be rebuilt. And the measuring line will be stretched out over Jerusalem,' declares the LORD Almighty.

"Proclaim further: This is what the LORD Almighty says: 'My towns will again overflow with prosperity, and the LORD will again comfort Zion and choose Jerusalem' " (vv. 14–17).

Several elements of this vision deserve special consideration, for they illuminate the message just quoted. First, the myrtle trees of the vision probably represent Israel and are so interpreted by most commentators. The myrtle is a small evergreen that never gets above eight feet tall. It has dark green leaves and white, star-like clusters of fragrant flowers, the petals of which emit a rich fragrance when crushed. Being an evergreen, the myr-

---

[1] Charles Haddon Spurgeon, *Lectures to My Students* (Grand Rapids: Zondervan, 1972), pp. 349–52.

tle illustrates the Jewish people's staying quality through history. Being small, it illustrates the insignificant state of the nation when compared with the gentile world powers. Israel is not likened to a cedar of Lebanon, which is majestic, or an oak tree, which is strong. Having blossoms that emit a sweet fragrance when crushed, the myrtle illustrates the strange grace of Israel in affliction. When Zechariah notes that the trees were in a ravine or low-lying area, he is probably pointing to the particularly low state of the Jewish people at the time of the vision.

The second important element is the identity of the man seated upon the red horse. If it were not for verse 11, we would regard the man as nothing more than a man, perhaps a representative figure of the powers arrayed on Israel's side. But verse 11 identifies him with "the angel of the LORD," and this brings in an entirely new dimension of imagery. This personage occurs at strategic points throughout the Old Testament.

The first appearance of the angel of the Lord is in Genesis 16:7, in the story of Hagar's flight from Sarah because of hard feelings between the two women. He instructs Hagar to return to Sarah, promising that she will have a child who will be named Ishmael. Then we read, "She gave this name to the LORD who spoke to her: 'You are the God who sees me' " (v. 13). In this verse the angel of the Lord is surprisingly but clearly identified with Jehovah.

The same thing is even more apparent in the next incident. In Genesis 18 Abraham is seated at the entrance to his tent near the great trees of Mamre. There "the LORD appeared" to him (v. 1). The story identifies the figures who appeared as three men. One of them has special significance and later converses at length with Abraham. He tells Sarah that she will have a son by the same time the next year (v. 10), speaking as God. Then in verse 13 we read, "The LORD said to Abraham . . ." Again, in verse 17 the text reads, "Then the LORD said, 'Shall I hide from Abraham what I am about to do?' " These references, and the fact that the angel of the Lord is consistently recognized as divine by those to whom he appeared, cause us to think of this figure as a pre-incarnation manifestation of the Second Person of the Trinity.

Joshua provides us with another example. After the crossing of the Jordan River on the way to the conquest of the Promised Land, a figure appeared to Joshua standing with a drawn sword in his hand. He identified himself as "commander of the army of the LORD" and was then worshiped by Joshua (Josh. 5:13–15). This person required Joshua to remove his shoes because the ground on which he was standing was holy, a clear throwback to Moses' earlier meeting with God at the burning bush (Exod. 3:5).

This is the figure Zechariah identifies as standing among the myrtle trees, which, as we have seen, represent Israel. So Zechariah is saying that God is with and in the midst of His people.

But now, having noticed what the vision signifies, can we miss the fact that this is also the specific content of the message added to the vision (vv. 14–17) and a specific fulfillment of the promise given in the opening six verses of the prophecy. The first sermon of Zechariah said, " 'Return to me,' declares the LORD Almighty, 'and I will return to you,' says the LORD Almighty" (Zech. 1:3). Presumably the people had returned to God, and now the second half of that message is fulfilled: God is returning to His people. The angel of the Lord and the angelic troops mounted upon their red, brown, and white horses had been about the earth, but now they had returned and were in Israel's midst. Moreover, this is exactly what is said later: "This is what the

LORD says, 'I will return to Jerusalem with mercy, and there my house will be rebuilt. And the measuring line will be stretched out over Jerusalem,' declares the LORD Almighty. . . . 'My towns will again overflow with prosperity, and the LORD will again comfort Zion and choose Jerusalem' " (vv. 16, 17).

It is hard to study this without thinking of the parallel vision in the first chapter of Revelation. The passage occurs toward the end of the New Testament just as Zechariah's vision occurs toward the end of the Old. In Revelation Jesus is pictured as standing in the midst of "seven golden lampstands," which are explicitly identified as representing the church (v. 20). From this position He speaks comfort and challenge to God's people.

Is this not a comfort to you? In Zechariah's time Jesus was in the midst of His people Israel. He is also in the midst of His chosen people, the church, composed of both believing Jews and believing Gentiles. He is in the midst of whatever true Christian gathering you may belong to, and He is with you whoever you may be—so long as you have really turned from sin to follow Jesus as your Lord and Savior. Moreover, He is there to challenge you. He comforts you by the teachings and promises of Scripture. He challenges you by His own life and by calling you to discipleship. He says, "If anyone would come after me, he must deny himself and take up his cross daily and follow me" (Luke 9:23). He adds, "Surely I will be with you always, to the very end of the age" (Matt. 28:20).

Four Horns and Four Craftsmen

The second of Zechariah's nine visions, a vision of four horns and four craftsmen, follow logically on vision one. In the first vision God has expressed His anger against Israel's enemies. In this, the second vision, He shows how He has raised up leaders of

His own to terrify, overthrow, and scatter them.

Of the two main parts of this vision the first is easier to pin down. The people of the East have always been a predominantly pastoral people. Therefore, noting that the strongest animals in a herd were furnished with horns, horns became for them a natural symbol of power and pride. To lift up the horn was to be proud or even arrogant about one's strength and position. To have horns coming out of the hands was to have power in the hands, and so on. In Daniel this imagery had been used to symbolize the nations coming together to oppose God (Dan. 7). Here there were ten horns, plus another little one which uprooted three of the ten. They are explicitly identified as kings in conflict, all of whom are to be overthrown by the Ancient of Days and the "one like a son of man" who rules for Him. It is clear that Zechariah's use of the horn image conforms to this, for the angel explains the horns, saying, "These are the horns that scattered Judah, Israel and Jerusalem" (v. 19).

It is not so easy to say whom the horns represent specifically. It is tempting to identify them with the gentile powers of this period: Syria, Assyria, Babylon, and Egypt. But Egypt did not really scatter the Jewish people, and any attempts at identification always seem to break down under the details of the period. Most commentators suggest that "four" is therefore probably just a representative number. It may indicate the four points of the compass, with the suggestion that God is against whatever powers may be arrayed against Israel.

The same situation prevails with the craftsmen the vision indicates will be raised up to destroy the horns. It would be tempting to identify them with Zerubbabel, Joshua, Ezra, and Nehemiah. But they do not relate to four world kingdoms in any way; and if they are intended, then the horns would have to be identified with small local kingdoms such as Samaria. This seems to be getting off the track. Probably, if the horns are symbolic (representing any and all world powers), then the craftsmen are also symbolic. It would be Zechariah's way of saying that whatever the power raised against God's people, God also has His power and representative to oppose it and throw it down.

History shows this to be fact. In the early days of the church, when unbelievers in the guise of clerics were attacking belief in the deity of Jesus Christ, God raised up Athanasius (A.D. 293–373) to contend for Christianity. He was reviled, banished five or six times, physically attacked. But he hung on throughout a long lifetime and eventually defeated Arianism, which would have returned Christianity to paganism. "To have set a dam against this process the whole force of a mighty personality constitutes the importance of Athanasius in the world's history."[2]

A century later the church was threatened by Pelagianism and other heresies. God raised up Augustine. With the skill and perseverance of a master craftsman, this intellectual giant scattered Pelagianism.

So it has been in all ages. Enemies rise against the church from all directions, but there has never been an age in which God did not raise up people equal to the task to scatter those who have scattered the flock of Christ.

I notice one more point. In the Hebrew text the word translated "craftsmen" (NIV) is *charash*, which may mean a worker in wood, stone, or iron, hence the variety of translations in the Bible versions. The New International Version opts for "craftsmen" being a general term, since it does not specify the

medium in which these individuals are supposed to work. But if we think of carpenters, for example, we do not get a very clear image of how they are supposed to throw down the four horns. It may be in this case, that the New English Bible is better when it translates the word as "smiths," meaning "blacksmiths." These men work with hammers on anvils, and it is easy to see how they might use their hammers to beat down the four horns.

Here I go a step further to ask: What are the hammers with which these craftsmen of God do the work of throwing down the enemies of God's people, if they are indeed to be supposed to use hammers? There can only be one answer to that question. Their weapon is the Word of God. Jeremiah says, " 'Is not my word like fire,' declares the LORD, 'and like a *hammer* that breaks a rock in pieces?' " (Jer. 23:29). This tool is mighty. It is effective by means of God's own power. This is why the servants of God triumph. It is why the apostle Paul can say, "The weapons we fight with are not the weapons of the world. On the contrary, they have divine power to demolish strongholds. We demolish arguments and every pretension that sets itself up against the knowledge of God, and we take captive every thought to make it obedient to Christ" (2 Cor. 10:4, 5). If that is our tool, we should use it. If the Word is our weapon, we should wield it forcefully in battles that bring glory to the Lord.

A Man With a Measuring Line

Like the second of Zechariah's visions, the third vision builds on the earlier ones. In the first vision God had mentioned a measuring line, saying, "The measuring line will be stretched out over Jerusalem" (Zech. 1:16). This is

---

[2] "Athanasius" in *The Encyclopedia Britannica,* eleventh edition (New York: The Encyclopedia Britannica Company, 1910), vol. 2, p. 827.

described in the third vision. Zechariah sees a man with a measuring line in his hand, and when he asks, "What are you doing?" the answer is given, "To measure Jerusalem, to find out how wide and how long it is" (Zech. 2:2). It turns out that the measurement shows an increasingly expanding city. It will be a city without walls because of the great numbers of people and livestock in it. If the question is then raised, as it would be in the minds of most hearers, "But what, then, will Jerusalem do for defense?" God replies, "I myself will be a wall of fire around it . . . and I will be its glory within" (v. 5).

What follows is a verbalized statement of the vision's message, much as in chapter 1. " 'Come! Come! Flee from the land of the north,' declares the LORD, 'for I have scattered you to the four winds of heaven,' declares the LORD.

" 'Come, O Zion! Escape, you who live in the Daughter of Babylon!' For this is what the LORD Almighty says: 'After he has honored me and has sent me against the nations that have plundered you—for whoever touches you touches the apple of his eye—I will surely raise my hand against them so that their slaves will plunder them. Then you will know that the LORD Almighty has sent me.

" 'Shout and be glad, O Daughter of Zion. For I am coming, and I will live among you,' declares the LORD. 'Many nations will be joined with the LORD in that day and will become my people. I will live among you and you will know that the LORD Almighty has sent me to you. The LORD will inherit Judah as his portion in the holy land and will again choose Jerusalem. Be still before the LORD, all mankind, because he has roused himself from his holy dwelling' " (Zech. 2:6–13).

The vision and its accompanying message have two main parts, just as the earlier visions did. Part one is the expansion and prosperity of Jerusalem. It had a temporal, physical fulfillment, because Jerusalem did indeed expand and become a great city. It became quite prosperous. But it is also clear, particularly from the final paragraph of chapter 2, that the fulfillment in view was to be more than merely temporal and physical. It was to be timeless and spiritual also. The ultimate fulfillment was to involve the expansion of God's spiritual city to include many nations and peoples. That is, the people of God were to be enlarged beyond Judaism to include the Gentiles, as happened in the establishment and growth of the Christian church.

Part two of the vision is the new presence of God among His people, which results in security from enemies without and glory within. What better security can the people of God have than God Himself? If He is present, there is no need for walls. If He is absent, nothing will be an adequate defense against enemies. The promise that God will be the glory of the city carries our minds to the end of Revelation where it is said of the new Jerusalem: "The city does not need the sun or the moon to shine on it, for the glory of God gives it light, and the Lamb is its lamp. The nations will walk by its light, and the kings of the earth will bring their splendor into it" (Rev. 21:23, 24).

What are the practical teachings of this vision? I turn to a list in Thomas V. Moore's commentary on Zechariah. Moore had the habit, which he learned from some of the Puritans, of following his expositions with a list of what he termed "practical inferences"—in this case the following:

"1. Although Zion has not yet lengthened her cords and widened her stakes to her appointed limits, yet the measuring line has gone forth that gives her bounds to be the habitable earth. Hence, if this future extension was a motive to the Jew, in his work of earing the temple of wood and stone, much more is it to us in our work of erecting the great spiritual temple on he foundation, Jesus Christ (vv. 1–4).

"2. We learn here the true glory of the church. It is not in any external pomp or power of any kind; not in frowning battlements, either of temporal or spiritual pretensions; not in rites and ceremonies, however moss-grown and venerable; not in splendid cathedrals and gorgeous vestments and the swell of music and the glitter of eloquence, but in the indwelling glory of the invisible God. Her outward rites and ceremonies, therefore, should only be like what the earth's atmosphere is to the rays of the sun, a pure, transparent medium of transmission (v. 5).

"3. The punishment of the wicked as truly declares the glory of God as the salvation of the righteous (v. 8).

"4. The wicked shall ultimately be slaves of their own lusts, those appetites and passions that were designed to be merely their obedient servants, shall become their tormenting and inexorable tyrants (v. 9).

"5. The incarnation of Christ, and his indwelling in the church, are grounds of the highest joy (v. 10).

"6. Christ is a divine Savior. In verses 10, 11, we have one Jehovah sending another, and the Jehovah sent is identified with the angel of the covenant, who was to come and dwell in the church, whom we know to be Christ. Hence, unless there are two distinct Jehovahs, one divine and the other not, Christ, the Jehovah angel of this passage is divine.

"7. The church of God shall cover the earth and become in fact what it is in right, the mightiest agency in human history. Though now feeble and despised, she shall one day include many nations, and every knee shall bow and every tongue confess that Jesus is Lord to the glory of God the Father (v. 11).

"8. Delay of punishment is no proof of impunity. God often seems to be asleep, but he is only awaiting the appointed time. In the end, when all seems as it was from the foundation of the world, the herald cry shall go forth, 'Be silent, O earth, for Jehovah is aroused to his terrible work, and the day of his wrath is come.' Let man kiss the Son whilst he is yet in the way, before his anger is kindled but a little, and they perish before him like stubble before the whirlwind of flames."[3]

The chapter's application relates to Moore's last point: "Flee from the land of the north. . . . Escape, you who live in the Daughter of Babylon" (vv. 6, 7). The Jews were to flee from those lands upon which God's judgment was to fall, just as we are to flee from God's final judgment by turning to the Lord Jesus Christ. However, "flee" is not the only imperative we find here. We also have the word "come," and that is repeated. "Come! . . . Come! . . . Come!" says God. And then to encourage us even in that invitation, "For I am coming, and I will live among you" (v. 10). What greater encouragement could there be? God has come to us and now invites us to come to Him to escape the sure wrath to come.

[3]Thomas V. Moore, A Commentary on Haggai, Zechariah and Malachi (Edinburgh and Carlisle, Pa.: Banner of Truth Trust, 1979), pp. 145–47. Original edition 1856.

21

Clean Garments for God's Priest

(Zechariah 3:1–10)

Then he showed me Joshua the high priest standing before the angel of the LORD, *and Satan standing at his right side to accuse him. The* LORD *said to Satan, "The* LORD *rebuke you, Satan! The* LORD, *who has chosen Jerusalem, rebuke you! Is not this man a burning stick snatched from the fire?"*

Now Joshua was dressed in filthy clothes as he stood before the angel. The angel said to those who were standing before him, "Take off his filthy clothes."

Then he said to Joshua, "See, I have taken away your sin, and I will put rich garments on you."

Then I said, "Put a clean turban on his head." So they put a clean turban on his head and clothed him, while the angel of the LORD *stood by.*

The angel of the LORD *gave this charge to Joshua: "This is what the* LORD *Almighty says: 'If you will walk in my ways and keep my requirements, then you will govern my house and have charge of my courts, and I will give you a place among these standing here.*

" 'Listen, O high priest Joshua and your associates seated before you, who are men symbolic of things to come: I am going to bring my servant, the Branch. See, the stone I have set in front of Joshua! There are seven eyes on that one stone, and I will engrave an inscription on it,' says the LORD *Almighty, 'and I will remove the sin of this land in a single day.*

" 'In that day each of you will invite his neighbor to sit under his vine and fig tree,' declares the LORD *Almighty."*

John Wesley never forgot a terrible night of his childhood. He was only six years old at the time, and he had awakened in the family's old rectory to find it ablaze from top to bottom. Everyone else had been dragged from the building, but by some extraordinary oversight he had been forgotten. At the very last moment, just before the roof fell in with a crash, a neighbor climbed on another's shoulders and pulled the terrified child from a window. Later that scene was drawn for Wesley, and he kept it until the day of his death. He wrote under it a verse taken from the third chapter of Zechariah: "Is not this a brand plucked from the burning?" (v. 2b, old KJV text).

Wesley's experience in being literally saved from fire was unusual, but all of God's people experience it in a far more important sense. Jesus Christ has rescued us from the fires of hell.

JOSHUA THE PRIEST

The verse that meant so much to Wesley occurs in the middle of the fourth of Zechariah's visions, seen on the twenty-fourth day of the eleventh month of the second year of King Darius. There had been three visions before this: (1) a man seated upon a red horse among some myrtle trees (1:7–17), (2) four horns and four craftsmen raised up to terrify and scatter them (1:18–21), and (3) a man with a measuring line going out to measure Jerusalem (2:1–13). These were encouraging. They showed that God was again among His people, intending to bless and prosper them; that God would raise up servants equal to any enemy or emergency that might threaten Israel; that Jerusalem and the land of Judah would prosper beyond the people's fondest dreams.

Zechariah must have wondered at this point how God could possibly bless His people after all they had done. Their sin had led to their exile in Babylon. Had it also removed them forever from the place of blessing?

The fourth and most dramatic vision seems like an answer to just such questions. Zechariah saw Joshua the high priest standing before the angel of the Lord. Although he does not say so, it probably took place in the remembered or anticipated temple in Jerusalem where Joshua would be performing his functions as priest. As Joshua performed his important function of representing the people before God, Sátan appeared at his right side to accuse him. Since we are told later that Joshua was clothed in filthy clothes, representing his and the people's sin, Satan must have been pointing to those and declaring forcefully that Joshua was unfit to stand before the Lord in this office.

Joshua said nothing. Presumably he had nothing to say. He was sinful and, being sinful, *was* unworthy. But God spoke, and His words were a rebuke to Satan: "The LORD rebuke you, Satan! The LORD who has chosen Jerusalem, rebuke you! Is not this man a burning stick snatched from the fire?" Then Joshua's filthy clothes were taken away, and rich garments and a clean turban were put on him, while the angel of the Lord stood by.

There are a number of important doctrines in this story. We see the deity of the "angel of the LORD " clearer here even than in the previous chapter. It is he who speaks to Satan, saying, "The LORD rebuke you!" but he is himself called the Lord: "The LORD said to Satan, 'The LORD rebuke you!' " Another doctrine is God's divine choice or election, for "the LORD . . . has chosen Jerusalem." It is not Jerusalem that chooses Him. Again, the picture speaks of God's grace.

More important than any of these other doctrines, however, is the picture of salvation presented by the clothing of Joshua in clean garments. This taps into a rich stream of biblical imagery. In Isaiah 64:6, in a passage that would no doubt be known to Zechariah and the biblically literate, returning exiles, Isaiah wrote: "All of us have become like one who is unclean, and all our righteous acts are like filthy rags." Job said, "I put on righteousness as my clothing; justice was my robe and my turban" (Job 29:14). One of the Psalms of Ascent, sung by the people as they made their way up to Jerusalem for the feasts, says, "May your priests be clothed with righteousness; may your saints sing for joy" (Ps. 132:9). Isaiah speaks of the Messiah being clothed with righteousness: "Righteousness will be his belt and faithfulness the sash around his waist" (Isa. 11:5) and "He put on righteousness as his breastplate" (Isa. 59:17). Toward the end of his prophecy Isaiah rejoiced that he was clothed in God's righteousness:

> I delight greatly in the LORD;
>   my soul rejoices in my God.
> For he has clothed me with
>   garments of salvation
> and arrayed me in a robe of
>   righteousness,

as a bridegroom adorns his head
    like a priest,
and as a bride adorns herself with
    her jewels (Isa. 61:10).

We see the same ideas in the New Testament. On one occasion Jesus told a parable about a wedding in which a guest came without wearing a wedding garment. The king asked him, "Friend, . . . how did you get in here without wedding clothes?" When the man was speechless, the king told the attendants, "Tie him hand and foot, and throw him outside, into the darkness, where there will be weeping and gnashing of teeth" (Matt. 22:12, 13). On the other hand, in Revelation 19:7, 8 the bride of Christ is described as clothed in fine linen: " 'His bride has made herself ready. Fine linen, bright and clean, was given her to wear.' (Fine linen stands for the righteous acts of the saints.)"

These images are descriptive of our justification through the work of Christ. So it is not surprising that the poets of the church have seized upon them in preparing hymns for worship. Zinzendorf wrote:

Jesus, thy blood and righteousness
My beauty are, my glorious dress;
'Midst flaming worlds, in these
    arrayed,
With joy shall I lift up my head.

Bold shall I stand in thy great day;
For who aught to my charge shall
    lay?
Fully absolved through these I am
From sin and fear, from guilt and
    shame.

O let the dead now hear thy voice;
Now bid thy banished ones rejoice;
Their beauty this, their glorious
    dress,
Jesus, thy blood and righteousness.

Edward Mote had similar thoughts:

When he shall come with trumpet
    sound,

O may I then in him be found,
Dressed in his righteousness alone,
Faultless to stand before the throne.

The question posed by this vision is whether we are clothed in Christ's righteousness and are therefore found fit to appear before God or whether we are still clothed in the filthy robes of our own righteousness, which makes us unfit and will eventually condemn us.

A CHARGE TO KEEP

The story of the justification of Joshua does not stop with the priest's change of clothing, for immediately after this the angel of the Lord gives Joshua this charge: "This is what the LORD Almighty says: 'If you will walk in my ways and keep my requirements, then you will govern my house and have charge of my courts, and I will give you a place among these standing here' " (vv. 6, 7).

It brings to mind something Jesus did during the days of His earthly ministry. On one occasion the enemies of the Lord brought Him a woman they had trapped in adultery. Everyone knew that the ministry of Jesus had been marked by compassion and that He could be expected to forgive the woman's sin. But the law of Moses had fixed the penalty for adultery as death. Christ's enemies asked Him what should be done, knowing that if He said to obey the law and kill her, He would be discredited as a compassionate man, and that if He said the opposite and forgave her, He could be accused of violating the law of Moses. It was a real problem. Indeed, it was the problem of all problems. How can God show love to the sinner without being unjust? How can the love of God and the justice of God be harmonized?

We know the story. Jesus told the one who was without sin to cast the first stone at her, and they, being convicted by their own consciences, went out one by one until only the woman was left. Then Jesus forgave her, undoubtedly on the basis of His imminent death for sinners. In this He was doing precisely what was earlier done for Joshua. He was clothing her in the robes of His own righteousness.

But then He said, as He also said to Joshua, "Go now and leave your life of sin" (John 8:11).

This command always follows upon forgiveness, for we cannot be justified by God and then do as we please. We must stop sinning. At the same time we can be glad the order is as Christ gives it. He did not tell the woman, "Go now, leave your life of sin and I will not condemn you." He said, "Neither do I condemn you. . . . Go now, and leave your life of sin." Similarly He said to Joshua, "See, I have taken away your sin, and I will put rich garments on you," and only after that did He say, "If you will walk in my ways and keep my requirements, then you will govern my house and have charge of my courts, and I will give you a place among these standing here." If we have experienced God's forgiveness, we must live for Him. In particular, we must "walk in [His] ways and keep [His] requirements," for only then will we have a proper work and place among God's servants.

Our Great High Priest

The last section of this chapter develops the imagery of Joshua's priesthood in a new and unexpected way. For this reason special attention is called to it: " 'Listen, O high priest Joshua and your associates seated before you, who are men symbolic of things to come: I am going to bring my servant, the Branch. See, the stone I have set in front of Joshua! There are seven eyes on that one stone, and I will engrave an inscription on it,' says the Lord Almighty, 'and I will remove the sin of this land in a single day. In that day each of you will invite his neighbor to sit under his vine and fig tree,' declares the Lord Almighty" (vv. 8–10).

This is a great messianic passage, containing some of the key symbols for the Messiah. He is the Servant (see Isa. 42:1; 49:3, 5; 52:13; 53:11; Ezek. 34:23, 24), the Branch (see Isa. 4:2; 11:1; Jer. 23:5; 33:15; Zech. 6:12), and the Stone (see Ps. 118:22; Isa. 8:14; 28:16), although "the stone" in this chapter may not be a messianic reference.[1] The reference to removing the sin of this land in a single day foretells the Atonement.

The emphasis of this paragraph is not on the identity of the Messiah as the Servant, Branch, or Stone, however. It is on Christ as priest, since the opening words speak of Joshua and his associates as "symbolic of things to come" (v. 8). The verse is saying that the one who was already known as the Servant, Branch, and Stone will fulfill the priestly function, removing the sin of the land in a single day and thus providing for the very cleansing of Joshua and the others about whom the vision has been speaking.

The Book of Hebrews develops these themes in the fullest measure and is therefore in some sense a New Testament commentary on Zechariah. It shows that Jesus fulfilled this function

---

[1] Zechariah 3:9 is one of the most difficult verses in the prophecy. The stone has been viewed as a foundation stone of the temple, a stone crowning the temple structure, the stone that took the place of the Ark of the Covenant in the Holy of Holies, a symbol of Israel or the church, a precious stone in the crown worn by Zerubbabel, a similar stone adorning one of his outer garments, an amulet, a signet stone worn by God Himself, a stone of remembrance on the breastplate or shoulder of the high priest, the altar, and a memorial stone like those often found in Babylon. For a discussion of these possibilities see Joyce G. Baldwin, *Haggai, Zechariah, and Malachi* (London: InterVarsity Press, 1972), pp. 116–18; H. C. Leupold, *Exposition of Zechariah* (Grand Rapids: Baker, 1978), pp. 77–80; and Charles L. Feinberg, *God Remembers: A Study of Zechariah* (Portland: Multnomah Press, 1979), pp. 51–53.

in two ways, by offering Himself up as a sacrifice for sin (which the Old Testament priests could not do) and by interceding for His people in heaven.

That Jesus is Himself the sacrifice for sins makes clear that His priesthood is different from and superior to the Old Testament priesthoods. There are other differences too. To begin with, the Old Testament priests were sinful and were required to offer a sacrifice for themselves as well as for those they represented. For example, before the high priest could go into the Holy of Holies on the Day of Atonement, which he did once a year, he first had to offer a bullock as a burnt offering for his sin and that of his household (Lev. 16:6). Only after that was he able to proceed with the ceremonies connected with the scapegoat and the offering whose blood was to be sprinkled upon the mercy seat within the Holy of Holies. Again, the sacrifices the priests of Israel offered were inadequate. They taught the way of salvation through the death of an innocent victim. But the blood of sheep and goats could not take away sins, as both the Old Testament and the New Testament recognize (Amos 5:22; Mic. 6:6, 7; Heb. 10:4–7). Finally, the sacrifices of the earthly priests were also incomplete. They had to be offered again and again. In Jerusalem, for example, the fire on the great altar of sacrifice never went out; and on a great sabbath such as the Passover, hundreds of thousands of lambs would be offered.

In contrast to this earthly priesthood, *the sacrifice of Jesus is by one who is Himself perfect* and who therefore has no need that atonement be made for Him. The author of Hebrews says, "Such a high priest meets our need—one who is holy, blameless, pure, set apart from sinners, exalted above the heavens. Unlike the other high priests, he does not need to offer sacrifices day after day, first for his own sins, and then for the sins of the people" (Heb. 7:26, 27).

Second, being Himself perfect and at the same time the sacrifice, it follows that *the sacrifice made by Jesus was itself perfect.* Hence, it could actually pay the price for sin and remove it, as the sacrifices in Israel could not. They were a shadow of things to come, but they were not the reality. Jesus' death was the actual atonement on the basis of which God declares the sinner righteous. The author of Hebrews makes this point in chapter 9: "When Christ came as high priest of the good things that are already here, he . . . did not enter by means of the blood of goats and calves; but he entered the Most Holy Place once for all by his own blood, having obtained eternal redemption. The blood of goats and bulls and the ashes of a heifer sprinkled on those who are ceremonially unclean sanctify them so that they are outwardly clean. How much more, then, will the blood of Christ, who through the eternal Spirit offered himself unblemished to God, cleanse our consciences from acts that lead to death, so that we may serve the living God!' " (vv. 11–14).

Finally, unlike the sacrifices of the Old Testament priests which had to be repeated daily, *the sacrifice of Jesus was complete and eternal.* This is confirmed by the fact that He is now seated at the right hand of God. In the Jewish temple there were no chairs. This signified that the work of the priests was never done. "But when [Christ] had offered for all time one sacrifice for sins, he sat down at the right hand of God. Since that time he waits for his enemies to be made his footstool, because by one sacrifice he has made perfect forever those who are being made holy" (Heb. 10:12–14).

Teaching about priests and sacrifices is hard for most people today to understand. We do not have sacrifices in most of the civilized world and do not understand the terminology. But it was not that easy to understand in antiquity either. The author of Hebrews acknowledges this in a parenthetical remark occurring in the midst of his own exposition ("We have much to say about this, but it is hard to explain because you are slow to learn," 5:11). That is why God gave elaborate instructions for the performances of sacrifices—to teach both the serious nature of sin and His provision for forgiveness. The sacrifices taught two great lessons. First, sin means death. It is a lesson concerning God's judgment. It means that sin is serious ("The soul who sins is the one who will die," Ezek. 18:4). Second, there is grace. The significance of the sacrifice is that by the grace of God an innocent substitute can be offered in the sinner's place. The

goat or lamb was not that substitute. It could only point forward to it. But Jesus was and is, for all who will have Him as Savior. He is the only, perfect, all-sufficient sacrifice for sin on the basis of which God counts the sinner justified.[2]

Only on the basis of Jesus' sacrifice can anyone properly sit under his vine and fig tree, enjoying the blessings of this life—as the last verse of the chapter reminds us. If we are not justified, prosperity is a fatal illusion. It tempts us to believe that all is well when all is not well. It lures us to the fires of hell. It is only when we are justified that we can see these things as having come to us from the hands of God and praise Him for them.

---

[2]The discussion of Jesus' priesthood is borrowed in part from James Montgomery Boice, *God the Redeemer* (Downers Grove, Ill.: InterVarsity Press, 1978), pp. 168–71.

22

Five More Visions

(Zechariah 4:1–6:15)

Then the angel who talked with me returned and wakened me, as a man is wakened from his sleep. He asked me, "What do you see?"

I answered, "I see a solid gold lampstand with a bowl at the top and seven lights on it, with seven channels to the lights. Also there are two olive trees by it, one on the right of the bowl and the other on its left." . . .

I looked again—and there before me was a flying scroll!

He asked me, "What do you see?"

I answered, "I see a flying scroll, thirty feet long and fifteen feet wide." . . .

Then the angel who was speaking to me came forward and said to me, "Look up and see what this is that is appearing."

I asked, "What is it?"

He replied, "It is a measuring basket." And he added, "This is the iniquity of the people throughout the land." . . .

I looked up again—and there before me were four chariots coming out from between two mountains—mountains of bronze! The first chariot had red horses, the second black, the third white, and the fourth dappled—all of them powerful." . . .

The word of the LORD came to me: "Take silver and gold from the exiles Heldai, Tobijah and Jedaiah, who have arrived from Babylon. Go the same day to the house of Josiah son of Zephaniah. Take the silver and gold and make a crown, and set it on the head of the high priest, Joshua son of Jehozadak. Tell him this is what the LORD Almighty says: 'Here is the man whose name is the Branch, and he will branch out from his place and build the temple of the LORD. It is he who will build the temple of the LORD, and he will be clothed with majesty and will sit and rule on his throne. And he will be a priest on his throne. And there will be harmony between the two.' The crown will be given to Heldai, Tobijah, Jedaiah and Hen son of Zephaniah as a memorial in the temple of the LORD. Those who are far away will come and help to build the temple of the LORD, and you will know that the LORD Almighty has sent me to you. This will happen if you diligently obey the LORD your God."

I do not know if Charles Dickens read Zechariah, but the experience of Ebenezer Scrooge accompanied by the ghosts of Christmas past, Christmas present, and Christmas future bears a strange resemblance to the experiences of Zechariah accompanied by the interpreting angel. Like Scrooge's visions,

174

all were received in one night. Like Scrooge's ghosts, the interpreting angel was present throughout to probe Zechariah's understanding and explain the visions.

There have already been four visions. In the first, Zechariah saw a man, later shown to be the angel of the Lord, seated upon a horse among some myrtle trees in a ravine. It symbolized the renewed presence of God with His people, which was how the angel explained it: "This is what the LORD says, 'I will return to Jerusalem with mercy, and there my house will be rebuilt. And the measuring line will be stretched out over Jerusalem,' declares the LORD Almighty" (1:16). The second vision was of four horns and four craftsmen raised up to scatter them. The angel explained this as the destruction of those "who lifted up their horns against the land of Judah to scatter its people" (1:21). In the third vision a man was seen going out to measure Jerusalem. The angel explained that Jerusalem "will be a city without walls because of the great number of men and livestock in it" (2:4). The fourth vision, which rounds out the first set, showed Joshua the high priest standing before the Lord with Satan at his right side to accuse him. He was clothed in filthy garments. But they were taken from him, and he was reclothed with clean garments and a clean turban. On this occasion the angel had a charge for Joshua which then passed over into a great messianic prophecy concerning God's servant, the Branch. It was said that by him God would remove the sin of this land in a single day" (3:9). The first four visions reach an early and unexpected climax in this statement.

In chapter 4 the movement leading up to a scene involving the high priest begins again. This time there are four clear visions: a gold lampstand with two olive trees (4:1–4), a flying scroll (5:1–4), a woman representing wickedness seated in a basket (5:5–11), and four chariots going out into the whole world (6:1–8). Strictly speaking, the last scene is not a vision—it is a revelation of an action Zechariah was to take after the visions ended. But it belongs with these later visions and is a climax to them, just as the other scene involving Joshua was a climax to the first three.

In each of these the angel is present to explain the vision and convey the message of the Lord embodied in it.

THE GOLD LAMPSTAND

The first of Zechariah's second set of visions, the fifth in the series, was of a gold lampstand consisting of seven lights. It had a bowl at the top, containing oil, and there were channels or conduits to the lights. Also there were two olive trees, one placed by each side of the bowl. Since this lampstand was of gold and had seven lamps as part of it, there can be little doubt that it is intended to resemble the seven-branched menorah originally fashioned for the Jewish tabernacle (cf. Exod. 25:31–40; 37:17–24). On the other hand, it had features that the menorah did not have: the bowl on top, the channels or conduits to the seven lights, and the two olive trees. These added features signify an unlimited and uninterrupted supply of oil to the lamps. Indeed, later on in the chapter (v. 12), it is shown that two branches from the two olive trees were constantly pouring out golden oil.

The central feature of this vision is not hard to explain. The lampstand represents the elect people of God— first Israel and then later the church— as many references throughout the Old and New Testaments make clear. Isaiah wrote of Israel, "Arise, shine, for your light has come, and the glory of the LORD rises upon you. See, darkness covers the earth and thick darkness is over the peoples, but the LORD rises upon you and his glory appears over you. Nations will come to your light, and kings to the brightness of your dawn" (Isa. 60:1–3). Again, "For Zion's sake I will not keep silent, for Jerusalem's sake I will not remain quiet, till her righteousness shines out like the dawn, her salvation like a blazing torch" (Isa. 62:1). In the New Testament Jesus called his disciples "the light of the world" (Matt. 5:14). He told them to "let your light shine before men, that they may see your good deeds and praise your Father in heaven" (Matt. 5:16). He said, "Keep your lamps burning" (Luke 12:35). In Revelation 1 we have the New Testament equivalent of Zechariah's vision: Jesus standing among seven golden lampstands. On this occasion Jesus explains, "The seven stars are the angels of the seven churches, and the seven lampstands are the seven churches" (Rev. 1:20).

The oil of Zechariah's vision is also not obscure in meaning. It is a pervasive image of the Holy Spirit and of the power of the Spirit which is supplied to God's people in abundant measure.

In his valuable commentary on Zechariah, Charles L. Feinberg makes a major point of this, showing why oil is such a good symbol for the Spirit of God or the Spirit's work. "First, oil *lubricates*, thus abolishing friction and promoting smoothness. The Holy Spirit it is who gives smoothness and abolishes wear in every service for God. Second, oil *heals*. In Biblical times wine and oil were applied to wounds (cf. Luke 10:34). No one but the Spirit of God can heal the heart wounded by life's cares, sorrows, or unpleasantness. . . . Third, oil *lights*. It is the Holy Spirit who illuminates the sacred page and the pathway of the believer. . . . Fourth, oil *warms*. Whether it be the sad plight of the lost soul, or the need of a fellow-member in the Body of Christ, or the truth of God, our cold hearts are unresponsive and impregnable except the warming, glowing, pulsating power of the Spirit of God penetrates and diffuses genial and welcome warmth. Fifth, oil *invigorates*, it increases the energy of the body. . . . Sixth, oil *adorns*. It was used in the feasts of Old Testament times, and was never applied in times of sorrow or grief (cf. 2 Sam. 12:20; Ps. 104:15; Isa. 61:3). . . . The life lived under the control of the Spirit of God is radiant with the joy of the Lord and fragrant with the perfume of the presence of the Lord. Seventh, oil *polishes*. The Spirit takes the rough edges from the character of the believer."[1]

However, when Zechariah asks for an explanation of the vision, the angel tells him that it is a message to the chief civil ruler of Israel, Zerubbabel. Thus, the fourth chapter of the prophecy is a message of encouragement to this civil ruler just as the third chapter was a message of encouragement to the chief religious ruler, Joshua, the high priest.

The message to Zerubbabel has several parts: first, a general principle: " 'Not by might nor by power, but by my Spirit,' says the LORD Almighty" (v. 6); second, a reference to obstacles: "What are you, O mighty mountain? Before Zerubbabel you will become level ground. Then he will bring out the capstone to shouts of 'God bless it! God bless it!' " (v. 7); third, a promise that Zerubbabel will complete the temple construction: "The hands of Zerubbabel have laid the foundation of this temple; his hands will also complete it. Then you will know that the LORD Almighty has sent me to you" (v. 9), and "Who despises the day of small things? Men will rejoice when they see the plumb line in the hand of Zerubbabel" (v. 10).

[1] Charles L. Feinberg, *God Remembers: A Study of Zechariah* (Portland: Multnomah Press, 1979), pp. 59, 60.

This is where the vision encourages us. Zerubbabel was a man beset by many problems in his attempts to carry God's work forward. He was fighting lethargy, smallness of vision, and lack of faith within Israel. Without, he was fighting the determined opposition and evil cunning of God's enemies. These forces undoubtedly did seem like a "mighty mountain" before him. They were an obstacle human power could not remove. But God urged him to be strong in completing his task, knowing that the Lord Himself would reduce the mountain to level ground. The victory would be won by God's Spirit, not by human power.

There were no shortcuts, however. The work still had to be done: the stones still had to be laid. Any worthwhile work always begins small and progresses from that point to become bigger. As I counsel with people in our day, many of them young people, I am convinced that one of their biggest problems is that they expect shortcuts. They want a simple principle which will explain all the Bible and eliminate the need for concentrated and prolonged Bible study. They want an experience that will set them on a new spiritual plateau and eliminate the need for hard climbing up the steep mountain paths of discipleship. They want a fellowship that has all the elements of a perfect heavenly fellowship without the work of building up those elements by their own hard work and active participation. This is not the way God has ordered things. He could have given shortcuts, but He has not. Even Zerubbabel, who was the leader of Israel at this time and who in this vision receives a promise that he will live to see the completion of the temple—even Zerubbabel, who is promised the fullness of the Holy Spirit to complete his work—even Zerubbabel still had to take his plumb line in hand and work away at the mountain one day at a time.

It was about four years after this that the temple was completed.[2] Those four years contained much hard, grueling work often hindered by Zerubbabel's internal and external enemies. Should it be easier for us? Should we expect shortcuts? On the contrary, victories will be won now as then only by those who advance toward them one step at a time.

After the angel had applied this fifth vision to Zerubbabel's task, Zechariah seems to have had questions about the olive trees and the two branches that he noticed pouring oil into the bowl for the lamps. The angel answered by saying, "These are the two who are anointed to serve the LORD of all the earth" (v. 14). In the immediate context they must be Joshua and Zerubbabel, the religious and the civil heads of the nation mentioned in chapters 3 and 4.

But there is more to it. For one thing, Joshua and Zerubbabel are identified as two branches of the two olive trees, not the trees themselves. Second, the promises made to Joshua in the preceding chapter were immediately carried over into a prophecy concerning the Messiah, "my servant, the Branch" (3:8). Third, the section of the book containing these visions ends with a renewed reference to Joshua and speaks of one who is coming who will be both a priest and king (6:12, 13). Given these facts, the olive trees undoubtedly represent the priestly and kingly offices in Israel, of which Joshua and Zerubbabel were then the officeholders. The true supply of oil is from Him who is both priest and prophet, namely, Jesus Christ. It is He who gives the Holy Spirit in abundance (cf. John 14:16, 17; 15:26; 16:7–15).

[2]Zechariah received his visions on the twenty-fourth day of the eleventh month, the month of Shebat, in the second year of King Darius (Zech. 1:7). The temple was completed on the third day of the month of Adar, in the sixth year of the reign of King Darius (Ezra 6:15).

VISIONS OF JUDGMENT

The first five of Zechariah's visions are extremely encouraging, for they point out days of blessing and prosperity for Israel. They tell of the renewed presence of God with His people; the raising up of leaders equal to every threat against the reestablished nation; the prosperity and growth of Jerusalem; the purification of the people symbolized by the purification of Joshua, their representative; and finally, the role of Zerubbabel in completing the temple, leading to a vision of the great priest-king, the Messiah. These are all uplifting. But, as David Baron says, "Before that longed-for day of blessing can at last come—before the beautiful symbolism of the fifth vision shall at last be realized and Israel's restored candlestick shall once again, and in greater splendor and purity than ever before, shed abroad the light of Jehovah throughout the millennial earth—both the land and people must be cleansed from everything that defileth, or worketh abomination, or maketh a lie."[3] This is the meaning of the next three visions (judgments), found in 5:1–6:8.

The Flying Scroll (5:1–4). In the sixth vision Zechariah sees a flying scroll that measures thirty feet long and fifteen feet wide. The dimensions are unusual and quite impossible for a literal scroll, which has led some commentators to connect it with the identical dimensions of the porch of Solomon's temple (1 Kings 6:3), where the Law was usually read. It is most likely that the enlarged measurements simply enforce the serious nature of this judgment. When Zechariah describes it, the angel tells him that "this is the curse that is going out over the whole land; for according to what it says on one side, every thief will be banished, and according to what it says on the other,

everyone who swears falsely will be banished" (v. 3). This judgment was already in motion, and it had the effect not only of judging the thief and liar but even destroying the timbers and stones of the houses in which they lived.

It is tempting to limit this judgment to thieves and liars only and even then to limit it only to those who were offending in Israel at that time or in some special way. But the vision is probably to be taken in a broader manner. Stealing and lying are no doubt representative vices by which all others are to be included. It is a way of saying that God will judge all sin in the land.

The Woman in a Basket (5:5–11). The idea that thieves and liars are representative of all other sinners finds support in the seventh vision where wickedness is symbolized by a woman sitting in a basket. The measuring basket is actually an *ephah*, the largest dry measure in Israel. It contained about thirty-nine American quarts. The woman is described as "wickedness." While Zechariah watches, the woman is pushed down into the basket, a lead cover is placed over its mouth and two winged women arrive to carry the basket to Babylon where a place is to be prepared for it. There is no particular interpretation of this vision beyond the description of the woman as wickedness, but the idea is clear enough. Just as the vision of the flying scroll shows that evildoers are to be judged, this vision goes a step further to show that even the principle of wickedness will be removed from the nation.

Four Chariots (6:1–8). The eighth vision has the fewest details. It mentions four chariots coming out from between two bronze mountains, the color of the chariot horses (red, black,

---

[3]David Baron, *The Visions & Prophecies of Zechariah* (Grand Rapids: Kregel, 1975), p. 143. Original edition 1918.

white, and dappled), and the directions in which the chariots are said to go. What is emphasized is that the chariots are to go out into every part of the earth. Three of the horses and their chariots go north, west, and south; the east is not mentioned. Then it says, "When the powerful horses went out, they were straining to go *throughout the earth*. And he said, *'Go throughout the earth!'* So they went *throughout the earth*" (v. 7). As a result of the work of the chariots that went north the Spirit of God is said to have been given rest.

Presumably the picture is one of judgment upon the gentile nations, and in this the three visions of chapters 5 through 6:8 go together. First, there is judgment upon the wicked in Israel. Second, there is the sending away of even the principle of wickedness within Israel. Third, there is judgment upon the wickedness of the nations round about.

The big question about these visions concerns the time to which they apply. Indeed, most differences of interpretation can be traced to confusion over this prior question. There are three main views. The first looks backward. That is, it regards the carrying away of the woman in the basket as the deportation of Judah to Babylon, something that had already happened. It then sees a corresponding judgment on the surrounding nations that gives Zerubbabel and the Jews of the restoration peacein which to build the temple. The difficulty with this interpretation isthat Zechariah's other visions concern things yet to come.

According to the second interpretation these visions were about the present or immediate future—that is, the days that lay immediately ahead. The visions promised a purging of the nation from all sin, thus paving the way for fullness of blessing. The problem with this view is that those events did not take place. Evildoers were not pun-

ished, wickedness was not rooted out of Israel, and the surrounding nations were not judged for their wickedness— at least not quickly or in any comprehensive way.

According to the third interpretation, which is my own, they refer to a future age of millennial blessing, when evil will indeed be purged out of Israel and the nations will indeed be judged. This is related to my conviction, on the basis of other passages, that there will be such a millennium; but it is also consistent, I believe, with the flow of the visions themselves. They move from God's blessing upon the nation of Israel under Zerubbabel's rule, to the coming of the Branch who shall "remove the sin of [the] land in a single day," to the removal of sin from Israel, the judgment of the nations, and the final rule of the Messiah, the only true priest-king of Israel.

This may be why there is a special emphasis on the judgment of Babylon, the country of the north, in Zechariah 6:8. Baron says, "God's wrath is specially spoken of in this last vision as being caused to rest on 'the north country,' because not only was it there that the attempt was first made to array a world-empire against God, and where apostasy sought, so to say, to organize and fortify itself; not only did Babylon also, at a later time, become the final antagonist and subduer of God's people and the destroyer of his temple, but probably because there, 'in the land of Shinar,' the metropolis of world power, Babylon, the great rival of the city of God—wickedness, as we have seen in the consideration of the last vision, will once again establish itself, and all the forces of evil again for a time be concentrated.

"Then God's judgments shall be fully poured out, and anti-Christian world power be finally overthrown to make room for the Kingdom of Christ, whom the Father has invested with all power and dominion and glory, 'that all nations and languages should serve him.' His dominion is an everlasting dominion, 'and His Kingdom shall never be destroyed.' "[4]

THE CROWNING OF JOSHUA

Strictly speaking, the last verses of Zechariah 6 are not a vision. Yet this portion is so closely connected with what has gone before that it is actually a continuation of and a climax to the earlier visions. Moreover, it parallels the incident involving Joshua the high priest in chapter 3. In the earlier passage Joshua appeared as a representative and pointed forward to one who would perfectly fulfill the priestly office, thereby removing the sin of the land "in a single day." In this passage Zechariah is to crown Joshua with a crown made with silver and gold brought from Babylon, after which the crown was to be laid up in the temple as a memorial of this symbolic act. The act pointed forward to that greater priest who should wear the crown of His father David and who, according to this prophecy, would "branch out from his place and build the temple of the LORD. . . . He . . . will build the temple of the LORD, and he will be clothed with majesty and will sit and rule on his throne. And he will be a priest on his throne. And there will be harmony between the two" (Zech. 6:12, 13).

In the Hebrew text the word for "crown" (*'ataroth*) is plural. That has led some liberal scholars to imagine that two crowns are being discussed and to insert the words "and on the head of Zerubbabel the governor." This is not only an unjustified interpolation—a vice of which liberal scholars are all too often guilty—it also completely misses the point. In Israel the priestly and kingly offices were kept separate. The

priest never wore a crown or sat upon a throne. The king never performed the priestly functions. Yet here a crown is placed upon the head of *Joshua*, not Zerubbabel, pointing forward to the one who should be both king and priest. It is said that "he will be a priest on his throne" (v. 13).

Baron says of this text: "This is one of the most remarkable and precious Messianic prophecies, and there is no plainer prophetic utterance in the whole Old Testament as to the Person of the promised Redeemer, the offices he was to fill, and the mission he was to accomplish."[5]

This is one of those prophecies in which nearly every word is important. In the Hebrew text the prophecy begins "Behold the man," the very words Pilate used to present the beaten Christ to the people of Jerusalem: *"Ecce homo!"* On the occasion referred to in Zechariah it is not the humiliated Christ who is in view; it is Christ triumphant. The next key word is "Branch." It occurred earlier (in 3:8), but here its significance is expounded. He will have a small and insignificant beginning but will in time "branch out from his place" and dominate the world. Next we are told that He will "build the temple." What temple is this? It is not the temple to be built in Zechariah's day, for the completion of that work had been promised to Zerubbabel (4:9). This is Messiah's temple. It may be a literal temple built during the earthly millennium in which Christ shall rule, a temple into which the wealth of the Gentiles shall come (cf. Isa. 2:2–4; 56:6, 7; Ezek. 40–48; Mic. 4:1–7; Hag. 2:7–9). But it may also be the spiritual temple, the church, which Paul refers to as "a holy temple in the Lord" (Eph. 2:21).

Four Hebrew words, rendered "He will be a priest on his throne," portray

[4] Ibid., pp. 182, 183.
[5] Ibid., pp. 190, 191.

all that the prophets had spoken about the Messiah's person and work. "Here is the true Melchizedek, who is at the same time King of Righteousness, King of Salem, which is King of Peace, and the great High Priest, whose period, unlike the Aaronic, abideth 'for ever.' "[6] By sitting, He ends His work of atonement and assumes the rule of His church and world forever.

What is the result of His atonement and rule? The text describes it as "har-

mony" or peace. Harmony between whom? Not between the two offices; that relationship has been harmonious from the beginning. Not between God the Father and His servant the Son; that too has existed from eternity. The peace is between the holy God and sinners, between God and ourselves. Is Christ your peace? He has made that peace at His cross. It must be found there if you are to find it.

---

[6] Ibid., p. 200.

23

Call to True Religion

(Zechariah 7:1–8:23)

Then the word of the LORD *Almighty came to me: "Ask all the people of the land and the priests, 'When you fasted and mourned in the fifth and seventh months for the past seventy years, was it really for me that you fasted? And when you were eating and drinking, were you not just feasting for yourselves? Are these not the words the* LORD *proclaimed through the earlier prophets when Jerusalem and its surrounding towns were at rest and prosperous, and the Negev and the western foothills were settled?' "*

And the word of the Lord came again to Zechariah: "This is what the LORD *Almighty says: 'Administer true justice; show mercy and compassion to one another. Do not oppress the widow or the fatherless, the alien or the poor. In your hearts do not think evil of each other.' " . . .*

"These are the things you are to do: Speak the truth to each other, and render true and sound judgment in your courts; do not plot evil against your neighbor, and do not love to swear falsely. I hate all this," declares the LORD.

Again the word of the LORD *Almighty came to me. This is what the* LORD *Almighty says: "The fasts of the fourth, fifth, seventh and tenth months will become joyful and glad occasions and happy festivals for Judah. Therefore love truth and peace."*

Not long ago Dr. George Gallup, Jr., president of the American Institute of Public Opinion, delivered an address at Princeton Theological Seminary in which he asked the question: "Is America's Faith for Real?" He found many factors that might lead us to reply in the affirmative. Eighty-one percent of Americans claim to be religious, which places them second only to Italians, whose rating is 83 percent. Ninety-five percent of Americans believe in God; 71 percent believe in life after death; 84 percent believe in heaven; 67 percent believe in hell. Large majorities say that they believe in the Ten Commandments. Nearly every home has at least one Bible. Half of all Americans can be found in church on an average Sunday morning. Only 8 percent say they have no religious affiliation. Most say that religion plays a very important role in their lives. One-fourth claim to lead a "very Christian life."

Yet that is only one side of the story. Although four in five consider themselves to be religious, only one in five says that religion is the *most* influential factor in his or her life. Most want religious education for their children, but religious faith ranks far below many other traits that parents would like to see developed in their offspring. Only one in eight says that he or she would consider sacrificing everything for religious beliefs or God.

Gallup sees "a glaring lack of knowledge of the Ten Commandments and about the basic facts of our religious heritage, . . . a high level of credulity, . . . a lack of spiritual discipline" and "a continuing anti-intellectual strain" in the religious life of most Americans.[1]

In a nation that considers itself religious, only one individual in eight claims that religion actually makes a significant difference in his or her life.

FEASTING OR FASTING?

This matter of religious indifference fills the middle portion (chapters 7 and 8) of the Book of Zechariah. By the time these words were written, approximately two years had passed since the prophet had received the visions of chapters 1–6. The temple was now halfway to completion. Seeing this, a delegation from the outlying town of Bethel had come to Jerusalem to ask the priests and prophets whether it was proper for them to continue a fast marking the destruction of the temple that they and their fathers had been observing since the fall of Jerusalem seventy years before.

The Mosaic Law had established only one fast for Israel—the fast of the Day of Atonement, and even then the fast was only a part of that day's observance. But since the fall of Jerusalem to the Babylonians, the Jews of the Exile had been observing a series of fasts designed around significant moments in the siege of Jerusalem. On the seventeenth day of the fourth month, Thammuz (which corresponds roughly to our month of July), they mourned the capture of the city. On the ninth day of the fifth month, Ab (which corresponds to our August), they remembered the burning of the city and the destruction of the beautiful temple by Nebuchad-

nezzar. On the third of the seventh month, Tishri (October), they commemorated the assassination of Gedaliah and massacre of the eighty men from Shechem, Shiloh, and Samaria, as recorded in Jeremiah 4:1–10. On the tenth day of the tenth month, Tebeth (January), they fasted in memory of the day Nebuchadnezzar began his siege of the embattled city. The fasts were appropriate during the Exile as a device for keeping the memory of the people's past alive. But now that the temple was on its way to being rebuilt, it was a valid question as to whether a fast marking the destruction of the temple was appropriate.

Unfortunately, the people of Bethel had failed to see that in God's sight the matter was far more important than simply whether or not a traditional fast should be celebrated. This fast (and the others like it) had been perverted into what was by this time merely an empty and superstitious formalism, just as had happened earlier in Israel's history and has happened since in many religious communions. The reply of God was to move the people away from mere formalism toward seeking God.

GOD'S ANSWER

God's reply has several parts, each of which deserves careful study and consideration. They are: (1) a reproof of mere ceremonial religion (7:4–10), (2) an encouragement for the pursuit of true religion, based on the fate of the people's predecessors and the future blessing of Jerusalem (7:11–8:8), (3) a reminder of the people's present duty (8:9–13), (4) a prediction of the transformation of all fasts into joyful occasions (8:14–19), and (5) a forecast of the calling of the Gentiles to salvation (8:20–23).

1. *A reproof of mere ceremonial religion*

---

[1]George Gallup, Jr., "Is America's Faith for Real?" in *Alumni News*, vol. 22, no. 4, Summer issue 1982, pp. 15–17.

(7:4–10). When the delegation from Bethel came to Jerusalem to seek the mind of God about their fast, they must have expected a relatively simple answer. Yes, continue the fast! Or, No, abolish it! Instead, the word of God came to Zechariah with this answer: "Ask all the people of the land and the priests, 'When you fasted and mourned in the fifth and seventh months for the past seventy years, was it really for me that you fasted? And when you were eating and drinking, were you not just feasting for yourselves? Are these not the words the LORD proclaimed through the earlier prophets when Jerusalem and its surrounding towns were at rest and prosperous, and the Negev and the western foothills were settled?'. . . This is what the LORD Almighty says: 'Administer true justice; show mercy and compassion to one another. Do not oppress the widow or the fatherless, the alien or the poor. In your hearts do not think evil of each other' " (7:5–7, 9, 10). The point is clear. God is not content with mere ceremonial acts. On the contrary, He actually hates such acts if they are not preceded and accompanied by a genuine love for God and other people (cf. Amos 5:21–24).

When Zechariah quotes God as saying, "Are these not the words the LORD proclaimed through the earlier prophets. . . ?" he does not say what particular prophets the Lord has in mind. But it is not hard to bring forward some of them. In all the Old Testament the chief passage on fasting is undoubtedly in Isaiah 58. In that chapter the greatest of all the Jewish prophets refers to a question the people of the day had been asking. They had fasted, but God had not responded by giving them what they asked for. So they asked, "Why have we fasted . . . and you have not seen it? Why have we humbled ourselves, and you have not noticed?" (v. 3). They meant, "Why are we going to this trouble if what we are doing won't work?"

Isaiah quotes God as giving this reply:

> On the day of your fasting, you do
>   as you please
>   and exploit all your workers.
> Your fasting ends in quarreling and
>   strife,
>   and in striking each other with
>   wicked fists.
> You cannot fast as you do today
>   and expect your voice to be heard
>   on high.
> Is this the kind of fast I have
>   chosen,
>   only a day for a man to humble
>   himself?
> Is it only for bowing one's head like
>   a reed
>   and for lying on sackcloth and
>   ashes?
> Is that what you call a fast,
>   a day acceptable to the LORD?
>
> Is not this the kind of fasting I
>   have chosen:
> to loose the chains of injustice
>   and untie the cords of the yoke,
> to set the oppressed free
>   and break every yoke?
> Is it not to share your food with
>   the hungry
>   and to provide the poor wanderer
>   with shelter—
> when you see the naked, to clothe
>   him,
>   and not to turn away from your
>   own flesh and blood?
> Then your light will break forth like
>   the dawn,
>   and your healing will quickly
>   appear;
> then your righteousness will go
>   before you,
>   and the glory of the LORD will be
>   your rear guard.
> Then you will call, and the LORD
>   will answer;
>   you will cry for help, and he will
>   say: Here am I (Isa. 58:3–9).

This is the greatest passage on religious celebrations in the Old Testament. But it is not the only one. Shortly before this Amos had written:

I hate, I despise your religious
  feasts;
I cannot stand your assemblies.
Even though you bring me burnt
  offerings and grain offerings,
I will not accept them.
Though you bring choice fellowship
  offerings,
I will have no regard for them.
Away with the noise of your songs!
I will not listen to the music of
  your harps.
But let justice roll on like a river,
  righteousness like a never-failing
  stream! (Amos 5:21–24).

The same principle is found in
1 Samuel:

Does the LORD delight in burnt
  offerings and sacrifices
  as much as in obeying the voice
  of the LORD?
To obey is better than sacrifice,
  and to heed is better than the fat
  of rams (1 Sam. 15:22).

Deuteronomy says, "And now, O
Israel, what does the LORD your God
ask of you but to fear the LORD your
God, to walk in all his ways, to love
him, to serve the LORD your God with
all your heart and with all your soul,
and to observe the LORD's commands
and decrees that I am giving you today
for your own good?" (Deut. 10:12, 13).

In Zechariah's treatment there are
two things for which the people of his
day are faulted. First, the worshipers
were not seeking or serving God in
their fasting. This is the importance of
the words "for me" in verse 5 and "for
yourselves" in verse 6. In the first case
the reference is to fasting, and the point
is that the people were not doing it for
God. They were doing it for themselves. In the second case the reference
is to eating and drinking, and the point
is that the people were doing it for
themselves. In other words, it did not
make any difference whether they were
fasting or feasting. In each case, they
were pleasing themselves. Their cele-

brations had nothing to do with true
religion.

The second thing for which the people are faulted is that their worship,
whether by fasting or by anything else,
did not lead to acts of mercy to the
abandoned and oppressed. Yet this is
what Isaiah, Amos, Samuel, Moses,
and indeed all the prophets and writers
of Scripture called for. Without such
acts the forms of religion are no true
religion. Without justice the worship of
God, however intense or prolonged, is
blasphemy.

2. *An encouragement for the pursuit of
true religion, based on the fate of the
people's predecessors and the future blessing
of Jerusalem (7:11–8:8).* The second part
of God's answer to the delegation from
Bethel was an encouragement for them
to abandon their empty and superstitious formalism and to pursue instead
the kind of true and pleasing religion
He had just mentioned. That is, they
were to seek God and act with mercy
toward the oppressed and abandoned.

He uses two lines of argument. First,
He reminds them of the fate of their
predecessors. They had been informed
concerning the kind of worship God
desired, but they had hardened their
hearts and thus brought judgment
upon themselves. Zechariah writes,
"But they refused to pay attention;
stubbornly they turned their backs and
stopped up their ears. They made their
hearts as hard as flint and would not
listen to the law or to the words that the
LORD Almighty had sent by his Spirit
through the earlier prophets. So the
LORD Almighty was very angry. 'When I
called, they did not listen; so when they
called, I would not listen,' says the
LORD Almighty. 'I scattered them with a
whirlwind among all the nations,
where they were strangers. The land
was left so desolate behind them that
no one could come or go. This is how
they made the pleasant land desolate' "
(7:11–14).

The second line of argument is the promised future blessing of Jerusalem, which has been a theme throughout the book. Zechariah writes, "This is what the LORD Almighty says: 'I am very jealous for Zion; I am burning with jealousy for her. . . . I will return to Zion and dwell in Jerusalem. Then Jerusalem will be called The City of Truth, and the mountain of the LORD Almighty will be called The Holy Mountain. . . . Once again men and women of ripe old age will sit in the streets of Jerusalem, each with cane in hand because of his age. The city streets will be filled with boys and girls playing there. . . . It may seem marvelous to the remnant of this people at that time, but will it seem marvelous to me?' declares the LORD Almighty. . . . 'I will save my people from the countries of the east and the west. I will bring them back to live in Jerusalem; they will be my people, and I will be faithful and righteous to them as their God' " (8:2–8).

The remarkable thing about these incentives for true religion is that there is nothing remarkable or new about them. It is simply the old theme of Deuteronomy: Where there is obedience there will be blessing, where there is disobedience there will be judgment.

The history of Israel shows this to be true. So does George Gallup's report on religion in American life to which I referred earlier. Gallup was writing in general religious terms, of course. He was not distinguishing between Judaism and Christianity or between denominations. Yet he noticed some unique characteristics in the 12 percent of his survey that he classified as "spiritually committed" or spiritually mature: "The 12 percent who fit our category of 'highly spiritually committed' are a 'breed apart,' different from

the rest of the populace in at least four key respects:

"(1) They are more satisfied with their lot in life than are those who are less spiritually committed—and far happier. A total of 68 percent of the highly spiritually committed say they are 'very happy,' compared to 46 percent of the moderately spiritually committed, 39 percent of the moderately uncommitted, and 30 percent of the highly uncommitted.

"(2) Their families are stronger, with the divorce rate among this group far lower than among the less committed.

"(3) They tend to be more tolerant of persons of different races and religions than the less spiritually committed.

"(4) They are far more involved in charitable activities than are their counterparts. A total of 46 percent of the highly spiritually committed say they are presently working among the poor, the infirm and the elderly, compared to 36 percent among the moderately uncommitted, and 22 percent of the highly uncommitted." He concludes, "One's faith can often have a tremendous impact on one's sense of self-esteem and on his or her contribution to society."[2]

3. *A reminder of the people's present duty (8:9–13).* At first glance, the third part of God's answer to the delegation from Bethel appears out of place, for it concerns the rebuilding of the temple and is a reminder to get on with that work: "You who now hear these words spoken by the prophets who were there when the foundation was laid for the house of the LORD Almighty, let your hands be strong so that the temple may be built" (v. 9). What does this have to do with fasting? The reminder would be appropriate in Haggai, which is entirely about the rebuilding. It might even seem in place in the earlier chap-

---

[2] Ibid., p. 16.

ters of Zechariah, which speak of Zerubbabel's role in completing the temple's reconstruction. But why here? Why should it occur in a chapter about the nature of true religion?

The reason is that obedience concerns specifics—not just any specifics! It concerns the particular task or command God has laid upon us. In this case it concerned the command of God through His prophets to build the temple.

We like to talk about obedience in general terms without coming to grips with what God is requiring. Or we talk about specifics so long as we do not need to come to terms with doing them. Not long ago I talked to a young man who is making a shambles of his life. He had come to see me because things had gotten so bad for him that he just had nowhere else to turn. He knew that his sin was hurting him. He was aware that he was wasting good years in disobedience. He needed fellowship, Bible study, a regular job—all items that make for a sound and growing Christian experience. But the point of my story is that he already knew these things because *we had spoken of them several years before and again several years before that.* The man was not in doubt about what he should do. He knew what he should do. The problem was that he was not doing it.

You say, "But these things are so basic. Everybody knows that we should spend time with other Christians, read the Bible, work at a job." I ask, Who said anything about obedience being exciting? Who said that the necessary elements of a sound and growing Christian experience are thrilling? I confess that there are often exciting moments in following God. Some things *are* thrilling. But the more necessary things are more often simply hard work. It is by obedience in small matters that we show ourselves to be faithful and are given stewardship in greater matters.

4. *A transformation of all fasts into joyful occasions (8:14–19).* After the specific command to His people to be faithful in the task of rebuilding the temple, the Lord briefly reviews the ground already covered and gives His specific answer to the question posed by the delegation from Bethel. First, He reminds them of what He had said concerning judgment on their predecessors for their empty and offensive religious practices ("Just as I had determined to bring disaster upon you and showed no pity when your fathers angered me. . . ," v. 14). Second, He reminds them of His promise of future blessing ("So now I have determined to do good again to Jerusalem and Judah," v. 15). Third, He restates the definition of true religion that appeared in the previous chapter ("These are the things you are to do: Speak the truth to each other, and render true and sound judgment in your courts; do not plot evil against your neighbor, and do not love to swear falsely. I hate all this," vv. 16, 17). Then, having reviewed this ground, He gives His final answer to the question about fasts. The fasts of Israel will be transformed. "This is what the Lord Almighty says: 'The fasts of the fourth, fifth, seventh and tenth months will become joyful and glad occasions and happy festivals for Judah' " (v. 19).

When would this happen? It is tempting to say, "At once." Or at least, "As soon as the rebuilding of the temple is completed." But the fasts of Israel were not turned into happy festivals at that time. Indeed, it has not happened yet. The fasts of the fourth, fifth, seventh, and tenth months are still observed in Judaism.

Then when will this be? Here again, in my judgment, is another passage pointing forward to a restored Israel in the last days. Today, in a certain sense, the fasts of Israel have been turned into feasts for both Jew and Gentile within the fellowship of the church, for it is a fact that fasts disappeared as a rite of worship within Christianity from the very beginning. There are no general fasts for all Christians either referred to or prescribed anywhere in the New Testament. Yet that is true only within the church. It is not true for Israel generally. Is it not the case that the ultimate fulfillment of this prophecy will be in the days of a regathered Israel during the millennium, at which time the Jews will be witnesses to the reality of God's salvation?

"Let Us Go With You"

In my judgment, the last part of God's answer to the delegation from Bethel, *the forecast of the calling of the Gentiles to salvation (8:20–23)*, refers to this same period. It is a poetically beautiful picture, telling how in that future day the peoples and nations of the world will go up to Jerusalem to entreat the Lord and how many will take hold of the edge of the robe of one Jew to go up with him. "This is what the Lord Almighty says: 'Many peoples and the inhabitants of many cities will yet come, and the inhabitants of one city will go to another and say, "Let us go at once to entreat the Lord and seek the Lord Almighty. I myself am going." And many peoples and powerful nations will come to Jerusalem to seek the Lord Almighty and to entreat him.' This is what the Lord Almighty says: 'In those days ten men from all languages and nations will take firm hold of one Jew by the edge of his robe and say, "Let us go with you, because we have heard that God is with you" ' " (vv. 20–23).

In that day it will be known that the Jews have again found favor with God and that God is to be found through those who are again His chosen people. We Gentiles are not seizing hold of the edge of a Jew's robe to go up with him to Jerusalem today. In fact, we are praying for and witnessing to Jews that *they* might come to salvation. Nevertheless we are all clinging to the seamless robe of that *one* Jew, Jesus of Nazareth, who because of His work on the cross is the only basis on which anyone may approach God and entreat Him for spiritual blessings.

On this point, Thomas V. Moore, one of the best commentators on Zechariah, has written: "When this prediction was uttered nothing seemed more hopelessly improbable than its fulfillment. The Jews were a poor, despised, obscure tribe in the heart of Syria, whose existence was only known to the mighty world by their furnishing a trophy to the victorious areas of Babylon. Greece was just riding in the firmament of human history, and as she ascended to her brilliant zenith her track was marked by the sweeping of the phalanxes of Alexander and the legions of Antiochus over the hills and valleys of Judea. And yet this prophecy remained unfulfilled. Rome was then in the rugged feebleness of her world-nursed infancy and slowly continued to grow until she reached that gigantic stature in which she ruled the earth, and her conquering legions under Pompey again swept over this fated land and even desecrated the places of her holy solemnities. Five hundred years rolled away, and yet this prophecy remained unfulfilled, indeed seemed farther from fulfillment than when it was uttered.

"But at length the time arrived, and there came to Jerusalem 'men out of every nation under heaven—Parthians, Medes and Elamites, and the dwellers in Mesopotamia, and in Judea and Cappadocia, in Pontus and Asia, Phrygia and Pamphylia, in Egypt, and in the parts of Libya about Cyrene, and strangers of Rome, Jews and proselytes, Cretes and Arabians'—all came up to Jerusalem to seek the face of Jehovah, and from the lips of a Jew they heard words that caused them to cry out, 'Men and brethren, what shall I do?' They scattered to their own homes again and carried with them the strange words that had so deeply moved their souls, and being followed by these wonder-working men, there soon began to work a new life among the nations of the earth, and this life took hold in its origin and efficacy upon *a Jew*. Greece with her polished dialectics, Rome with her mailed mightiness, Asia with her soft voluptuousness—all submitted to the authority of a Savior who was a Jew; all rested their hopes for eternity upon a Jew; and soon received as divinely inspired the words and writings of men who were Jews. And for nearly two thousand years the mightiest intellects and largest hearts of the race have breathed the spirit and studied the words of men who were Jews and have sought as the most precious boon of existence the privilege of being covered with a robe of righteousness that was wrought by the divinely incarnated hands of one who is of the seed of Abraham after the flesh, though as to his higher nature, God over all, blessed forever. And at this day there are literally men of all nations and kindreds and tribes and people who are laying hold of the skirt of him that is a Jew, and casting in their lot with those whom God chose to be a people for himself, and resting their hopes on that crucified Jew, who is the Saviour of the world."[3]

If you have not done that, the last words of Zechariah 8 are for you especially. They are a response to the invitation of God given in 2:6, 7. In that earlier chapter God invited the people to come to Him: "*Come! Come!* Flee from the land of the north. . . . *Come*, O Zion! Escape, you who live in the Daughter of Babylon!" In chapter 8, the Gentiles respond to this call and reply, "Let us *go*." They say, "Let us go at once to entreat the LORD and seek the LORD Almighty. . . . Let us go with you, because we have heard that God is with you" (vv. 21, 23). Happy is the one who is among those who hear that call and go with Jesus.

---

[3]Thomas V. Moore, *A Commentary on Haggai, Zechariah and Malachi* (Edinburgh and Carlisle, Pa.: Banner of Truth Trust, 1979), pp. 209–11. Original edition 1856.

24

Israel's Shepherd-King

(Zechariah 9:1–10:12).

Rejoice greatly, O Daughter of Zion!
Shout, daughter of Jerusalem!
See, your king comes to you,
righteous and having salvation,
gentle and riding on a donkey,
on a colt, the foal of a donkey.
I will take away the chariots from Ephraim
and the war-horses from Jerusalem,
and the battle bow will be broken.
He will proclaim peace to the nations.
His rule will extend from sea to sea
and from the River to the ends of the earth.

Moses, the great law-giver of Israel, lived 120 years. As the time of Moses' death drew close, God caused him to climb Mount Nebo from the plains of Moab and there showed him the whole land of Canaan, which the people he had led through the wilderness for forty years were about to conquer. The text says, "There the LORD showed him the whole land—from Gilead to Dan, all of Naphtali, the territory of Ephraim and Manasseh, all the land of Judah as far as the western sea, the Negev and the whole region from the Valley of Jericho, the City of Palms, as far as Zoar" (Deut. 34:1–3).

As we come to the final section of Zechariah and approach the end of the Old Testament (only Malachi, the last of the minor prophets, is later), we discover a phenomenon similar to Moses' final vision. Up to this point most of the events foretold by the prophets have concerned their immediate future, primarily the fall of the northern kingdom of Israel and the fall of the southern kingdom of Judah, with judgment against such additional kingdoms as Syria, Philistia, Edom, Ammon, Moab, Assyria (Nineveh, its capital), and Babylon brought in along the way. From time to time there were prophecies of the coming of Christ or of more distant events such as the regathering of Israel to her own land in the last days. But these were rarely extensive. Now this changes, and, like Moses on Mount Nebo, we are given the widest possible vision of the land before us. Our vision involves extensive prophecies of the person and work of Christ and many details of the future of Israel leading up to and following the Lord's first advent. As Charles L. Feinberg says in his commentary, "The last six chapters of this prophecy constitute an incomparable treasury of prophetic truth."[1]

Chapters 9–14 of Zechariah contain two oracles: chapters 9–11 and 12–14 respectively. David Baron describes the first oracle as "the judgment through which Gentile world-power over Israel is finally destroyed and Israel is endowed with strength to overcome all their [sic] enemies." He describes the second as "the judgment through which Israel itself is sifted and purged in the final great conflict with the nations and transformed into the holy nation of Jehovah."[2]

In the first of these sections, chapters 9 and 10 form one unit and should therefore properly be considered together, just as chapters 7 and 8 form a unit and were considered together in the last study.

WHO WROTE THESE CHAPTERS?

Before plunging into a detailed examination of these chapters, it is important to deal with a critical problem that has hovered over them: the matter of authorship. Is Zechariah 9–14 by the same person who composed the earlier portions of the book? Discussion of this problem has a long history. One of the earliest writers to question Zechariah's authorship was Joseph Mede, an Englishman who was born in 1586 and died in 1638. He had the highest possible view of inspiration and was not at all concerned to discount chapters 9–14 as being part of the Word of God. On the contrary, it was his concern for the inspiration and inerrancy of Scripture that got him involved in this problem in the first place. He noted that in Matthew 27:9, the prophecy in Zechariah 11:12, 13 is ascribed to Jeremiah. Therefore, he reasoned, why not accept Mat-

thew's testimony that someone other than Zechariah wrote it? His views were adopted by scores of other commentators both in England and on the continent.

With the coming of the higher criticism more radical views were advanced. The higher critics approached Scripture with an antisupernaturalistic bias that discounted even the possibility of true prophecy. Therefore, the "prophecies" of battles involving Israel and other nations either had to refer to events that had occurred earlier than Zechariah's time and were written about in retrospect, or they had to concern events that transpired later and were written about then by some other writer.

The higher critics had two chief reasons for discounting Zechariah's authorship of chapters 9–14. First, they pointed to major *differences in style* between the first half of the book and the second. The first portion contains careful indications of author and date, the visions being placed in the eleventh month of the second year of King Darius and the question to the priests about fasting with its accompanying promises of blessing being placed in the ninth month of the fourth year of King Darius. There are no time indications in chapters 9–14. The first portion has clearly defined sections and bold outlines. The second section is harder to sort out. It contains difficult references to a variety of battles, and there are scattered references to the future work of Christ. Phrases like "this is what the LORD Almighty says" or "the word of the LORD came to me," which occur frequently in section one, are said not to occur in section two (but see Zech. 11:4, 13, 15; 12:1, for evidence to the contrary). The caption "An Oracle," which introduces 9–11 and 12–14, is not used earlier.

---

[1]Charles L. Feinberg, *God Remembers: A Study of Zechariah* (Portland: Multnomah Press, 1979), p. 117.

[2]David Baron, *The Visions & Prophecies of Zechariah* (Grand Rapids: Kregel, 1918), p. 285.

What shall we say about these differences? Obviously they exist. But equally obvious, they are hardly as weighty as the more radical critics suggest. The use of Zechariah's name early in the book is clearly appropriate, particularly since the early portions have to do with events in which he was participating. The use of his name is less appropriate and not at all necessary later. Similarly, the specific time references suit the earlier material, while the later material is more like the undated prophecies of Isaiah, Jeremiah, and other prophets. Differences just as great occur in prophecies whose authenticity has never been questioned— those of Amos, to give just one example.

More conservative scholars explain the differences in part as a difference in Zechariah's age when each was written—the first half of the book being composed when Zechariah was a young man and the second half much later—and in part as a difference in the author's aim in writing.

Second, critical scholars point to *the nature of the prophecies.* These arguments take different forms, but a typical one might be directed at Zechariah 9:1–8, to give an example. These verses accurately describe the invasions of Syria, Phoenicia, and Judah by Alexander the Great; the destruction of Damascus, Tyre, and Sidon, Ashkelon, Gaza, Ekron, and Ashdod, and the contemporaneous and unaccountable sparing of Jerusalem. Such detailed prophecies are impossible, such a critic might argue. Therefore, the "prophecy" itself must have been written after the events took place, or at least contemporaneously with them. Is this argument valid? Obviously it is only valid on the critic's assumption of an antisupernaturalistic world order. If God reveals the future to His chosen agents, there is no reason for using this unbelieving mind-set as an argument against Zechariah's authorship of the section.

Against both of these views, one may properly argue that there are genuine prophecies in both portions of Zechariah and that there are far more similarities of style and even of specific themes than there are differences. One example of the latter is the images used to characterize the work of the Messiah.[3]

But there is still Matthew's ascription of Zechariah 11:12, 13 to Jeremiah. What about that? The solution to this difficulty is to recognize that Matthew is referring to two passages from the prophets: Zechariah 11:12, 13, which he quotes most closely, and Jeremiah 32:6–9, which he quotes less closely but which actually concerns the main point of his own narrative concerning the purchase of the potter's field with the betrayal money originally paid to Judas. The passage in Zechariah mentions the thirty pieces of silver for which the Lord was betrayed, but it says nothing about the purchase of a field. In fact, it does not mention a field at all. Jeremiah has many references to a potter and his work, used symbolically of God's work with Israel (cf. Jer. 18:2; 19:1, 11), and the purchase of the field in Anathoth is a major symbolic incident. Apparently, Matthew combined and summarized elements of prophetic symbolism from both Zechariah and Jeremiah. But since Jeremiah is the more prominent of the two prophets, he mentioned his name rather than that of the minor prophet. A similar case occurs in Mark 1:2, 3 which attributes to Isaiah a combined quotation actually found in Malachi 3:1 and Isaiah 40:3.[4]

The conclusion is that there is no

---

[3]See Earl L. Brown, "Portrait of the Messiah from Zechariah 9–14: The Unity of Zechariah Demonstrated by Messianic Motifs," unpublished dissertation, submitted to Biblical Theological Seminary, 1979.

[4]Cf. Gleason L. Archer, *Encyclopedia of Bible Difficulties* (Grand Rapids: Zondervan, 1982), p. 345.

compelling reason to believe that Zechariah 9–14 was written by any author other than the author of the first half of the book. On the contrary, there are good reasons for considering both to have been composed by Zechariah.

THE COMING OF ALEXANDER

The opening title of chapters 9–11 (and again of chapters 12–14) is "An Oracle" from the Hebrew word *massa'*, which actually means "a burden." At first glance it is a strange word for a book that is largely a collection of encouragements for the Jewish people in the days leading up to the coming of Christ. *Massa'* refers most naturally to a judgment. But there *is* a judgment in these chapters. As indicated at the very beginning, in a quotation from David Baron, the first section contains a judgment against the gentile world powers for the benefit of Israel, while the second contains a purifying judgment against Israel herself.

The remarkable thing about the first section of this rehearsal of judgment against the gentile world powers is that it accurately foretells the conquest of the eastern Mediterranean coastlands by Greek armies under the command of Alexander the Great. Alexander, the young commander of the Macedonian forces, crossed the Hellespont into Turkey shortly after the death of his father Philip in 336 B.C. He defeated the armies of the frontier governors of King Darius at Granicus and later overwhelmed the armies of Darius himself at the decisive battle of Issus in 333 B.C. After that he marched south against Damascus, Tyre, and Sidon, and the cities of Philistia, precisely as Zechariah foretells in 9:1–8.

Alexander's siege of Tyre is worth elaboration. At one time the city stood on the mainland, but in order to ensure Tyre's greater safety a new city had been constructed on an island located about a half mile offshore. This island was surrounded by a double wall 150 feet high that was filled in with 25 feet of earth. This wall, plus the surrounding sea, seemed to make the city impregnable. Tyre prospered from this secure position. Thus, when the armies of Alexander appeared on the shore she felt she could easily defy the invasion. After all, Tyre had withstood a five-year siege by the Assyrians and a thirteen-year siege by the Babylonians. Surely she could defy Alexander. Alexander took the city in just seven months! At incredible effort he had his armies fill in the half-mile channel to the island, using stones, timber, and other material from the remains of the old city on the shore. This Tyre was literally scraped flat, thus fulfilling the prophecy of Ezekiel, who had said: "They will break down your walls and demolish your fine houses and throw your stones, timber and rubble into the sea. . . . I will make you a bare rock, and you will become a place to spread fishnets. You will never be rebuilt" (Ezek. 26:12, 14). Tyre has not been rebuilt to this day, and the causeway of Alexander remains, a monument to the truth of prophecy and the folly of human pride.

Verse 8 of this chapter says that during this invasion of Alexander, Jerusalem and its people would be spared. ("But I will defend my house against marauding forces.") Josephus tells how this happened. When Alexander was besieging Tyre he sent a letter to the high priest, who lived in Jerusalem, requesting him to send him assistance and to supply his army with provisions. The priest declined to do this because, as he said, he had sworn an oath of loyalty to King Darius, which he would not break so long as Darius was alive. This infuriated Alexander, and he determined to besiege and sack Jerusalem as soon as the coastal conquests were behind him.

When the seven-month siege of Tyre

and the two-month siege of Gaza were over, Alexander started for the Jewish capital. Jaddus, the high priest, was terrified, not imagining how he could meet the victorious forces of Alexander and fearing the worst for his people. He therefore ordered the Jews to make sacrifices to God and ask for deliverance from the advancing danger. That night, after the sacrifice, God spoke to Jaddus in his sleep, telling him to take courage. He was to adorn the city with wreaths and then open the gates and go out to meet the invaders. The people were to be dressed in white garments and the priests in the robes prescribed by law. Josephus writes: "When Alexander while still far off saw the multitude in white garments, the priests at their head clothed in linen, and the high priest in a robe of hyacinth-blue and gold, wearing on his head the mitre with the golden plate on it on which was inscribed the name of God, he approached alone and prostrated himself before the Name and first greeted the high priest."

Alexander's men were astonished at this, and Parmenion, his second-in-command, asked why he had bowed down to the Jewish high priest. Alexander replied, "It was not before him that I prostrated myself but the God of whom he has the honor to be high priest, for it was he whom I saw in my sleep dressed as he is now, when I was at Dior in Macedonia. As I was considering with myself how I might become master of Asia, he urged me not to hesitate but to cross over confidently, for he himself would lead my army and give over to me the empire of the Persians. Since, therefore, I have beheld no one else in such robes, and on seeing him now I am reminded of the vision and the exhortation, I believe that I have made this expedition under divine guidance and that I shall defeat Darius and destroy the power of the Persians."[5]

Most scholars are skeptical of this account, but it is a fact that Jerusalem and the surrounding cities of the Jews were not destroyed by Alexander and most of the gentile cities were.

The Coming of Israel's King

If the ninth chapter of Zechariah were organized along strictly chronological lines, the next two verses (vv. 9, 10) would be out of order. They speak of the coming of the Messiah, which occurred not only after the invasion of Alexander the Great described in verses 1–8, but also after the Maccabean revolt against the Greek armies described in verses 11–17. But, of course, the order is theological rather than chronological. After a prophecy of the coming of King Alexander, the proper next step is a prophecy of the coming of Zion's King.

Few Messianic prophecies are better known than this, chiefly because of its quotation in Matthew 21:5 and John 12:15 as being fulfilled by the triumphal entry of Jesus into Jerusalem on what we traditionally call Palm Sunday.

> Rejoice greatly, O Daughter of Zion!
>   Shout, daughter of Jerusalem!
> See, your king comes to you,
>   righteous and having salvation,
>   gentle and riding on a donkey,
>   on a colt, the foal of a donkey
>   (v. 9).

The next verse tells how this righteous yet gentle King will bring peace to the nation and extend His rule over the entire earth.

The passage mentions four characteristics of this King. First, He is *just*, or *righteous*. In the context of Zechariah 9 this probably does not refer to His own personal righteousness, either active or

---

[5] Josephus, *Jewish Antiquities*, trans. by Ralph Marcus for "The Loeb Classical Library" (Cambridge: Harvard University Press, 1958), vol. 7, pp. 461–79. By Josephus's divisions the relevant material is in XI, viii, 3–5.

passive, but rather to the righteousness or justice that will characterize His rule. Since He is the one who brings peace, this teaches that there can never be any strong or lasting peace apart from justice. Second, the Messiah-King has *salvation*. The Hebrew verb *nosha'*, which is used here, can mean either that the Messiah Himself is saved by God or that He somehow has or possesses salvation and can thus bestow it on others. Probably the latter is meant. That is, the King is salvation for all who belong to Him. Third, He is *gentle*, or *lowly*. This characteristic is hardly to be expected of kings. Alexander and those of his kind have always been precisely the opposite. They come with pageantry and pride. The Messiah comes "riding on a donkey, on a colt, the foal of a donkey." He did not come "to be served, but to serve, and to give his life as a ransom for many" (Mark 10:45).

David Baron has pointed out that "Christ is the only person in all history whose character and experience answer to the description of the ideal king in this prophecy. He alone, among the sons of men, can be described as the true *Tsaddik*—the righteous One, who did no violence, nor was deceit found in his mouth. . . . The Lord Jesus Christ for us men and our salvation also became 'poor' and 'afflicted'—so poor that he himself could say: 'The foxes have holes, and the birds of the air have nests, but the Son of Man hath not where to lay his head.' And of him alone also is it true that he is endowed with and is the bringer of salvation, because he was himself 'saved' or 'delivered' or 'made victorious' . . . in the great conflict which he came to wage on our behalf with the powers of darkness."[6]

Verse 10 tells of the final victories of the Messiah as a result of which war will be abolished and peace will extend to the ends of the earth. This is the eventual outcome of Messiah's reign, but we do not see it yet. Therefore, the entire church age may rightly be said to intervene between verses 9 and 10 of this chapter.

WARS OF THE MACCABEES

The verses which follow the prophecy of the coming of Israel's king do not have the same clear reference to historical events as the first eight verses, so it is difficult to tell precisely what they refer to. The opening verses refer to the conquests of Alexander the Great. These latter verses could refer to any future Jewish victory—with the sole exception of verse 13, which is therefore the key to understanding them. That verse says, "I will rouse your sons, O Zion—against your sons, O Greece." Since the only time in history that the Jews have been at war with Greeks was during the period of the Maccabean revolt, the passage must refer to those years.

After the death of Alexander in 323 B.C., the empire divided into three parts: Greece itself, under a variety of rulers; the eastern lands, including Judah, under the Seleucids; and Egypt, under the Ptolemies. If Judah had been ruled by the milder Ptolemies, the nation might have drifted gently toward a pagan culture. But the Seleucid kings ruled ruthlessly. Moreover, they repeatedly offended the Jews' religious sensibilities. A climax came with the rule of Antiochus IV, known as Antiochus Epiphanes (175–163 B.C.). He suspended the daily sacrifices, abolished the sabbath, destroyed copies of the Scriptures, forbade circumcision, and erected pagan altars. To crown it all, in December, 167 B.C., he introduced the cult of the Olympian Zeus into the

---

[6] Baron, *The Visions & Prophecies of Zechariah*, pp. 310, 311.

temple by setting up a pagan altar and offering swine's flesh on it. This is probably the "abomination that causes desolation" spoken of in Daniel 11:31 and 12:11 (cf. also 1 Macc. 1:54).

Against this offensive and autocratic rule, the areas of Judah and Ephraim (that is, the northern and southern parts of the ancient Jewish nation) were indeed around, as Zechariah prophesied (v. 13). The spark was struck in Modein, a little town in the hill country northwest of Jerusalem. A Syrian officer had demanded that the people make pagan sacrifices. But when a Jew came forward to make the sacrifice, a local priest named Mattathias rose up and killed both the Jew and the Syrian officer. Then he fled to the wilderness with his five sons: John, Simon, Judas, Eleazar, and Jonathan. Others gathered around them, and a guerrilla war commenced. When Mattathias died soon after the outbreak of the rebellion, leadership passed to Judas, who became known as Judas Maccabeus, which means "the hammer." Judas won stunning victories against a number of Antiochus's generals and eventually occupied Jerusalem and purified the temple. The Maccabees were able to achieve a century of Jewish independence that lasted until the coming of the Roman ruler Pompey in 63 B.C.

The Lord Is My Shepherd

At some point in these verses—it is hard to tell when—attention passes from the time of the Maccabees to a more distant time or at least to a more general consideration of God's provision. I think the transition begins with verse 14. But whatever the case, somewhere between the mention of Greece in 9:13 and the end of the chapter, Zechariah begins to show how the one who was earlier introduced as a king would actually function as a shepherd to His people, unlike the harsh rulers defeated by the Maccabees. The shep-

herd theme grows in importance until almost the end of the prophecy. This section tells of four things the Shepherd-King does.

1. *The Shepherd saves His people (9:14–17).* This is stated for the first time in verse 16, where it is still probably related to the deliverance under the Maccabees: "The LORD their God will save them on that day as the flock of his people." The earlier verses use military language:

Then the LORD will appear over them;
his arrow will flash like lightning.
The Sovereign LORD will sound the trumpet;
he will march in the storms of the south,
and the LORD Almighty will shield them (vv. 14, 15).

This sounds like the Maccabean warfare. But when the verses go on to speak in other terms, saying that the people "will sparkle in his land like jewels in a crown" (v. 16), they seem to imply a later and greater deliverance.

David Baron writes, "Jehovah in that day shall 'save them.' This does not mean here merely that he will help and deliver them. This, as another writer points out, would affirm much too little after what has gone before. 'When Israel has trodden down his foes, he no longer needs deliverance.' The meaning is rather that God will in that day endow them with salvation, not only in the negative sense of deliverance, but in the *positive* sense; and, if we want to know what is implied in it, we have it in the figure of the next clause. He will do for them and be to them *all that a shepherd does and is to his flock,* which implies that he will not only *seek* and *deliver* and gather them, but he himself in the person of the Messiah, as all the prophets bear witness, will *tend* and *feed* and lead and rule over them. . . . The most beautiful 'nightingale song,'

Psalm 23, which is so precious to us now, will then express the experience of saved Israel."[7]

2. *The Shepherd provides for His people (10:1, 2).* In the past Israel had looked to idols for the blessings God stood ready to give the people if they had only asked Him. In those days they were like sheep without a shepherd, lost and oppressed by their enemies. In the latter days, about which these verses speak, the people will ask God for blessings and will find them. These verses speak of an Israel that is delivered, not only from her political enemies, such as the Seleucids, but from the idolatry that had been the cause of her downfall for so many generations.

3. *The Shepherd purifies His people (10:3–5).* Israel's lack of a true shepherd in verse 2 leads to the thought that the people were nevertheless afflicted by false shepherds, whom the true Shepherd now intends to punish. Who are these false shepherds? Some interpreters believe they are the pagan kings of Greece and other nations who ruled over Palestine. (This would fit in with the immediate context of the allusions to the wars of the Maccabees.) Others believe them to be Israel's own bad kings and false prophets, along the lines of important references in Jeremiah (chap. 23) and Ezekiel (chap. 34). Probably all false prophets, kings, or other leaders, both Jew and Gentile, are meant.

Ultimately, there is only one true leader: the Lord, the Shepherd of Israel. That is why verse 4 must refer to the Messiah. In one sense, it could refer to whatever good rulers God Himself brings forth from Judah—rulers like the Maccabees and others. But in the ultimate sense, only Jesus of Nazareth is the "cornerstone," the "tent peg," and the "battle bow."

The cornerstone is one of the most important messianic images in the Bible. An exposition is chiefly a presentation of the key texts. Undoubtedly the original idea goes back to Isaiah 28:16, where the prophecy occurs: "See, I lay a stone in Zion, a tested stone, a precious cornerstone for a sure foundation; the one who trusts will never be dismayed," and to Psalm 118:22, 23, which says, "The stone the builders rejected has become the capstone; the LORD has done this, and it is marvelous in our eyes." This was applied to Himself by Jesus in Matthew 21:42, and to Jesus by Peter in Acts 4:11. Later, in 1 Peter 2, the apostle quotes both texts (plus Isa. 8:14, "a stone that causes men to stumble and a rock that makes them fall") to make the point: "As you come to him, the living Stone—rejected by men but chosen by God and precious to him—you also, like living stones, are being built into a spiritual house to be a holy priesthood, offering spiritual sacrifices acceptable to God through Jesus Christ" (1 Peter 2:4, 5). Paul wrote, "You are no longer foreigners and aliens, but fellow citizens with God's people and members of God's household, built on the foundation of the apostles and prophets, with Christ Jesus himself as the chief cornerstone. In him the whole building is joined together and rises to become a holy temple in the Lord. And in him you too are being built together to become a dwelling in which God lives by his Spirit" (Eph. 2:19–22).

There were two kinds of pegs to which the word in the Hebrew text of Zechariah 10:4 may refer: an outer peg that held the rope of fabric of a Bedouin tent (cf. Judg. 4:21, 22) and an inner peg, either in a tent or house, on which utensils or valuable objects of the family were hung (cf. Ezek. 15:3). Either could

---

[7] Ibid., p. 330.

be meant here. But probably the key to understanding Zechariah's reference is Isaiah's prophecy of the replacing of the wicked treasurer of Jerusalem, Shebna, with Eliakim son of Hilkiah, of whom it is said, "I will drive him like a peg into a firm place; he will be a seat of honor for the house of his father. All the glory of his family will hang on him: its offspring and offshoots—all its lesser vessels, from the bowls to the jars" (Isa. 22:23, 24). The image points to the intrinsic strength of the Messiah.

The battle bow refers to the warlike functions of the one who is to come. He is pictured as a conquerer both in the Old Testament and the New (cf. Isa. 63:1–4; Rev. 19:11–16). This warrior will subdue all enemies.

4. *The Shepherd gathers His people (10:6–12).* The last section of Zechariah 10 tells how the Great Shepherd of Israel will restore the people by regathering them from the distant reaches of the earth. This theme is introduced in verse 6 ("I will restore them because I have compassion on them") and comes to a great climax in verses 10 and 11.

"I will bring them back from Egypt
    and gather them from Assyria.
I will bring them to Gilead and
    Lebanon,
    and there will not be room
        enough for them.
They will pass through the sea of
    trouble;
    the surging sea will be subdued
    and all the depths of the Nile will
        dry up.
Assyria's pride will be brought
    down
And Egypt's scepter will pass away.
I will strengthen them in the LORD
    and in his name they will walk,"
                declares the LORD.

The imagery of these verses is from the miracles accompanying the exodus of Israel from Egypt under Moses. This passage refers to a future regathering— not the regathering of the people from Babylon following the Exile. That was already history at the time of the writing of this chapter. The prophecy must concern a yet future day. The regathering may have begun with the reestablishing of the modern state of Israel. This will be a great regathering in which the scattered flock of the Messiah is returned to its own land and to great material and spiritual blessing.

OUR SHEPHERD-KING

I argue here, as elsewhere,[8] that verses like these refer to a literal future blessing upon a regathering and believing Israel. This is their meaning. Nevertheless, it is true that we who have been brought to faith in Jesus Christ as Savior can see ourselves in the points of this prophecy. Has the Lord not done each of these great things for us? He has saved us by His death. He has provided for us and encourages us to come to Him in prayer, asking for anything we lack. He is purifying us. He is also gathering us—both Jew and Gentile—from the farthest reaches of this world.

What we mean by this is that the Lord is not merely the Shepherd-King of Israel. He is our Shepherd too. And Israel's shepherd psalm is also our psalm.

The LORD is my shepherd, I shall
    lack nothing.
    He makes me lie down in green
        pastures,
he leads me beside quiet waters,
    he restores my soul.
He guides me in paths of
    righteousness
    for his name's sake.
Even though I walk

---

[8]Cf. "Days of Fruit and Wine" (Amos 9:11–15) in James Montgomery Boice, *The Minor Prophets*, vol. 1 (Grand Rapids: Zondervan, 1983), pp. 179–86; and "New Day Dawning" (Zeph. 3:9–20), pp. 129–34 in the present volume.

through the valley of the shadow
of death,
I will fear no evil,
for you are with me;
your rod and your staff,
they comfort me.

You prepare a table before me
in the presence of my enemies.
You anoint my head with oil;

my cup overflows.
Surely goodness and love will follow
me
all the days of my life,
and I will dwell in the house of the
LORD
forever.

Praise God that we have such a
Shepherd!

25

Rejection of the Good Shepherd

(Zechariah 11:1–17)

This is what the LORD my God says: "Pasture the flock marked for slaughter. Their buyers slaughter them and go unpunished. Those who sell them say, 'Praise the LORD, I am rich!' Their own shepherds do not spare them. For I will no longer have pity on the people of the land," declares the LORD. "I will hand everyone over to his neighbor and his king. They will oppress the land, and I will not rescue them from their hands."

So I pastured the flock marked for slaughter, particularly the oppressed of the flock. Then I took two staffs and called one Favor and the other Union, and I pastured the flock. In one month I got rid of the three shepherds.

The flock detested me, and I grew weary of them and said, "I will not be your shepherd. Let the dying die, and the perishing perish. Let those who are left eat one another's flesh."

Then I took my staff called Favor and broke it, revoking the covenant I had made with all the nations. It was revoked on that day, and so the afflicted of the flock who were watching me knew it was the word of the LORD.

I told them, "If you think it best, give me my pay; but if not, keep it." So they paid me thirty pieces of silver.

And the LORD said to me, "Throw it to the potter—the handsome price at which they priced me! So I took thirty pieces of silver and threw them into the house of the LORD to the potter.

Then I broke my second staff called Union, breaking the brotherhood between Judah and Israel.

If there was any question about the use of the word "oracle" (Heb. *massa'*, "a burden") to introduce Zechariah 9–11 (in Zech. 9:1), it should be dispelled now. For the encouragements of chapters 9 and 10 are followed in chapter 11 by one of the darkest prophecies in the entire body of Israel's prophetic literature.

This chapter falls into three distinct parts. The first (vv. 1–3) is a poetic description of a coming judgment on and desolation of Israel. It is a terrible section, though Charles Feinberg rightly calls it "the most poetic section of the whole book of Zechariah."[1] The second section (vv. 4–14) describes a symbolic action undertaken by Zechariah, reminding us of similar actions by Ezekiel and other prophets. In this case, Zechariah was to assume the role of a shepherd and portray events to be fulfilled in the coming rejection of the Messiah, the Lord Jesus Christ. He was

[1]Charles L. Feinberg, *God Remembers: A Study of Zechariah* (Portland: Multnomah Press, 1979), p. 154.

to serve the people, be rejected by them, and then abandon them to the consequences of that rejection for a time. This section contains the prophecy of the pricing of the shepherd at thirty pieces of silver quoted in Matthew 27:9, 10. The third section (vv. 15–17) describes a second symbolic act in which Zechariah assumes the role of a wicked shepherd in anticipation of an additional judgment upon the nation.

DESTRUCTION OF THE LAND

There can be little doubt that the first three verses of chapter 11 describe a coming judgment upon the land beginning with Lebanon in the north and continuing to Bashan and the Jordan. After the assurances of God's provision and care for His people in just the previous chapter, the prophecy comes unexpectedly, but its meaning is clear. The only question concerns the events to which these verses refer.

Not a few commentators content themselves with general statements about the passage, suggesting that it may refer to any future invasion of Israel by gentile powers. But if the previous chapters are as specific as I have tried to indicate—that is, if Zechariah 9:1–8 refers to the invasion of the land by Alexander the Great and if Zechariah 9:11–13 (and perhaps some of the following verses) refers to the wars of the Maccabees—then we are probably right in expecting a specific historical reference for this passage also. What can it be? The only real possibility is the destruction of Jerusalem and the surrounding towns by the Roman armies in the war of A.D. 66–70. These verses might have described the Babylonian invasion if they had been written earlier; but that was past history by Zechariah's time. There is nothing in the history of the people that a comprehensive destruction of the land can refer to prior to the terrible destruction ordered by Vespasian and his successor Titus.

The story is told at length in Josephus's *The Jewish War*. For years before this war the country had been in turmoil, various small skirmishes against the existing authorities being commonplace. At last revolutionaries gained control of Jerusalem and massacred the Roman garrison stationed there. The year was A.D. 66. In the next year General Vespasian, dispatched by Nero, arrived in Antioch. From there he moved first against the fortified towns of Galilee, subduing or arranging the surrender of each, and then against Jerusalem.

In A.D. 68 Nero died, and after a considerable delay Vespasian was proclaimed the new emperor. He returned to Rome, leaving his second-in-command, Titus, to carry on the war. By this time Jerusalem was host to three rival factions, which made negotiations with the Romans impossible and greatly intensified the coming tragedy. Jerusalem was surrounded. Food was cut off. People starved; some even resorted to cannibalism. Steadily the Romans broke through wall after wall, defense after defense, and the defenders were driven back to the temple. On July 17, A.D. 70, the daily sacrifices came to an end for lack of men to offer them. At last the gates of the temple were burned and then the temple itself. Thousands were crucified. The victorious Titus set up Roman standards in the temple court and returned to Rome to celebrate his triumph in the year A.D. 71. Through this great war and a later series of rebellions and reprisals, Judaism ceased to exist politically, and the Jewish people were widely scattered throughout the known world.

THE GOOD SHEPHERD

The second portion of Zechariah 11 is so difficult that we would find it almost impossible to interpret except for the acknowledged fulfillment in the earthly ministry of Jesus Christ. Apparently,

Zechariah was instructed to act out Christ's shepherd role over Israel and thus experience the rejection the true Shepherd was later to experience even more intensely. Verses 4–6 explain what Zechariah was to do and forecast the outcome. He was to pasture "the flock marked for slaughter." This would not have a fortunate outcome. His work was to be symbolic of God's last approach to the people through His own Son, the Messiah, whom they would reject. As a result of this rejection—which is stated later but presupposed here—God says that He "will no longer have pity on the people of the land. . . . I will hand everyone over to his neighbor and his king. They will oppress the land [as in the opening three verses], and I will not rescue them from their hands."

In verses 7–14 Zechariah tells how he carried out the Lord's instructions. He did pasture the flock, using two staffs to which he gave the symbolic names *Favor* and *Union*. He does not elaborate upon these staffs except to say later that he broke them. He does not need to. *Favor* symbolizes the favored status of Israel as the chosen people of God. *Union* symbolizes the internal harmony of the people that was lost at the time of the siege of Jerusalem.

What does Zechariah mean when he says that "in one month I got rid of the three shepherds"? Presumably, the need to get rid of these shepherds betrays opposition to his work and symbolizes opposition to the future work of Jesus. But it is still hard to place these three "shepherds" specifically. One commentator lists forty different solutions to the problem! The best explanation is probably the oldest, which sees the three shepherds not as three individuals but as three classes of individuals, namely: the prophets,

priests, and kings of Israel. Thomas V. Moore sees it thus: "The obscurity of this phrase would have been more easily removed by interpreters, if the three-fold nature of Christ's work had been recollected, and its relation to the Jewish polity. He was the great antetype, of which that polity was the complex type. Now he, as our Redeemer, appeared as a Prophet, a Priest and a King, and thus fulfilled all the significance of these three orders in the old dispensation. He was the promised prophet, the one and only priest, and the king in Zion, and hence his appearing brought these respective orders in the theocracy to an end, since they were only designed to foreshadow his advent and kingdom. This was done in judicial anger also; they were deposed because of their unfaithfulness in the discharge of their duties."[2]

If this is not the proper explanation of this verse, it is nevertheless significant that the prophetic, priestly, and kingly offices did cease following the Jewish rejection of Christ and the overthrow of Jerusalem. According to Jesus, John the Baptist was the last of the prophets. The priesthood ceased with the destruction of the temple where alone the sacrifices were permitted to be performed. Again, after this shattering and terribly destructive period, no king has ever ruled over a Jewish state.

Verse 9 seems to describe the horrors of the siege of Jerusalem: the "dying" of the warriors, the "perishing" of those who (presumably) were stricken by plague and illness, and the eating of "one another's flesh" by the starving. In verse 11 there may be a specific prophecy of an unusual event that took place during this siege. This verse speaks of God revoking the covenant of favor that had been established with the people, which is clear enough if the

[2]Thomas V. Moore, *A Commentary on Haggai, Zechariah and Malachi* (Edinburgh and Carlisle, Pa.: Banner of Truth Trust, 1979), p. 262. Original edition 1856.

passage is referring to the destruction of Jerusalem and its temple. But then it goes on to say: "So the afflicted of the flock who were watching me knew it was the word of the LORD." These "afflicted of the flock" may be the Christians who were in Jerusalem at the time of the Roman siege. When Titus unaccountably raised the siege for a few days, the Christians remembered Jesus' warning to flee to the mountains (Matt. 24:16) and left the city for Pella. They thereby escaped the fate of those who remained and thus proved the words of this prophecy to be true.

The next verses (vv. 12, 13) describe the final rejection of the Good Shepherd. Thirty pieces of silver was the price of a servant who was gored by an ox (cf. Exod. 21:32). So to pay Zechariah this sum was to say that at any time the people could buy a slave that would be as useful as he had been. Zechariah ironically calls it a "handsome price." So also was the Lord of glory valued, Judas betraying him for a similarly insulting amount. When Judas later wished to return this blood money and ended up by throwing it down before the priests in the temple, he unintentionally fulfilled verse 13.

It is hard to leave this elaborate development of the shepherd theme in Zechariah 11 without thinking of the use Jesus made of it in the teaching recorded in John 10. So far as we can tell, Jesus did not refer to Zechariah specifically, any more than He referred to Psalm 23 or any other of the great Old Testament passages that use this imagery. But He knew these passages, and they were all undoubtedly in His mind as He explained to His disciples: "I tell you the truth, the man who does not enter the sheep pen by the gate, but climbs in by some other way, is a thief and a robber. The man who enters by the gate is the shepherd of his sheep. The watchman opens the gate for him, and the sheep listen to his voice. He calls his own sheep by name and leads them out. When he has brought out all his own, he goes on ahead of them, and his sheep follow him because they know his voice. But they will never follow a stranger; in fact, they will run away from him because they do not recognize a stranger's voice" (John 10:1–5).

In this parable the thieves and robbers are the false shepherds of Israel, which is what Zechariah called them. The sheepfold is Judaism. The ones who hear Christ's voice and respond to His call are those of His own within Israel. (The man born blind, whose story is told in the immediately preceding chapter of John's gospel, is one example. Those who believed Christ and fled from Jerusalem at the time of its encirclement by the armies of Titus are others.)

What are the lessons of this parable? There are several.

First, the parable teaches that *the Lord Jesus Christ knows His sheep* and that it is a wonderful thing to be known by Him. This truth is implied in verse 3: "He calls his own sheep by name." It is stated even more explicitly in verse 14: "I am the good shepherd; I know my sheep and my sheep know me." According to the teaching of this chapter, the sheep are known to Christ because they have been given Him by the Father (v. 29), and it is for these and not for all sheep that the Shepherd dies (vv. 14, 15). What a wonderful collection of truths that is! God has given a certain number of individuals to Christ, Jesus knows who they are, and He has died for them to provide their way to heaven.

Second, the parable teaches us that having known His sheep, *Jesus calls them* and that He does so *by name* (v. 3). This is the doctrine of election. It is not liked. Often it is not preached. But it is in Scripture and must be preached, above all by anyone who is serious about expounding the whole of God's counsels. For election is the central point of Christ's parable! God has given some sheep to the Lord Jesus, and Jesus comes to the gate of the sheepfold, knowing His sheep in advance, calls to them, and leads them out. Not all are saved. Jesus did not call the Pharisees. But those are saved whom God has given to Jesus, and all of them are saved. Indeed, they shall never perish, and no one shall snatch them out of Christ's hand (v. 28).

This is not an impersonal, still less arbitrary decree, however, though some have charged this. It is a very tender and personal thing; for Jesus says that the Shepherd calls His own sheep *by name*. Being called by name, they follow Him.

Finally, the parable teaches that having known His own sheep and having called them, *the Lord leads them out* (v. 3). He leads them out from anything that would keep them from Him and into His own great flock the church. Jesus led the man who had been born blind out of Judaism. But there are other examples. Jesus has led some out of paganism. He has led others out of Western materialism. He has led some out of communism, some out of the worship of knowledge, some out of the rat race generated by our competitive society. These latter are contemporary sheepfolds. Perhaps He is calling you from some other sheepfold today.

THE WORTHLESS SHEPHERD

In the last section of Zechariah 11 (vv. 15–17), the prophet is given a second symbolic commission. Just as he had been told to represent the true Shepherd in verses 7–14, so now is he to represent a false or wicked shepherd.

The character of this man is described both negatively and positively. Negatively: "I am going to raise up a shepherd over the land who will not care for the lost, or seek the young, or heal the injured, or feed the healthy." This shepherd will be the exact opposite of the kind of shepherd Jesus was in His earthly ministry. Positively: " . . . but will eat the meat of the choice sheep, tearing off their hoofs." (This shepherd uses the sheep selfishly for *his* benefit. By contrast, Jesus gave Himself *for* the sheep.)

Who is this shepherd? Again, there have been many interpretations. For the most part, Jewish commentators see him as Herod. Christian commentators are often quite general, assigning the image to all evil rulers collectively. Some refer this to the Roman emperors, noting that in their rejection of Jesus at His trial the leaders of Israel shouted out, "We have no king but Caesar" (John 19:15). This last suggestion is quite plausible, for in rejecting their true Shepherd-King, the people obtained a king who would eventually destroy both their city and nation.[3]

However apt this image may be as a designation of Rome or the Roman emperor, it is probable that it has its full and final realization only in the Antichrist of end-time prophecy. This is the figure described in Daniel 7:8–12; 11:36–38; 2 Thessalonians 2:1–12; 1 John 2:18–27; 4:1–3; 2 John 7; and Revelation 13. In Daniel 7, in the context of a vision involving four great beasts, Antichrist is described as "a little horn" who destroys three other horns. In the language of these visions a horn is a king or ruler. So the statement indicates that Antichrist will be a political figure, a king, who is able

---

[3] Moore sees a broader reference to Rome, finding support in the prophecy of the end of the false shepherd when, like an "old lion," withered in strength and failing of sight, the empire lay down to die. "The sword of the barbarian was added to her own blinded and palsied weakness, and thus judgment inflicted in exact accordance with the words of this prophecy" (Moore, *Commentary on Haggai, Zechariah and Malachi*, p. 271).

to overcome three other kings. The vision says that "this horn had eyes like the eyes of a man, and a mouth that spoke boastfully." This suggests that the Antichrist will be keen of insight and will have great oratorical ability.

Revelation 13 links up with Daniel 7, for in it the vision of the beasts and horns reappear. John writes, "I saw a beast coming out of the sea. He had ten horns and seven heads, with ten crowns on his horns, and on each head a blasphemous name. The beast I saw resembled a leopard, but had feet like those of a bear and a mouth like that of a lion. The dragon gave the beast his power and his throne and great authority" (Rev. 13:1, 2). Every image in this vision refers back to Daniel, only here the beast (rather than his horn) is the Antichrist. The reference to the horns tells us that the Antichrist controls ten kingdoms but that there are only seven heads of state. As in Daniel, the Antichrist has conquered and displaced three of them.

The description of the beast is particularly interesting, for it combines features of the first three beasts seen by Daniel. These beasts represent three former world powers. So to combine them in the figure of the fourth beast is to suggest that the Antichrist will combine the strengths of each of those former kingdoms in his own. His kingdom will have the ferocity of the lion, the strength of the bear, and the speed of the leopard. The verses also indicate that the possession of the ten kingdoms and the strengths of the former three kingdoms are given to Antichrist by the Devil.

In 2 Thessalonians 2:3 we are told more. Here the Antichrist is described as "the man of lawlessness" who "opposes and exalts himself over everything that is called God or is worshiped, and even sets himself up in God's temple, proclaiming himself to be God." This adds the thought that the Antichrist will also serve a religious as well as a political function, and reminds us of the place occupied by the later emperors of Rome who became both political and religious heads for those under them.

Zechariah tells us what will happen to this satanic figure. "The sword [will] strike his arm and his right eye." That is, he will be judged in the very areas— his superhuman strength and insight— in which he takes most pride.

RUIN OF THE WICKED

I end with these "practical inferences" from the exposition of Thomas Moore:

"1. No defence shall protect the wicked from punishment when God's time has come. Though they tower as high and strong as Lebanon, the storm shall bow their summits, and though they hide themselves as deep as the lairs in the creeping thickets of Jordan, the tempest shall find them out and wrap them in ruin (vv. 1–3).

"2. Sin is always folly and the sinner always a fool, for he secures the great evil of punishment in exchange for the small good of gratification and therefore always makes a fool's bargain (vv. 4, 5).

"3. Wicked rulers are a curse of God on a wicked nation. As religion tends to prevent such rulers or at least prevent their choice, there is an obvious connection between politics and religion. Church and state may and ought to be separated; politics and religion ought not, for thus the state becomes exposed to the curse of God and political evil follows in the train of moral evil (v. 6).

"4. Blessed are the poor in spirit, for theirs is the kingdom of heaven (v. 7).

"5. Union of feeling in a people is a mark of the favor of God, and disunion a token of his wrath (v. 7). . . .

"6. Christ cannot be rejected with impunity. Even the Jews, who 'did it ignorantly in unbelief,' paid a terrible penalty for their crime; how much more terrible will be the punishment of those who have all their unbelief without any of their ignorance (vv. 8–11).

"7. Men now sometimes reject Christ for a far less reward than thirty pieces of silver, and of course with far more guilt than Judas (vv. 12, 13).

"8. God may bear long with the wicked, but there is a point where the piling avalanche will cease to be held back and descend in fearful ruin (vv. 14–17)."[4]

This grim chapter of the otherwise uplifting Book of Zechariah is a sobering look at the results of unbelief, particularly unbelief that leads to the rejection of Jesus Christ as one's personal Lord and Savior. Still it has blessed many by causing them to reject that rejection and follow the Good Shepherd.

---

[4]Ibid., pp. 271–73.

26

Mourning for the Good Shepherd

(Zechariah 12:1–14)

And I will pour out on the house of David and the inhabitants of Jerusalem a spirit of grace and supplication. They will look on me, the one they have pierced, and mourn for him as one mourns for an only child, and grieve bitterly for him as one grieves for a firstborn son. On that day the weeping in Jerusalem will be great, like the weeping of Hadad Rimmon in the plain of Megiddo. The land will mourn, each clan by itself, with their wives by themselves: the clan of the house of David and their wives, the clan of the house of Nathan and their wives, the clan of the house of Levi and their wives, the clan of Shimei and their wives, and all the rest of the clans and their wives.

The last three chapters of Zechariah contain a second "oracle," or "burden" (Heb. *massaʾ*) of the prophet, corresponding to the burden of chapters 9–11. But in the first section the burden is laid upon Hadrach, a gentile nation, while in the second section the burden is laid upon Israel. This points to the chief difference between the two oracles. To go back to the words of David Baron, the first oracle concerns "the judgment through which gentile world-power over Israel is finally destroyed and Israel is endowed with strength to overcome all their [sic] enemies," while the second concerns "the judgment through which Israel itself is sifted and purged in the final conflict with the nations and transformed into the holy nation of Jehovah."[1]

The events of these last chapters belong to the same time period, as a careful reading shows. Characteristic of these chapters is a reiteration of the phrase "on that day," found in 12:3, 4, 6, 8, 9, 11; 13:1, 2, 4; and 14:4, 6, 8, 9, 13, 20, 21. Since this begins as early as 12:3 and continues to the last verse of chapter 14, it is hard to miss that the events all belong together.

OUR TIMES OR END TIMES?

But to what period do they belong? And to what people? They obviously follow the first coming of Jesus Christ, for 12:10–14 describes a universal repentance in which people mourn for "the one they have pierced" (v. 10). But does that concern events shortly after Jesus' death, perhaps events accompanying the first preaching of the gospel at Pentecost or shortly thereafter? Does it refer to the expansion of Christian preaching and church growth throughout all subsequent ages? Or does it relate to something special to happen at the end of this age? Quite a few reformed thinkers pick the second

[1]David Baron, *The Visions & Prophecies of Zechariah* (Grand Rapids: Kregel, 1918), p. 285. See my earlier discussion in chapter 24 ("Israel's Shepherd-King"), pp. 190–99.

207

possibility and see the blessing of these chapters as belonging to the church, not to Israel nationally. This is probably the majority view in reformed circles, due to the more basic conviction that the people of God are one, the church being an extension of Israel, and that reversion to a day of national Jewish blessing would be a step backward from the fulfillment of all prophecy in Christ.

Unfortunately for this view, the chapter does not speak generally about "the people of God" or even merely about "Israel." It repeatedly stresses the names of Jerusalem and Judah. And when it talks about Israel's repentance, it does so by reference to the specific Jewish clans or tribes: "the clan of the house of David and their wives, the clan of the house of Nathan and their wives, the clan of the house of Levi and their wives, the clan of Shimei and their wives, and all the rest of the clans and their wives" (Zech. 12:12–14). There is probably no more specifically Jewish prophecy in the book.

But if these chapters refer to Jews specifically and not to the church as the New Testament Israel, then the events to which they refer must be future. For it is certain that there has not yet been a national repentance by Israel nor an enjoyment by them of the blessings here enumerated. And if this is the case, then the battle referred to in Zechariah 12:1–9 must be the last great battle, Armageddon, and the repentance of verses 10–14 a time of national salvation prior to the second coming of the Lord. Indeed, when the chapters are viewed in that light, the repeated "on that day" is seen quite naturally to refer to that last and great day of the Lord's return in judgment. These chapters are a prophecy of the events of those end times.

Earlier I said that this is not the majority view of reformed thinkers (though it is the general view of American Evangelicalism). But it is worth adding that it has nevertheless been the view of some in the reformed camp. For example, although the publishers of the 1958 reprint of Thomas V. Moore's *A Commentary on Haggai, Zechariah and Malachi* felt compelled to add an appendix, showing that reformed thought generally assigns these chapters to the church age, they nevertheless explored the other possibility (the one introduced here) thoroughly, concluding: "While agreeing with Chambers [Thomas W. Chambers of New York] that it is generally right to regard the church as the New Testament Israel, we are, like Moore, not satisfied that the meaning of these closing chapters of Zechariah can be fully explained in that way."[2] The publishers then quote seventeenth-century Scottish expositor George Hutcheson as saying, "The conversion of the Jews or Israel unto the Messiah is not to be of some few only but national of the body of that people, and there will be real repentance among many of them." Thomas Boston, the eighteenth-century Scottish Evangelical wrote in regard to Romans 11 that Paul "shows that the blindness of the Jews is only in part, and to last only to a certain time, when there shall be a national conversion, and so all Israel shall be saved. This is not meant of the spiritual Israel, for their conversion could be no mystery as this is. But as the conversion of the Gentiles themselves under the Old Testament (Eph. 3:3–6), so is that of the Jews to the Gentiles and Jews themselves under the New Testament. And as many Jews then would not believe the one, so many Christians now believe not the other." They even quote Charles

---

[2]Thomas V. Moore, *A Commentary on Haggai, Zechariah and Malachi* (Edinburgh and Carlisle Pa.: Banner of Truth Trust, 1979), p. 330.

Hodge as teaching that Zechariah 12:12 is one of the "express predictions of their [the Jews'] national conversion to faith in him whom they had rejected and crucified."[3]

If this is right, then there is no reason to discount these last chapters of Zechariah as giving a forecast of scores of events associated with the end times.

Charles Feinberg says, "The actual events, world-embracing in character, which are presented include the world confederacy against Jerusalem; the victory of God's people, empowered of the Lord; the conviction of Israel nationally by the Spirit of God; the presentation of Christ as their rejected Messiah; the national Day of Atonement; the cleansing of the hearts of the nation; the purging of the land from idolatry and false prophets; parenthetically, the crucifixion of the Messiah; the time of Jacob's trouble; the partial success of the nations invading Palestine and besieging Jerusalem; the appearance of the Messiah for his people; their rescue and his coming with his saints; the changed and renovated Holy Land; the establishment of the Messianic kingdom; the punishment of the nations for their futile assault on Israel; the celebration of the kingdom feast, the Feast of Tabernacles; and the complete restoration of the people of God to a holy nation."[4] It would be hard to find a more complete treatment of the events of the end times in all Scripture.

A THEMATIC STATEMENT

The oracle begins with a thematic statement in which God first identifies Himself and then tells what He is going to do: "This is the word of the LORD concerning Israel. The LORD, who stretches out the heavens, who lays the foundations of the earth, and who forms the spirit of man within him,

declares: "I am going to make Jerusalem a cup that sends all the surrounding peoples reeling" (vv. 1, 2).

The identification of God as He who "stretches out the heavens, who lays the foundation of the earth, and who forms the spirit of man" is significant for several reasons. For one thing, it summarizes the creative movement of the opening chapter of Genesis in which God first makes the heavens, then creates the earth and everything on it, and finally breathes life into the man He has formed from the dust. No doubt, this identification is meant to recall that original creation and identify the God of the end events with the God of the beginning. The verse is also striking for another reason. The words translated "stretches," "lays," and "forms" are present participles. They do not say: God "*stretched* out the heavens," "*laid* the foundation of the earth" or "*formed* the spirit of man," referring to some past activity, but rather He is stretching, laying, and forming things now. That is, the world we see may be said to exist, not because God originally wound it up like a mechanical clock and then left it alone, but because He continually re-creates (or at least preserves) it, apart from which it would instantly vanish.

It is more natural for us to say that God brought things into being by the sheer word of His power and that He now preserves what He has created. "But when we reflect," as John H. Gerstner wrote, "that we who are brought into being by him have no substance of our own which could possibly perpetuate our own being and that, as Augustine observes, the natural tendency of created being is to nonbeing, we may feel that God, when he

---

[3] Ibid., pp. 331, 332.

[4] Charles L. Feinberg, *God Remembers: A Study of Zechariah* (Portland: Multnomah Press, 1979), pp. 169, 170.

upholds the universe, is constantly re-creating it."[5] Whether this is the actual case or not, there is no doubt that Zechariah rightly stresses God's continuing involvement with His universe. He created it, is with it now, and will be with it at the end. That is the significance of this thematic introduction.

The second part of the statement tells what God is going to do. He is going to make "Jerusalem a cup that sends all the surrounding peoples reeling" (v. 2). Jerusalem and the surrounding area of Judah will be besieged; this will be the time of Jacob's trouble. But out of that will come the judgment on the gentile nations that the next verses describe. The cup is the cup of God's wrath or judgment (cf. Isa. 51:17; Jer. 25:15–28; 49:12; Ezek. 23:31–34; Rev. 14:9, 10; 16:19).

ARMAGEDDON

Since the first half of Zechariah 12 tells of God's final judgment and the destruction of the gentile nations that have made war against Israel, after which they pass from history, it is worth noting that the last act of these gentile world powers is warfare. "Men since the beginning of time have sought peace," wrote General Douglas MacArthur in *Reminiscences*.[6] But war is man's chief legacy.

Each treaty of history was hailed by someone at some time as the road to a just and lasting disarmament, but the ink had scarcely dried on most of these treaties when the guns began to sound for the next encounter. Each new weapon discovery—gunpowder, tanks, airplanes, missiles, nuclear weapons—has been said to make war

far too horrible to contemplate. But human experience indicates that there is never a horror so great that someone will not use it to enforce his designs on others or to seize others' possessions.

This judgment is not merely an expression of the fading hopes of our century. It is vindicated by historical records. One of the earliest of all historical records, a Sumerian bas-relief sculpture from Babylon (c. 3000 B.C.), shows soldiers fighting in close order, wearing helmets and carrying shields. Wars fill the history of every ancient culture—Babylon, Syria, Assyria, Egypt, Phoenicia. The twenty-seven-year-long Peloponnesian War destroyed Greece at the height of the great civilization she had created during Athens' Golden Age. Rome made war a way of life, but even she was eventually defeated and overrun by barbarians. In the Middle Ages war ravaged Europe, culminating in the horrors of the Thirty Years' War, which ended in 1648. The *Encyclopedia Britannica* calls the Thirty Years' War "the most horrible military episode in western history prior to the 20th century."[7] By early estimates three-fourths of the German-speaking peoples died in that war. But even by the more cautious estimate made later, about seven million people (one-third of the population) are judged to have lost their lives.[8] We come to modern times, and we find that World War I was even more destructive, killing approximately twenty million people.[9] Men and women were horrified.

But within one quarter of a century a similar war was fought in the same amphitheater by the same parties and

[5]John H. Gerstner, "Man as God Made Him" in James M. Boice, editor, *Our Savior God: Studies on Man, Christ and the Atonement* (Grand Rapids: Baker, 1980), p. 21.

[6]Douglas MacArthur, *Reminiscences* (New York: McGraw-Hill, 1964), p. 276.

[7]"War" in *Encyclopedia Britannica*, vol. 23, p. 198.

[8]Ibid., p. 199.

[9]Ibid., p. 201. In addition twenty million more lost their lives due to war-related epidemics and famines.

for much the same reasons. World War II resulted in a loss of sixty million lives, triple the loss of the earlier conflict, while the costs quadrupled from an estimated $340 billion to an estimated $4.5 trillion.[10]

"Since World War II there have been at least 12 limited wars in the world, 39 political assassinations, 48 personal revolts, 74 rebellions for independence, 162 social revolutions, either political, economic, racial or religious." So wrote *U.S. News and World Report* in the September 25, 1967, issue. By now the totals need to be increased substantially in each category. The sad lesson is that people do not learn from history and that Armageddon is always at the door.[11]

This final war is now described in Zechariah. Apparently the nations of the world will combine in a final deadly onslaught against the state of Israel. But God will strengthen the nation to resist: "On that day, when all the nations of the earth are gathered against her, I will make Jerusalem an immovable rock for all the nations. All who try to move it will injure themselves" (v. 3). God will call forth strong leaders: "On that day I will make the leaders of Judah like a firepot in a woodpile, like a flaming torch among sheaves" (v. 6). Indeed, He will make heroes even of the least of the people: "On that day the LORD will shield those who live in Jerusalem, so that the feeblest among them will be like David, and the house of David will be like God, like the Angel of the LORD going before them" (v. 8). In all this, God's hand will be seen. The victory over the nations will be His: "On that day I will strike every horse with panic and its rider with madness. . . . I will keep a watchful eye over the house of Judah, but I will blind all the horses of the nations" (v. 4). "On that day I will

set out to destroy all the nations that attack Jerusalem" (v. 9).

The judgment against the nations will be an accelerating one, to judge from the increasing intensity of the verbs used in this section: *reeling* (v. 2), *injured* (v. 3), and *destroyed* (v. 9).

MOURNING FOR JESUS

This battle, in which God intervenes at the crucial moment on behalf of His people, will be the greatest victory the nation of Israel has achieved—greater even than its conquests in the day of King David, greater than the deliverance of the Maccabees, greater than the conquests of the Sixty Day War or any other. But just at the time of this, their greatest victory, God intervenes in another way to achieve His final conquest *over them:* "And I will pour out on the house of David and the inhabitants of Jerusalem a spirit of grace and supplication. They will look on me, the one they have pierced, and mourn for him as one mourns for an only child, and grieve bitterly for him as one grieves for a firstborn son" (v. 10).

Apart from the incarnation of the Second Person of the Trinity, Jesus Christ, these words must remain a mystery, as they in fact are for the host of unbelieving Jewish commentators who generally try to relate the piercing to Israel and speak of mourning for her. But the Jews will not mourn for themselves. "They [that is, the Jews] will look on . . . the one they [again, this must mean the Jews] have pierced." This one is someone other than the nation. But who is he? The text calls him "me," that is Jehovah. But no one can pierce or wound God . . . not unless God first takes on human flesh and dwells among us. Is that the meaning? Indeed, it is, for this is what happened in Jesus Christ. He is "God

[10] Ibid., p. 202.
[11] See a longer treatment of this theme in James M. Boice, *The Last and Future World* (Grand Rapids: Zondervan, 1974), pp. 98–113, from which parts of the above have been taken.

with us." He is God come to die. As Isaiah declared,

Surely he took up our infirmities
    and carried our sorrows,
yet we considered him stricken by
    God,
    smitten by him, and afflicted.
But he was pierced for our
    transgressions,
    he was crushed for our iniquities;
the punishment that brought us
    peace was upon him,
    and by his wounds we are
    healed.
We all, like sheep, have gone
    astray,
    each of us has turned to his own
    way;
and the LORD has laid on him
    the iniquity of us all (Isa. 53:4–6).

Perception of these truths will come about by the power of God's Holy Spirit, for it is only as God pours out "a spirit of grace and supplication" that the repentance and turning depicted in these verses occurs.

It is only by the power of God's Holy Spirit that they occur anywhere or to anyone. But where the Holy Spirit is present, there is first, a mourning for personal and national sin and second, a turning from that sin to look in faith to the Lord Jesus.

Baron writes wisely, "The ultimate literal fulfillment of [these verses] lies yet in the future, in the day for which we watch and pray, when our Lord Jesus shall, according to his promise, appear in his glory and the Jewish nation shall literally look upon him whom they have pierced and be, as it were, 'born in a day.' But there is a forestallment, so to say, in the fulfillment of this prophecy in the case of the individual even now. 'And thus,' to quote the words of an honored Hebrew Christian brother and true master of Israel, 'every Jew who, by the grace of God since the Day of Pentecost, had been brought to Christ fulfills this prediction; he looks unto him whom he has pierced. It is the look of repentance; for only a sight of the crucified Jesus shows us our sin and grief. It is the look of supplication and faith; for he only can bless and save, and he saves all who believe. It is the look of peace and adoration; for his love is infinite, unchanging and omnipotent. It is the look which never ceases and never ends; for now the veil is taken away, and we with open face, beholding the glory of the Lord, are changed into the same image from glory to glory' (Adolph Saphir).

"And as it is with the individual Jew, so it is with the individual Gentile. Yes, thanks be to God, as we all, whether Jew or Gentile, had our share in the guilt of Christ's crucifixion because of our common sin, so also may all have their share in the salvation which comes through a penitent look of faith on him whom we have pierced."[12] May God give many that look of saving faith before the day of His announced and final judgment dawns.

---

[12]Baron, *The Visions & Prophecies of Zechariah*, pp. 454, 455.

27

A Fountain Opened in Israel

(Zechariah 13:1–9)

On that day a fountain will be opened to the house of David and the inhabitants of Jerusalem, to cleanse them from sin and impurity. . . .

> *"Awake, O Sword, against my shepherd,*
> *against the man who is close to me!"*
> *declares the LORD Almighty.*
> *"Strike the shepherd,*
> *and the sheep will be scattered.*
> *and I will turn my hand against the little ones.*
> *In the whole land," declares the LORD,*
> *"two-thirds will be struck down and perish;*
> *yet one-third will be left in it.*
> *This third I will bring into the fire;*
> *I will refine them like silver*
> *and test them like gold.*
> *They will call on my name*
> *and I will answer them;*
> *I will say, 'They are my people,'*
> *and they will say, 'The LORD is our God.' "*

Chapter 13 of Zechariah is closely linked to chapter 12, so closely that we can almost wish there had been no chapter division. There is both chronological connection and even more importantly, a theological connection in which the cleansing from sin depicted in chapter 13 follows the repentance of chapter 12.

The joining of the two sections by language is most evident. The thirteenth chapter begins with the words "on that day," which occur just two verses earlier in 12:11. (They are found a total of nine times in the two chapters.) The descriptive phrase "the house of David and the inhabitants of Jerusalem," also in 13:1, occurs in 12:10. These details show that the chapters (particularly 12:10–14 and 13:1–6) are dealing with the same people and concern the same period of time. The people are Jews. The time is the period of final repentance at the end of world history in which "all Israel shall be saved" (Rom. 11:26). Chronologically this means that the blessing of the purifying of the nation described in chapter 13 will follow the repentance of the nation described in chapter 12.

213

It is always the case that repentance must precede cleansing and that cleansing from sin follows genuine repentance. This is the point of 2 Chronicles 7:14: "If my people, who are called by my name, will humble themselves and pray and seek my face and turn from their wicked ways, then will I hear from heaven and will forgive their sin and will heal their land." It is the theology of 1 John 1:9: "If we confess our sins, he is faithful and just and will forgive us our sins and purify us from all unrighteousness."

FORGIVENESS AND CLEANSING

Chapter 13 begins with a verse that must be taken by itself: "On that day a fountain will be opened to the house of David and the inhabitants of Jerusalem, to cleanse them from sin and impurity."

The idea of God being a fountain to His people is found frequently in the Old Testament, but Zechariah's treatment is possibly the richest of all. Psalm 36:9 says, "For with you is the fountain of life; in your light we see light." Jeremiah uses the image in two key places. He says:

"My people have committed two sins:
They have forsaken me,
    the spring of living water,
and have dug their own cisterns,
    broken cisterns that cannot hold .
        water" (Jer. 2:13).

Again,

"Those who turn away from you
    will be written in the dust
because they have forsaken the
    LORD,
the spring of living water" (Jer.
    17:13).

Ezekiel uses the image positively: "I will sprinkle clean water on you, and you will be clean; I will cleanse you from all your impurities and from all your idols. I will give you a new heart and put a new spirit in you; I will remove from you your heart of stone and give you a heart of flesh" (Ezek. 36:25, 26). This passage may have been in Zechariah's mind as he composed his writings, for the verses in Ezekiel relate to the end times when God will gather His people from all the countries into which they have been scattered and "bring [them] back into [their] own land" (v. 24).

Zechariah speaks of a twofold effect of the cleansing God provides. He cleanses us from *sin* and *impurity*. We could also say that He cleanses us from *sin's penalty* and *sin's power*. That is, the salvation of God's people is not merely from the condemnation due to them for their sin; it is, in addition, a progressive (and eventually a full) deliverance from the power and presence of sin in their lives.

Where does this cleansing from sin's power and defilement come from? It comes from the fountain. And what is that? Clearly, the "fountain" that will be opened to the house of David and the inhabitants of Jerusalem is the blood of the Messiah whom they have pierced.

This is what was in the mind of John the Evangelist when he called attention to the fact that blood and water issued from the side of Jesus when He was pierced by a soldier's spear at the Crucifixion. In this account, John briefly reports Jesus' death but then takes seven verses to show how His legs were not broken, as were the legs of the two thieves who were crucified with Him, and how Jesus was pierced with a spear. This was in fulfillment of prophecy, he says. The first situation was a fulfillment of Psalm 34:20, the second of Zechariah 12:10. This was remarkable in itself, of course. One of these prophecies was negative (the Savior's legs must not be broken), the other positive (the Savior's side must be pierced), but neither was what might have been expected. It was normal to break legs of crucified prisoners so that they might die quicker. It was not normal to pierce them with a spear. That each of these happened to Jesus was a remarkable fulfillment of Scripture and a clear proof that God was controlling these circumstances.

But this was not all that was involved. John was impressed with the fact that when Christ's side was pierced the piercing was accompanied by "a sudden flow of blood and water" (John 19:34). This was so remarkable that John calls attention to it, saying, "The man who saw it has given testimony, and his testimony is true. He knows that he tells the truth, and he testifies so that you also may believe" (v. 35). It is after this that he gives his two texts, including the one from Zechariah.

What did John have in mind? When he saw the surprising issue of blood and water from the side of Christ, he must have remembered (what Jew would not!) that in the Old Testament sacrificial system, blood was the appointed means of cleansing sin, and that in the temple ceremonies, water was used for ceremonial purification from uncleanness. Moreover, he would have known that the passage he was quoting from Zechariah (Zech. 12:10, "They will look on . . . the one they have pierced") is followed four verses later by the text we are considering, namely, "On that day a fountain will be opened to the house of David and the inhabitants of Jerusalem, to cleanse them from sin and impurity" (13:1). Seeing the flow of blood and water and putting these two bits of information together, John must have concluded that deliverance from sin's penalty and cleansing from its defilement are to be found in the death of Jesus only.

This is the theology that William Cowper, the English poet, pictured so beautifully in his great hymn of the crucifixion.

There is a fountain filled with
   blood,
   Drawn from Immanuel's veins;
And sinners, plunged beneath that
   flood,
   Lose all their guilty stains.

The dying thief rejoiced to see
   That fountain in his day;
And there have I, as vile as he,
   Washed all my sins away.

E'er since by faith I saw the stream
   Thy flowing wounds supply,
Redeeming love has been my
   theme,
   And shall be till I die.

Dear dying Lamb, thy precious
   blood
   Shall never lose its power,
Till all the ransomed church of God
   Be saved, to sin no more.

Zechariah is saying that in the last great day of national repentance by Israel that fountain will be opened to Israel nationally. But it is not necessary for you to wait for that day. In fact, it may be fatal for you to delay repentance and faith in Christ even for a moment. If you have not yet turned to look upon the Son of God who was pierced for your sin, you should cry out at once, as Augustus Toplady did:

Foul, I to the Fountain fly;
Wash me, Saviour, or I die.
Rock of Ages, cleft for me,
Let me hide myself in thee.

PURIFICATION OF THE LAND

No one can be forgiven and cleansed of sin in the way the opening verse of this chapter describes without that person's environment being affected. Since this cleansing is to affect the people as a whole, the environment as a whole is also to experience cleansing. David Baron says, "From the inward cleansing of the people from the guilt and moral defilement of sin, the prophet passes in verses 2–6 to the cleansing of the land and the purification of the environment in which the forgiven and sanctified people shall then live and move. Nothing that defileth shall be permitted in the restored Jewish state."[1]

The purification of the land will cleanse it of every possible appearance of evil. Of the many that might be mentioned, however, Zechariah singles out only two evils that plagued the nation before the fall of the northern kingdom to Assyria in 721 B.C. and the fall of the southern kingdom to Babylon in 586 B.C.: idolatry and false prophecy.

These went together. In the age of Ahab and Jehoshaphat, when Micaiah was called to prophesy the death of Ahab by Ramoth Gilead, there were 400 false prophets but only one prophet of the Lord (1 Kings 22). Moreover, when Elijah appeared on Mount Carmel, there were 450 prophets of Baal but only one Elijah (1 Kings 18). Later, in the southern kingdom, Jeremiah was plagued by the many false prophets who predicted peace for Jerusalem when actually destruction was coming (Jer. 6:13, 14; 8:10, 11). When times were bad, idolatry and false prophecy went together and were widespread. In the prophesied day of genuine national repentance, both will be put away.

Zechariah makes three points about this time of purification. First, the idols will be so thoroughly removed that even the memory of them will be forgotten. That is a great promise, for anyone who has ever wrestled with sin knows that the memory of sin (accompanied by a persistent desire for it) often continues long after the sin itself has been repudiated. We remember Augustine's description of trying to free himself of sexual sins but finding even in his seclusion that his mind was thinking about the dancing girls in Rome. Sin lingers in the mind. But in

this day, even the memory of idols will be taken away from God's people.

Second, zeal for the Lord will be so great that the people will no longer even tolerate the existence of false prophets. Zechariah makes this point by saying that if a false prophet should emerge, his own father and mother would be the first to see that he is executed in obedience to Deuteronomy 13:6–10 and 18:20. "If your very own brother, or your son or daughter, or the wife you love, or your closest friend secretly entices you, saying, 'Let us go and worship other gods' (gods that neither you nor your fathers have known, gods of the peoples around you, whether near or far, from one end of the land to the other), do not yield to him or listen to him. Show him no pity. Do not spare him or shield him. You must certainly put him to death. Your hand must be the first in putting him to death, and then the hands of all the people. Stone him to death, because he tried to turn you away from the LORD your God, who brought you out of Egypt, out of the land of slavery" (Deut. 13:6–10). "But a prophet who presumes to speak in my name anything I have not commanded him to say, or a prophet who speaks in the name of other gods, must be put to death" (Deut. 18:20).

Third, Zechariah shows that even those who have been false prophets will be so ashamed of their past prophesying that they will do everything possible to deny and hide it. They will put away their hair garments and return to their farms, claiming always to have been farmers.

Verse 6 is difficult, but it is generally taken to refer to wounds inflicted on themselves by false prophets in moments of prophetic fervor or frenzy. This was the case with the prophets of

---

[1]David Baron, *The Visions & Prophecies of Zechariah* (Grand Rapids: Kregel, 1975), p. 463. Original edition 1918.

Baal who, we are told, "slashed themselves with swords and spears, as was their custom, until their blood flowed" (1 Kings 18:28). Apparently, in Zechariah's hypothetical situation, wounds like these are noticed on one who had formerly been a prophet of one of the idol gods. When they are pointed out, the false prophet denies their origin, saying, "The wounds I was given at the house of my friends." (This may mean that he received the wounds elsewhere, perhaps in his family as a youth or child. Or it may be an ironic reference to the house of the idols, which he used to regard as "friends" but no longer does.)

The Smitten Shepherd

Having spoken concretely of the repentance and purifying that is to take place among the Jews in the days prior to the consummation of all things, Zechariah now introduces one of those flashbacks that are common in his prophecy and would be taken as an error in chronology if one were not aware that his concerns at these points are theological rather than chronological. The clearest example of this was in chapter 9, where verses describing the coming of Christ to Jerusalem riding on a donkey come before those describing the wars of the Maccabees. Chronologically this is out of order. But theologically it is in perfect order, since it describes the true King immediately after verses depicting the great Greek king, Alexander of Macedonia. It is the same here. Having spoken of Israel's repentance through looking to the one they had pierced, Zechariah now glances back to that piercing to analyze it theologically. Having spoken of the false prophets, Zechariah now speaks of the true and reliable Prophet, who fulfills all prophecies.

The most remarkable thing about these verses is that they describe God the Father as Himself striking the Savior, just as Isaiah did in the well-known fifty-third chapter of his prophecy ("we considered him stricken by God, smitten by him, and afflicted," v. 4; "the LORD has laid on him the iniquity of us all," v. 6; "it was the LORD's will to crush him and cause him to suffer," v. 10). Zechariah says:

> "Awake, O sword, against my
> shepherd,
> against the man who is close to
> me!"
> declares the LORD Almighty.
> "Strike the shepherd,
> and the sheep will be scattered
> . . . " (Zech. 13:7).

This would not be so remarkable if it were spoken against the three false shepherds of Zechariah 11:8 or the foolish shepherd of 11:15–17. In fact, with no textual warrant whatever, some critical scholars have rearranged the text to place Zechariah 13:7–9 at the end of chapter 11—for just this reason. Judgment upon the wicked or derelict shepherds seems proper. But this is not a judgment against a false shepherd, but against one whom the verses themselves say is "close" to God and whom God Himself identifies as "my shepherd."

Indeed, it is even stronger than this. For the words translated "close to me" are actually parallel to "my shepherd" and literally mean "my fellow" in the sense of "my close relation" or "blood associate." The great Bible commentator C. F. Keil writes of this word: "God would not apply this epithet to any godly or ungodly man whom he might have appointed shepherd over a nation. The idea of nearest one (or fellow) involves not only similarity in vocation, but community of physical or spiritual descent, according to which he whom God calls his neighbor cannot be a mere man, but can only be one who participates in the divine nature, or is essentially divine."[2]

The solution to this problem is the *Incarnation,* and the meaning of the verse is the *Atonement.* It is God the Father striking His own Son, the Lord Jesus Christ, in our place as our sin-bearer. It is Jesus suffering for us in order that we might be delivered from the wrath of God against sin and be released to serve the Lord effectively.

In Zechariah's treatment of this passage, the immediate consequence of the smiting of the shepherd is the scattering of the sheep, which is the way Jesus referred to it prior to His arrest and crucifixion: "This very night you will all fall away on account of me, for it is written: 'I will strike the shepherd, and the sheep of the flock will be scattered' " (Matt. 26:31; cf. Mark 14:27). This was a first and immediate fulfillment, but its fullness has been seen throughout history in the scattering of Israel, which is to continue until the time of Israel's regathering at the end of time.

This scattering is to be intense and filled with suffering. In that day, "two-thirds will be struck down and perish" (v. 8). One can argue that this has already been fulfilled. Probably as many as two-thirds of the Jews living in Palestine perished at the time of the Roman victory in A.D. 70, when Jerusalem and Masada were overthrown, and at the time of the punishments associated with the Bar Cochba revolt a generation later. During the Middle Ages there were intense purges against the Jews, so much so that at the beginning of the sixteenth century, by reliable computation, there were only about one million Jews left in the entire world.[3] Hitler exterminated six million Jews during World War II. Yet in spite of these terrible purges, there will be even worse slaughter in the final days, described as "Jacob's trouble" (cf. Jer. 30:7).

Yet the grace of God shines through even here. For although two-thirds of the people may be cut off and perish, yet one-third will remain and will be purified by God for His own purposes.

"In the whole land," declares the
   LORD,
  "two-thirds will be struck down
    and perish;
  yet one-third will be left in it.
This third I will bring into the fire;
  I will refine them like silver
  and test them like gold.
They will call on my name
  and I will answer them;
I will say, 'They are my people,'
  and they will say, 'The LORD is
   our God' " (vv. 8, 9).

This is probably also the meaning of the sentence, "I will turn my hand against the little ones" (v. 7). In English it sounds as if God's judgment is going to be turned against children as well as adults. But the Hebrew actually says, "I will cause my hand to come back to (or upon) the little ones"—that is, God's hand was removed from these people, but now His hand will come back to them in blessing. If this is the meaning, "little ones" probably means "those who make themselves little" or "are humble." It is a promise of blessing upon those who do look to Him whom they have pierced and turn from sin. The text says that God has been preserving a remnant of the Jewish people so that they might do just that.

About one hundred years ago the king of Prussia, Frederick the Great, was having a discussion with his chaplain about the truth of the Bible. Frederick had become skeptical and unbelieving, largely through the influence of the infidel Voltaire. So he said to his

---

[2] Carl Friedrich Keil, *The Twelve Minor Prophets,* vol. 2 (Grand Rapids: Eerdmans, 1965), p. 397. Trans. James Martin.

[3] Baron, *Visions & Prophecies of Zechariah,* p. 484.

chaplain, "If your Bible is really true, it ought to be capable of very brief proof. So often when I have asked for proof of the inspiration of the Bible I have been given some enormous volume that I have neither the time nor disposition to read. If your Bible is really from God, you should be able to demonstrate the fact simply. Give me the proof of the inspiration of the Bible in a word."

The chaplain replied, "Your majesty, it is possible for me to answer your request quite literally. I can give you the proof you ask for in a single word."

Frederick looked at the chaplain with some amazement and asked, "What is this magic word that carries such a weight of proof?"

The chaplain answered, "Israel, Your Majesty."

The continued existence of the Jewish people in spite of centuries of persecution is one proof of the Bible's inspiration and of the existence of the God who has promised to preserve them and bring them to a time of great national blessing in the last days.

"My People, My God"

The last lines of this chapter—almost the last of the Book of Zechariah and close to the last lines of the Minor Prophets—carry us back to the prophecy of Hosea, which we saw at the beginning of these studies. It is likely that Zechariah is thinking of it explicitly.

Hosea had been telling of his marriage, which was a pageant ordained by God, upon which the message of the book turns. He had been told to marry a wife who proved unfaithful to him, but after they were married and before that happened, his wife had three children. Each of these children was given a symbolic name. The first was Jezreel, which means "scattered," because God was going to scatter the people all over the world, as Hosea, Zechariah, and other prophets foretold. The second child was called Lo-Ruhamah, which means "not loved" or "not pitied," because a time was coming when God was no longer going to have pity on the people due to their unbelief. The third child was called Lo-Ammi, which means "not my people," because they would no longer be God's people in any special sense. It is a bleak picture but one that accurately describes the past thousands of years of Jewish history: "scattered," "not loved," "not my people."

But then, as Hosea tells his story, we learn that God is going to regather His people and turn them to Himself once again. The names of the children will be changed. Jezreel will be changed from Jezreel meaning "scattered," to Jezreel meaning "planted"; for God will plant the Jews in their land once again. Lo-Ruhamah, meaning "not loved" or "not pitied," will be changed to Ruhamah, meaning "loved" or "pitied"; for God will show pity once more. And Lo-Ammi, meaning "not my people," will be changed to Ammi, meaning "my people"; for in that day they will again become the people of the living God (cf. Hos. 1:10).

Hosea concludes, "I will say to those called 'Not my people,' 'You are my people'; and they will say, 'You are my God' " (Hos. 2:23).

These are almost the identical words with which Zechariah 13 closes: "I will say, 'They are my people,' and they will say, 'The LORD is our God' " (v. 9). But notice: this comes in Zechariah, after the destruction of the northern kingdom by the Assyrians and the destruction of the southern kingdom by the Babylonians. This comes after the Babylonian captivity. By now many new scatterings have taken place. But God is faithful to His promise. Nothing can ever separate us from the love of such a great God.

28

Consummation of All Things

(Zechariah 14:1–21)

A day of the LORD is coming when your plunder will be divided among you.

I will gather all the nations to Jerusalem to fight against it; the city will be captured, the houses ransacked, and the women raped. Half of the city will go into exile, but the rest of the people will not be taken from the city.

Then the LORD will go out and fight against those nations, as he fights in the day of battle. On that day his feet will stand on the Mount of Olives, east of Jerusalem, and the Mount of Olives will be split in two from east to west, forming a great valley, with half of the mountain moving north and half moving south. You will flee by my mountain valley, for it will extend to Azel. You will flee as you fled from the earthquake in the days of Uzziah king of Judah. Then the LORD my God will come, and all the holy ones with him.

On that day there will be no light, no cold or frost. It will be a unique day, without daytime or nighttime—a day known to the LORD. When evening comes, there will be light.

On that day living water will flow out from Jerusalem, half to the eastern sea and half to the western sea, in summer and in winter.

The LORD will be king over the whole earth. On that day there will be one LORD, and his name the only name. . . .

On that day HOLY TO THE LORD will be inscribed on the bells of the horses, and the cooking pots in the LORD's house will be like the sacred bowls in front of the altar. Every pot in Jerusalem and Judah will be holy to the LORD Almighty, and all who come to sacrifice will take some of the pots and cook in them. And on that day there will no longer be a Canaanite in the house of the LORD Almighty.

It is not very often that a person finds Martin Luther at a loss for words, but there is something close to this in his handling of Zechariah 14. Luther did two commentaries on this prophet: one in Latin, which was published first, and a second in German, which he may have intended as a definitive edition of the first. In the first of these there is *no* treatment of chapter 14. The manuscript just stops at 13:9, with no expla-nation. In the second commentary, chapter 14 is briefly treated. But it begins with the words: "Here, in this chapter, I give up. For I am not sure what the prophet is talking about."[1] This may explain why there is no commentary in the earlier version!

Not all commentators admit to being as baffled as Luther. But most acknowl-edge that in a difficult book this chapter is probably the most difficult of all—or

[1]Martin Luther, *Luther's Works*, vol. 20, *Lectures on the Minor Prophets: III, Zechariah* (Saint Louis: Concordia, 1973), p. 337.

at least the final chapters of Zechariah (chaps. 12–14) are most difficult.

The chief problem is that nothing in this chapter fits historical events. So either the chapter is descriptive of events yet future, or it is to be considered figuratively as describing this present age. H. C. Leupold takes chapter 14 in this second sense. "Our verses do not, therefore, apply to any one situation. They do not describe a siege, capture and captivity which actually occurred. By means of a figure they describe a situation which obtains continually through New Testament times. God's people shall continually be antagonized and suffer bitter adversity at the hands of their foes and shall in consequence be brought low; but there shall always be an imperishable remnant, and that not so extremely small."[2]

This will not do. Scholars who apply these prophecies to God's people in this age take "Israel" as meaning "true Israel (or the church)." Yet when a statement of judgment occurs, as in the prophecy that two-thirds of the people will be struck down or cut off (Zech. 13:8), they usually view them as literal Jews and the land as literal Palestine. When it is a question of a prophecy which has already been fulfilled, such as the piercing of the Messiah (Zech. 12:10) or the scattering of the sheep (Zech. 13:7), they take it literally. It is inconsistent to do this and then give spiritual meanings to portions of the book which have not been fulfilled. If one portion of these last chapters refers to literal events, the other portions must refer to literal events too, even if, from our particular viewpoint, we are not able to explain all the details accurately.

I think David Baron is right when he says, "We have a great and solemn prophecy which will yet be literally fulfilled in the future. And when it is objected by some of the modern writers that the literal fulfillment is 'impossible,' because it would involve not only national upheavals, but physical convulsions of nature, our answer is that *this is just what the prophet declares as most certainly to take place.*"[3] We should treat the chapter for what it teaches and leave the possibility (or impossibility) of these things in God's hands, knowing that for God "all things are possible." (Matt. 19:26).

THE LAST BATTLE

The place to begin is by noting that the first verses of Zechariah 14 obviously amplify upon the last three verses of chapter 13 and probably also carry us back to the battle with which the oracle (chaps. 12–14) begins. In other words, these chapters belong together, which is what we have already concluded on the basis of the sixteen occurrences of the phrase "on that day" spread throughout them. The ending of chapter 13 spoke of the destruction of two-thirds of the people and the preservation and purification of the remaining one-third. This is consistent with the sacking of Jerusalem described in 14:2 and the preservation of a remnant described in 14:5. In general terms, 14:1–5 is also consistent with 12:1–9, although the earlier passage does not say that Jerusalem will be overrun *before* God intervenes to save it and its people.

Next we will need to see precisely what the passage teaches. There are a number of items. First, the passage presupposes that there will be a Jewish nation centered about Jerusalem in the last days. Today, with the existence of the modern state of Israel a reality, this does not seem to be terribly

---

[2]H. C. Leupold, *Exposition of Zechariah* (Grand Rapids: Baker, 1978), p. 259.

[3]David Baron, *The Visions & Prophecies of Zechariah* (Grand Rapids: Kregel, 1975), p. 491. Original edition 1918.

remarkable. But we forget how improbable it seemed for the thousands of years that passed between the final scattering of the Jews by the Romans in the first Christian century and the establishing of the modern state of Israel in 1948.

Before World War II many commentators mocked even the possibility of a reestablished Israel. But David Baron, whom I have been quoting favorably and who wrote in 1918 (between the world wars), predicted the regathering of the Jews on the basis of this prophecy: "It seems from Scripture that in relation to Israel and the land there will be a restoration, before the second advent of our Lord, of very much the same state of things as existed at the time of his first advent, when the threads of God's dealing with them nationally were finally dropped, not to be taken up again 'until the times of the Gentiles shall be fulfilled.' There was at that time a number of Jews in Palestine representative of the nation; but compared with the number of their brethren, who were already a diaspora among the nations, they were a minority, and not in a politically independent condition. So it will be again. There will be at first, as compared with the whole nation, only a representative minority in Palestine, and a Jewish state will be probably formed, either under the suzerainty of one of the Great Powers, or under international protection. . . . Around this nucleus a large number more from all parts of the world will in all probability soon be gathered."[4] Since the conditions for the events described in Zechariah 14 seem to be receiving a literal fulfillment, why should we not expect that the events themselves will be literal when they unfold?

Second, the chapter speaks of a gathering of the nations of the world against the Jews and Jerusalem. We do not know what the immediate occasion of this invasion might be, but we can imagine any number of scenarios in light of current world politics, not to mention the possibility that world conditions could change substantially before such events happen. It is helpful to remember that Zechariah 14 is not the only passage in the Bible to predict a great final battle in the last days. Ezekiel describes it in chapters 38 and 39 of his prophecy. There is another description in Daniel 11. In these passages the kings of the earth unite against God's people, but God intervenes and they are soundly defeated. God's victory is followed by the great golden age.

Third, at the apex of this destruction—when the nations are dividing the spoil of the city and the inhabitants of Jerusalem are being led away to exile—God appears to fight for His people as He did many times previously. The text says, "Then the LORD will go out and fight against those nations, as he fights in the day of battle. On that day his feet will stand on the Mount of Olives, east of Jerusalem, and the Mount of Olives will be split in two from east to west, forming a great valley, with half of the mountain moving north and half moving south. You will flee by my mountain valley, for it will extend to Azel. You will flee as you fled from the earthquake in the days of Uzziah king of Judah. Then the LORD my God will come, and all the holy ones with him" (vv. 3–5).

Moore has a puzzling comment at this point, saying, "It is impossible for us to take this whole passage literally, for God cannot literally place his feet on the Mount of Olives."[5] But surely God has already done it in the person of Jesus Christ. What is more, the angels

[4]Ibid., pp. 492, 493.
[5]Thomas V. Moore, *A Commentary on Haggai, Zechariah and Malachi* (Edinburgh and Carlisle, Pa.: Banner of Truth Trust, 1979), p. 307. Original edition 1856.

who appeared at Christ's ascension said, "Men of Galilee, . . . this same Jesus, who has been taken from you into heaven, will come back in the same way you have seen him go into heaven" (Acts 1:11). What is more natural than that the second coming of Christ should be at this place and at the moment of a desperate need on the part of the Jewish people?

BLESSING ON THE LAMB

Following Zechariah's description of the final great battle and the Lord's return, the prophet zeros in on the blessings of the age which follows. These fall into four categories, focusing on: (1) light (vv. 6, 7); (2) water (v. 8); (3) the king (v. 9); and (4) the city (vv. 10, 11).

1. *Light*. It is hard to tell how far Zechariah's references to light and dark, cold and frost, day and evening are to be taken literally and how far figuratively. But in view of similar descriptions in the Book of Revelation it may be that they are to be taken as actual fact. Zechariah says, "On that day there will be no light, no cold or frost. It will be a unique day, without daytime or nighttime—a day known to the LORD. When evening comes, there will be light" (vv. 6, 7). In Revelation heaven is described as being filled with light: "The city does not need the sun or the moon to shine on it, for the glory of God gives it light, and the Lamb is its lamp. The nations will walk by its light, and the kings of the earth will bring their splendor into it. . . . There will be no more night. They will not need the light of a lamp or the light of the sun, for the Lord God will give them light" (Rev. 21:23, 24; 22:5). If this is not a literal light of a messianic age (or heaven), the passage is saying that "in the hour of deepest gloom and blackness God causes the bright light of his deliverance to shine forth for the distressed ones."[6]

2. *Water*. In a semiarid country such as Palestine, water was always a great blessing. Hence, in the golden age, water will flow forth abundantly from Jerusalem, according to Zechariah. "On that day living water will flow out from Jerusalem, half to the eastern sea and half to the western sea, in summer and in winter" (v. 8).

In view of the convulsions of the land which both the earlier and later verses describe, it is not inconceivable that this too is quite literal. The earthquake of verse 4 (cf. v. 5) that splits the Mount of Olives and levels other portions of the land (v. 10) could conceivably cause a literal river to flow forth from the environs of Jerusalem. But even if that is the case, it is clearly also a visible symbol of the mighty river of God's salvation, which will flow to the nations from Jerusalem during this period. Ezekiel describes a river "coming out from under the threshold of the temple toward the east" (Ezek. 47:1; cf. vv. 1–12). John also describes the river in the Book of Revelation: "Then the angel showed me the river of the water of life, as clear as crystal, flowing from the throne of God and of the Lamb down the middle of the great street of the city" (Rev. 22:1, 2). God is the source of this river, for He is the source of all spiritual blessings the nations need.

3. *The King*. "Thy kingdom come." Thus have Christian people prayed singly and in unison ever since the Lord first taught His disciples to pray in that manner. The kingdom has come— wherever the gospel has been preached and men and women have responded to the message of the cross. Still, we continue to look for that day when Christ will have "destroyed all domin-

---

[6]Charles L. Feinberg, *God Remembers: A Study of Zechariah* (Portland: Multnomah Press, 1979), p. 198.

ion, authority and power" (1 Cor.
15:24) and will have "everything under
his feet" (v. 27). This is what Zechariah
describes. "The LORD will be king over
the whole earth. On that day there will
be one LORD, and his name the only
name" (Zech. 14:9).

4. *The City.* Strictly speaking, the
fourth blessing is upon the entire land,
which, says the chapter, "will become
like the Arabah," that is, the flat fruitful
plain of the Jordan. But the focus is
Jerusalem. By contrast to the flatness of
the land round about, Jerusalem will be
lifted up as the holy mountain of God
(vv. 10, 11). This is the vision also seen
by Isaiah:

"Behold, I will create
   new heavens and a new earth.
The former things will not be
      remembered,
   nor will they come to mind.
But be glad and rejoice forever
   in what I will create,
for I will create Jerusalem to be a
      delight
   and its people a joy.
I will rejoice over Jerusalem
   and take delight in my people;
the sound of weeping and of crying
   will be heard in it no more. . . .

"Before they call I will answer;
   while they are still speaking I will
      hear.
The wolf and the lamb will feed
      together,
   and the lion will eat straw like
      the ox,
   but dust will be the serpent's
      food.
They will neither harm nor destroy
   in all my holy mountain" (Isa.
      65:17–19, 24, 25).

Isaiah shows that the outward changes
in the land are symbolic of what will
also be spiritually true. Evil will be
eliminated from the city. God will be
with His people, and salvation will flow
like a stream from Zion.

JUDGMENT ON THE NATIONS

When we review the blessing of God
upon Israel and the land of Palestine,
we think of the condition of those who
resist God's rule. This is brought before
us in the next section of the chapter (vv.
12–19).

It involves a strange description of
God's judgment. On the one hand,
God will bring a particularly grim
plague on the nations that fought
against Jerusalem: "Their flesh will rot
while they are still standing on their
feet, their eyes will rot in their sockets,
and their tongues will rot in their
mouths. On that day men will be
stricken by the LORD with great panic.
Each man will seize the hand of another, and they will attack each
other. . . . A similar plague will strike
the horses and mules, the camels and
donkeys, and all the animals in those
camps" (vv. 12, 13, 15). Chronologically
these verses follow verse 3, and perhaps also belong with the opening
section of chapter 12. The nations who
had come up against Jerusalem had
looked on her in haughty scorn; hence
the judgment affecting the soldiers'
eyes. They had spoken against God,
like the field commander of Sennacherib before the armies of Hezekiah;
hence the judgment on their tongues.
The mention of a "plague" recalls the
judgments of God against Egypt at the
start of Israel's history as a nation.

On the other hand, over against this
particularly grim plague is a description
of blessing for those nations that learn
righteousness and pay their proper
homage to God. Zechariah says, "Then
the survivors from all the nations that
have attacked Jerusalem will go up year
after year to worship the king, the LORD
Almighty, and to celebrate the Feast of
Tabernacles" (v. 16). Not all will want
to do this; apparently the hearts of
many will remain unchanged. God will
withhold rain from those who refuse

and bring other judgments on them (vv. 17–19). Those who obey will participate with Israel in the material and spiritual blessings of that day.

HOLY TO THE LORD

The prophecy ends with an emphasis upon holiness: "On that day HOLY TO THE LORD will be inscribed on the bells of the horses, and the cooking pots in the LORD's house will be like the sacred bowls in front of the altar. Every pot in Jerusalem and Judah will be holy to the LORD Almighty, and all who come to sacrifice will take some of the pots and cook in them. And on that day there will no longer be a Canaanite in the house of the LORD Almighty" (vv. 20, 21). What is Zechariah talking about here? Why horse bells and cooking pots? The point is that the people and city will be so holy that even these insignificant things will be fully dedicated to the Lord. All of life will have the glory and enjoyment of God as its object.

Have you ever thought of holiness in terms of your destiny as a child of God? You are not holy now. You are sinful; the more you live, the more you will be aware of it. But your destiny is holiness. God has determined that we are to be holy through the work of the Lord Jesus Christ. We find this determination four times in Leviticus: "Be holy, because I am holy" (two times, Lev. 11:44, 45), "Be holy because I, the LORD your God, am holy" (Lev. 19:2), and "Be holy, because I am the LORD your God" (Lev. 20:7). Peter writes: "But just as he who called you is holy, so be holy in all you do; for it is written: 'Be holy, because I am holy'" (1 Peter 1:15). The

author of Hebrews speaks of "holiness," without which "no one will see the Lord" (Heb. 12:14). Our destiny is to be holy—like the Lord.

We think of things relationally today. Because God is a person and we are like Him in having personalities, we think of our destiny in terms of our relationship to God. We look forward to the day when we will be able to express our love to Him fully and know the full measure of His love to us. This is not wrong, of course; we are persons, and our future is to be enfolded in the all-embracing love of God. But this is not the way the Bible speaks of our destiny. It is not the love relationship that is emphasized. The Bible emphasizes that which is the basis of all other experiences: holiness. The reason why our relationship to God is not all it should be is that we are not holy. The reason why our relationships with other people are not all they should be is that we are sinful. We need holiness. On the day that we pass from earth to heaven we will be holy, for we will be like Jesus, since we will see Him as He is (1 John 3:2).

Then we must strive to be holy now. That is what 1 John 3 emphasizes. It says that we will be like Jesus (v. 2), but immediately after this it says, with reference to this present life, "Everyone who has this hope in him purifies himself, just as he is pure" (v. 3). We emphasize so many other things. Instead of these, we must find and fulfill God's emphasis, knowing that one day HOLY TO THE LORD will be inscribed on us and we will be the Lord's holy people forever.

MALACHI

29

Mirror of This Age

(Malachi 1:1–5)

An oracle: The word of the LORD *to Israel through Malachi.*
"I have loved you," says the LORD.
"But you ask, 'How have you loved us?'
"Was not Esau Jacob's brother?" the LORD *says. "Yet I have loved Jacob, but Esau I have hated, and I have turned his mountains into a wasteland and left his inheritance to the desert jackals."*
Edom may say, "Though we have been crushed, we will rebuild the ruins."
But this is what the LORD *Almighty says: "They may build, but I will demolish. They will be called The Wicked Land, a people always under the wrath of the* LORD. *You will see it with your own eyes and say, 'Great is the* LORD—*even beyond the borders of Israel!' "*

Over thirty years ago on the first Friday night of September I was sitting at the dining-room table with my family in western Pennsylvania talking to Donald Grey Barnhouse who was beginning a Bible conference in our area. We were talking about schooling. I was thirteen at the time, and Barnhouse was asking me if I would be interested in attending the Stony Brook School on Long Island for eighth grade. He asked, "Jimmy, would you go to Stony Brook this year if your parents send you?"

I remember thinking that this was no idle inquiry. It was the time of year schools started, and I thought that an affirmative answer would probably mean an immediate and major transformation of my life.

"Yes," I said. "I would like to go to Stony Brook."

At this point, even though we were still midway between the main course and dessert, Barnhouse got up from the table, went into the next room, and called Frank E. Gaebelein, the school's headmaster. "I have a boy for you," he said. It is harder to be admitted to Stony Brook today, but I was accepted on the spot. The next day, Saturday, my mother bought me some appropriate school clothes, and on Sunday my mother and father drove me to Long Island where I began what were to be five good years.

What a transition! From the past to the future! From a sheltered home environment to the beginnings of a new life on my own!

END OF AN ERA

The Book of Malachi is located at a point of transition too. It comes at the end of the Old Testament, but it anticipates the New Testament.

Frequently in our study of the Minor Prophets it has been necessary to profess ignorance of the period in which one or another of these brief prophecies was written. This is not true in the case of Malachi. It is evident even from a quick reading that it is post-exilic, that is, that it was composed after the Jews who had been exported to Babylon and Nebuchadnezzar returned under Zerubbabel, the new governor of Judah, and Joshua, the high priest. A careful reading can narrow the dating down even further than this. Many years ago a Roman Catholic scholar named Vitringa did this so convincingly that most scholars since have followed him (*Observations Sacrae*, bk. 6, chap. 7). He argued that: (1) in Malachi's day the temple was apparently rebuilt (Mal. 1:13; 3:1, 10), which places him after Haggai and Zechariah; (2) the Jews were under a civil ruler (Mal. 1:8), which places him before the death of Nehemiah, who was the last civil ruler; and (3) the offenses rebuked by Malachi are precisely the abuses Nehemiah corrected, namely, the practice of mere formal religion, mixed marriages, and the neglect of tithes (Mal. 1:6–14; 2:10–17; 3:6–12). Since Nehemiah corrected the abuses during his second residence in Jerusalem, the period of Malachi's prophesying must be either in the period between Nehemiah's first and second residence or during the second residence itself. Malachi's ministry bears the same relationship to Nehemiah as Haggai and Zechariah's ministries bore to Zerubbabel and Joshua. He describes Israel as it existed at the very end of Old Testament history.

Malachi returned to Judah from Persia between the thirty-second year of Artaxerxes Longimanus, about 432 B.C., and 424 B.C. when Artaxerxes died. Consequently, Malachi prophesied approximately one hundred years after Haggai and Zechariah, the two writers who immediately precede him in our English Bibles.

But Malachi is not only oriented to the past as the last of the Old Testament prophets, bemoaning the decline of godliness in Israel. He is also oriented to the future, which is what makes him significant as a transitional figure. Like the prophets before him, Malachi looks forward to God's coming. He is specific. Malachi prophesies the coming of that "messenger" who will prepare the way for God—that is, John the Baptist, who will prepare the way for Jesus. Malachi writes, "See, I will send my messenger, who will prepare the way before me. Then suddenly the LORD you are seeking will come to his temple; the messenger of the covenant, whom you desire, will come" (Mal. 3:1). He ends by saying, "See, I will send you the prophet Elijah before that great and dreadful day of the LORD comes. He will turn the hearts of the fathers to their children, and the hearts of the children to their fathers; or else I will come and strike the land with a curse" (Mal. 4:5, 6).

This was the text the disciples were thinking of when they asked Jesus "Why then do the teachers of the law say that Elijah must come first?" (Matt. 17:10). Jesus replied by reference to John the Baptist. "To be sure, Elijah comes and will restore all things. But I tell you, Elijah has already come, and they did not recognize him, but have done to him everything they wished. In the same way, the Son of Man is going to suffer at their hands" (vv. 11, 12; cf. Matt. 11:11–15; 16:13, 14, 15; Mark 8:27, 28; 9:11–13; Luke 1:17; 9:18, 19; John 1:21, 25). After Malachi the voice of prophecy ceased in Israel until John the Baptist appeared four hundred years later to announce the arrival of the Messiah.

So Malachi really is the last of the old and the anticipation of the new. T. V. Moore says wisely of this book, "It is the transition-link between the two great dispensations of redemption—the last note of that magnificent oratorio of revelation, whose wailings of sorrow and breathings of hope were soon to give place to that richer song, which should be not only of Moses, but also of the Lamb; and tell not only of Eden and Sinai, but also of Calvary and Heaven."[1] The transitional nature of Malachi makes the book particularly interesting to anyone concerned with the relationship between Christianity and Judaism as well as with the overall history of revelation and redemption.

THIS PRESENT ERA

But Malachi is interesting for another reason also. It is true that it is a link between the old covenant and the new, between Judaism and Christianity. But in describing the Judaism of Malachi's day the book also vividly describes the moribund religiosity of any era, including our own. We can go further. Perhaps more than any other Old Testament book, Malachi describes that modern attitude of mind that considers man superior to God and which has the audacity to attempt to bring God down to earth and measure Him by the yardstick of human morality.

This attitude is a recurring theme in Malachi, and it is expressed by a recurring word. The word is "how" as in "How have you loved us?" (1:2). This word appears seven times in this last of the Old Testament books, and in every case it expresses a state of mind that challenges God's statements, demanding that He give an accounting of Himself in human terms. It is worth previewing these seven instances.

1. In 1:2, God begins His message to the people with the words, "I have loved you." But the people reply in critical unbelief, *"How* have you loved us?" Behind this question is a bitter complaint about the way the people felt they had been treated by the Deity. As we read on in this book we discover that the religion of the people was

formal, empty. Yet they were satisfied with it. Indeed, they considered themselves to be doing quite well, even doing God a favor by the quantity of their religious activities. God had not prospered them in return as they thought they deserved. They were still a relatively weak nation. They were not particularly wealthy. So they ask, "How have you loved us?" The implication is that if God really did love them, He would make them rich.

2. In verse 6 of the same chapter, God speaks to the religious leaders, saying, "It is you, O priests, who despise my name." But they reply, *"How* have we despised your name?" As we read on we find that they had been offering blind, crippled, or diseased animals in sacrifice—that is, the animals nobody else wanted. As they did they even complained about the weariness of thus serving God. "You profane it [God's service] by saying of the Lord's table, 'It is defiled,' and of its food, 'It is contemptible.' And you say, 'What a burden!' and you sniff at it contemptuously" (vv. 12, 13). This was no proper attitude for God's servants. Yet the priests considered themselves to be doing God a favor, while despising His service. What cause did He have to complain? "How have we despised your name?" they counter angrily.

3. In verse 7, after God says, "You place defiled food on my altar," the priests reply, *"How* have we defiled you?" The attitude behind this question is the same as behind the preceding verse. The clergy considered themselves to be going beyond what was required even though they were offering deformed animals and were performing their duties with a fault-finding and bitter attitude.

4. In 2:17, Malachi says, "You have wearied the Lord with your words."

---

[1]Thomas V. Moore, *A Commentary on Haggai, Zechariah and Malachi* (Edinburgh and Carlisle, Pa.: Banner of Truth Trust, 1979), p. 347. Original edition 1856.

But the people reply, *"How* have we wearied him?"* The next lines explain the problem. Apparently, the people had been faulting God for His management of the world's affairs. As they observed things, those who did good (they meant themselves) suffered misfortune, while those who did evil (they meant everyone else) were blessed. This was unjust in their opinion. Their exact words were, "All who do evil are good in the eyes of the LORD, and he is pleased with them" and "Where is the God of justice?" The flaw in this argument is not that God must act justly. Abraham expressed that view to God and was not rebuked for it (Gen. 18:25). The flaw is that the people were considering themselves to be among the righteous when they were actually acting wickedly. They wanted justice from God. They should have been thankful that instead of justice they had actually been the recipients of God's grace.

5. In 3:7, God admonishes the people: "Return to me, and I will return to you." This was the same challenge God had voiced through the first of the minor prophets, Hosea, more than three hundred years earlier: "Return, O Israel, to the LORD your God. Your sins have been your downfall!" (Hos. 14:1). But the people had not returned then, and they do not return now. Instead they reply, *"How* are we to return?"* The reply does not mean that they are ignorant of the proper stages of repentance and want to learn these steps so they can genuinely turn from sin and please God. They mean, "How can you say that we should return when we are already as close to you and as obedient as we can possibly be? What can we do that we have not already done?"

6. The next verse pursues this further. God declares, "Will a man rob God? Yet you rob me," to which the people retort, *"How* do we rob you?"* They mean, "Don't throw wild charges about, God. If you think we are deficient in anything owed you, declare what you believe is owed specifically. We will defend ourselves, and you will discover that we are actually models of spiritual accountability. You will have to eat your words." God replies curtly that they have robbed Him in tithes and offerings.

7. The last time we see this sequence of question and answer is in verse 13 of the same chapter, which is similar to Malachi 1:6. Here God says, "You have said harsh things against me." The people reply, *"What* have we said against you?"[2] Apparently the people had been speaking against God all along—questioning His love, despising His name, defiling His sacrifices, attacking His justice, questioning His commands, and withholding His tithes. But so self-righteous had the people and their priests become that they considered their remarks and actions to be entirely justified and their alleged slander nonexistent. "What have we ever said against you?" is their astonished reaction.

A FORM OF GODLINESS

There is a sense in which the attitude of the people depicted in Malachi is a mirror of our present secular world, for people today also want to measure God by the standards of human justice—if they do not want to do away with God entirely. Yet Malachi hits even closer to home than this. He not only describes the secular world of our age, but also the secular church of which we are often all too unfortunate examples.

One of the most helpful writers on Malachi is the late G. Campbell Mor-

---

[2]The New International Version uses the word *what* in this verse instead of the word *how,* presumably because it is more idiomatic in English to say "What have we said against you?" than "How have we spoken against you?" But it is the same word in Hebrew. Interestingly, the Authorized Version also makes a change at this point from *wherein,* which was used in 1:2, 6, 7; 2:17; 3:7, 8, to *what.*

gan, who carefully links the erroneous and arrogant spirit of the people of Malachi's day with the identical attitude that prevails in so many alleged Christian circles. "These people are not in open rebellion against God, nor do they deny his right to offerings, but they are laboring under the delusion that because they have brought offerings they have been true to him all along. Theirs is not the language of a people throwing off a yoke and saying, 'We will not be loyal,' but of a people established in the temple. It is not the language of a people who say, 'Let us cease to sacrifice and worship, and let us do as we please'; but it is the language of a people who say, 'We are sacrificing and worshiping to please God,' and yet he says by the mouth of his servant, 'Ye have wearied me; ye have robbed and spoken against me.' They have been most particular and strict in outward observances, but their hearts have been far away from their ceremonials. They have been boasting themselves in their knowledge of truth, responding to that knowledge mechanically, technically, but their hearts, their lives, their characters, the inwardness of their natures, have been a perpetual contradiction in the eye of heaven, to the will of God. And when the prophet tells them what God thinks of them, they, with astonishment and impertinence, look into his face and say, 'We don't see this at all!' To translate it into the language of the New Testament— 'having the form of godliness, they deny the power.' "[3]

That is precisely what thousands of self-righteous church-going people do. They do not consider themselves irreligious. On the contrary, they think of themselves as people whom God in the very necessity of the case must approve. But whenever they have a problem in life—if a job falls through, if a romance goes sour, if sickness or death touches someone close to them, or even if they fall sick themselves—they immediately blame God, holding Him accountable.

Moreover, people who think this way are capable of living the most corrupt lives. The last sentence of the quotation from G. Campbell Morgan refers to 2 Timothy 3:5 ("having a form of godliness but denying its power"), and it is significant that this biblical reference is from a chapter describing the most deficient morality. Paul is writing of the notorious last days of this world's history: "There will be terrible times in the last days. People will be lovers of themselves, lovers of money, boastful, proud, abusive, disobedient to their parents, ungrateful, unholy, without love, unforgiving, slanderous, without self-control, brutal, not lovers of the good, treacherous, rash, conceited, lovers of pleasure rather than lovers of God" (2 Tim. 3:1–4). We read those verses and immediately translate Paul's phrases into our terminology: the "new narcissism," materialism, arrogance, "Letting it all hang out," the generation gap, the "new morality," hedonism, and so on. It is a dreadful picture. But what makes it even more dreadful is the context in which Paul places this depravity. Paul is not writing about the world at large, the secular world of this or any other time. He is writing about the nominal church and describing the morality of those who have "a form of godliness" but deny its power.

ESAU AND JACOB

Each of the seven objections of the self-righteous religious people of Malachi's day is answered in turn in the course of this book. We will study them all in subsequent chapters. But here it is

---

[3]G. Campbell Morgan, *Malachi's Message for Today* (Grand Rapids: Baker, 1972), pp. 30, 31.

worth looking at God's reply to them first. God tells the people, "I have loved you," and they reply, "How have you loved us?" To this God answers, "Was not Esau Jacob's brother? . . . Yet I have loved Jacob, but Esau I have hated, and I have turned his mountains into a wasteland and left his inheritance to the desert jackals." Esau may express a desire and will to rebuild. But God replies to that: "They may build, but I will demolish. They will be called The Wicked Land, a people always under the wrath of the LORD. You will see it with your own eyes and say, 'Great is the LORD—even beyond the borders of Israel!' " (1:2–5).

We remember from Obadiah that God had prophesied a future destruction of Edom for its pride and the accompanying unbrotherly conduct toward the citizens of Jerusalem in the day of their misfortune. This judgment had apparently come to pass by this time and is here declared by God to be permanent. Edom has been wiped off the map, and the citizens of that nation would never be able to rebuild it, God declares.

This striking comparison—between Jacob and Esau, Judah and Edom—is to remind the self-righteous, critical citizens of Jerusalem of the unmerited and therefore electing love of God. They have had the audacity to demand that God show how He has loved them, utterly disregarding their unique status as His elect people. This is what God now brings to their willfully negligent attention. By birth Esau was as much a privileged child as Jacob; both were twin sons of the same Jewish father and mother, Isaac and Rebekah. Yet God had loved Jacob with a gracious love.

All God's dealing with Jacob and his descendants was in love. When they were ignorant, He blessed them with a true knowledge of Himself. When they were weak and defenseless, He empowered them and shielded them from enemies. When they strayed, He disciplined them. When they persisted in wickedness, he eventually sent the Babylonian captivity, as the prophets had warned He would do over many generations. Then He brought them back to Judah, established them within the walls of a refortified Jerusalem, and had them rebuild the temple. There was blessing and judgment, building and destruction. But in all these things God had loved them and was continuing to work with them in order that they might be a precious and holy people. Edom perished utterly.

That is how God is working with you if you are one of His precious people through faith in the work of Jesus Christ. Do not ever say, as those in Israel said, "How have you loved us?" Instead, confess the greatness of God's love as well as your own paltry love for Him, and determine that you will be a mirror of His grace rather than a mirror of the times in which you live.

30

Curse on the Clergy

(Malachi 1:6–2:9)

"A son honors his father, and a servant his master. If I am a father, where is the honor due me? If I am a master, where is the respect due me?" says the LORD Almighty. "It is you, O priests, who despise my name.

"But you ask, 'How have we despised your name?'

"You place defiled food on my altar.

"But you ask, 'How have we defiled you?'

"By saying that the LORD's table is contemptible. When you bring blind animals for sacrifice, is that not wrong? When you sacrifice crippled or diseased animals, is that not wrong? . . .

"Because of you I will rebuke your descendants; I will spread on your faces the offal from your festival sacrifices, and you will be carried off with it. And you will know that I have sent you this admonition so that my covenant with Levi may continue," says the LORD Almighty. "My covenant was with him, a covenant of life and peace, and I gave them to him. . . . True instruction was in his mouth and nothing false was found on his lips. He walked with me in peace and uprightness, and turned many from sin.

"For the lips of a priest ought to preserve knowledge, and from his mouth men should seek instruction—because he is the messenger of the LORD Almighty."

There are some things that are difficult for a preacher to talk about, and one of these, perhaps the hardest, is the sin of those of his own profession, the clergy. Yet that is required in any faithful treatment of Malachi. Malachi discusses the clergy's sins in 1:6–2:9, and he is not sparing in his criticism. In the first part of this section (1:6–14) he cites the priests of his day for offering defiled sacrifices on God's altar, harming the people, disparaging God's service as a contemptible and intolerable burden, and defying God. In the second part (2:1–9) he calls for repentance and warns of a curse on the priests if they do not repent.

Puritan Richard Baxter worked among ministers who (by comparison with ourselves) maintained an extremely high standard of piety and church discipline. Yet his great classic, *The Reformed Pastor*, is a devastating exposure of the clergy's sins and a call to them to reestablish a high and God-honoring standard of church life. Baxter wrote, "The great and lamentable sin of ministers of the gospel is that *they are not fully devoted to God*. They do not give themselves up wholly to the blessed work they have undertaken to do.

"Is it not true that flesh-pleasing and self-seeking interests—distinct from

235

that of Christ—make us neglect our duty and lead us to walk unfaithfully in the great trust that God has given us? Is it not true that we serve God too cheaply? Do we not do so in the most applauded way? Do we not withdraw from that which would cost us the most suffering? Does not all this show that we seek earthly rather than heavenly things? And that we mind the things which are below? While we preach for the realities which are above, do we not idolize the world?

"So what remains to be said, brethren, but to cry that we are all guilty of too many of the aforementioned sins. Do we not need to humble ourselves in lamentation for our miscarriages before the LORD?"[1]

WAY OF THE UNGODLY

If the priests of Israel, whatever their sins, had been as humble and repentant as Richard Baxter, there would have been hope for renewal. But the priests of Israel showed exactly the opposite attitude. Instead of humbling themselves before God, they tried to justify themselves and thus moved even farther from Him.

God's indictment of the clergy comes at the end of this section and is in two parts. God says that the priests: (1) "have turned from the way" and (2) "by [their] teaching have caused many to stumble" (2:8). In other words, the problem of the nation was traceable to failure in the personal life and devotion of those whom God had called to serve Him.

The personal failures of the priests are detailed in Malachi 1:6–14, as indicated. There are four of them.

1. The priests of Israel were *offering defiled sacrifices* on God's altar. They were unwilling to admit this, of course. When God said, "It is you, O priests,

who despise my name," they replied, "How have we despised your name?" (v. 6). When God replied, "You place defiled food on my altar," they answered, "How have we defiled you?" (v. 7). Whether they acknowledged it or not, this is what they were doing. The text says that they were offering blind, crippled, and diseased animals on God's altar. That is, they were offering animals no one else wanted. The Lord says ironically, "Try offering them to your governor! Would he be pleased with you? Would he accept you?" (v. 8).

We do not have literal altars today, at least in Protestant churches. But many clergymen nevertheless offer God defiled sacrifices in the way they do their work. In 1966 at the first World Congress on Evangelism, held in Berlin, Germany, Billy Graham addressed the more than twelve hundred evangelical delegates from more than one hundred countries on the theme "Stains on the Altar," suggesting that many of even these outstanding evangelical leaders had been offering God defiled sacrifices in these areas:

Their conversion. Many preach who are not genuinely saved. Richard Baxter said in the work referred to earlier, "God never saved any man for being a preacher."

Their call to service. Many preach who have no call from God to do so, and thousands more are not sure they belong in the ministry. Many (no doubt rightly) drop out each year to enter secular professions.

Their devotional life. In a recent survey conducted at a theological seminary in the United States ninety-three percent of the students acknowledged that they had no devotional life whatever.

Their message. Countless preachers offer a watered-down, man-pleasing

---

[1] Richard Baxter, *The Reformed Pastor: A Pattern for Personal Growth and Ministry*, abridged and edited by James M. Houston (Portland: Multnomah Press, 1982), pp. 61, 62. A longer, more original text can be found in The Banner of Truth Trust edition (1974).

message instead of the true and disturbing message of the Word of God.

Their social concern. We are surrounded by people with immense social needs. Many pastors as well as laymen are unconcerned.

Their evangelism. One of the great old preachers said, "I preach always as a dying man to dying men." Yet many preachers talk as if life is unending, hell is a fantasy, and faith in the Lord Jesus Christ is unnecessary for salvation. How can ministers of the Word of God become so unconcerned, so careless?

Their relationship to their brethren. Many preachers have allowed minor doctrinal matters and jealousies to divide them and weaken their ministries.[2]

I am particularly concerned about the sermons many preachers offer to God on Sunday mornings. Years ago a distinguished preacher who had spent a summer listening to others preach told me, "It was all pretty thin gruel." This is my judgment too, if indeed my own assessment is not worse. Where are the great themes of Scripture? You do not find them in the majority of sermon topics listed in the Saturday edition of most city newspapers. Where is the effort that is necessary to make a sermon say something worth crossing town or even crossing the street to hear? God can no doubt rightly say of many ministers today, "It is you, O priests, who despise my name. . . . You place defiled food on my altar."

2. The priests of Israel were *harming the people,* according to this same section. Again, they would have denied it. They would have said that they were serving the people—taking their sacrifices, offering the sacrifices, perhaps even doing various sacrificial good deeds to help the needy among them. But God indicates that their despising

of God led others (even other nations) to do so also, thus harming their people.

This is what is involved in God's reference to His name being great "among the nations," which is found three times in this section (vv. 11, 14). If God's ministers are godly, the people of God will tend to be godly also and even the ungodly will have some cause for honoring the Lord's name. If ministers are unfaithful—if they suggest by their conduct that God is contemptible and His service a burden—then the people will not be edified, their lives will not exhibit the excellencies of God's character, and God will be despised among the heathen for their sake.

Paul talks about this in the second chapter of Romans where he criticizes the nominally religious people of his day: "Now you, if you call yourself a Jew; if you rely on the law and brag about your relationship to God; if you know his will and approve of what is superior because you are instructed by the law; if you are convinced that you are a guide for the blind, a light for those who are in the dark, an instructor of the foolish, a teacher of infants, because you have in the law the embodiment of knowledge and truth—you, then, who teach others, do you not teach yourself? You who preach against stealing, do you steal? You who say that people should not commit adultery, do you commit adultery? You who abhor idols, do you rob temples? You who brag about the law, do you dishonor God by breaking the law? As it is written: 'God's name is blasphemed among the Gentiles because of you' " (Rom. 2:17–24).

It is a fatal mistake to break the law of God, a more dreadful mistake to do so carelessly and willingly. But it is even more dreadful to cause others to

---

[2]Billy Graham, "Stains on the Altar" in *One Race, One Gospel, One Task,* official reference papers of the World Congress on Evangelism, Berlin, 1966 (Minneapolis: World Wide, 1967), vol. 1, pp. 151–60.

dishonor God and stumble because of your transgressions.

3. Malachi suggests, in the third place, that the priests of Israel were to be blamed for *disparaging the priest's office,* which means holding the service of God in contempt. We have already suggested this problem in remarks above, but it is stated explicitly in verse 12: " 'You profane it by saying of the LORD's table, "It is defiled," and of its food, "It is contemptible." And you say, "What a burden!" and you sniff at it contemptuously,' says the LORD Almighty."

Here is how Theo. Laetsch, one of the best commentators on the minor prophets, expresses the priests' thinking at this point. "Far from possessing the humble spirit which later characterized the great apostle (1 Cor. 2:1–6; 3:5; 15:8f.), they felt that they were shamefully underprivileged people. The 'fruit'—the food, the grain, the living we get from our job, the 'bread'—the food we receive for our service at the altar, how contemptible it is! What the people cannot sell, what they refuse to eat, all the sick, the old and defective animals are palmed off on us, and the best parts, the fat, must be offered on the altar, while we get what is left! And what a weariness (v. 13) to stand all day long and be ready whenever someone feels like bringing his sacrifice, to slay it, and skin it, and gut it, and cut it up, a filthy, bloody job, and what do we get out of it? A few pieces of tough meat, unfit for food! Dissatisfied, they fault the Lord for conditions they themselves have brought about."[3]

I find that condition today. I have known men who complained about how little their people cared about the church's work or services. But these same men skimped on the preparation of sermons and rushed through ser-

vices as if the best blessing of a Sunday morning were to get out of church and go home. They did not seem to love God. They did not seem to love His word, His people, or His work. Some even joked about their ministry only half concealing their resentment of their calling. What a travesty! What a vivid example of the very attitude reproved by Malachi!

4. The final point of Malachi's criticism of the clergy is their brazen *defying of God.* It is the attitude we have already seen in our overview of Malachi, the characteristic attitude of the time. When God says, "It is you, O priests, who despise my name," the priests reply, "How have we despised your name?" (1:6). When God replies, "You place defiled food on my altar," they answer, "How have we defiled you?" (v. 7). The priests considered themselves to be righteous at this point, but their answers are not the answers of righteous men. They are the answers of the self-righteous. The righteous do not defend themselves arrogantly when God criticizes.

Job illustrates the attitude of the righteous. In the opening chapter of Job, Job is called a righteous man. But he suffers the loss of his wealth, family, and health in spite of his righteousness. The bulk of the book is an account of his attempt to understand these devastating reversals in the face of the facile and cruel explanations of his "friends." At last God speaks, calling Job to account. God reminds him of his ignorance, taking several chapters to stress his own might and wisdom as contrasted with Job's weakness and ignorance. When it is over Job does not answer with a self-righteous "But God. . . ." Instead, he says, "My ears had heard of you but now my eyes have seen you. Therefore I despise

---

[3]Theo. Laetsch, *Bible Commentary: The Minor Prophets* (Saint Louis: Concordia, 1956), p. 519.

myself and repent in dust and ashes" (Job 42:5, 6).

That is what we must do—and will do—when we truly meet with God. Like Richard Baxter, we will "humble ourselves in lamentation" for our sins.

There is one more interesting point in this section. It is the suggestion in verse 10 that it would be better in God's sight for the Jerusalem temple to be closed than for such contemptible service to continue: " 'Oh, that one of you would shut the temple doors, so that you would not light useless fires on my altar! I am not pleased with you,' says the Lord Almighty, 'and I will accept no offering from your hands.' " It is an interesting footnote to this text that the Qumran or Dead Sea Community later used it to justify their own rejection of the Jerusalem temple and its priests.[4]

God's wish that someone might close the doors of the temple veils a threat that God would Himself bring the temple worship to an end, which He did forever by the agency of the Roman armies under Titus in A.D. 70. Should not the same judgment rightly apply today? We are much concerned with evangelism, church planting, and church growth. But the cause of Christ would be better advanced in some instances by closing some churches than by opening them. By the existence of unbelieving churches the gospel of Christ is diluted and even contradicted in our land.

Call to the Clergy

At this point the prophet drops his rehearsal of the sins of God's priests and instead calls them to a genuine and thorough repentance. He calls them to listen to what the Lord is saying and to set their hearts on honoring Him. If they do not, He promises to send a curse on them and their descendants (Mal. 2:1–9).

What impresses me most about this section is the brief but excellent portrait of a true minister interjected into the middle of God's rebuke of the unbelieving clergy (vv. 5–7). There God looks back to Levi, the father of the tribe of priests, and notes how Levi revered God and honored his profession. The text says, "My covenant was with him, a covenant of life and peace, and I gave them to him; this called for reverence and he revered me and stood in awe of my name. True instruction was in his mouth and nothing false was found on his lips. He walked with me in peace and uprightness, and turned many from sin. For the lips of a priest ought to preserve knowledge, and from his mouth men should seek instruction— because he is the messenger of the Lord Almighty." It tells how a minister (or anyone else who is called to speak in God's name) should live and testify. Like the longer section dealing with the clergy's faults, it too has four divisions.

1. The first mark of a true minister is a proper relationship to God, which Malachi calls *reverence*. ("This called for reverence and he revered and stood in awe of my name," v. 5.) Most people are aware that the word "fear," often used in translations of Old Testament texts, actually means "reverence," so that when the psalmist writes, "The fear of the Lord is the beginning of wisdom" (Ps. 111:10), he is actually saying that true knowledge begins with a reverential awe of God. All things spiritual begin with such reverence, and God's ministers need to cultivate it more than anything else.

2. The second characteristic of the man God holds out as an example to the false priests of Israel is personal *commitment to the truth* of God's Word ("True instruction was in his mouth and nothing false was found on his

---

[4]"The Damascus Rule," VI. 11–13. See Eduard Lohse, ed., *Die Texte aus Qumran* (Darmstadt: Wissenschaftliche Buchgesellschaft, 1964), pp. 77, 79.

lips," v. 6). To speak the truth, the whole truth, and nothing but the truth, is a large assignment were it not for the written Word of God, which it is the preacher's duty to proclaim. Left to ourselves we could speak little but error or at best truth mixed with error. But when we proclaim God's Word we proclaim what is eternally truthful— not only true for a particular moment of history or a particular person, but true for all time and for all people. To proclaim that Word is a great responsibility.

3. The true minister of God is to be marked by godlike *character and piety* ("He walked with me in peace and uprightness, and turned many from sin," v. 6). The essential requirement here is godliness. It is what I most appreciate in the prayers of others when they pray for me personally. I do not care much if they request that I become a great preacher or become successful as the world defines that term. I want them to pray that I might be faithful to the teachings of Scripture and that I might be godly. God honors it more than anything else.

4. Finally, Malachi quotes God as saying that a priest (or minister) "ought to *preserve knowledge,* and from his mouth men should seek instruction" (v. 7). It is evident, I am sure, that Malachi is not talking here about the mere conveyance of information, as if the preacher were to be merely a storehouse of details about the history of the Hebrew kings, the background of the New Testament, the fine points of theology, or quotations from the giants

of church history. Malachi is talking about the knowledge of God, which is salvation (John 17:3), and about the way to live a God-pleasing life. The godly minister passes this on, and the sheep look to him for the instruction and are fed.

In his commentary on this text Martin Luther stresses how important it is to do this through preaching, contrasting the spoken word with written words, which in his judgment, are more likely to produce trickery. "Certainly God could with his Spirit instruct and justify those whom he would, but it has pleased his wisdom more to instruct and justify those who believe through the foolishness of preaching. The Word is the channel through which the Holy Spirit is given. This is a passage against those who hold the spoken Word in contempt. The lips are the public reservoirs of the church. In them alone is kept the Word of God. . . . Unless the Word is preached publicly, it slips away. The more it is preached, the more firmly it is retained. Reading it is not as profitable as hearing it, for the live voice teaches, exhorts, defends, and resists the spirit of error. Satan does not care a hoot for the written Word of God, but he flees at the speaking of the Word. . . . This penetrates hearts and leads back those who stray."[5]

May God give us many such ministers. May He make those He has given faithful to that task. May He give us all ears to hear what the Spirit says to us through them for the church's benefit.

[5]Martin Luther, *Luther's Work,* vol. 18, *Lectures on the Minor Prophets, I: Hosea, Joel, Amos, Obadiah, Micah, Nahum, Zephaniah, Haggai, Malachi,* edited by Hilton C. Oswald (Saint Louis: Concordia, 1975), p. 401.

31

God, Divorce, and Apostasy

(Malachi 2:10–16)

Have we not all one Father? Did not one God create us? Why do we profane the covenant of our fathers by breaking faith with one another?

Judah has broken faith. A detestable thing has been committed in Israel and in Jerusalem: Judah has desecrated the sanctuary the LORD loves, by marrying the daughter of a foreign god. As for the man who does this, whoever he may be, may the LORD cut him off from the tents of Jacob—even though he brings offerings to the LORD Almighty.

Another thing you do: You flood the LORD's altar with tears. You weep and wail because he no longer pays attention to your offerings or accepts them with pleasure from your hands. You ask, "Why?" It is because the LORD is acting as the witness between you and the wife of your youth, because you have broken faith with her, though she is your partner, the wife of your marriage covenant.

Has not the LORD made them one? In flesh and spirit they are his. And why one? Because he was seeking godly offspring. So guard yourself in your spirit, and do not break faith with the wife of your youth.

"I hate divorce," says the LORD God of Israel, "and I hate a man's covering himself with violence as well as with his garment," says the LORD Almighty.

So guard yourself in your spirit, and do not break faith.

The marriage vow is the most solemn, official commitment a person can make. What could be more serious or official than the promise made before a minister of the gospel to take your spouse as husband or wife "in plenty and in want, in joy and in sorrow, in sickness and in health as long as [you] both shall live"? If you are a naturalized American citizen, you have sworn loyalty to the United States of America. But you can reverse that commitment, becoming an expatriate, and no one—certainly not God—will be offended. In the army, you took an oath of obedience to your commanding officers, but only for a short period of time. Even if you make a career of the military, it is only for twenty or so years. The only thing I can think of that is more solemn than the commitment one makes in marriage is the commitment Christians make to Jesus Christ as Savior and Lord. But even that is not always so formal and, in any case, the two commitments are related to each other, as I hope to show.

So I repeat: no commitment you or I can make is as solemn or as official as the one we make to our husband or wife in the marriage ceremony. It is a commitment involving the other person, the state, and God. Yet here is the anomaly. In spite of marriage commencing with a commitment of this nature, marriages are breaking up at a previously unheard of rate. As a result, our society is suffering disastrously.

Do we need statistics? Almost fifty years ago the original speaker on "The Lutheran Hour," Walter A Maier, wrote the best book on marriage I have ever read. In it he deplored the increasing divorce statistics of his day, complaining that if the trends of the 1930s continued, by 1950 one-fourth of all marriages made in the United States would end in divorce, and by 1990 that figure would be one in two.[1] It was so outrageous a suggestion for the 1930s that Maier had to be defensive. He argued that his prophecy was "no harebrained" hallucination. But today, as we look back on Maier's words, we find that he was far too sanguine. In 1920 there was one divorce for every seven marriages. In 1940 there was one divorce for every six marriages. In 1960 there was one divorce for every four marriages. In 1972 there was one divorce for every three marriages. And by 1977 (thirteen years ahead of Maier's timetable) there was one divorce for every two marriages. In that year alone there were more than a million divorces in the United States of America.

The divorce rate doubled in the decade between 1967 and 1977, and at the present rate there will soon be one divorce for every marriage!

A Sin of Evangelicals

What is the cause of this problem, a problem that involves our national character and has untold evil effects on society? There are many causes, of course, depending on how the subject is treated. But like most problems the underlying causes are spiritual, and among these spiritual causes is the breakdown of faithfulness to God's teaching on the evils of divorce.

That is where the teaching of Malachi comes in! Malachi 2:10–16 contains some of the most forceful teaching in the Bible on divorce and remarriage. Not surprisingly, many contemporary books on marriage advocating a more permissive attitude in this area ignore the passage. But ignoring Malachi's teaching is part of the problem. It is our contemporary version of the very problem Malachi is writing about. In Malachi's day there were many divorces and many mixed marriages of God's people with unbelievers, which is a matter related to divorce. Worse yet the problem even existed among the priests, who should have resisted the breakups of godly homes in Israel but who encouraged them instead.

Malachi words his condemnation of mixed marriages and divorce broadly to include lay people as well as priests. But he has just been talking about the sins of the priests, and we are no doubt to assume that this (though also a sin of the people) was among their faults.

We remember from our discussion of the dating of Malachi's book that this last of the prophets was writing contemporaneously with Nehemiah's second residence in Jerusalem, at which time Nehemiah rebuked the marital infidelity of the priests. Nehemiah gives an example. In Nehemiah 13:28 the governor mentions the case of "one of the sons of Joiada son of Eliashib the high priest" who was "son-in-law to Sanballat the Horonite." This is a clear example of a mixed marriage, involving the grandson of the high priest himself. Nehemiah explains how he drove this individual away from him, concluding, "Remember them, O my God, because they defiled the priestly office and the covenant of the priesthood and of the Levites" (v. 29). This is the very language used and the charge leveled by Malachi.

---

[1]Walter A. Maier, *For Better, Not for Worse* (Saint Louis: Concordia, 1935), p. 371.

The point I am making is that the priests' permissive attitude toward divorce and their own bad examples contributed greatly to the loose moral climate of Malachi's day. And ministers are doing the same thing today—even in so-called evangelical circles. They are a major part of the problem.

In preparation for this study I looked through a sizable collection of contemporary books on marriage, divorce, and remarriage, and my impression is that in all but a very few cases the overall tendency of the books is to lower the standards previous generations have set and propose that the world's contemporary low practices are not so bad after all. One writer has even gone so far as to suggest that remarriage, even when there have been unbiblical grounds for divorce, "is desirable." I think this is sinful and tragic.

Let me acknowledge that there are ambiguities in some cases. There are also cases where remarriage is permissible. Jesus spoke of Moses granting the right of divorce because of the hardness of people's hearts (Matt. 19:8). Paul recognized cases in which an unbelieving spouse departs from the marriage and nothing can be done to bring the spouse back. In that case the believer is not in the wrong and is not bound to the marriage (1 Cor. 7:15). Jesus spoke of the possibility of divorce for the cause of fornication (Matt. 5:32). I believe that in the case of a person who was married and divorced and then, subsequent to the divorce, became a Christian, it is right for him or her to marry again for the first time as a Christian, since "if anyone is in Christ, he is a new creation; the old has gone, the new has come!" (2 Cor. 5:17). Unfortunately, these few and carefully qualified exceptions have been used to excuse almost anything and open the door to remarriages that in the vast majority of cases must be judged offensive to God on the basis of Malachi 2:16 and other passages.

I am charging evangelical ministers with being part of the breakdown in our national marriage morality. I am not asking them to ignore the exceptions. But I am challenging them to limit them as severely as the Bible itself does and to let the clear cry of the evangelical pulpit be that God hates divorce and stands against it as a witness to the original contract of a man and woman in marriage.

Marriage Is of God

This brings us to the first point that Malachi makes. The basis of all he will say is that God has created marriage, that it was His idea. It was God, not man, who made the race male and female (Gen. 1:27). It was God who looked at the man in his singleness and judged, "It is not good for the man to be alone. I will make a helper suitable for him" (Gen. 2:18). It was God who brought the first woman to the first man and, as it were, performed the first marriage ceremony (Gen. 2:22). It was God who said, "Be fruitful and increase in number" (Gen. 1:28). It is to this original creation of man and woman and of God uniting them in one permanent marriage that Malachi refers: "Has not the LORD made them one? In flesh and spirit they are his. And why one? [That is, why did God not make more than one wife for Adam or more than one husband for Eve?] Because he was seeking a godly offspring. [That is, godliness is linked to marriage faithfulness. Divorce, which is itself a sin, leads to other sins.] So guard yourself in your spirit, and do not break faith with the wife of your youth" (Mal. 2:15).

Marriage is not only a divine institution. It is the first of all institutions and is therefore the basis of the institutions that follow it. From marriage and the relationships that exist within the home have come various forms of government, educational institutions, and medical care. Destroy marriage, as so many today are trying to do, and these other beneficial institutions will fall with it.

I quote here from Walter Maier. "Because marriage comes from God above and not from man or beast below, it involves moral, not merely physical problems. A sin against the commandment of purity is a sin against God, not simply the outraging of convention, the thoughtlessness of youth, the evidence of bad taste. The Savior tells us that, when God's children are joined in wedlock, they are united by God, and beneath the evident strength and courage and love that this divine direction promises there is a penetrating, ominous warning. Those who tamper with God's institution have lighted the fuse to the explosive of retributive justice. Marriage is so holy that of all social sins its violation invokes the most appalling consequences. Sodom and Gomorrah were burned out of existence because of the vile disregard of the holiness of marriage. David's rule over Israel was blackened by his marital follies and by the royal lust that forgot God and dedicated itself to raging passion. The Hebrew people dropped out of the family of nations largely because of the vicious practices associated with Baalim worship."[2]

Instead of trying to find loopholes in God's commandment or trying to convince ourselves that our spouse is not a Christian or is at least not behaving as one and is therefore divorceable, we ought to be shouting the holiness of marriage from the housetops. It is better to endure much personal unhappiness than to treat as expendable the solemn vows of the wedding service.

Mixed Marriages

There are two specific violations of God's word that Malachi tackles in this passage. The first is mixed marriage. It is never God's will that a believer marry an unbeliever—either in a first marriage, which is one obvious sin and error (2 Cor. 6:14), or in a second marriage, which seems to have been a frequent fault in Israel. The men had been divorcing their Jewish wives for the daughters of the heathen.

"But surely an unbelieving spouse can be saved by the consistent testimony of a believing wife or husband," someone protests. "Paul says so."

I acknowledge that is so. But notice. Paul's words are given as encouragement to one who was married as an unbeliever and then became a believer. Such a person might wonder whether he or she should divorce the unbelieving wife or husband. Paul's answer is No. God does not want divorce. Then he adds a word of encouragement. God has called the believing spouse to faith. He will most likely work in the unbelieving partner's life too. It is no promise that the unbelieving spouse will necessarily be saved, but it is an encouragement along those lines. It is not at all an authorization for a believer to marry a non-Christian.

God is gracious. We must acknowledge that sometimes when a Christian marries one who is not a Christian, God graciously draws the non-Christian to Christ. We praise God when that happens. But it is not the usual outcome. More often the mixed marriage brings great sorrow and pain to the Christian.

The marriage of Olivia L. Langdon to the American writer Mark Twain is a tragic case in point. Olivia Langdon had been raised in a Christian home by devout parents and professed Christianity. But when Twain, an open critic of religion, came calling, she eventually accepted his proposal, no doubt secretly cherishing the hope that he might

---

[2] Ibid., p. 83.

in time be converted to Christ by her example. At first this seemed to be happening. Albert Biglow Paine in his comprehensive biography of Twain records that "his natural kindness of heart, and especially his love for his wife, inclined him toward the teachings and customs of her Christian faith. . . . It took very little persuasion on his wife's part to establish family prayers in their home, grace before meals, and the morning reading of the Bible chapter." One of Clemens's friends, who knew him to be a great skeptic, recorded his surprise at visiting the home and discovering Twain praying and otherwise joining in the family worship.

Unfortunately, in time Twain began to express distaste for this worship and told his wife, "Livy, you may keep this up if you want to, but I must ask you to excuse me from it. It is making me a hypocrite. I don't believe in the Bible; it contradicts my reason. I can't sit here and listen to it, letting you believe that I regard it, as you do, in the light of the Gospel, the Word of God."

This alone would have been a great tragedy; it must have marked the end of Olivia's hopes for her husband. But something even worse followed. Mark Twain's unbelief had a disastrous influence on his wife and Olivia gradually progressed from doubt to the death of her religion. One day when she and her sister were walking across the fields she confessed with sorrow that she had drifted away from her orthodox views. She had ceased to believe in a personal God who exercised personal supervision over every human soul, she said. Years later, in a time of bereavement, Twain tried to strengthen his wife with the words, "Livy, if it comforts you to lean on the Christian faith, do so."

She replied, "I can't, Youth [her favorite designation for her husband]. I haven't any."[3]

If you willfully disobey God and marry a non-Christian, do not beguile yourself with the belief that you will be the cause of your husband or wife's conversion. By the grace of God that may possibly happen. But it usually does not. Mixed marriages usually end in great unhappiness or divorce. And even if that is not the case, you will certainly bring much unnecessary sorrow upon yourself by disobedience.

WHAT GOD HATES

The Bible teaches that God hates sin, but it rarely says that about a particular sin. So it should be especially striking when we read in Malachi 2:16 that God hates divorce. The text teaches that He hates it the same way He hates violence. Why does God hate divorce so fiercely? We can suggest a number of reasons. First, it is a matter of a man and a woman breaking faith with his or her spouse. God, who is a God of faithfulness and truth, hates infidelity. The marriage vow speaks of union "in plenty and in want, in joy and in sorrow, in sickness and in health." We cannot guarantee anyone happiness, not even ourselves. We cannot guarantee affluence or health. But we can guarantee that we will stick by our word, that we will not break faith just because fidelity is difficult or because another way or person becomes more attractive. God hates divorce because it breaks faith, because it violates truth's standard.

Second, God hates divorce because it is harmful. It is harmful to the couple involved, generally leaving scars that never truly heal. It is harmful to society. Above all it is harmful to whatever children may be involved.

Divorcing persons generally do not want to admit this, and their reluctance is understandable. They have to raise

---

[3] Ibid., pp. 243, 244.

their children, and it is difficult to do this if they are laboring under guilt that the divorce has done the children great harm. But admit it or not, divorce does harm children. Oh, some cope better than others. Many children of divorced parents get on with life somehow. But all are harmed, and some are harmed deeply and irreparably. We live in a day of "human rights." Everyone is fighting for his or her rights, so it seems. Even divorcing persons fight for their supposed right to be happy. What about the children? I maintain that they also have rights: a right to a mother *and* a father, a right to a stable home environment, a right to an actualized biblical model of what a God-blessed home should be. Divorce deprives them of that and often leads them into a self-destructive life pattern. The great majority of children appearing in juvenile court are from broken homes. The vast majority of prison inmates have the same background.

In the final analysis, however, the fundamental reason why God hates divorce is that God created marriage to illustrate the most blessed of all spiritual relationships—the union of a believing man or woman with Christ, the divine bridegroom of the church—and divorce must therefore illustrate apostasy or the falling away of a man or woman from God, which is damnation.

People in the reformed tradition are strong in insisting that the work of God in the life of one of His believing sons or daughters is never frustrated and that the one He has called to Himself will never be lost. God is the active agent in salvation: He elects, He regenerates, He calls, He justifies, He sanctifies, and at last, He glorifies. We are right to insist on such a perfect gospel, for it is what Scripture teaches about salvation from the beginning of Genesis to the end of Revelation. But if that is the case, how then can we possibly compromise on God's marriage standard and imply that divorce (and, even worse, remarriage) is permissible or even desirable because of our merely human condition? Far be it from us! One writer declares, "I am convinced that if a strict view on divorce and remarriage were taught in our churches, there would be fewer divorces among believers. Marriage would be entered into with more caution, and marriage partners would seek to preserve that union at all cost."[4]

I believe that as well, and I affirm that God, who "hates divorce," would bless our stand, deepen our marriages, and begin the long and difficult task of healing our sick land.

---

[4]J. Carl Laney, *The Divorce Myth* (Minneapolis: Bethany House, 1981), p. 123.

32

The Day of His Coming

(Malachi 2:17–3:5)

You have wearied the LORD *with your words.*
"How have we wearied him?" you ask.
By saying, "All who do evil are good in the eyes of the LORD, *and he is pleased with them"*
or "Where is the God of justice?"
"See, I will send my messenger, who will prepare the way before me. Then suddenly the
Lord you are seeking will come to his temple; the messenger of the covenant, whom you
desire, will come," says the LORD *Almighty.*
But who can endure the day of his coming? Who can stand when he appears? For he will
be like a refiner's fire or a launderer's soap. He will sit as a refiner and purifier of silver; he
will purify the Levites and refine them like gold and silver. Then the LORD *will have men*
who will bring offerings in righteousness, and the offerings of Judah and Jerusalem will be
acceptable to the LORD, *as in days gone by, as in former years.*
"So I will come near to you for judgment. I will be quick to testify against sorcerers,
adulterers and perjurers, against those who defraud laborers of their wages, who oppress the
widows and the fatherless, and deprive aliens of justice, but do not fear me," says the LORD
Almighty.

Between the portion of Malachi 2 that deals with the sin of the people in divorcing their spouses and marrying unbelievers and the part of Malachi 3 that deals with their sin of robbing God of tithes and other obligations, there is a section dealing with the coming of the Lord in judgment (Mal. 2:17–3:5). But the coming of God is not the initial thrust of the passage. It begins with the people's complaint that God's rule is not just. God replies that He is just but that His coming in justice will mean judgment for the very people who are raising this objection.

"How Have We Wearied Him?"

The verses begin with an exchange that should be familiar by now to any

student of Malachi. Seven times in this book God makes a statement either directly or indirectly critical of the people, and they reply by challenging the statement. Generally their challenge begins with the word "how," though in one instance the New International Version translates the same Hebrew word as "what."

In Malachi 1:2 God tells the people, "I have loved you."

This statement of fact is also a veiled criticism of the people's indifference to God's love for them. They respond by asking, *"How* have you loved us?" God's love surrounded them in spite of their half-hearted devotion and open sin. But they are so insensitive to that

247

love that they actually consider God remiss in His favors. They think He has not loved them to the degree that He should.

The second and third exchanges occur just verses later. There God says, "It is you, O priests, who despise my name."

The priests reply, *"How* have we despised your name?"

God answers, "You place defiled food on my altar."

They reject this explanation in spite of the fact that they have been offering blind, crippled, and diseased animals, and answer God, *"How* have we defiled you?" (Mal. 1:6, 7).

We find this same type of exchange at the beginning of the section we are now studying, where it says that the people "have wearied the LORD with [their] words."

They reply, *"How* have we wearied him?" (Mal. 2:17).

How indeed? When we see the word "wearied" we think of repetitious entreaties that tire the person hearing them. As it turns out, it is not so much the repetitiousness as the nature of the complaints that bothers God. God is offended that the people accuse Him of injustice. They say, "All who do evil are good in the eyes of the LORD, and he is pleased with them." That is, evildoers prosper materially. The wicked get rich. By contrast, they imply, "We who do good [they considered themselves to have been quite good, as we have seen] are evil in the eyes of the LORD, and he is not pleased with us." They mean, "We are not getting rich. Where is the God of justice?"

We need to see two things about accusing God of injustice. First, it is *horribly arrogant.* It demands that the only wise, holy, omniscient, sovereign God of the universe come down to our level and defend Himself before our petty human standards of justice. God was managing the universe quite well

long before we were even born. He raises nations up and brings nations down. He imposes judgment upon individuals through the inevitable outworkings of sin in their lives and the lives of those with whom they come in contact. Eventually He punishes the wicked in hell and brings the redeemed to heaven. God does all this perfectly without our help. Yet when something does not go the way we like, we immediately accuse God of injustice and call Him to an accounting. How dare we behave in this fashion? How dare we accuse God of doing wrong?

Second, accusing God of injustice is *distressingly frequent.* We see this at the beginning of the Old Testament. When Adam and Eve sinned and God came to them in the garden, asking, "Have you eaten from the tree that I commanded you not to eat from?" Adam replied, "The woman you put here with me— she gave me some fruit from the tree and I ate it" (Gen. 3:11, 12).

In a similar way, when God asked the woman, "What is this you have done?" She replied, "The serpent deceived me, and I ate" (v. 13).

On the surface these statements seem to be honest admissions of guilt. But beneath the surface Adam and Eve were doing their best to shift the blame. Eve tried to implicate the serpent. True, she had eaten, but the Devil made her do it, she said. Adam blamed the woman and then with characteristic male arrogance hinted that the whole thing was God's fault: "the woman you put here with me" is to blame. Like the people in Malachi's time, Adam was arguing that the current evil state of things, which was actually the result of his own sin, was God's fault.

Moreover, although the woman did not say so openly, she too was blaming God. Eve blamed the Devil. But is that reply any different from Adam's? Not really! We see the similarity of the two excuses when we ask: But who made the Devil? Or, who let the Devil into the garden? Every attempt to excuse ourselves is in the final analysis an attempt to blame God. It is saying, as Martin Luther in his lectures on Genesis accused Adam of saying, "Thou, Lord, hast sinned."[1]

What do you blame for your misfortunes? Is it circumstances? God made the circumstances. Is it other people? God made them and has permitted them to come into your life. If you do not admit your own guilt in a matter (or at least acknowledge that God may be delaying the full execution of His justice for reasons that seem both wise and right to Him), then you are saying that God acts sinfully. You are saying, as these people did, "All who do evil are good in the eyes of the LORD, and he is pleased with them" (Mal. 2:17).

"WHERE IS GOD?"

Christians affirm that God is a God of justice, but we all know that injustices occur in this life. We believe that God will judge all evil one day, but in the meantime the evil *do* prosper, the righteous sometimes *are* afflicted, and evils go unchecked. What are we to make of this?

The next verses deal with that question. They make two points. First, God *is* coming and there will be a judgment. Second, *all* evildoers will be judged including those who object to God's management of the world's affairs. The unspoken inference of these first points is that if God does not come in judgment immediately, it is because He is a God of grace as well as a God of justice. He has not come in judgment because, if He were to come none could possibly stand before Him. All would perish. All would be consigned to the lake of fire.

It is important to see what God promises to do. First, He promises to send His "messenger, who will prepare the way before" Him (Mal. 3:1). It is interesting that in the Hebrew the phrase translated "my messenger" is actually the word *Malachi*, the name of the prophet. Malachi means "my messenger." But Malachi is not thinking of himself when he records this important promise of God. The words "prepare the way before me" are a clue that Malachi is thinking of the well-known prophecy of Isaiah 40:3–5, a prophecy that was extremely popular with the Jews of this period. Isaiah wrote:

A voice of one calling:
"In the desert prepare
the way for the LORD;
make straight in the wilderness
a highway for our God.
Every valley shall be raised up,
every mountain and hill made
low;
the rough ground shall become
level,
the rugged places a plain.
And the glory of the LORD will be
revealed,
and all mankind together will see
it.
For the mouth of the LORD has
spoken."

This is the messenger who was to prepare for God's Messiah. And we have the united witness of the four evangelists who declare that Isaiah 40:3 was fulfilled in the person of John the Baptist, the forerunner of the Lord Jesus Christ. Each of the evangelists quotes at least part of this text (Matt. 3:3; Mark 1:3; Luke 3:4–6; John 1:23), and Matthew also quotes the text from Malachi, thus linking the two pronouncements. "This is the one about whom it is written:

" 'I will send my messenger ahead
of you,
who will prepare your way before
you' " (Matt. 11:10).

---

[1]Martin Luther, *Luther's Works*, vol. 1, *Lectures on Genesis Chapters 1–5*, edited by Jaroslav Pelikan (Saint Louis: Concordia, 1958), p. 175.

In each case the messenger is identified as John the Baptist.

The second thing God promises is to come Himself. This is an astonishing promise, of course. It is one thing for God to send a messenger. Indeed, that is what God had been doing for many hundreds of years. He had sent messengers like Isaiah, Jeremiah, Ezekiel, and Daniel. He had sent the so-called Minor Prophets: Hosea, Joel, Amos, Obadiah, Jonah, Micah, Nahum, Habakkuk, Zephaniah, Haggai, and Zechariah. Now He is sending Malachi, and He is promising to send John the Baptist too. They were all great messengers, great gifts to God's people. But they were men after all. It is not all that extraordinary that God should communicate with His people by this means. But now the truly incredible thing is that God is promising to dispense with the messengers and come Himself. "See, I will send my messenger, who will prepare the way before *me*. Then suddenly *the Lord* you are seeking will come to his temple; *the messenger of the covenant* [this 'messenger' is not the forerunner, but rather the Lord Himself], whom you desire, will come" (v. 1).

Surprising as this is, it is nevertheless exactly what Isaiah had declared earlier: "A voice of one calling: 'In the desert prepare the way for *the LORD*; Make straight in the wilderness a highway for *our God*'" (Isa. 40:3). It is what John the Baptist had in mind when he said, "After me will come *one who is more powerful than I*, whose sandals I am not fit to carry" (Matt. 3:11). When Jesus was revealed to John on the occasion of His baptism, John declared unequivocally, "This is *the Son of God*" (John 1:34).

These texts are testimony to the deity of Jesus Christ! There are other things that attest to Jesus' deity, of course. There was the voice from heaven at the baptism and again on the Mount of

Transfiguration: "This is my Son, whom I love; with him I am well pleased" (Matt. 3:17; 17:5; cf. Mark 1:11; 9:7; Luke 3:22; 9:35). There were Christ's own claims: "I and the Father are one" (John 10:30); "Anyone who has seen me has seen the Father" (John 14:9). There were the miracles, the Resurrection. But among these many claims and evidences, the great Old Testament prophecies stand out. Who is the messenger if not John the Baptist? Who is the Lord for whom he was to prepare if not Jesus? If Jesus is not the Son of God, then these prophecies have not been fulfilled, and the Bible (thus far at least) is unreliable.

GRACE AND JUDGMENT

At this point another remarkable thing happens, and it is even more remarkable than the prophecy that God will Himself come to His temple. To see it we have to reconstruct the reasoning thus far. Malachi began with the complaint of the people that God had been unjust in withholding what they considered their proper measure of material blessings. Even worse, they had accused Him of favoring evildoers. "Where is the God of justice?" they complained. To this God replied that although His coming had been long delayed, it had nevertheless not been canceled. "Where is the God of justice?" These verses teach that the God of justice is coming.

So what should we expect at this point? The people had asked for justice. Justice is what they should get. The God of justice who is also the God of judgment should come, destroy their land, obliterate their city, and confine every last one of them to hell for their wickedness.

It is true that God does speak of judgment. Verse 5 declares, "So I will come near to you for judgment. I will be quick to testify against sorcerers, adulterers and perjurers, against those who defraud laborers of their wages, who oppress the widows and the fatherless, and deprive aliens of justice, but who do not fear me." But even here, although God says that He is coming in judgment, it is only to *testify* against sinners. And the verses that come before this speak, not of a final judgment that results in men and women being sent to hell, but of a purification process in which the priests and Levites will be refined like gold and silver and the Lord "will have men who will bring offerings in righteousness, and the offerings of Judah and Jerusalem will be acceptable to the LORD, as in days gone by, as in former years" (vv. 3, 4).

According to this image, God will be like a refiner of silver. Workers of silver can still be seen today in oriental bazaars. They melt the ore in small, portable furnaces. As the ore melts, the dross rises to the top and is then scraped off by the refiner. The workman keeps peering into the crucible, removing dross until he can see his face in the molten metal as in a mirror and knows that the work is done. In such a manner, God will apply the heat of affliction and discipline until He can see His image in His people.[2]

In spite of the people's demand for justice, when God should come to His people in the person of His Son, the Lord Jesus Christ, it would not be for an immediate judgment on sin—however much they deserve it—but for God's own gracious work of redemption. He would come to seek and to save the lost, to bring healing, and to purify His elect people. Only after that gracious work would the judgment come.

The Lord Himself taught this when He eventually came—four hundred years after the age of Malachi. Jesus had returned to Nazareth after His baptism by John and His temptation by Satan, to begin His ministry, and He went into the synagogue of Nazareth on the Sabbath. He was asked to take part in the service and was given the scroll of Isaiah from which He was to read the day's lesson. He unrolled it, found the sixty-first chapter and read:

> "The Spirit of the Lord is on me,
>   because he has anointed me
>   to preach good news to the poor.
> He has sent me to proclaim freedom
>   for the prisoners
>   and recovery of sight for the
>   blind,
> to release the oppressed,
>   to proclaim the year of the Lord's
>   favor" (Luke 4:18, 19; Isa.
>   61:1, 2).

Jesus then announced that this remarkable prophecy had been fulfilled in Himself. He was the One who had come to do these things, as God had promised. But the most remarkable thing about Jesus' handling of this passage is what He did not read. If you look at Isaiah 61, you find that the very next line of the prophecy, indeed the completion of the sentence with which Jesus stopped, says: "and the day of vengeance of our God" (Isa. 61:2). Vengeance (or judgment) is part of Isaiah's great prophecy. One day it will come. But it did not come with Jesus' first appearing. Indeed, by His very citation of this prophecy He indicated that a day of grace would precede the final judgment.

The Silence of God

We are in that day of grace now, and we should be thankful that it is so. It is a day for repentance and salvation. We should use it as such before the day of final judgment comes. We should never say, "Where is the God of justice?" We should never ask for judgment.

---

[2] The image of the refiner also occurs in Isaiah 1:25; 48:10; Jeremiah 6:29, 30; Ezekiel 22:17–22.

Robert Anderson wrote one of the most original and stimulating books I have read. It is called *The Silence of God*. It asked why in our time, if God is as omnipresent, omniscient, and caring for us as we imagine Him to be, He does not speak. He spoke in the past through prophets. From time to time there was even a voice from heaven. Certainly we would like to hear God speak today. In a number of penetrating chapters Anderson presents how even strong believers would like a whisper of explanation in moments of personal suffering, a pointed, directing word in crisis, a shout of vindication when non-Christians seem to have the upper hand. Yet God does not speak. We refer to the four hundred silent years that intervened between the words of God through Malachi and the coming of John the Baptist and Jesus Christ. But since the time of Jesus nearly two thousand years (five times the other silent period) have gone by.

Why is God silent? Why does the God of all the universe not speak? Anderson answers that God has already spoken everything that can probably be spoken graciously. Jesus is the ultimate, final word of God in that area. Not a syllable can be added. The only words that remain to be spoken are the final words of judgment. And God is silent now because, when He speaks audibly again, that judgment will come.[3]

Do not argue with God. Do not try to bring God down to the level of your own petty justice or understanding. On the contrary, accept that God is good, that today is the day of His grace. And come to Him through Jesus while there is still time.

[3]Robert Anderson, *The Silence of God* (Grand Rapids: Kregel, 1965).

33

Robbers! Robbers of God!

(Malachi 3:6–12)

"I the LORD do not change. So you, O descendants of Jacob, are not destroyed. Ever since the time of your forefathers you have turned away from my decrees and have not kept them. Return to me, and I will return to you," says the LORD Almighty.

"But you ask, 'How are we to return?'

"Will a man rob God? Yet you rob me.

"But you ask, 'How do we rob you?'

"In tithes and offerings. You are under a curse—the whole nation of you—because you are robbing me. Bring the whole tithe into the storehouse, that there may be food in my house. Test me in this," says the LORD Almighty, "and see if I will not throw open the floodgates of heaven and pour out so much blessing that you will not have room enough for it. I will prevent pests from devouring your crops, and the vines in your fields will not cast their fruit," says the LORD Almighty. "Then all the nations will call you blessed, for yours will be a delightful land," says the LORD Almighty.

I was counseling a young man whom I had known for years. Earlier he had made a commitment to Jesus Christ as Lord that had been growing in intensity, but he had also been involved in sexual sin and seemed unable to shake it. I had told him that he needed to be obedient to Christ in this as in other areas, but the struggle went on. In this particular session he told me that several months previously he had decided to stop having sexual relations with his girlfriend to see if that would help get his life straightened out and bring the kind of blessing he expected from Christianity. "But it hasn't worked," he told me. He had done his bit—a great deal in his opinion—but God had not responded as he expected.

This was exactly what was happening with those of Malachi's day. Ac-

cording to the prophet, the people were guilty of many serious sins. The priests were offering blemished animals in a formal but insincere religious ritualism. Many were divorcing their wives to marry unbelieving women. Most had been disobeying God's law by withholding tithes of their harvests. And they were all accusing God of loving them only half-heartedly and of being unjust in His dealings with them—because He had not prospered them adequately. If they could have put their feelings into words other than those recorded by Malachi, they might have said, "We have been utterly faithful in fulfilling our responsibilities toward God. Never mind the divorces and mixed marriages. Never mind the tithes. We keep our side of the bargain through many things that seem important to us. The problem is that God has not kept His side of the bargain. We have been faithful; He is unfaithful. In short, obedience to God does not work. God has not prospered us as we think He should, and the fault is God's alone.

The answer, of course, is that God had not changed. It is the people who had changed, falling away from a true love for Him and from the truly righteous life their forefathers once had (Mal. 3:4). But in another sense, the problem is that the people—we must include ourselves at this point—had changed so little. Though fallen from their original, early devotion to God, they were nevertheless exactly as they had been for much of their history. They were exceedingly sinful and self-righteous, and they needed to repent.

GOD HAS NOT CHANGED

Once when I was preaching through the Book of Malachi and dealt at length with God's indictment of divorce and mixed marriages in Malachi 2:10–16, I was approached afterward by a man who identified himself as a Baptist. He said, "I have never heard a sermon on the second chapter of Malachi, but I have heard dozens of sermons on Malachi 3." He was referring to the fact that in Malachi 3:10 God challenges the people to "bring the whole tithe into the storehouse, that there may be food in my house, . . . and see if I will not throw open the floodgates of heaven and pour out so much blessing that you will not have room enough for it." This is a great text for a sermon on stewardship, which is what this man had so often heard. But it is striking that the context for God's words about tithes is the teaching that God is faithful. The matter of tithes is only an illustration of that teaching.

In theology this doctrine is called immutability. It means that, being perfect, God cannot and does not change.

In order to change, a moral being must change in either of two ways. Either he must change for the better, or he must change for the worse. God cannot get better, because that would mean that He was less than perfect earlier, in which case He would not have been God. But God cannot get worse either, because in that case He would become imperfect, which He cannot be. God is and must remain perfect in all His attributes.

Malachi 3:6 is a classic statement of immutability: "I the LORD do not change." But we immediately ask, "What are the specific areas in which God does not change?" And "Why does God mention this particular doctrine here?"

It would be a valid exposition of this text to list every one of God's attributes and show how God does not change in any of them, attributes like sovereignty, wisdom, holiness, self-existence, self-sufficiency, knowledge, and justice. But the relevant attributes here are His love, mercy, grace, and faithfulness. Malachi 3:6 says that it is because of God's immutability in these areas that the people have not been destroyed. At first glance this is surprising, because the theme of the preceding verses has been the people's complaint: "Where is the God of justice?" In such a context, if God replies that He has not changed, we should expect Him to mean, "I have not changed in my demand for justice, and I will judge the ungodly."

Instead, we find that the emphasis is on His grace and mercy. Even when we were looking at the previous verses we saw that God was coming, not to judge, but to save His people. The messenger was to prepare the way for Jesus, who would redeem and purify them. We find the same thing here. God emphasizes His immutability to say that He is unchanging in His faithfulness, which is why the people have not been destroyed for their transgressions.

How gracious of God! The people were accusing Him of changing, of having become unfaithful. God replies that He is unchanging precisely in His faithfulness, which is why these very people had not been cast off.

WE MUST CHANGE

It is this unchangeableness of God that gives us a chance to change. For, of course, that is what we must do. It is why the passage goes on to speak of repentance or returning to God: " 'Return to me, and I will return to you,' says the LORD Almighty" (v. 7). "How are we to return?" someone asks. That is what the people of Malachi's day asked, and God's response to them in the first instance was that they had robbed Him of tithes and offerings. The word "tithe" means "tenth." It refers to that tenth of the people's produce or income that was owed to God for the temple service and other social obligations. The basic tenth was paid to the Levites for their maintenance (Lev. 27:30–33), and from this tenth the Levites themselves paid a tenth to the ministering priests (Num. 18:25–32). Additional tenths may have been paid on other occasions (cf. Deut. 14:28, 29). That is what the people had not done. They had undoubtedly made some small contributions to the Levites and temple service as part of their ritualistic practice of religion. But they had not given the "whole tithe" (v. 10), and they had certainly not presented even what they did give with a willing and thankful heart. They had to change in this area.

Many believers today also need to change. Sometimes in question-and-answer periods I am asked whether Christians today are obliged to tithe. I suspect the questioner wants to know how little he must give to Christian causes and how much he can keep for himself. I reply with what I believe to be a proper statement of the case, namely, that the tithe was an Old Testament regulation designed for the support of a particular class of people. It was not carried over into the New Testament. Nowhere in the New Testament are believers instructed to give a specific tenth or any other proportion of their income to Christian projects.

On the other hand, I also point out that although the tithe is not mentioned, the giving of weekly offerings is (1 Cor. 16:2). And more importantly, it is generally the case that in the New Testament the obligations of the Old Testament legislation are heightened rather than lessened. That is, the law is interpreted in the fullest measure. So while we are not required to give a specific tenth of our income, it is hard to think of a normal Christian, blessed with the fullness of the gospel of Jesus Christ, doing less. Under reasonable circumstances any true believer in Christ should give more than the tenth, for all we have is the Lord's.

I wonder how many believers today even approach that ideal. I wonder if God would not say to most today, "You rob me" (Mal. 3:8). Why should this be? Why should we who have been blessed so abundantly be so ungenerous?

I think the reason is that we really do not trust God to take care of us. We think we have to store up the money for ourselves against the day when money may run out and God will be unable to provide. This was Oswald J. Smith's problem, as he tells about it in his classic story of his introduction to sacrificial missionary giving. He was the newly installed minister of the People's Church of Toronto, Canada, and it was the church's missionary week. He was sitting on the platform when the time came for the ushers to collect the faith promises for the coming year's missionary program. One of them, as he said, had the "audacity" to walk up to the platform and hand him an envelope. He read on it: "In dependence upon God I will endeavor to give $_____ toward the missionary work of the church during the coming year."

He had never seen such a thing before, and he began to protest inwardly. He was the minister. He had a wife and child to support, and at that time he was earning only twenty-five dollars a week. He had never given more than five dollars to missions at any one time previously, and that was only once. He told the Lord, "Lord God, I can't do anything. You know I have nothing. I haven't a cent in the bank. I haven't anything in my pocket. Everything is sky-high in price."

But the Lord seemed to say, "I know all that. I know that you are getting only twenty-five dollars a week. I know that you have nothing in your pocket and nothing in the bank."

"Well, then," he said, "that settles it."

"No, it doesn't," the Lord answered. "I am not asking you for what you have. I am asking you for a faith offering. How much can you trust me for?"

"I guess that's different," said Smith. "How much can I trust you for?"

"Fifty dollars."

"Fifty dollars!" he exclaimed. "That's two weeks' salary. How can I ever get fifty dollars?" But God seemed to be making the matter clear, and with a trembling hand Oswald Smith signed his name and put the amount of fifty dollars on the envelope. He has written since that he still does not know how he paid it. He had to pray each month for four dollars. But God sent the money, and at the end of the year, not only had he paid the whole amount, but he had himself received such a blessing that he doubled the figure at the next year's missionary conference.

Can God take care of us? Can God care for His people and at the same time use their willing generosity to provide for Christian work here and in other lands? Of course, He can! To doubt Him in this and give little (in some cases, nothing) is to rob God and slander His sovereignty.

KEEPING GOD'S DAY

There is another area in which many professing Christians rob God. It concerns the Lord's Day and what we do with it. Here again we have a situation analogous to the Old and New Testaments' view of tithing. According to the law of Israel, keeping the Sabbath was a solemn obligation (cf. Exod. 20:8–11). It is the most elaborated section of the Decalogue. Indeed, so solemn are these instructions for a proper keeping of the Sabbath that many Christians carefully observe Sunday or the Lord's Day in this fashion. For my part, I believe that there is a marked biblical difference between these two days. The Jewish Sabbath was a day of somber inactivity and reflection. The Christian Sunday is a day of joy, activity, and spiritual expectation.[1] But the fact that the character of the two days differs (in my opinion) does not mean that Sunday is any less the Lord's Day than the Old Testament Sabbath or that we are any less obligated to use it in a way that honors God.

In actual fact, in this age all our days are God's days—whether Sunday, Monday, Tuesday, or any other day of the week—and we have a special obligation to use Sunday to serve Him.

One person who believed this passionately was the great late eighteenth- and early nineteenth-century Welsh preacher John Elias. In his day there was an annual harvest fair held in the North Wales town of Rhuddlan, a town that has given its name to one of our

---

[1]I have expressed my understanding of the Sabbath and the Christian Sunday in *The Gospel of John*, vol. 2 (Grand Rapids: Zondervan, 1976), pp. 26–54.

great hymn tunes. At Rhuddlan Fair farmers would be hiring laborers, and many things would be sold for work on the land. The fair was held on Sunday, and crowds of people would throng into the town. The bars were all open. There was music and singing. The laws of God were broken in a variety of ways.

Elias knew about Rhuddlan Fair and was increasingly disturbed that people from that part of Wales should be so disobedient to God. One day he decided to go to Rhuddlan Fair to preach. He took a number of Christians with him, and together they arrived at Rhuddlan in the afternoon when the fair was at its busiest. They went to one of the public houses or bars called the New Inn. It had three steps in front leading to a small porch, so John Elias climbed those steps and told the Christians who had accompanied him to sing Psalm 24:

> The earth is the LORD's, and
>   everything in it,
>   the world, and all who live in
>   it. . . .
>
> Who may ascend the hill of the
>   LORD?
>   Who may stand in his holy place?
> He who has clean hands and a
>   pure heart,
>   who does not lift up his soul to
>   an idol
>   or swear by what is false (vv. 1,
>   3, 4).

Surprisingly, it seemed, the noise of the fair began to die down and people by the thousands came close to the New Inn to see what was going on. By the time the singing had stopped there was already a change. Many were struck even by Elias's earnest appearance. Some started to hide what they had purchased.

Elias started to pray. As he prayed tears ran down his cheeks. Silence crept over the crowd. It was astonishing. When Elias had finished praying he opened his Bible and read, "Six days you shall labor, but on the seventh day you shall rest; even during the plowing season and harvest you must rest" (Exod. 34:21). Then he started to preach as a divine messenger sent that day to Rhuddlan Fair. His listeners became afraid, and many began to weep when Elias shouted out, "O robbers! Robbers! You are robbing the Lord; you are robbing my God of His day!"

When John Elias finished preaching that summer afternoon in 1802, that was the end of the fair. There has never been another Rhuddlan Fair.

I wonder what John Elias would say if he could see how Christians spend Sunday today. Would he not say that we too are robbers of God, that we are robbing God of His day?

LIVING SACRIFICES

The end of this matter is that not merely our money or time, but our whole selves—body, soul, and spirit— are God's, and therefore we are to honor God wholly with all we are. Paul wrote, "You are not your own; you were bought at a price. Therefore honor God with your body" (1 Cor. 6:19, 20). He said, "Therefore, I urge you, brothers, in view of God's mercy, to offer your bodies as living sacrifices, holy and pleasing to God—which is your spiritual worship" (Rom. 12:1). That is the essence of it. So long as we are thinking legalistically in terms of financial percentages and portions of the week we will be exactly like the self-righteous sinners of Malachi's day. We will do little and think it much. We will resent God who, in our judgment, should do more for us. On the other hand, if we give God ourselves as living sacrifices, then the most we give will seem to be little and we will be overwhelmed that God is willing to use us in His service.

Will you try it God's way? Will you put God to the test? This is what God challenges the people to do in verses 10–12. The text has four parts.

First, God calls for obedience: "Bring the whole tithe into the storehouse, that there may be food in my house." All spiritual relationships with God start with obedience.

Second, God issues a challenge: "Test me in this."

Third, God accompanies His call and challenge with a promise: "See if I will not throw open the floodgates of heaven and pour out so much blessing that you will not have room enough for it. I will prevent pests from devouring your crops, and the vines in your fields will not cast their fruit."

Fourth, God speaks of the ultimate result: "Then all the nations will call you blessed, for yours will be a delightful land."

God's challenge in this great passage from Malachi is identical to the one we have already seen in Haggai, recorded by him approximately seventy-five years before. In Haggai's day the people had been neglecting the rebuilding of the temple, which was God's announced will for them at that period. As a result, God had withheld rain and had not prospered the crops. Much of the first portion of Haggai deals with this situation and challenges the people to take note of it and acknowledge God as the cause. Then God says, "Give careful thought to this from this day on—consider how things were before one stone was laid on another in the LORD's temple. When anyone came to a heap of twenty measures, there were only ten. When anyone went to a wine vat to draw fifty measures, there were only twenty. . . . From this day on, from this twenty-fourth day of the ninth month, give careful thought to the day when the foundation of the LORD's temple was laid. Give careful thought. . . . From this day on I will bless you" (Hag. 2:15, 16, 18, 19). Before they obeyed God the people experienced frustration and physical want. But from that point on they were to experience satisfaction and material blessings—if they obeyed God.

Are you bold enough to accept this challenge personally—as stated either here or in Malachi? Usually we try to shy away from anything as tangible as this, for we are afraid that our faith or testimony will be shaken if we try it and God does not come through. But it is not my idea to put God to the test with obedience. This is God's challenge. It is God who says, "Test me in this . . . and see . . ." (Mal. 3:10).

Why not obey God in this matter? Why not put God first in the use of your financial resources, your time, above all in what you do with yourself—and see if He will not "throw open the floodgates of heaven and pour out so much blessing that you will not have room enough for it"?

34

Last Words of the Old Covenant

(Malachi 3:13–4:6)

"You have said harsh things against me," says the LORD.
"Yet you ask, 'What have we said against you?'
"You have said, 'It is futile to serve God. What did we gain by carrying out his requirements and going about like mourners before the LORD *Almighty? But now we call the arrogant blessed. Certainly the evildoers prosper, and even those who challenge God escape.' "*

Then those who feared the LORD *talked with each other, and the* LORD *listened and heard. A scroll of remembrance was written in his presence concerning those who feared the* LORD *and honored his name.*

"They will be mine," says the LORD *Almighty, "in the day when I make up my treasured possession. I will spare them, just as in compassion a man spares his son who serves him. And you will again see the distinction between the righteous and wicked, between those who serve God and those who do not.*

"Surely the day is coming; it will burn like a furnace. All the arrogant and every evildoer will be stubble, and that day that is coming will set them on fire," says the LORD *Almighty. "Not a root or a branch will be left to them. But for you who revere my name, the sun of righteousness will rise with healing in its wings. And you will go out and leap like calves released from the stall. Then you will trample down the wicked; they will be ashes under the soles of your feet on the day when I do these things," says the* LORD *Almighty.*

"Remember the law of my servant Moses, the decrees and laws I gave him at Horeb for all Israel.

"See, I will send you the prophet Elijah before that great and dreadful day of the LORD *comes. He will turn the hearts of the fathers to their children, and the hearts of the children to their fathers; or else I will come and strike the land with a curse."*

The books of the Hebrew Bible do not have the same order as the books in our Bible. Our Bibles end with the minor prophets. The Hebrew Bible has the prophets in the middle, its order being: (1) the law, (2) the prophets, and (3) the writings. Second Chronicles actually ends the Hebrew Old Testament. On the other hand, the Greek (Septuagint) and Latin (Vulgate) versions have our order, which is where the English order comes from. So the majority of all Bibles, whether measured by the number of languages into which the Bible has been translated or merely the number of Bibles in existence, end with Malachi.

That presents a problem! The problem is that Malachi (and therefore also the Old Testament) does not end the way we might wish it did.

259

First, the final words of Malachi are "or else I will come and strike the land with a curse" (Mal. 4:6). They do not seem appropriate. We like upbeat endings. We think novels should end "and they lived happily ever after." Isn't that the kind of ending we expect to God's great plan of creation and redemption? God's people will be saved. Christ will see the travail of His soul and be satisfied. God will be perfectly and eternally glorified. Why then should the Old Testament end with the word "curse"? The Masoretes, who have given us most of the copies of the Hebrew Old Testament we have and who added the vowel points to the Hebrew text, were so bothered by this that they repeated the next-to-the-last verse of Malachi after the last verse.[1] Similarly, the Septuagint reverses the last two verses so the Old Testament ends, not with a curse, but with a blessing.

The second problem is different from this, but I suspect that it is a more basic reason why the ending of the Old Testament does not seem proper to us. The entire last portion of the book contains nothing that can really be called new material. Oh, there are a few ideas that do not occur elsewhere—the "scroll of remembrance," in which the names of the righteous remnant are recorded, and the image of the "sun of righteousness," to give just two examples. But basically the material of these verses is "old hat." It is a reminder of things said already, and we react to that the way a child reacts to a repeated warning: "Mother, you've already told me that." We do not want to be reminded yet another time.

Yet that is what we need. God reminds us of five things in these verses.

A Faithless People

The first thing these verses remind us of is that the people are still unchanged. This is the theme developed in the last chapter; indeed, it is a major theme of Malachi as a whole. For hundreds of years God had remonstrated with the people. He had sent famine and plagues. Eventually He had sent armies from the surrounding nations to overthrow first the northern and then the southern kingdoms (cf. Amos 5:6–13). But there had been no basic changes. Here at the last the people are much as they had been at the beginning.

This point is vividly made by the specific complaint of the people and God's response to it recorded in Malachi 3:13–15. These verses contain the last of those seven cavils marked by the word *how* (or, in this case *what*) that provide one possible outline of the book. When God said, "I have loved you" (Mal. 1:2), the people replied, *"How* have you loved us?" When God said, "It is you, O priests, who despise my name" (Mal. 1:6), the priests answered, *"How* have we despised your name?" When God explained, "You place defiled food on my altar" (Mal. 1:7), they defend themselves by retorting, *"How* have we defiled you?" When Malachi told the nation, "You have wearied the LORD with your words" (Mal. 2:17), the people responded, *"How* have we wearied him?" In chapter three God declared, "Return to me" (Mal. 3:7) and "You rob me" (Mal. 3:8). They said, *"How* are we to return?" and *"How* do we rob you?"

These statements and retorts reveal six very distinct transgressions, which G. Campbell Morgan calls profanity,

---

[1] The Hebrew text of Malachi has no chapter 4, our chapter 4 being a part of the Hebrew chapter 3. So the Masoretic text ends with Malachi 3:23, rather than with 3:24.

sacrilege, greed, weariness in service, honoring of vice, and robbery.[2] But although Morgan gives a separate name to this last cavil—blasphemy—it is really no different from the truth and is actually a summary of all of these. The people were saying that God did not love them, that He was not worthy of the best sacrifices, that He was unjust, did not deserve a full tithe, and was unreasonable to call for repentance. The seventh and last complaint summarizes their thoughts as: "It is futile to serve God. What did we gain by carrying out his requirements and going about like mourners before the LORD Almighty? But now we call the arrogant blessed. Certainly the evildoers prosper, and even those who challenge God escape" (vv. 14, 15). The people are blind to the fact that among those who had been challenging God they were themselves most guilty.

But there is another way in which the situation had not changed, and this is the first encouraging note in what is otherwise a distressing picture. There was a remnant. As in all previously grim centuries there were some who actually reverenced the Lord, and God noted and remembered them. This classic text says in reference to them: "Then those who feared the LORD talked with each other, and the LORD listened and heard. A scroll of remembrance was written in his presence concerning those who feared the LORD and honored his name" (Mal. 3:16).

This was true in earlier days too. We think of the faithful few during the days of the judges when the majority ignored God and did what was right in their own eyes (Judg. 21:25). The judges were themselves a remnant. God remembered them. Or we think of the seven thousand of Elijah's day who, although unknown to the prophet, had

not bowed down their knees to Baal (1 Kings 19:18). God took note of them also.

Here is a contemporary example. One of the inmates of the notorious Russian prisons was a Jewish doctor by the name of Boris Nicholayevich Kornfeld. He was a political prisoner of the Stalinist era. But he was treated better than most simply because doctors were scarce. Guards got sick as well as prisoners, and no prison officer wanted to end up in the hands of a prisoner he had cruelly abused. Boris Kornfeld was filled with hate. He considered himself innocent of all crime, and he was by our standards. But he would gladly have killed all his persecutors if the path had been open to him. There was a Christian in the camp. He was another one of those nameless persons who perished by the millions in those days. But he spoke to Kornfeld, and through his witness this Jewish atheistic doctor became a believer in Jesus.

The most extraordinary changes followed. The conversion was itself astonishing, but Kornfeld now began to live the faith he professed. He began to pray for the guards, above all for forgiveness for himself for the hatred he had once had for them. He stopped signing forms that permitted the guards to confine those they disliked to dark torture cells where most died. Even more significant, he turned in an orderly who had been stealing food from the most seriously ill patients. It was the equivalent of signing his own death warrant, for although the orderly was placed in a punishment block for three days, he was inevitably released and could be expected to try to kill Kornfeld at the first opportunity.

The doctor took to sleeping in the hospital, where he had his best chance of survival. Still, having accepted the

---

[2] G. Campbell Morgan, *Malachi's Message for Today* (Grand Rapids: Baker, 1972), p. 43.

possibility, even the probability of death, Kornfeld now experienced freedom to live as God's man. Hatred vanished from his life. He did what he could for the prisoners.

One night Kornfeld began to tell a patient what had happened to him. This man had been operated on for cancer of the intestines and probably had little time to live. As the doctor talked, the patient kept drifting in and out of consciousness. He was an unlikely person to hear the Jew's testimony. But Boris Kornfeld spoke of Jesus as his Savior and confided, "On the whole, you know, I have become convinced that there is no punishment that comes to us in this life on earth which is undeserved. Superficially, it can have nothing to do with what we are guilty of in actual fact, but if you go over your life with a fine-tooth comb and ponder it deeply, you will always be able to hunt down that transgression of yours for which you have now received this blow."

It was a remarkable confession, and it touched the patient deeply in spite of his pain-wracked condition! (The people of Malachi's day who considered God unjust and themselves innocent lacked that remarkable spirit of humility and repentance.)

The patient awoke the next morning to the sound of running feet. The commotion concerned his new-found friend, the doctor. During the night, while Boris Kornfeld slept, someone had crept up on him and had shattered his skull with eight blows of a plasterer's mallet. It was the end of Boris Nicholayevich Kornfeld! Yet not the end, because Kornfeld's testimony lived on through the life and witness of that one single cancer patient with whom he had shared it. The patient's name was Aleksandr Solzhenitsyn.[3]

These are the remnant. They are those who fear the Lord and talk with each other, whom the Lord remembers.

GOD IS UNCHANGED

The second reminder of these concluding verses is this. Just as the situation among the people had remained unchanged, so too God was unchanged. The Lord had stated this explicitly in the verses immediately before this: "I the LORD do not change" (Mal. 3:6). But these verses make the point again by bringing some of God's immutable attributes before us as the book closes. God is unchangeable in His knowledge; He knows the faithful and the faithless (Mal. 3:14–17), the righteousness and the wicked (v. 18). God is unchangeable in His holiness; His standard remains that righteousness which the law embodies (Mal. 4:4). God is unchangeable in His judgments; though postponed, the reality of judgment still looms before the wicked (Mal. 4:1–3). God is unchangeable in His promises; He still speaks of a day of blessing in which the hearts of the fathers will be turned to their children and the hearts of the children to their fathers (Mal. 4:6).

Men and women wish that they could get God to change. They do not like Him for His godly attributes: sovereignty, holiness, omniscience, justice, wrath—even love, because it is a holy love. But they could endure these perfections if it were possible to think that given time God might change in some of them.

We could endure God's sovereignty if we could think that given a bit more time God's grip on the universe might weaken and another strong personality might take over. Perhaps we could take over. Maybe men could be sovereign. We could endure God's holiness if

---

[3]I have found Boris Kornfeld's story in Charles W. Colson, *Loving God* (Grand Rapids: Zondervan, 1983), pp. 27–34. It originates in Aleksandr Solzhenitsyn, *Gulag Archipelago* (New York: Harper and Row, 1975), pt. 4, chap. 1.

we could think that given a bit more time His tough moral standards might change. What we are forbidden to do now we might be able to do then. We could wait to sin.

We could endure omniscience if given the passage of years it might be possible for God to forget. We could wait for Him to become senile.

We could endure His justice if with the passage of time it might become more of an abstract ideal than a reality.

We could even endure His love if it could cease to be the perfect and properly jealous love the Bible describes it to be.

But God does *not* change. God is the same today as He has always been; He will be the same in what we would call billions of years from now. God will always be sovereign. He will always be holy. He will always be omniscient. He will always be just. He will always be loving. It is appropriate that we be reminded of this in the closing pages of the Old Testament.

A CERTAIN JUDGMENT

Because God is unchanging in His holiness and justice, it follows that the inevitability of His judgment upon the wicked is unchanging also. The final chapter of Malachi virtually shouts for us to see this, for it begins, "*Surely* the day is coming . . ." (v. 1). The judgment of God may be postponed. For the most part it has been postponed for the long years of human history—postponed but not forgotten. Delay is not elimination. Judgment will come.

The image of a furnace, used earlier (in 3:2), reappears in this portrayal. Earlier the image was used to describe a future work of purging or purifying, as a result of which God would cleanse His people and establish a generation of those who would live righteously and worship Him in truth. It is the kind of discipline Jesus spoke of through His use of the image of the vine and its branches. He spoke of trimming the branches (John 15:2). It is a blessed thing for God's people, though painful. However, the second use of the image of a furnace (in 4:1) is quite different. Here the object of the burning is not purification but rather the destruction of the wicked: " 'All the arrogant and every evildoer will be stubble, and that day that is coming will set them on fire,' says the LORD Almighty. 'Not a root or a branch will be left to them' " (v. 1). This is a judgment to be feared.

But even here we find the same encouraging note we saw when considering the unchanged character of the people. Most had remained unchanged in their arrogance. But among them were those who constituted a genuinely godly remnant (Mal. 3:16). Here, even in the midst of a terrible reminder of God's judgment, God nevertheless also speaks of those who "revere [His] name," upon whom the "sun of righteousness" will rise with healing in its wings" (Mal. 4:2).

The church fathers from Justin onward have almost universally understood the "sun of righteousness" to be Christ. Martin Luther in particular said, "Under the Law there is weakness and condemnation; under the wings of Christ, under the Gospel, there is strength and salvation."[4] This is proper theology, of course, and the earlier prophecy of God's sending a messenger to prepare the way before Him (Mal. 3:1) does encourage us to think forward to the coming of Jesus. Still it is probably not the correct interpretation of "sun of righteousness." Carl Friedrich Keil, author of one of the most analytical and accurate commentaries on the twelve minor prophets, argues

---

[4]Martin Luther, *Luther's Works*, vol. 18, *Lectures on the Minor Prophets, I: Hosea, Joel, Amos, Obadiah, Micah, Nahum, Zephaniah, Haggai, Malachi*, Hilton C. Oswald, editor (Saint Louis: Concordia, 1975), p. 418.

that the context does not support this interpretation and simply means that righteousness is itself to be like a sun in the day of God's judgment. He calls "righteousness" an "epexegetical genitive of apposition." "*Ts^edaqah* is here, what it frequently is in Isaiah (e.g., Isa. 45:8; 46:13; 51:5, etc.), righteousness in its consequences and effects, the sun and substance of salvation. . . . As the rays of the sun spread light and warmth over the earth for the growth and maturity of the plants and living creatures, so will the sun of righteousness bring the healing of all hurts and wounds which the power of darkness has inflicted upon the righteous. Then will they go forth from the holes and caves into which they had withdrawn during the night of suffering and where they had kept themselves concealed, and skip like stalled calves (cf. 1 Sam. 28:24) which are driven from the stall to the pasture. . . . They will acquire power over the ungodly. They will tread down the wicked, who will then have become ashes and lie like ashes upon the ground, having been completely destroyed by the first of the judgment (cf. Isa. 26:5, 6)."[5]

Understood in this way, the verses are not a prophecy of Christ's future work, though they depend on that work for their fulfillment, but rather of the vindication and triumph of the righteous. They refer to us, if we are God's people. They are meant to establish us and encourage our obedience.

AN INFLEXIBLE STANDARD

The fourth reminder of these closing verses of the Old Testament is of God's law, which remains an inflexible standard. The people are unchanged. God is unchanged. God's judgment is unchanged. *God's law is unchanged.* Because God remains unchanged in His

righteousness, so does the expression of His righteousness in the law remain unchanged from generation to generation.

Moreover, not only does God's law remain unchanged, so also does our obligation to live by that standard. This is conveyed by the word "remember." "*Remember* the law of my servant Moses, the decrees and laws I gave him at Horeb for all Israel" (Mal. 4:4). In Deuteronomy, the heart of the law, "remember" is used thirteen times to bring God's saving acts before the minds and consciences of God's people. The key verse is from the Decalogue: "Remember that you were slaves in Egypt and that the LORD your God brought you out of there with a mighty hand and an outstretched arm" (Deut. 5:15). In Malachi the word is used of the law itself, as the people are admonished to remember all the decrees and laws God gave through Moses at Mount Horeb.

The two go together. There are always people who want to hold forth the law apart from God's personal intervention in their lives; they become legalists. But there are others—they are more numerous and a greater danger today—who want to exalt their experience of God to the neglect of obedience. That cannot be done, simply because the God who acts is also the God who speaks. If you claim to have a relationship with God, then you must heed Malachi's warning: "Remember the law" and do it.

STANDING ON THE PROMISES

The last two verses of Malachi remind us that just as the people, God, judgment, and the laws of God are unchanged, so also are the promises of God unchanged. It is as Paul says in 2 Corinthians 1:20. "No matter how

---

[5]Carl Friedrich Keil, *The Twelve Minor Prophets*, vol. 2, in S. F. Keil and F. Delitzsch, *Biblical Commentary on the Old Testament* (Grand Rapids: Eerdmans, 1965), pp. 468, 469.

many promises God has made, they are 'Yes' in Christ. And so through him the 'Amen' is spoken by us to the glory of God." Malachi reminds us of these promises when he repeats his prophecy of the coming of God's messenger who will prepare the way before Him. This is said for the first time in Malachi 3:1–4. It is repeated in Malachi 4:5, 6, where the messenger is said to be (or be like) Elijah.[6]

What are we to do with these great promises of God? There is only one thing to do. We must believe them and take our stand upon them. As Paul wrote, we must speak our "Amen" to those promises and thus glorify God until the day when they are all fulfilled and we see God face to face. *Amen* is the Hebrew for *true* or *truth*. That is why it is sometimes translated "truly, truly" or "verily, verily" in our Bibles. Frequently it is spoken by Jesus as a preface to some great saying. It means, "Listen to this; what I am about to say is important; it is very true." More often *amen* is used by men and women as a conclusion to some statement. On our lips it generally means, "Yes, Lord, what you have said to me is true; I believe it and will live by it." Think of some of those statements.

In Deuteronomy 27, after God had given a large portion of the law involving curses on all who dishonor their parents, move boundary stones, or commit a variety of sexual sins, the people responded by saying, "Amen" (Deut. 27:15–26).

In 1 Chronicles 16, after a great prayer of David in which the acts, laws and promises of God were rehearsed in the hearing of the people, we read:

"Then all the people said, 'Amen'" (v. 36).

When Ezra the scribe read the law in the hearing of the people, praising the Lord who gave it, "all the people lifted their hands and responded, 'Amen! Amen!' Then they bowed down and worshiped the LORD with their faces to the ground" (Neh. 8:6).

Psalms 41, 72, and 89 end, "Amen and Amen."

Jesus said, "Amen, Amen, I tell you, everyone who sins is a slave to sin" (John 8:34, my translation).

Our hearts echo sadly, "Amen, Amen."

Jesus said, "Amen, Amen, I am the gate for the sheep" (John 10:7, my translation).

We hopefully echo, "Amen."

"Amen. Amen, whoever hears my word and believes him who sent me has eternal life and will not be condemned; he has crossed over from death to life. Amen, Amen, a time is coming and has now come when the dead will hear the voice of the son of God and those who hear will live (John 5:24, 25, my translation).

We joyfully echo, "Amen."

We come to the very last words—not of the old covenant, which ends with a curse, but of the new covenant of Revelation, and we hear a last great promise: "He who testifies to these things [that is, Jesus] says, 'Yes, I am coming soon.'"

We respond, "Amen. Come, Lord Jesus" (Rev. 22:20).

The last verse says, "The grace of the Lord Jesus be with God's people. Amen" (v. 21). Amen and Amen!

---

[6]John the Baptist denied that he was Elijah when questioned by the religious authorities from Jerusalem (cf. John 1:21), but Jesus said that He fulfilled Elijah's role in preparing for His own public ministry and that John was Elijah if people were willing to accept it (cf. Matt. 11:14). In that latter passage Jesus seems to link Malachi 3:1 (in Matt. 11:10) with Malachi 4:5 (in Matt. 11:14). Luke quotes Malachi 4:5, 6 in recording the announcement of the birth of John the Baptist to his aged father Zechariah by the angel (Luke 1:17).

Indexes

Subject Index

Scripture Index